INNS AND TAVERNS

THE ILLUSTRATED HISTORY OF DERBY'S PUBS

THE ILLUSTRATED HISTORY OF DERBY'S PUBS

Maxwell Craven

breedon **books** PUBLISHING

First published in Great Britain in 2002 by

The Breedon Books Publishing Company Limited

Breedon House, 3 The Parker Centre,

Derby, DE21 4SZ

Dedication
Ivor Alex Clissold
(1942–1997)
and Derby CAMRA

ISBN 1 85983 330 6

Printed and bound by Butler & Tanner, Frome, Somerset, England.

Cover printing by Lawrence-Allen Colour Printers, Weston-super-Mare, Somerset, England.

Contents

Introduction

I

THERE have been inns since Roman times in these islands of ours. Excavations have revealed them extensively on the continent, especially at Pompeii, and examples have come to light in Britain, too. But the Roman inn or alehouse, along with the *mansiones* (hostels) on the important main roads, is a tradition which was interrupted by the Dark Ages, and for that long period, evidence is quite lacking.

Hence it is necessary to look to the Middle Ages in order to trace the unbroken thread of the English inn and English public hospitality. The earliest inns began as houses of rest and refreshment provided by the multifarious religious orders, which flourished in mediaeval times. The object was partly charitable, partly to encourage pilgrimage to the shrines inevitably kept by all but the most impoverished monasteries. The visitors to these shrines were an important source of revenue to the monks, and providing a decent inn made good business sense.

There were, of course, also alehouses in towns to provide for the needs of those trading in the market places, but records of these are generally scant and many may have been ephemeral affairs, combining the sale of beer with other sources of income.

In Derby there were six monastic institutions, of which the combined college of St Alkmund and All Saints' held the shrine of the important Northumbrian saint, Alkmund. The convent of St Mary de Pratis (Kingsmead) preserved the shirt of St Thomas of Canterbury – an object of reverence, we are told, to pregnant women - and the others no doubt sported similar relics of veneration as well. These bodies undoubtedly offered the pilgrim hospitality and their places of refreshment evolved into inns through time.

The earliest reference we have to an inn in Derby is in a Darley Charter which refers to William the Innkeeper *(Hostilarius)* having some meadows in Alvaston c.1260. His son, Roger, 'son of William the Innkeeper' sub-let one of these meadows for a grain of pepper per annum – a peppercorn rent – at the same period. Unfortunately, there is nothing to tell us where the inn was, but as the transactions were conducted with the Abbot and Canons of Darley, it may be that he kept the Abbey's inn.

As pilgrims tended to enjoy the hospitality they were offered, the monastic inn would have been a separate building from the monastery itself in order not to tempt or taint the members of the order with the aggressively secular ambience of the hostelry. To identify these establishments, they acquired signs, invariably of a religious nature, giving birth to the inn sign as we know it today. Typical ones were

Dolphin motif from the Queen Street inn.

named after saints' symbols and other religious themes. For example the *Angel* (Cornmarket), was the inn built to serve the Canons of the College of All Saints' and is the earliest named inn in Derby. It survived, much rebuilt, into the 20th century. Names like the *Dolphin*, the *Bell* and the *Anchor* also have religious origins.

As the Middle Ages waned, and with the Dissolution of the Monasteries under Henry VIII and Edward VI, more and more hostelries began to open under the aegis of private landlords in market towns (such as Derby), at important staging and goods consignment posts, and at seaports. Further, with the end of the Wars of the Roses in 1485, more settled conditions had led to increased security of travel on the nation's roads, and this accelerated the process, fed by an ever-increasing number of travellers.

In many towns, for instance, the last inn on the road to a neighbouring settlement was given a name echoing the latter, as in Derby, the *Nottingham Castle* stood on St Michael's Lane, the earliest route from Derby to

Nottingham, and the *Burton Inn* on the Burton Road, and so on.

By the 18th century, there had grown up a distinct division between an inn and a tavern; the former was a coaching house or a place equipped with ostler and stables where even a gentleman might put up for the night without qualms; at the very least it was able to provide a bed for the night. A tavern, however, was in reality merely a drinking-house, usually in times past with food on offer, frequented by all manner of people, much less well appointed than inns. They were regulated by an ancient Act of Parliament which also attempted to control prices: '...and if any taverners exceed [the rates laid down] their doors shall be shut.' Yet somehow they are evocative of the rebellious soldiery of the Civil War, of the whorehouse, of bucolic revels and of the worst excesses of the lower social grades of the 18th century as depicted so graphically in the work of Hogarth: Gin Lane was full of them.

Taverns especially clustered around the areas of the town where there was markets and fairs held. Thus in Derby the Market Place, where ironmongery, household requisites and dry goods were traded, was crowded with them, as was Cornmarket (grains), the west end of Nuns' Green, later Friar Gate (livestock) and The Morledge and Cockpit Hill (wool, textiles and some vegetables) were all the focus of a cluster of taverns.

There were also alehouses, the simplest of those outlets in former times where alcohol could be imbibed and which boasted little more than crude seats, ale and straw or sawdust to cover the floor.

Inns and post-houses, on the other hand, were an aping of the lesser country house, wherein any traveller of means could demand and legally expect hospitality of a tolerably high order. The highest order of such was the coaching inn or post house. These catered for the better-off travellers, even to crowned heads - after all the King of Denmark stayed at the *George* and Louis IX of Hesse Darmstadt with the exotic cross-dresser the Chevalier d'Eon, too. Here coaches from distant destinations paused, often for as little as 15 minutes, to change horses, afford 'comfort' for their passengers and a quick snack and then off. Such stops could take place at any time in the day or night, too, the coach sounding a horn or bugle - a distinctive call for each different coach - to give a precious few minutes' warning to the staff of the inn; it made Derby's streets incredibly noisy places: it is no wonder that the Duke of Devonshire forsook his town house in the Cornmarket for the quieter Judges' Lodgings in St Mary's gate, once they were completed in 1811.

Derby was liberally endowed with both in the 18th century; indeed, it has been calculated that there was an alehouse or inn for every 88 people in 1761. In that year there were 108 public houses functioning in the town, of which but 12 could claim the distinction of being inns, and even then it was more often reflected in the addition of that word to the sign than to the facilities on offer.

By 1861 there were more than 170 drinking establishments, including 18 inns, and two hotels, a new concept then. Included in the statistics were the 50 or so beerhouses, which were the last vestiges of the common alehouse, the category having been brought into being through late 18th-century taxation and under an Act of Parliament passed by the Duke of Wellington's administration in 1830, both of which sought to protect the lower orders from the evils of gin ('mothers' ruin') by allowing the sale of beer on the premises, but not wine or spirits. The 1830 act required only a two guinea (£2 – 10p) excise licence for the occupier of any premises to open as a beer house. These establishments were, much later, enabled to apply for full licences (allowing them to become public houses in the full sense) under the terms of the 1902 Licensing Act. Until the early 20th century, all applications to the Licensing Bench were dealt with on 26th August each year.

Chronicling the vicissitudes of the beer houses of Derby has been one of the most exacting tasks in revising this book, and they constitute the bulk of the entries. Because the licences were so easily obtained, they became increasingly numerous – the 'corner pubs' of recent folk lore. Their demise through death of landlord, loss of trade or demographic change, was just as unpredictable and confusing as their establishment, not to mention frequent changes of name and even location. Close analysis of their addresses and street numbering has, however, allowed many of the 1992 entries to be amalgamated, with the names being cross-referenced. It has also been possible to push back the date of foundation of a considerable number.

There were attempts to outlaw or at least circumscribe Sunday drinking, usually at local level. In 1767 the mayor of Derby, Alderman Samuel Crompton, issued an ordnance which stated:

'...and whereas it is notorious that several public houses suffer tippling therein on the said days and frequently during the time of Divine Service; it is therefore to discharge all such persons from permitting the same as they will answer the contrary at their perils' (*DM* 23/12/1767).

In practice, most Derby beerhouses which survived into World War Two obtained full licences either during' that conflict or in 1949-52. Some, however, in the West End and in the Siddals Road area, lingered on until their demise as beerhouses.

A anonymous locally-written saga (really a travelogue) based entirely on the names of pubs, probably of early

20th-century date, has come to hand and is worth recording:

'I set out one night for a nice walk. It was a grand night, for there was only a *Half Moon* and *Seven Stars*. Continuing my journey I tripped over a *Flower Pot* that had been thrown at the *Lamb*. Being anxious to escape the *Eagle and Child*, I slipped into the *Nottingham Castle* but noticed that I was being pursued by a *Dolphin* which somehow had got on to the wrong side of the *Iron Gates*. So I ran around the *Globe* into the *Rodney* yard, where I thought my troubles were over, but I was wrong for I was there attacked by a *Tiger*. I had almost given up hope when an *Angel* appeared bearing a *Royal* bar. She pointed to the *Queen's Head* and it slunk into the *Post Office*. By now, things were improving, for I noticed *Lord Nelson* gazing earnestly at a *Buck in the Park* whilst the *Rising Sun* in the vicinity made a grand picture. By now I was feeling somewhat weary, so I tried to beg a ride from a *Gallant Hussar*, but he had unfortunately lost a *Wheel* running over a *Greyhound*. Anyway, I managed to get into a *Waggon and Horses* and I went to where the *Travellers Rest* and was there provided with a meal of *Swan and Salmon*. Feeling refreshed I wended my way to where I could picture in the distant past *Victoria* discussing currant (sic) topics with *Lord Raglan*. As I continued, I was sorry that the *Duke of Cambridge* was quarrelling with the *Prince of Wales*, who threw a *Malt Shovel* at him causing him to take refuge in an *Elm Tree*, like *Napoleon* procured a *Horse and Groom*. By now the *Pheasant* stood preening himself, whilst the *Wood Lark* sang merrily from the top of a *Holly Bush*. By this time I arrived home after an enjoyable but exciting time.'

II

THE great age of the inn was from the Restoration until the coming of the railways finally killed off the coaching routes. In Derby this led to the demise of those unable to adapt to the new dispensation although some, like the New Inn, under the vigorous and entrepreneurial proprietorship of William Wallace Wallis (who moved into omnibuses and freight chartering) survived. Some flavour of the English inn is caught by a German traveller of the late 18th century.

He wrote: *On the Continent, the pleasant amenities offered by the English inn are unknown. In general, that is to say in the towns also, English inns are most praiseworthy: rooms, beds, service and cleanliness surpass anything one encounters in other countries. We might even assert that the good inns in the countryside surpass those in the towns to the same degree as English inns on the whole surpass their German counterparts.*

Prices are not as high as one is inclined to think, once one has grown familiar with the customs of the country. For example, the fact that one does not ever eat by portion is certainly disagreeable. The stores of the house, meat, fish, vegetables, all that sort of thing, are displayed in a glass case in the hall, arranged with the greatest neatness and elegance. Apart from some pastry and confectionery, nothing is prepared in advance. The exception to this rule is at those inns where public conveyances stop at appointed hours. There the table is set at noon and in the evening, and the travellers arriving eat at a set price, and in company, should they wish. Otherwise the traveller must choose for himself from the store and state the manner in which he wishes his meal to be cooked.

Then he must wait patiently until it is ready. Should he choose a roast of mutton or beef or any large joint, it will be brought to the table whole and he has to pay for the whole even if it goes out with only a small portion carved. This is certainly not satisfactory, but anyone acquainted with the country knows how to arrange matters and only orders simple, easily prepared dishes.

Lodgings are not expensive. The room in which one eats and spends the day is usually not charged, even over longer periods unless, of course, one uses the room and eats elsewhere. In the bedroom one pays only for the bed which is seldom more than a shilling a night – and what a bed! There are the finest mattresses, the best sheets and blankets, with beautiful curtains round the bed, while in front of it lies a pretty little rug. A fine white nightcap and a pair of slippers are never missing and the English travellers, who carry very little luggage, use these without the slightest hesitation.

It has always struck us how this nation, with all its care for cleanliness, does not worry about a thousand little considerations which, to the German and even more to the Frenchman, have become second nature. For example, no Englishman, unless belonging to the highest rank, would refuse to drink with somebody from the same glass or porter jug, and should there be a shortage of accommodation, he will share a bed at the inn with an acquaintance or a complete stranger.

Even in the towns, the host appears at once to welcome the stranger the moment he steps from the coach. In the country one has the feeling that one has arrived on a long-expected visit. The innkeeper himself opens the carriage door and helps the traveller alight. His wife, standing in the doorway with the most friendly expression in the world, curtsies half a dozen times, seizes the lady travellers and takes them to a special room where she attends to their every comfort, while her husband does the honours to the gentlemen.

Even if one only changes horses without stopping for a meal, the courtesy remains every bit the same. The innkeeper and his wife accompany the traveller to the coach, thank him for the honour of the visit and ask him to return soon. To be sure, in every case the innkeepers make some profit, for they service the traveller's coach.

The farther one travels towards the north of England and Scotland, the more the courtesy of the innkeeper seems to increase, showing a cordiality it is a pleasure to encounter. The host always carries the first course to the table, even though the inn may be large and handsome. He is followed by his wife and all the children old enough for the task. They walk in procession, according to their age, all bearing something. Often we saw a little cherub with a head of golden curls bringing up the rear, perhaps only three or four years old, busily tripping along, pepper-box in hand. All rooms have bells in good working order and the English traveller uses these to his heart's content.

As there are no more attentive innkeepers than in England, there are equally no more demanding guests. But somehow the running of an inn is handled like that of a factory: everyone has his department, which makes for order and quick service. Horses are looked after by the groom, called an ostler, who must surely keep menials in the stable to do the actual work, as he himself looks far too elegant for manual tasks. Then there is the shoeblack. This lad, usually the most crafty and intelligent of the staff, called simply Boots, is a most important person in the establishment. He manages to attend to all external matters, carries out commissions, takes strangers round the town and has an answer for everything. High falsetto cries constantly echo through the house, shouting 'Boots' and always he is there at once.

On going to bed at night the chambermaid is called. She appears, wearing a fine cotton dress with a snow-white apron and a pretty little lace cap, in fact dressed in as neat and ladylike a manner as can be imagined. It is her duty to light a candle on the visitor's bedside table, and, irrespective of person or sex, she also escorts him to his bedroom and sees to his every comfort. This happens every night, even if one should spend a month in the place. On taking one's farewell, waiter, ostler and Boots appear and finally the chambermaid who, with a pretty curtsey, says: 'Don't forget the chambermaid'. One does not give these people very much, considering how expensive things are in their country, but one gives with pleasure for one has had good service.

This was the 18th-century inn: more than just a catering establishment. In the urban context inns also doubled as active community centres (to adopt current usage). Their premises were let for a wide variety of purposes which, later on, in the 19th century, mostly graduated to specialist outlets. Certainly animals figure high on these: Vets practised by 'being in attendance' in hostelries:

John Fowk the famous cow doctor from Kilburn is now removed from the Saracen's Head [St James' Lane] to the Bell [Sadler Gate] where his drinks are to be had at any time.

Heaven knows when his professional advice was to be had!

Game conservation was thought a fit subject for a session at the King's Head. In 1750, the High Sheriff, a grand jury and *other gentlemen* met to discuss the preservation of game. Inns also acted as clearing houses for lost property: horses, dogs, watches and wallets being the commonest. Animals were available to offer services themselves too:

There is now at the Blue Boar on Nuns' Green a high bred Berkshire Boar (how appropriate, and how typical of a semi-literate age!) *that will brim sows at reasonable rates*

and

Stallion available, a chestnut Yorkshire horse, Nimrod, to cover 12/6 [62p] and mare and 1/- [5p] servant at the Nag's Head, 17 April 1772.

It is notable that pubs are chosen with names associated with the animals offered, no doubt as an *aide-memoire* for slow-witted country yeomen.

Advertising was pub-oriented in other ways, being centred on such things as buying land, jobs, shows, assemblies, creditors' meetings and sales. Most of the inns benefited in being the venues for many of the events they advertised:

Auction in the great dining room of Brentnall's Wine Vaults [Market Place] a collection of prints and drawings belonging to Thomas Smith of Derby painter. The Freeholders of Littleover are invited to The George to consider an application to Parliament for dividing and inclosing the Common and open fields there.

The *George* even took over temporarily as the venue of the Post Office from 1766, whilst that in Queen Street was being rebuilt.

Salesmen also set up in pubs, for instance, as the *celebrated Italian artists* exhibiting *a set of grand fireworks at the Ostrich Inn (Sadler Gate)* in 1772. The advertisement went on:

Rockets to begin at 5.30pm (this was in January).
The artist Joseph Rose [who executed the stucco work for Robert Adam at Kedleston Hall] to teach gentlemen to make fireworks at the same place.

Pubs were certainly in those days at the heart of politics. The George and King's Head were prominent during the hectic days of the '45. In 1761, Sir Henry Harpur paid for drinks in nearly half the pubs in town in the hope of influencing the electors. Lord Scarsdale's son *entertained at* the George and King's Head a great number of freeholders and several barrels of ale were given to the populace as the price of his being elected unopposed (as a Tory) in 1775. Conclaves of myopic grandees also met in the George or King's Head to select the candidates.

We also see pubs as the venues for Derby School old boys' dinners, school rooms – as at the King's Head and the Dolphin – community meetings, charity trustees, Licence Commissioners, civic meetings of the 'smoke-filled room' type, and quack doctors.

> Mr Page of Breadsall, author of the Grand Restorative for Consumption may be spoke with at the Seven Stars [King Street] every Friday... he may be consulted gratis on many disorders.

There were more respectable practitioners too. Dr Timon of London, operator for the ears was at the Bell in 1760, Dr Taylor, the Royal oculist, was at the George in 1748 and the grandiosely-styled Chevalier John Taylor, Opthalmic surgeon to the Pope and the Holy Roman Emperor, was there 11 years later.

Nor did the pubs eschew duty as funeral parlours, for Godfrey Heathcote, the Duke of Devonshire's comptroller, lay-in at the George en route for burial at Chesterfield in 1773, whilst Mrs Curzon was brought, encoffined, to the King's Head in 1754. The landlords of both the King's Head and New Inn had hearses for hire. More recently, Mr Scotton, senior, landlord of the Falstaff, Silver Hill Road, was 'laid out in the tap room for three days' whilst his numerous family, friends and devoted customers paid their respects.

Theatre and concert-tickets were invariably to be had at hostelries, too, and landlords were not loth to promote even cultural events. At the George in 1766, indeed, a concert of vernacular music was held in order to benefit a blind man called George Mullin (plainly an Irishman) tickets being 1s (5p). Before the theatre was built in 1773, large rooms in pubs were useful for theatrical performances. Plays were performed in the ballroom of the George, in a room in Irongate and even at the County Hall.

III

IF it was the railways which dealt the death-blow to the coaching age and the turnpikes – and hence the coaching inns which served them – they also spawned the modern hotel. Derby's Midland Hotel, built in 1840-41 and designed by the North Midland Railway's highly competent architect Francis Thompson, is arguably the earliest railway hotel in the country. Bradbury and Keene say of it in 1884:

> It must be regarded as the leading hotel of the town, if not the Midland Counties.

> It embraces the best features of the English, American, and Continental systems of hotel-keeping, with the quiet-

ness and retirement of a private house. The history of the Midland Hotel like that of the British Constitution – is one of change combined with immutability, alteration associated with stability, and improvement linked with permanence. The wing nearest to the Station was opened in 1840 [sic] as a private hotel, offering, by its proximity to the trains, special accommodation to the travelling community. Another wing was added shortly afterwards.

The 'caravanserai', however, does not appear to have been, under private proprietorship, a paying concern; and it was not until it was purchased by the Midland Company – about 1860 – that it became a popular and profitable establishment. A further wing was added in 1872, and structural enlargements and improvements have since taken place. It has its own steam laundry, Vienna bakery, and all the latest modern appliances. A pleasant feature in connection with the establishment is the lawn-tennis ground and gardens attached to the house. Towle, the administrator of

An advertisement for luncheon baskets to be provided by the Midland Hotel in 1875.

the 'Midland', is intimately associated with the success of the Midland Hotel, and its wide-spreading dependencies, which include the Dining Rooms at Derby, the Midland Hotel at Morcambe Bay, the refreshment 'buffets' at Derby, Normanton, Lincoln, Bradford, Leicester, Trent, Nottingham, Burton, Gloucester, Hellifield, and Bedford. An interesting fact is that owing to the improvement in the service of nonintoxicants, with lower prices, the sale of tea, coffee, and milk is much greater than beer, the latter being in most refreshment rooms the staple commodity.

Sir William Towle (1849-1929), long-time manager of the Midland Hotel.

William Towle (1849-1929) later went on to a knighthood and a directorship of the Midland Railway: not bad for a Twyford-born Derby publican!

The *Royal Hotel* was built and opened but a year or two before the *Midland*, and its original purpose was to replace the town house for county gentlemen come to town for business or pleasure. A third major hotel was to join this pre-eminent pair in the late 1860s: the *St James's*. It replaced the old *King's Head* on almost the same site, although it faced the widened St James's Street instead of Cornmarket.

The Derby Improvement and Hotel Company which built it in 1865 sold the lease to Mr Wagstaff, and the hotel

sported a public room (later Richardson & Linnell's auction room and now a ladies' gymnasium) which seated 400.

Nevertheless Bradbury and Keene commented: *St James' Hotel is no doubt, more in accordance with the demands of modern civilisation, but there was nevertheless, a charm not readily replaced about the Old King's Head, upon whose site the new 'caravanserai' now stands. The Royal Hotel is an ornament to Victoria Street; but to the old inhabitants it does not carry with it the associations which attended the Red Lion and the White Lion, the two quaint hotels of the brave coaching days, which stood in friendly rivalry on the ground occupied by 'The Royal', with the Markeaton Brook running, a duck-haunted stream, through Victoria Street (then called Brookside) and crossed in the Cornmarket by the old Jail Bridge.*

The *Royal*, as we have seen, included the Athenaeum Club, where its gentlemen-members could rub shoulders with the upper echelons of Derby society in mutual intellectual and radical pursuits. Not to be outdone, the *St James's* included the premises of the County Club and the Derby Conservative Club, later renamed the Beaconsfield Club (after Disraeli) and from the turn of the century until 1932 located in Erasmus Darwin's old house in Full Street.

Today, although part of the old *Royal*, after 40 years as DHSS offices, has reopened as a banqueting suite, using the finest of the old public rooms on *the piano nobile*, the *St James's* is still in thrall to shops and offices, its hospitable element reduced to the tawdry *Sugaz*, the palest shadow of its former glories. Only the *Midland*, once again free of direct railway control and in private hands, survives from this pioneering trio of the post-coaching age.

Over the past decades another hotel has also been mooted, promoted by the 1978-88 City Council. This was to have been a five-star establishment, but the site – opposite the Council House and adjoining the Market Place – was never large enough to allow a viable size. Only by producing plans for a building of quite outstanding height and hideousness was it possible to include the necessary 200-plus rooms. In addition, four developers failed to raise the finance for the project, even with a generous amount of municipal pump-priming. Much to everyone's relief, the local election manifesto of the successful party in the 1992 local election pledged to buy back the site and develop it sympathetically, enlarging the Market Place at the same time. In practice, this meant the laying out of the Sir Peter Hilton memorial garden, something of an improvement upon the reeking water-filled pit that had marked the site during the years it was earmarked for an hotel. Nevertheless, a further hotel appeared on the former Chaddesden Sidings, now the Wyvern Park, and the *Mickleover Court*, opened less than a decade ago, at least provides the city with 5-star comfort. Despite this the current City Council is still angling for an hotel in the city centre; MetroHolst's planned development of the 'bus station site was originally going to have one, but by 2002, its site was redesignated (without demur of the Council's part) as residential.

IV

THE keeping of inns was always a specialised trade, and families remained in it from generation to generation. The earliest such dynasty was that of More, in the 16th century. Roger More was by no means the first of his family to be an inn-holder, and his will, proved in March 1545, establishes that he was the proprietor of an otherwise unknown *Crown*, in St Michael's parish. Yet his family were on the up: his son became a draper and Citizen of London in 1577, having represented Derby in Parliament in 1553-4 and 1562. He married Anne, daughter of Robert Newton of Chaddesden – a landed gentlemen of distinguished Welsh descent and ancestor of the Newtons of Mickleover Manor. Roger's daughter, Alice, married Humphrey Sutton of The College (d.1556), a brazier who seems, on the basis of Roger's career, to have become a vintner too.

Strangely, a distant kinsman of these Mores, John Moore (spelling of surnames was not a precise art until the later 19th century) married Mary, daughter of George Campion in 1689. Their nephew, Thomas Campion, was a Derby landlord, and his two sons, George (1713-1766), and, John, became landlords too. George was proprietor of the *Anchor*, St Peter's Street in 1761, where his wife, Sarah Bernard, succeeded him on his death.

John was the West India merchant who returned to Derby and took the *Bell*, Sadler Gate, in the 1760s. He was succeeded there by his son John (born 1769) and his grandsons, George and John (born 1799). Over the three generations they ran the *Bell* for just on a century. Other members of the family also kept pubs in the 18th century, including Harry (*Hare and Hounds*, 1761) and Robert, who in 1763 forsook the *Swan*, St Peter's Street, and took the *Rising Sun*.

Another inn-keeping dynasty was that of Brentnall. The Brentnalls appear to have come from Morley in the early 18th century. William Brentnall was born at Kirk Langley in 1724 (his father having forsaken Morley for that village due to marriage with an heiress) and ran the *Spread Eagle*, London Street, in the 1750s and was also the last proprietor of the *Virgin's Inn*, Market Place, before its sale to the Cox family. He ended up as the landlord of the *Talbot*, Irongate.

His cousin, George, a prominent vintner, kept the *Wine Vaults*, Market Place (as *Brentnall's Wine Vaults*). William's eldest son, however, Charles, became a farmer. Nevertheless, his grandson, Charles (1810-1886), became an opulent maltster.

William Brentnall's second son, Francis, was a grocer,

but his son, John (b.1792), kept the *Earl Grey*, Uttoxeter Old Road, from 1843 to c.1860. Francis's brother, Thomas, also avoided the inn trade, working as a watchmaker *next to the Old Talbot* (his father's inn).

Another cousin was Thomas Brentnall, brother of George, a wine merchant, who went bankrupt in March 1781. He was a cousin of Joseph, whose son, William Palmer Brentnall, kept the *Duke of Clarence*, Mansfield Road, in the 1840s, before moving to the *Windmill*, Willow Row, and then the *Durham Heifer*, Morledge, by 1857; all something of a come-down from the elite inns in the family in the 18th century.

At the time that the Brentnall's 150 years of innkeeping was ending, the Fearns were one of many families also heavily involved in the trade. George and Benjamin were sons of Ralph and Mary Fearn; George had three sons and a daughter: Frederick, John Samuel, Charles Henry and Harriet. Frederick also had a son, Alfred. Between them they ran 17 Derby pubs between 1860 and 1900. This involvement is best tabulated as under:

Name	Inn	Dates
George	*Bull's Head*, Full Street	1864-1871
	Corporation Hotel, Cattle Market	1871-1876
	Duke of York, Burton Road	1871-1874
	Bay Horse, Uttoxeter Old Road	1876-1878
Benjamin	*Royal Oak*, Market Place	1875-1885
Frederick	*Rose & Thistle*, Chapel Street	1875-1877
	Old Angel, Cornmarket	1877-1885
	Telegraph, Morledge	1885-1889
	Globe, Iron Gate	1889-1891
John Samuel	*Old Shakespeare*, Bold Lane	1871-1876
	Star Vaults, Albert Street	1876-1885
	Old Angel, Cornmarket	1885-1887
	Nag's Head, St Peter's Street	1886-1893
Charles Henry	*Vulcan Arms*, St Thomas's Road	1889-1894
	Freehold Tavern, Freehold Street	1894-1898
	Pear Tree Inn, St Thomas's Road	1898-1902
Alfred	*White Swan*, (*Swan & Salmon*) Ashbourne Road	1874-1893

John Samuel took over the *Old Angel* from his brother, Frederick, and he later took over the *Nag's Head* from Mary Huntsworth, wife of Joseph Wilde, whose nephew married Alfred's sister. George's daughter, Harriet, married in 1876, the Chellaston artist Frank Gresley. (I am indebted to Mr S.J. Wilde of Mackworth and another member of the family for his information.)

Another notable dynasty, whose careers were confined almost exclusively to the smaller beerhouses in the West End, was that of Newbold. Benjamin Newbold was landlord of the *Black Horse*, Nuns' Street in 1842/1846, moving on to the nearby *Dove*, and working as a joiner to make ends meet. His widow Eleanor later kept the *Alma*, York Street in 1878. Their son John succeeded to the *Dove* in the 1870s, and the other son, Edmund started off in Normanton (in 1878 he is listed as 'inn-keeper' but no pub name is given, although it certainly wasn't the *Normanton Arms*, as the landlord there was someone else entirely). He then moved to the *Brown Bear*, Lodge Lane (1891) before taking the *Hollybush* in the West End in 1893, remaining there until World War One, dying aged 80 in 1935 at 12, Madeley Street. A cousin was William Newbold of the *Malt Shovel*, Kedleston Street in the 1890s, and a sister-in-law, Emma, was landlady of the *Duke of York*, Burton Road. It is conceivable that the James Newbold who in 1849 married Charlotte Hollis of Rosliston was another cousin, especially in view of the fact that her probable great niece, Mabel Florence Hollis – daughter of Edward, second generation landlord of the *Old Spa Inn* – had married Edmund Newbold's son Reginald Arthur, who took the *Spa* over from his father-in-law.

These are only two of the more remarkable dynasties; numerous others are noted under the individual pub headings in the gazetteer section, and without doubt there are others that have escaped the author's attention.

There have been notable recent dynasties, too, like the Roberts' (*Melbourne Arms*, Siddals Road) and the Coneeleys (*Market Tavern*, Meadow Road). Not all inns paid well enough to keep their landlords. The *Mitre*, Amen Alley, was the 'fall-back' of Abraham Denstone, the plasterer who created the fine ornate ceilings in some of the houses built by Joseph Pickford. He died in 1779, leaving it to his heir. Elliott, who kept The *Napoleon*, Parker Street, in the 1890s, was also foreman compositor at Harwood's printing works; his son trained as a plumber and married a daughter of the landlord of the *Cheshire Cheese*, who himself doubled as odd job man at Atkey's Garage, itself much later on the *Flamingo & Firkin*. The last landlord of the *Royal Oak*, Market Place, also had a second job, at British Celanese; the increase in the demand for his services forced the closure of the inn, for good, not long afterwards.

V

THE families which made the beer sold by those mentioned above were also of interest. Nor should it be forgotten that until the beginning of the 19th century, Derby was renowned throughout the Kingdom for the quality of its beer, long before Burton-upon-Trent overtook it. As early as 1673 the town was so noted: *The principal trade*, wrote William Woolley in 1713, *is that of malting, with which many good estates have been raised.*

Twenty years earlier, Fuller had written, *Never was the wine of Falernum better known to the Romans than the Canary [Ale] of Derby to the English.* To which we might add the words of his contemporary Charles Cotton (1630-1687): *Nay, I am for the Country liquor, Derbyshire Ale, if you please; for a man should not, methinks come from London to drink wine in the Peak.*

The Derby malt was being exported to London in the 1730s, and Thomas Cox said of it: *This drink is made here in such perfection, that wine must be very good to deserve a preference.*

The same author gave us a wonderfully apposite piece of Latin doggerel on the subject, which, in translation, reads:

Of this strange drink, so like the Stygian Lake,
Men call it Ale, I know not what to make.
They drink it thick and piss it wondrous thin:
What store of dregs must needs remain within?

Why Derby Ale should have been called Canary is quite obscure, unless it be based on the colour. The water-meadows east of the Derwent, now crossed by Derwent Street, were also called Canary Island, but no obvious connection between the two presents itself.

In 1577, Thomas Alsop and Robert Stringer are listed as vintners, but no brewers appear, although they undoubtedly existed if only amongst the innkeepers. Indeed, Alsop was the ancestor of a long line of such, although the family left Derby in the earlier years of the 18th century. They were a cadet branch of the gentry family of Alsop of Alsop Hall, Alsop-en-le-Dale, and it was not unusual for members of such families to enter the malting trade at least, as with George Buxton, of the Bradbourne Hall family, in the 1660s. Buxton built and operated a malthouse in Walker Lane in 1661 on land leased from the Mosleys of Rolleston Hall, Staffordshire. By 1705, Buxton's son, another George, also owned the *Bull's Head*, Queen Street, which he left to his son, Samuel, and which was let to Robert Sergeant and Joseph Stephenson.

The case of the Alsops (this family subsequently spelt their name Allsopp) – whose posterity are attested as brewers in the 17th century – is echoed in William Frith, 'bear-bruer', who in 1619 leased a house in Rotten Row, Market Place with 'half a cellar' from the Corporation. The Alsops operated from a stone house (with malthouse and brewery behind) in the Wardwick, opposite St James's Bridge. In 1708 this house was replaced by the elegant Queen Ann building which is today the *Wardwick Tavern*; a few fragments of the previous building can still be seen embedded in the fabric.

Nevertheless, the Alsops transferred the business to John Lowe, another maltster who may have been a kinsman: he too was a scion of a county family, the Lowes of Aldgreave Hall. His son Thomas actually founded the business in 1767. The Alsops retired to Burton to take a hand in the process that eventually caused that town to surpass Derby as a brewing centre.

With the modification of smaller taverns as the town expanded, the practice of brewing beer on the premises was not always convenient. Hence the Lowes switched from malting to brewing and supplying ale to local outlets, leaving others – especially large-scale bakers like the Sowter family, with extensive premises in Queen Street and on Dayson Lane (later Curzon Street) – to undertake the necessary malting. Even the Derby Royal Theatre in Bold Lane was created, probably by Joseph Pickford, in 1773, from a redundant malthouse of 40 years before. An advertisement from the *Derby Mercury* (*DM*) from the 1780s is instructive:

'Wanted, a person who is a good brewer and baker that can be well recommended immediately in a Gent's family. The wages paid will be £10 per annum.'

John Lowe's son, Thomas, greatly expanded the Wardwick brewery and became very opulent in the process and served as Mayor of Derby four times before his death in 1831. His eldest son did not succeed him (except, unusually, in the Mayoralty for 1821) for he was a parson, but the next brother, Charles did, until selling out to Moreton Charles Wedge in 1837.

The other brewers at the start of the 19th century were the Ash Close Brewery (of 1804 near the north end of the Duffield Road), Wheeldon and Gibson (Navigation Brewery Nottingham Road, 1830), and Gisborne and Watson of Friar Gate. The latter was started in 1811 in Dayson Lane (Curzon Street) run by Henry Franceys Gisborne, another gentleman brewer. His partner, John Watson, continued the firm into the Victorian era, closing in November 1883 (*DM* 28/11/1883). They were joined in healthy competition by Henry Hunt (the Derby Brewery, Nottingham Road, 1835), Washington Pike, ironically the son of a notable Baptist minister (Parker Street) and John Porter's Manchester Brewery (hence his workers' cottages in Manchester Street) of Ashbourne Road in 1835.

By the 1850s, Hunt had been taken over by David Paine, but Pike, Porter and Watson flourished. Of these three, Pike continued until the late 1870s when he and his son, Baxter Pike, closed down and took the franchise to run the GNR's Friar Gate station refreshments rooms from 1877; Porter was bought out by Stretton's in 1865, and Watson survived a decade more on Uttoxeter New Road.

David Paine, in his turn, was taken over by L.W. Reynolds *c.*1860 and he was shortly afterwards (in 1871) bought out by Alderman Thomas Clarke (1814-1877) Mayor of Derby in 1862-3. He was grandson of John, a Nottingham Road cornfactor, who founded his malting business before 1791, and whose daughter married into the Wallis dynasty of the *New Inn*. Thomas also had a brother, John, a vintner in the Market Place; no doubt their enterprises were linked, as was that of his other brother, Robert who began brewing in 1830. Thomas, however, had inher-

ited through his wife – the grand-daughter and heiress of Robert Bloor – the Derby China Factory which he closed and asset-stripped before disposing of part of the site to the Sisters of Mercy and built his new brewery on the remainder. Following the repeal of the Malt Tax in 1880, he and his eldest son, Thomas were able to expand Robert's Nottingham Road Brewery, sandwiched between Nottingham Road and the canal and had grandiosely renamed it the Derby Brewery by 1874, having taken over Henry Hunt's original concern. It was fed by 16 'great malthouses', some on the modestly-named Clarke Street nearby and others in Beeston, Bedford and elsewhere. It was re-registered in May 1893 on taking over the non-Derby brewery of H.J.E. Scott and Hugh Bertie Craven, although the latter – a keen hunting man, but no relation – did live nearby, at Wheathills, Mackworth. The Derby Brewery Company was the first local brewery to install the telephone, in 1891. They had over 57 houses when taken over by Stretton's in 1899.

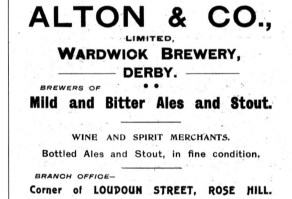

Alton & Co brewery advertisement.

In 1869, William Alton (who numerous tenancies are noted in the text) bought out M.C. Wedge of the former Lowe Brewery of 1788 behind 19-20 Wardwick and expanded it further with his partner, Edward Barnett, who subsequently took the business over, taking into partnership Alton's nephew (and adopted son), Hepworth Tropolet Tijou, later Alton, George d'Arcy Clark, an opulent attorney, and Arthur Walkden. The company was registered in 1888 and a new company in July 1899. They brewed on the Union System and were also maltsters. By 1899 they owned 91 licensed outlets in the area.

Another newcomer was Stretton's, established in Ashbourne Road in 1865 by taking over both Porter and Sarah Eyre (1821-1863). Her grandfather, Samuel, was a tenant farmer on the Radburne estate, son of Joseph, of Mickleover. The Poles of Radburne then gave him a tenancy at their Park Hall, Barlborough estate, sometime after the birth of his son, Elijah (1799-1863). Elijah went to King's Lynn, Norfolk, in the mid-1820s and became a brewer there in partnership with a Mr Slagg, whose daughter Jane he married at Barlborough in 1820. He later returned to Derby and established a branch of the brewery at the Ashbourne Road Old Brewery, 50 Ashbourne Road in 1852. Sarah was the eldest of his eight daughters, and in 1841 married her namesake, Thomas Eyre of the Liversage Brewery, Court No.2, Nottingham Road. Widowed by 1861, she died not long after her father (who left £60,000), and the business was disposed of by her son-in-law, Thomas Blake, then the manager of the *Royal Hotel*.

Most of Alton's large brewery, built in the 1860s and designed by George Henry Sheffield (1844-1882), survives, and has for years been earmarked for adaptation as flats, a notion which took a dent in the late 1990s when one entire range facing Surrey Street burnt to the ground, to be conveniently replaced by much cheaper new-build flats, completed in 2002. Stretton's had 154 pubs when they bought out Alton's in January 1903, but both were run separately until 1922, when the Wardwick operation closed. It was taken over by Samuel Allsopp in 1927, when the firm had 143 houses. The brewery closed in 1929 and was leased to Burrows & Sturgess, soft drinks manufacturers. In 1907, a member of the family, John Stretton, broke away and started his own brewery on Kedleston Road, by Cedar Street, formed from the business of Henry Sherwin (several of who kin ran pubs – see text), which collapsed in December 1905. His brewery was opened in 1907 and functioned until 1916, but the venture was thereafter (and prosaically) absorbed by the Derby Vinegar Company of Harvey & Harvey, formerly of Wood Street. The building, closed 1983, is now an old folks' home. Another Ashbourne Road brewery was that of B. & A. F. Weall, taken over by Altons in December 1897. Also in the late 1860s, Zachary Smith's brewery came into being, with operations in Derby and on the canal at Shardlow.

A final entry into the ranks of Derby breweries in the 19th century was George Offiler's Vine Brewery. Like many landlords of that era, George Offiler (1837-1899), licensee of the *Vine*, on the corner of Whitaker Street and Corden Street, brewed his own beer, but after less than two years in Derby, in 1877, began brewing a surplus and

Offiler's label of c.1930.

selling to neighbouring houses; in 1881 he employed three men.

He was attended with remarkable success, and in 1884 purchased the warehouse of the Star Tea Company, formerly the old Ordnance Depot, on Normanton Road (built to the designs of James Wyatt in 1806, but converted by Ambrose Moore into a silk mill in the 1820s) and converted it into the Vine Brewery. The architect, who mainly replaced Wyatt's building, was William Bradford of London and the tower principle was adopted.

By 1890, the year the company was registered, Offiler's were producing 509,000 gallons of ale per annum. In that year the brewery owned the following 14 Derby pubs: *Castle* (Castle Street), *Chequers* (Willow Row), *Crown* (London Road), *Golden Eagle* (Agard Street), *Green Lane House*, *Minstrel Boy* (Rose Hill Street), *New Inn* (Russell Street), *Park Street Tavern*, *Seven Stars* and *Stag & Pheasant* (Brook Street), *Stork* (Macklin Street, later sold to Alton's), *Union of Hearts* (John Street), *Victoria* (Cowley Street, the brewery's first purpose-built new pub) and, of course, the *Vine*. In addition they had five in Loughborough, six in Belper, two in Whitwick (Leicestershire), one in Shepshed (Leicestershire), and 12 others scattered around the Southern Derbyshire area, making 40 outlets altogether. Two years later the company reformed and re-registered.

George Offiler was the eldest of the four sons and three daughters of Samuel Offiler of Whitemoor Place, Basford, Nottinghamshire, whose father, David was a humble labourer. George's aunt Mary married, in 1844, a brewer, William Marshall of Hyson Green, who may have been the incentive behind George's subsequent career for, although a coal higgler at the tender age of 14 (Census, 1851), he too had set up as a brewer, at William Street, Basford by 1858 (at 21!). In 1871 he was landlord of the *Shoulder of Mutton* on Radford Road, Nottingham (now the site of a McDonald's), from whence he removed to Derby. He married, firstly, in 1858 Eliza Smart, mother of his daughter Lucy who was born and died in 1860, but would seem to have led an irregular personal life even before her death in 1870, for his only son, John Henry Mark Scott was born in May 1861, son of Mary Scott whom he did not marry until 1872. Henry Scott later took his father's surname and was George's partner by 1881 and his managing director in 1890. Mary died in 1885, and George married a third time, at the Osmaston Road chapel (he was then living close by at Brooklyn House, Charnwood Street) to Mary Ellen Slater.

On George's death, Henry Offiler (as he by then was) took over. He lived at Salisbury House, Mill Hill, again, not far from the brewery and in due course was succeeded by the eldest of his sons, (Henry) Cecil Offiler (1896-1971). As it turned out, Offiler's was the last independent brewer to survive in Derby, latterly with 238 houses in the region, finally being taken over by Charrington United Breweries in 1965, swiftly losing its identity, the old brewery closing on 30 September 1966. Charringtons were then shortly afterwards taken over by Bass.

Alton's had been taken over by Stretton's as early as 1903, but kept their identity for another 35 years, both names continuing on their pubs and products for decades more, despite a second takeover of the combined company by Samuel Allsopp & Company in 1927, but even then the name Stretton's appeared in conjunction with Ind Coope, who were a 're-branding' of Allsopp's.

This was the final irony, for the latter was the Burton brewing company once run by Sir Charles Allsopp, Bt, 1st Lord Hindlip, the direct descendant of the builder of that elegant house in the Wardwick where John Lowe had established his brewery in the 18th century. Thus, in the rate-books for 1933-8, the firms of Stretton, Alton and Allsopp are still differentiated from each other, although all three were controlled by the latter. Allsopps, of course, soon became Ind Coope (& Allsopp) later Ansell's, Allied Breweries, Carlsberg-Tetley and Allied-Domecq.

A 1908 advertisement for Pountain's, Market Place.

In 1899, the Derby Brewery Co had also fallen victim to Stretton's. Charringtons also had a considerable presence in Derby early in the century but they sold most of their Derby pubs at auction in 1926, which is ironic, in view of Charrington's take-over of Offiler's 40 years later. Many were bought up by Pountain's, wine merchants, of the Market Place, others going to Zachary Smith, James Eadie of Burton (whose proprietor lived at Barrow Hall) and various other breweries. Pountain's, who sold all 42 of their pubs in 1950-55 to Ind Coope (Ansell's), were also finally taken over by Bass post-war, the era in which Zachary Smith's brewery also ceased trading; the site of their works at Shardlow was built over in the early 1970s.

Despite the expansion of large-scale brewing in the 18th and 19th centuries in Derby, beer was still being made on the premises of around one-third of the individual houses at the beginning of the 20th century. John Houghton's account of brewing in Derby of 1693 makes no mention of

any large-scale brewing and the implication is that only malting was actually done on a general supplier basis and that each of the 120 alehouses which he records brewed their own ale.

He also records that the excellence of Derby ale was said to be due to the fact that the malt was dried with coke, which must be the earliest reference to the use of this fuel in British industry.

The trade of the town, wrote Defoe, *is chiefly in good malt and good ale; nor is the quantity of the latter unreasonably small, which, as they say, they dispose of among themselves, though they spare some to their neighbours, too.*

Thus, the retreat of on-site brewing seems to have begun at this juncture: in the third or fourth decade of the 18th century.

The art of small-scale brewing appears to have been passed on from father to son (or daughter). Roy Christian reported being told by the late Mrs Winter, who brewed at the *Copeland Arms* until she was 78, (in 1963) and was the last woman brewster: *I picked* [the art] *up by watching the men at work.*

John Houghton FRS records the brewing method in Derby: *The malt thus prepared is mashed with boyling liquor so as it may easily be stir'd about with the mashrule and having stood close covered about 2 hours (in which time more boyling liquor is got ready) it must be run off, and so much more hot liquor put on as will serve to fill the Vessel or Vessels design'd: which a tryal or two by the Brewing Vessels will easily discover.*

To a Hogshead of the first running is put about one pound of Hops: when as much Wort is gathered as will serve for the Ale, then the Grains must be filled up again with boyling liquor and so stand about half an Hour and then let run off, which will make good Beer; the Grains filled up again, and standing so another half Hour or more, will make small Beer very well worth boyling. The Ale or best Wort must boyl an Hour and half or two Hours before it be laded into the Cooler, and when it is cold enough, Yeast must be put to it. If it be good Wort and well boyled, it will have an oyl upon it, which you may perceive by rubbing it between your Forefinger and Thumb.

Nevertheless, 17 pubs were reported in one source as brewing on the premises in 1945, although by 1960, only a handful of Derby inns were brewing on the premises, including the *Green Man* (Kensington Street), *Seven Stars* and *White Bear.* The decline had been well under way between the wars and became terminal with the drain on manpower and shortages of raw materials during World War Two; only the most determined survived, numbering no more than 20 in 1950. By 1962, when it was taken over by William Younger's, the *Seven Stars* was one of the last.

Tom Roome, the 'jolly brewer' there, went briefly to *The Friary* but, until the opening of the *Flamingo and Firkin* in Becket Street, 20 years later, the tradition died. Tom Roome had gone to the *Seven Stars* in the Depression in the early 1930s to work for Thomas Henry, where he served a three year training period. Before the war, he recalled (*DET* 15/6/1962) brewing took place three or four times a week, but by the later 1950s it had become two or three times, excepting holiday periods. The process took him 11 hours, and visits to see him at work were highly prized concessions on the part of Thomas Henry's son and successor, Philip. Since the opening of the Becket Street establishment, the revived *Brunswick Inn* has also opened a brewery as, briefly, did the *Falstaff*, Silver Hill Road.

VI

FROM the earliest time public houses, taverns and inns have carried distinctive names, often imaginatively illustrated for the benefit of the illiterate, being then the case for the majority of the English population. Even in Roman times taverns were distinguished by names and signs.

In Roman times too, there lay along the course of the roads *mansiones* or small settlements, in many cases rarely bigger than a cluster of outbuildings round the *mansio* itself – situated about a day's march (25/30 Roman miles) apart where there was no town already existing. These had names not on the inn sign system, but like those of other Roman forts and settlements. But they are the direct antecedents of the coaching inn or post-house; indeed, it was at *mansiones* that the Imperial Post *(cursus)* could change horses.

Among the inn names with the oldest antecedents are, as we have seen, the religious ones: the *Cross Keys* – the Arms of the Papacy and symbol of St Peter; the *George* – the patron saint of the Knights Templar; the *Lamb* – as a symbol of Christ and others including the *Crown and Mitre* (Church and State), the *Virgin's* and the *Anchor*. Royal crests in the Mediaeval period were often adopted, especially where an inn was provided by a Town Corporation: *White Swan* (Henry IV); *White Hart* (Richard II); *White Lion* (Edward IV) and of course the *Rose and Crown*, representing the Tudor Dynasty.

Also in the Mediaeval period, trades' symbols came to be adopted: the *Ram* (wool trade; this sign nationally predates the legend of the Derby Ram, although the trade's success may have had a hand in fostering it); the *Dusty Miller*; the *Green Man* came to symbolise the forester, although the Green Man himself takes us back deep into pagan beliefs, and the *Coopers' Arms*.

Note that 'Trades' signs underwent a revival in an updated form during the 19th century: the *Plumbers' Arms*, the *Furnace Arms* and the *Moulders' Arms* – not to mention the various 'secret' societies like the *Freemason's Arms*, as well as Friendly Societies as the *Foresters' Arms*, the *Oddfellows' Arms* and the *Druids' Retreat*.

Other signs were merely whimsical, like the *Quiet Woman* which depicted a woman standing erect, but headless; and The *Five Alls*, the sign for which depicted the King *(I rule all)*, the Soldier *(I fight for all)*, the Farmer *(I work for all)*, the Parson *(I pray for all)*, and the Devil *(I take all)*; hardly an encouragement for the young Derby buff of the time *(I drink all)*! People gave their names to taverns, especially heroes, generals, politicians and local nobles – the list is full of them.

One presents an amusing anomaly: the *Richard Cobden* (Abbey Street) was represented on the sign as *Sir Richard Cobden* which in view of that gentleman's having refused a Baronetcy at least once in his long career, seems like taking enthusiasm too far. Lord Byron (and even his subjects) was also popular, not to mention George Hudson of York, members of the Royal Family, the Immortal Bard (both close to the Bold Lane Theatre) and his characters (two *Falstaffs*).

Public Houses erected on the limits of the town between the wars have not been graced with names that are either exciting or original; even the architecture is dull and pretentious. Post-war pub architecture has continued to decline, although names had become more interesting and original: others revive traditional names.

Much has been made of the signs themselves, but it is often forgotten that most urban inns had written rather than pictorial signboards, and in Derby until the early twentieth century virtually all were affixed flush to the façades of the buildings. Only a few coaching inns had pictorial signs, usually displayed across the entrance to the yard. The traditional sign hanging from a pole supported by a frame was anciently confined to country coaching inns; fewer still had signs which spanned the street, like that of the *Green Man and Black's Head* at Ashbourne, the *George* with one spanning Iron Gate being the only example recorded in Derby, and even that eventually collapsed, killing an unfortunate horse. In the 20th century, the urban inn has gradually switched from signs fixed to the building on the façade to one set on a bracket at right-angles. The incentive on the part of the brewers has been to appeal to nostalgia; the precedent (in Derby at any rate) is largely spurious.

Since the first edition of this book was published, there has been much ink spilled about the large proprietorial companies changing the names of local pubs at random, mainly at the whim of their marketing managers. Before the first edition Derby had seen the *Globe* become the *Mr Jorrocks*, the *Spotted Horse* become *Lloyd's* and the *Golden Eagle*, Agard Street, become the *Knight Fall*. Subsequently, a campaign was launched, to coincide with the 250th anniversary of Bonnie Prince Charlie's entry into Derby in the 'Forty Five, to persuade the brewery to rename the *Mr Jorrocks* the *George*, it being a portion of the original 1693 building. This having been triumphantly achieved by autumn 1995, within three years the brewery decided to re-brand it as an Irish theme pub *Lafferty's*. The *Green Man* soon followed, becoming *Ryan's* with the *Saracen's Head* not far behind, becoming *O'Neill's*, although it is not without *schadenfreude* that it was noticed that the latter has swiftly reverted to its previous (although not original) name. Even one of the city's newest inns, the *Jackie Stamps*, has been thoroughly gutted and reopened with an Australian theme as *Walkabout*. Indeed, so long drawn out has the process been that it would surprise no one if the Australian bubble has burst just as swiftly as the Irish one did.

Yet this is all very reminiscent of the 18th century and early 19th, when pub names changed with alarming rapidity, which bewildering changes, it is to be hoped, are accurately chronicled in the main text. Sometimes a land-lord would change pubs, taking the name of his old one to bestow on his new charge. There are several cases authenti-cated from the 18th century, and two of the most bizarre are that of the *Dove* and the *Three Nuns* nearby in Derby's West End in the 1870s and the earlier 30-year duplication of *Noah's Arks* in The Morledge. Pub name-changes are nothing new in themselves, what is new is the imposition of names from afar by a large company, especially when that name is repeated across the country under the same owner-ship, like the *Harvester*, Pride Park, or the *Pig & Truffle* (ex-*Lloyd's*, ex-*Spotted Horse*, ex-*Post Office Hotel*, etc. ad nauseam). In this way are uniqueness and character lost.

In the early 1970s, traditional ale was fast disappearing from Derby, and the Derby branch of the Campaign for Real Ale (CAMRA) was formed. A measure of their success over 20 or so years is the fact that in 1994 all but three pubs in central Derby sold real ale (the exceptions were the *Melbourne Bar*, the *Rhode Island Exchange* and the *Durham Ox*, although this is still regrettably true of the *Midland Hotel*). This process was greatly aided by legislation of around 1990 which laid down that the big brewers could have only a limited number of tied houses, obliging them to dispose of a considerable number locally. Whilst some failed to find buyers, most went to smaller chains or private owners, with beneficial results. The same legislation also obliged the breweries to allow their landlords to offer 'guest' ales. In 2001, however, some 60 city pubs sold no real ale at all. One unfortunate tendency which pre-dated these changes was the accountant-led decision of most of the big brewers with tied houses to force out their tenants and replace them with managers. This damaging policy has

destroyed individuality, continuity and in some cases the lives of tenants, forced out at a loss in middle age with little chance of alternative employment. A final modern trend has been to remove internal walls and partitions so that more customers can be crammed in and surveyed by CCTV cameras. Listed pubs cannot, in general, be so altered and the corollary is that more pubs need to be added to the Statutory List. Unfortunately, Secretaries of State over the last decade have been very reluctant to add any Derby ones, however eligible, as noted elsewhere.

VII

IF the two oldest sets of statistics are correct, the table below demonstrates unequivocally that the ratio of pubs to people in Derby has declined steadily!

Year	No. of Houses*	Population of City	No. of persons to one pub
1693	120	6,850	57
1761	113	9,970	88
1833	142	31,882†	224
1846	161	39,020	300
1883	335	85,874	254
1895	306	98,891	325
1935	230	145,106	631
1975	156	219,348	1,406
1992	142	216,410	1,524

*Excluding suburbs

†Population (1821 Census) was 19,648, illustrating a remarkable increase over 12 years. The increase over the years 1818-21 had been only 3,551.

Even adding the suburban inns to the latter statistics, the current figure of persons per pub only totals 1,035 – a stark contrast to the situation pertaining in, say, 1833, the year of the first reliable statistic! A current statistic has not been compiled, for, with the profusion of university students and 'café-bars', 'fun pubs' and the setting-up of establishments of a status that can be difficult to determine, firm statistics are had to come by. All those included here-under that are currently in existence (or were at the time of writing – changes are almost weekly) are one into which any reader of this book might wander and buy a drink without necessarily having to buy food or pay a member-ship fee. The same criterion applies to those no longer in existence. There may be some inadvertent exceptions listed, however.

VIII

The sources available are variable; early deeds have been searched, but largely in vain. The chief source for the 18th and 19th centuries is the *Derby Mercury [DM]*, started in 1732, and its pages are peppered with advertisements naming inns, for inns were the places where things happened, and all in intense competition with one another. It was also the chief place for advertising freeholds and leases.

From 1791 the chief source is the trade directories which list inns; previously only one significant one exists giving names and locations: the list of inns wherein potential voters could sample the free hospitality provided by Sir Henry Harpur of Calke, Bt, standing in the Tory interest for one of the two Derby seats. If it is appreciated that he was one of four candidates, then it might suggest that the list only represents 25 per cent of the total inns available to the candidates. In reality, it is known that Harpur was being far more generous than any of his rivals, and the list probably represents nearer 40 per cent of the whole.

The directories themselves run to 1965 and with them some reasonable precision may be derived, although some pubs are demonstrably absent from one or other of them when known from other evidence to exist. They can also be wayward when recording addresses, and much more attention has been given to precisely locating pubs through their addresses (and other means) in this edition, enabling many more re-namings to be recorded or confirmed. The earlier ones tend to list beer houses anonymously, which is a problem, for their addresses had to be compared with those of named pubs to sort out those already chronicled from those whose names are lost for ever. Nevertheless, the directory evidence forms the backbone of this book.

The other chief source is the form volumes of rate-assessment books, compiled from 1935, in most cases by the predecessors of Messrs Maynard, estate agents, on contract from the Borough Council. Each inn is described and illustrated by a plan, showing the number and layout of rooms. Other information includes landlord's name, owners names, brewery, whether beer is brewed in the premises and when it stopped, date of full licence if previously a beerhouse, turnover, and other notes at the discretion of the valuer. The books were kept up until 1952, so closure dates of pubs can be divined to within a year of the last yearly assessment, providing some real precision, where directory evidence can only be accurate to within a few years.

Beyond these sources, property deeds have been used (including a complete set for the *White Bear*, Derwent Row, courtesy the late Mr N.R. Beckett), deeds and newspaper reports' kept at Derby Local Studies Library, and other chance references whenever they have been made available. Other, printed, sources of varying usefulness are listed in the bibliography.

On local signs the only local source is Jewitt's long series of articles printed in the *Reliquary* in the 1860s and 1870s. Unfortunately, this names several inns without providing a date or a locale within the Borough. Some have been pinned down from other sources, others are merely names.

Publication inevitably attracts further and hitherto unsuspected material from readers, and the author does not doubt that this will be so in the case of this edition. Nor is total accuracy within these pages guaranteed: thus all corrections and amplifications will be most gratefully received and, if it proves sufficiently popular, can be incorporated in a third edition.

Acknowledgements

IT goes without saying that I owe much to many in the preparation of this book. The simple hand-list from which it grew was compiled when I was assistant museum education officer at Derby Museum in the mid-1970s, and without the support of my immediate superior Yvonne Adams and, later, the late Roy Hughes, it would not have been done. It also drew impetus from requests from the Geography Department of the old Bishop Lonsdale College (now Derby University) for town walks focusing on historic taverns, so to the survivors of this august body I also owe a debt! The project was kept alive by requests for lectures on the same topic, and I must acknowledge the late genial Ray Neave as a prime mover in this. Thanks are also due to members of Derby CAMRA from the 1970s for, although never a member, I had the pleasure of many helpful conversations with Reg Newcombe, John Arguile and Ivor Clissold.

The great advance in this research, however, and that which has made this book a real possibility, was that undertaken by my former colleague John Crossling, who spent many lunchtimes (when he could have been out researching the inns of the town in the field), going through 18th-century issues of the *Derby Mercury* and indexing each pub entry: to him and his wife, Helen, who typed them up, I owe an enormous debt. After his departure to Warwick Museum, I continued the task for a few more decades until the real burden – from 1790 – was taken on by the late and much missed Ivor Clissold. He industriously recorded all the public house notices of any kind in the *DM* and kept me furnished with copies as he went along. He had just reached 1891 when he unexpectedly and most tragically died. Yet the period he covered included the rise of the small beer house, and without his efforts, the full revision of this book would have been impossible. He also furnished me, in a series of very jovial letters, with a large quantity of comments, notes, corrections and pieces of Clissoldian wisdom, all of which have been incorporated. It would have been impossible to acknowledge these individually, but I hope very much that this note will itself be acknowledgement enough.

I am most grateful, too, for the opportunity to use photographs from Derby Museum's collections, as well as others from private sources including J. Sharpe, the late C.H. Burton, R.G. Hughes, S.J. Wilde Esq, E. Tranter, Esq, and Frank Gilbert, who shared much information on the family of his brewing ancestor, Sarah Eyre. Numerous other owners who modestly wished to remain anonymous have also been enormously helpful. I offer them all my warmest thanks.

For my own researches I must heartily thank Sylvia Bown, her successors and colleagues at the Derby Local Studies Library, and thanks also to James Darwin, now of the Georgian Group and Josef Lachowicz, on the buildings, and to their former colleagues in the Derby City Survey, who worked within my department at the Museum 1984-7 and whose research was an essential supplement to my own.

I owe a debt, too, to my friend the late George Rennie, chief conservation officer for the city, who frequently updated me in relation to pubs, and with whom my wife and I worked in 1994-5 when English Heritage put the word round that they would welcome applications to add hitherto neglected pubs to the Statutory List. Carole and I, on behalf of the Civic Society, with George, Dave George of CAMRA and one or two other willing experts, drew up a list of likely candidates, whittled it down to about eight, and then religiously visited them all to assess the likelihood of their being accepted. We put forward five including the *Exeter Arms, Woodlark* and the *Blue Boy* (as the least mauled of G.M. Eaton's three Art Deco inns). Not one was accepted by the EH inspector.

I would also like to thanks the many who read the original edition and contributed additions and corrections, especially Mr Ken Motley, who furnished me with a wealth of information, whom I have been able to cite as the authority in a number of instances. My heartfelt thanks also go to Pip Southall (editor of the *Derby Drinker*) who added much new information, my publisher Anton Rippon, O. Fox, N.R. Beckett, Roy Christian, Reg Fenton, Michael Stanley, Mr Wilde, Alan Millband, Richard Felix, Edward Saunders, the late Cliff Burton, Jeffery Tillett, the late Michael Fall and the late Guy Brighouse. To these and many others who I have not named individually, I owe a great debt.

Finally, to my dear wife, Carole, I would like to record my warmest thanks and regard. She has suffered the hours when I have been writing this book, helping without demur when asked, and undertaking the thankless and unrewarding task of accompanying me into numerous inns and plying me with drink in the course of research and photography. Poor thing, it must have been awful! Yet, without her, and her driving skills, this essential aspect would hardly have been possible. Since 1996, we have been accompanied on many of these expeditions by our daughter Cornelia, not always entirely welcome in some hostelries, but always unusually tolerant for one so young.

Maxwell Craven
Derby
2002

Town Centre Pubs

THE ENTRIES here are headed by the name, followed by the address or locality (where known) to the left. To the right are the dates: the first is that of the inn's first mention in the sources; if there is good reason to suppose that the establishment had been in existence before that date, 'by' is prefixed. The second is the last date known. If there is no date in the second column, it may be presumed that the pub is still functioning. Amplification where possible will be found in the paragraph that follows. A single date with dashes either side indicates a single reference only. Sources are gathered at the end of the entry, with abbreviations expanded in the bibliography.

In this second and wholly revised edition, a single asterisk (*) denotes an entry where new or revised information has been added; two asterisks (**) indicate a completely new entry.

Where there has been one of more changes of name, the inn has been listed under that best remembered one, and cross-referenced.

Words of a pub's title in round brackets are elements of the name occasionally omitted at some time in the history of the establishment. Entries are listed in alphabetical order of the main element of the title. Generally 'Old' is considered a subsidiary element, for instance, as in the *(Old) Seven Stars* – this is listed under *Seven Stars* and not under 'Old'.

There are a few exceptions, however, where the title makes little sense without the epithet, or where the qualifying element is unvarying as in the *New Inn, Old English Gentleman* or the *Old House at Home.*

Addresses were often given with a degree of imprecision both in directories and the local papers; over half Derby's streets were renumbered towards the end of the 19th century, occasionally more than once, their first numbering tending to exclude factories, yards and work premises, later brought into sequence. The previous street number, where it existed, is given in brackets after the later one, except where one or other doesn't apply. Where streets have been renamed the earlier name is also supplied in this way.

A number of Derby pub names were recorded by the 19th century antiquary Llewellyn Jewitt, in the journal he founded and edited, *The Reliquary,* mainly in a series of articles running from Vol. VI (1865-6) p. 50ff. to Vol. XI (1870-71); unfortunately he did not record either the location of these inns or the period of their existence. Except where research has resolved these questions, they are entered as *unknown location* and *before* [date of article] and with the word 'Jewitt' below. Any further comment follows. Abbreviations in the section below each entry can be found in the Bibliography.

ABBEY INN

54 Abbey Street   *by 1857-1936*
Named after the street which itself was pitched across the fields called Abbey Barns (because until 1537 they had been owned by the Abbey of Darley) in c.1824. Closed by Ind Coope & Allsopp trading as Strettons; the licence was transferred to the *Coronation*, Baker Street, c.1937.

ACORN

26 Queen Street   *by 1846-1926*
The name, frequently met with on inns, could be attributable to the Derby family of Oakes, later of Riddings, and long the proprietors of the *Nag's Head* St Peter's Street, who had a grant of arms incorporating three acorns in 1806. The building began as an impressive Carolean town house, erected by Stephen Flamsteed, the father of Revd John Flamsteed, FRS (1646-1719) England's first Astronomer Royal, which he inherited in 1688. It was extended at the rear in the 1730s, and equipped with a (lost) Robert Bakewell side gate. In 1764 it was refronted in Palladian style by Joseph Pickford for his friend John Whitehurst, FRS (1713-1788). In 1793, Whitehurst's nephew and successor, John Whitehurst II (1761-1834) moved the business and the house was sold to Thomas Bainbrigge of Rocester, who let it immediately to Joseph Wright ARA (1734-1797), who died there five years later. He was followed by Alderman John Hope (a former mayor) and John Hudson, a master at Derby School. Sometime before 1846 the building was divided one-third/two-thirds. The larger (northerly) portion was lived in for a time by John Wright, a surgeon, who was succeeded by John Smith (1813-1883), clockmaker, a former apprentice and employee of John Whitehurst III. The smaller portion was converted into the *Acorn Inn*, possibly as early as the period following Hope's death in 1819. The yard to the south became Acorn Yard. It was to let in 1869. In 1907 the pub had its licence withdrawn (as did several in this area) due to pressure on the Bench from Mrs Henry Boden and the Derby Temperance Society and it was vacated, acquired by Smith's and taken down to form a wide access to their works behind. In 1926-8 Queen Street was widened and Pickford's remaining façade removed with the rooms behind, J.E.H. Smith's friend, the newly-appointed Borough Architect C.H. Aslin, CBE stylishly refronting what remained for him. The clockmakers moved out in 1999 and the site was sold in 2001, but at the time of writing it is unclear what its fate would be. Proposed for Spotlisting, December 2001.   *DM 7/7/1869.*

ADAM & EVE

Unknown locale   *unknown date*
Jewitt.

(ADMIRAL) RODNEY

See RODNEY

ADMIRAL VERNON

Bridge Gate   *-1775-*
Named after a naval hero: the maverick Admiral Edward Vernon MP (1684-1757), the capturer (from Spain) of Porto Bello in the West Indies, 20-21 November 1739, with only six ships. This made him a popular hero, the subject of numerous medallions, and – as with Rodney (*qv*) – his surname became a popular Christian and pub name. His other connection with drink is that he also invented the Naval 'grog' ration, an effort to cut nautical drunkenness by diluting the rum ration by adding one quart of water to each half-pint of rum. Inn, to let in 1775, therefore perhaps established c.1740 and taken down to accommodate some new building, *eg* the Regency St Anne's Terrace.
DM 14/7/1775.

ALBERT VAULTS*

6 (3) Albert Street   *by 1874-1912*
Named after the street, itself pitched in 1848 and named after the Prince Consort. Mr Ragg, the licensee in 1863 organised the Licensed Victuallers' ball that year.
DM 4/2/1863.

ALBERT (VAULTS)*

2-4 Whitecross Street (corner Brook Street) by 1874-1963
Named after the Prince Consort, probably in the immediate wake of his death in 1861. H.D. Leonard brewed on the premises until sale to Stretton's in 1924. At this period, and for many years, HQ of the Derby Town Pigeon Club. Later purchased under a CPO in 1961, closed in 1963 and demolished shortly afterwards in slum clearance.

ALBERT VAULTS

See also NEW MARKET

ALBION*

9-10 Albion Street (corner Bloom Street)   by 1833-1965
A common name, being an ancient one for the British Isles. Probably adapted from a house (or a pair of terraced cottages) after the street was pitched and so named c.1815. First known from a spirit licence application on 26th August 1874; note that until the late 19th century all applications to the licensing Bench were made on or about this date. Cleared for the erection of the gross Eagle Centre, late 1960s. Formerly the *Black Boy*, under which name it was known from 1833 until 1873, the date it changed.
DM 26/8/1874.

Alexandra
Hotel, Siddals Road.
Drawing by Reg Newcombe.

ALEXANDRA*

203 Siddals Road   *1871-1987; 1989*

Named after HRH Princess Alexandra, daughter of Christian IX of Denmark, who married the future Edward VII on 10 March 1863. Built for Sir John ('Brassy') Smith by the architect G.H. Sheffield in 1871 in his usual exuberant gothic manner *(BBA)* with its first licence application made two years later. The building was originally a riot of polychrome brickwork with lancet style paired fenestration and polished limestone colonnettes for mullions, but all crudely harled over in the post-war era. Home brewing in the 1930s when owned by Strettons. In the 1960s an early haunt of the gay community before migration to the *Rising Sun*. Closed for demolition in 1987 and for two years boarded up and decaying before purchase by Messrs Bateman's brewery and full restoration. Now a free house owned by Tynemill Ltd.

ALEXANDRA VAULTS**

3-4 Bold Lane   *by 1878-1880*

In 1878 kept by W.V. Scholes, also listed (as 'bandmaster' at the same location) as the *Jolly Dogs* perhaps either a colloquial name for the house which confused the directory's compilers or even a band, mistaken for the inn's name! Possibly the renamed *Elephant & Castle*.

ALLIES, THE*

85 High Street   *by 1857-1895*

Although High Street was pitched within a year or two of the Napoleonic Wars, the title must refer to the victorious allies of the Crimean War, great rejoicings for the successful conclusion of which were held in Derby in 1856. This may indeed have been when it was founded, for an anonymous beer house appears at this address in the 1857 directory. However, it was briefly later called the *Prince Albert* in memory of the late Prince Consort (HRH Prince Albrecht v Saxe-Coburg und Gotha) who died in 1861, the pub being

so listed the following year, but it was certainly *The Allies* again by 1874 and so remained. It was for sale in 1882, but probably failed to make its way in the same street as the *High Street Tavern* and reverted to a house.
DM 9/8/1882.

ALMA, THE*

29 (2) York Street   *by 1862-1930*

Like High Street, York Street was pitched early in the 19th century (1828) but the fact that *The Alma* took its name from the Crimean river at which the first battle of the war in that peninsular was fought (20 September 1854) suggests that the inn was founded at around that time, probably after 1857, the date of *White's Directory* in which it does not appear, although it is the anonymous beer house listed at this address in 1862. Run in the 1870s by Mrs Eleanor Newbold (widow of John, of the *Black Horse* and *Dove*). Doubtless it was adapted from a pair of terraced artisans' cottages. Closed and the licence transferred to the *Osmaston Park Hotel*, 1930.

ANCHOR

See (CROWN &) ANCHOR

ANGEL*

2-4 Burton Road   *by 1833-1916*

Modest brick inn, probably built as part of Alderman Madeley's Little City estate. It was for sale in 1871 when it was 2 houses up from the end of Green Lane on the Little

Angel Inn, Burton Road, left, after 1905.

City side, and was so in the 1874 directory, too. Yet in the 1878 one, it is shown as next to the *Duke of York;* it presumably migrated. After closure, the building served as the meeting rooms of the Ancient Order of Druids friendly society and survived as a shop until c.1957.
DM 23/8/1871.

Old Angel, Cornmarket on the morning of Sunday 22 May 1932, the day of the Derby Flood, the 1836 façade of the former Rodney is to the left.

(OLD) ANGEL*

29 Cornmarket   *by 1549-1962*
All the evidence suggests that this inn was in existence prior to the dissolution of the College of All Saints' in 1549. In Queen Mary's charter of six years later it was confirmed to the Corporation as part of the endowment of All Saints' Church. An engraving shows a timber-framed building of mixed 15th and 16th century date with a brick façade to the street and what looks like a reset stone over the door with an angel under a crocketed ogiform Gothic arch. There is some evidence that, in the mid-18th century, it was for a time called the *(Nether) Ship* (qv). In 1645, 'Richard Cockeram was hanged on the gallows on Nuns' Green for killing one Mills, a servant at the Angel.' In the Civil War the vestry of All Saint's were all for selling it to the left wing Parliamentary firebrand Col. Thomas Sanders of Little

Ireton, but the deal fell through and Thomas Browne took a 60-year lease on it in 1656 instead, paying £10 per annum. This was surrendered in 1686, when a new lease of 100 years was granted to Charles Hacker, a scion of the Hackers of East Bridgford Hall. In the end, the freehold (including the Hacker family lease, then held by Charles's son Rowland) was sold by All Saints' parish vestry on 17 April 1732 to Alderman Henry Franceys, the apothecary, for £210, the money being spent on building the present gallery in the church, the work of Thomas Trimmer. Charles Hacker was then the tenant on a 100-year lease granted in 1686. It was then a timber-framed edifice rebuilt c.1660 with a brick façade incorporating a Dutch gable similar to that on the *Green Man*. It was to let in 1746, with 'stabling for 60 horses and a long garden' and was then the venue for cockfighting on race days. It nearly closed in 1867, being advertised for sale as a 'first class building site' and on condition that 'the licence is discontinued'; fortunately, this did not happen, and when it was rebuilt it was 30 years' later by Cox & Malin (see *Rodney*), who kept it going to boot! It was further altered in 1938 after which it bore a Guinness clock, and it was at this period when the illustrious boxer Joe Rostron took it on, coming from the *Woodlark* (qv in his biography), and moving on to the *Spotted Horse*. Closed in 1962, it was demolished in January 1969 to make way for Littlewoods, after over 400 years. It had a notable cock pit in the 18th century.
Allen (c.1964) 7; Cox & Hope (1881) 22; *DM* 6/2/1746 & 29/5/1867; *Reliquary* VII (1866-7) 179

Angel, Cornmarket, 1906.

ANGEL

Rotten Row   *–1673–*
A single reference occurs in Glover's *History and Gazetteer of the County of Derby* (1st Edn. 2 vols. [Derby 1829-31] II. 608).

ANTELOPE**

Unknown location   *before 1867*
Jewitt

APNA PUNJAB
See PEAR TREE

APOLLO
13 (9, 6) Ford Street (corner Willow Row) by 1833-1919
Stood opposite the *Silent Woman* by Brook Walk bridge and was to let in 1842. Named after the classical deity, but between 1857 and 1862 renamed the *Waterloo Tavern*. Closed by Stretton's just after World War One.

ARBORETUM
See LEOPARD

ARBORETUM HOTEL*
192 Osmaston Road (corner of Arboretum Street) by 1846-1994

Built between 1840 (when the Arboretum was opened) and 1846; a dignified brick and stucco building. It was envisaged that some of the middle-class visitors to the Arboretum itself would wish to stay here, and in consequence it began with high expectations, with six bedrooms, stabling for nine horses and room for two carriages. It was the scene of one of a number of sheep roasts to celebrate the 1856 peace at the end of the Crimean War. In 1935 Ind Coope and Allsopp remodelled the ground floor in Art Deco style with light horizontal bands on a black background, Crittall windows and a vertical internally-lit sign. Being close to the Derby China factory, it changed its name to the *Olde Avesbury* (a notable china pattern from the factory) to celebrate the centenary of the works in 1978. However, it was for sale in September 1993, closed in 1994 and was acquired by Royal Crown Derby which concern incorporated it into their new 'visitor centre', albeit without much concern for its function; most of it appears to be storage. The exterior was restored to some degree however.
DM 21/5/1856

ARKWRIGHT'S**
Market Place 1995-2001
When Sir Hugh Casson designed the new Assembly Rooms (completed in 1977) he provided shop units in the ground floor facing the Market Place, but these were plagued by seepage of sewage and damp problems, and in time only the Council could use the premises, and they were amalgamated to form a housing office. However, the problems were then soon acknowledged and cured, and in 1995 the area was let and converted into a café-bar called after Sir Richard Arkwright, the eminent local cotton spinning pioneer. There was scope for out-of-doors eating and drinking in fine weather at tables (the design of which the City Council made them change), but the bar

closed on 1 December 2001. At the time of writing it appeared that it would reopen as the *Co-Co Lounge* before Christmas 2002.

(ARMS OF THE ISLE OF MAN &) MOIRA**
48 Siddals Lane (corner John St) by 1832-1852
Offered for sale in 1832 and 1835 as the *Moira Arms* being the achievement of the Rawdon (later Rawdon-Hastings) family, Earls of Moira in the Irish peerage, big coal owners in the South Derbyshire/NW Leicestershire coalfield through having inherited the estates there of the Earls of Huntingdon in 1789 (for their later history see *Marquess of Hastings*). Sir John Rawdon, 2nd Earl of Moira, was a hero of the Napoleonic Wars. The arms are: *argent a fesse between three pheons sable*. How this beer house contrived to have the ArmS of the Isle of Man (*gules three legs in armour conjoined in pairle proper, spurred or*) added to its title is difficult to judge; perhaps a Manx-born landlord took it over before 1852, when this name was recorded. An anonymous beer house in 1850. Almost certainly renamed the Magnet.
DM 16/2/1832 & 11/3/1835

ARUBA
See BERLIN'S

ASTON COURT
See YORK

Babington Arms, at the junction of Babington and Green Lanes, 1925.

BABINGTON ARMS*
34 Babington Lane by 1850-1926
Handsome brick inn with stone dressings and distinctive wavy edged rusticated lintels built probably *c.*1810, perhaps as a residence, as it fails to appear as a pub in the street directories, at the intersection of Babington Lane and Green Lane. Named after the armorial bearings of the Babington family who had owned the land between the two streets to 1586, and after which Babington Lane (pitched

1789) was also named: *Argent ten torteaux four three two and one; crest: A dragon's head between two dragons' wings gules and out of the mouth an escroll; motto: 'Foy est Tout'* proudly emblazoned on the sign, affixed, old-style to the end wall. A sheep roast was held here to celebrate the peace of 1856. When for sale in 1879 it was described as an 'old established and well accustomed old public house'. Joseph Wagstaff was the landlord when it closed in 1926 and it was demolished the year following because of the widening of Babington Lane, and what remains of the site is still empty and untidy.
DM 21/5/1856 & 9/4/1879.

Babington Arms, Babington Lane, 2002.

BABINGTON ARMS**

2 Babington Lane   *1997*
About 1960, all the buildings between the Grand Theatre (by then the *Locarno* ballroom) and Sitwell Street, including the 1865 Swedenborgian Chapel, were swept away for redevelopment, which took the form of a tall, square and essentially rather brutal four-storey glass and steel block with brick and tile facings, set well back but with the ground floor being advanced to the edge of the street line as retail units. Into two of these, adjacent to the old Grand Theatre (nowadays *McCluskey's* night spot), Messrs J.D. Wetherspoon opened one of their characteristic establishments on 28 February 1997, tactfully reviving the name of the then long-defunct *Babington Arms*, albeit on a quite different site. The frontage folds open in summer, affording customers the opportunity of drinking on a dais-like platform a little above the street's edge.
DET 21 & 28/2/1997.

BANK TAVERN**

14 Friar Gate   *by 1835-1854*
Listed in 1852 and two years later the place wherein a Mr Ball 'conducted himself in a most indecent manner' (!)

Named, without doubt, after the Derby Savings Bank, established in 1817 by William Strutt, FRS, Thomas Cox and William Leaper Newton, and housed from 1840 in a muscular and elegant Greek-revival building by Henry Isaac Stevens, opposite which it stood, which was demolished to build the awful Heritage Gate in 1971. The inn was listed as an anonymous beer house in 1835 and 1850, and it was either renamed or closed before the 1857 directory, in which it fails to appear. The premises had become a fruiterer's shop by 1874 and are currently a charity shop.
DM 4/10/1854

BAR 2000**

87 Green Lane   *2000-2002*
A bar optimistically named after its millennium opening date, in a Victorian House next to the former Presbyterian Chapel, and in which Alderman Oswald Ling was living at the time of his mayoralty in 1922. It failed to pay its way and was closed by July 2002.

BARLEYCORN*

105 (47) Canal Street   *by 1846-1961*
This inn stood on north side of Canal Street near *New Inn*, and is listed as an anonymous beer house in 1846/50 and 1862. By 1908 when it had declined to a beer-retailership on licence, the lowest form of beer house. It was taken over and developed by Offiler's by 1935, brewing on the premises. It remained a beerhouse until a full licence was granted in 1950. De-licenced 1961 in advance of clearance of the area and sold in February 1963. The name derives from 'John Barleycorn', a euphemism for beer (and whisky north of the border) and celebrated in a famous ballad of the late 17th century.

BARLEY MOW*

35 East Street (Bag Lane)   *by 1818-1911*
A three-bay, three-storey brick inn of late 18th-century date, which stood on the corner opposite St Peter's Church – hence 'St Peter's Street' being given occasionally as the address – but replaced in 1878-9 two doors down East Street from its old site, with the famous Star music hall attached. Performers there are alleged to have included Vesta Tilley. It is unlisted in Pigot's 1818 directory, so may have been founded or renamed in that year. In its original guise, too, it was spacious enough for auction sales to be held there – as in 1819 – it was for sale in 1862 and 1878 (contents prior to moving) and to let in 1863 having just been relinquished by Joseph and Robert Russell, successors to their father, John, the landlord in 1827. Despite its comparatively generous size, it appears only to have been a beer house in the mid-19th century, a spirit licence application being made in 1872. Demolished to make way for

Boots the Chemist, completed 1912. A barley mow was a rick or stack of harvested barley.

DM 21/1/1819; 23/4/1862; 4/11/1863; 11/9/1872 & 13/11/1878.

BARLEY MOW*

Market Place (Leather Lane; Cornmarket)   by 1755-1829
This market inn was for sale as a going concern when advertised by Richard Woodhouse in 1755; he took the name with him to his new house in Sadler Gate (*qv*) and this one must have been renamed, although what to is quite unclear; there are several possibilities in this list. However, after Woodhouse's new *Barley Mow* was absorbed by the *George* the name was revived in its original place, and is so recorded in 1791 in the *Universal British Directory* [UBD]. Its site is fixed in an advertisement for sale in 1821 as a 'well accustomed public house situate near the Town Hall.' It then comprised:

> 'A front parlour, bar, kitchen and scullery on the ground floor, and dining room on the first floor, and six bedrooms together with the brew house and other conveniences and stabling for 20 horses now in the occupation of Richard Orme. Also all those six messuages [houses] or tenements lying behind the said public house... and also the stable and slaughterhouse situate at the bottom of Barley Mow Yard... the above premises comprise about 15 feet in front to the Market Place and 200 feet and upwards in depth and the right of carriage, horse and footway... along the common yard from the Morledge.'

The footprint of the inn demonstrates dramatically the long narrow shape of the burgage plots which were laid out, narrow end to the road, when the Borough was founded in the 10th century. The Guildhall, or Town Hall, then stood clear of the Market Place's south side, but in 1828-9 a new Guildhall was built to the designs of Matthew Habershon in its present position, and the inn was one of the buildings demolished to make way for it.

DM. 4/11/1755; 30/6/1785; 9/5/1821 & 23/7/1823.

(OLD) BARLEY MOW*

1 Russell Street (corner of Osmaston Road)   by 1862
Built, in all probability, at the time of Alderman Robert Russell's foundry here (hence the street name) in brick, later stuccoed. Colloquially known at 'Bottom House', the *New Inn* Gilman Street being 'Middle House' and the *Litchurch Inn* 'Top House'. In 1977 it lost its name and was thereafter called the *Jubilee City* to mark the raising of the Borough to city status by HM the Queen on the occasion of her Silver Jubilee that year, when she visited the town, although the *Barley Mow* was hardly on her itinerary!

Damaged by fire 1996 and reopened the following year as the *Old Barley Mow*.

BARLEY MOW

Sadler Gate   by 1755-1785
Name transferred by landlord Richard Woodhouse when he sold the *Barley Mow* in Rotten Row, to an inn adjacent to the *George* in Sadler Gate previously called the *Sun*. In 1785 it was sold and demolished to extend the *George*, the name being revived back in its original location in Leather Lane (*qv*).   *DM 26/9 & 3/10/1755; 30/6/1785.*

BARLEY MOW

See also SUN

BARRELL (OF BEER)*

14 Walker Lane   by 1835-1862
Name echoes the related craft of cooperage. Advertised as the *Barrell of Beer* in 1840 but listed in 1846 merely as the *Barrell*, and probably to be equated with an anonymous beer house in this street listed in 1835 and at No.14 in 1862. Doubtless closed or renamed thereafter.

BASEBALL HOTEL*

173 Shaftesbury Crescent (corner Vulcan Street)   1890-1994
A handsome pub of brick with stone dressings built in 1890 with curving façade to fit the site, the main bar within elegantly following the shape, designed, along with the original stadium, by E.R. Ridgeway of Long Eaton. It took its name from the Derby County FC's ground, which was laid out on a site given by the local foundry owner, Sir Francis Ley, Bt, who came back from the USA in 1881, keen to promote a baseball league. When this lost support a decade later, its place was taken by the football club, originally founded in 1884 as an offshoot of Derbyshire County Cricket Club. Tied to James Eadie & Co in the 1930s, subsequently a Bass house, but freehold from around 1989 owned by the Barker dynasty (cf. *Dolphin, Greyhound, Victoria*). Following the dissolution of that grouping, it was run to a local entrepreneur, the freehold remaining with the Football Club. In 1993 it was resolved to vastly expand the ground, and the inn was closed in 1994 and peremptorily demolished 28 June, despite an attempt to have it spotlisted. To add insult to injury, a few months later, the club's board decided to move to a new site on Pride Park and start again, leaving the old ground in occasional use and, since 2000, subject to a planning application to demolish and develop with housing – much opposed locally – in an area singularly lacking community facilities and open spaces. The area was once surrounded by foundries, hence Vulcan Street.

BASEBALL BAR & GRILL**

Pride Park   *1997*

Built as part of the new Pride Park stadium of Derby County FC on its NW side and opened shortly after the stadium was ready to host its first football match. The name Baseball Bar and Grill is a welcome reminder of the club's former home, the Baseball Ground. Fittings from the Baseball Hotel, which stood next to the old ground, were incorporated into the pub at the new ground. Also featured are turnstiles from the Baseball Ground, and photographs and shirts from various periods in the club's history. There is a members-only policy on match days.

BATH*

7 (6) Amen Alley   *by 1835-1912*

Housed in a building of venerable antiquity which stood until 1873 on the Full Street corner; legend had it that, before the Reformation, it was a shop which sold missals. There was a jettied end gable to Full Street and two gables facing Amen Alley, and the portion of the building under the westernmost gable was the inn. It seems to have had a previous existence under another name, and was probably the beer house listed anonymously in Pigot's directory of 1835. Whatever its original name – quite possibly the *Old Mitre* – it without doubt changed to the *Bath* to reflect the erection in 1852 of the Corporation's first public baths opposite, designed by Henry Isaac Stevens. When John Davis & Sons bought the site in 1870, they knocked this range down and built a new precision- and mining-implement factory, rehousing the tavern one door further up the street, and it clung on to life until shortly before World War One, when it closed and Davis's used the premises for offices.

BAY COB**

8 Colyear Street   *by 1848-1852*

Probably rather short lived; it was next door to the contemporary *Scarsdale Arms* (both are listed in 1850/2, this one as an anonymous beer house) so perhaps absorbed into it. Horsey name.

BAY HORSE

1 Uttoxeter Old Road (corner Ashbourne Road)   *by 1833-1911*

One of many inns and alehouses situated at the west end of Friar Gate where, until 1861, beast and cheese markets were held (hence the wideness of that part of the street). For sale in 1848 and spirit licence approval sought in 1874. After the market moved to The Holmes, the number of inns gradually declined. The name is of an heraldic derivation, but not one easy to pin down to a specific (local) family, unless it refers to one of the supporters of the Eyre Earls of Newburgh, one of whose kinsmen had a house in Friar Gate

at this period. More likely it merely reflects the nature of the market itself, which included horses.
DM 31/5/1848 & 26/8/1874.

BEAR

See BROWN BEAR

BECKET'S

See THOMAS-À-BECKET

Bedford Arms, Bedford Street, 1930.

BEDFORD ARMS

2 Bedford Street   *by 1874*

Brick-built inn on west side of street near Hoult Street corner, with busy quoins not only at the angles but all around the door, all now masked by subsequent rendering. Purchased by Strettons from Charringtons, 1926, for £4,600. The street was one of several neighbouring ones named after contemporary grandees (*eg* Leicester, Arundel), and thus commemorates Sir Francis Russell, 9th Duke of Bedford KG (1819-1891), who succeeded in 1872; his mother was local, being a niece of 1st Marquess of Hastings. As with several Derby inns, it took its name from the street.

BEE HIVE

90 Devonshire Street   *by 1833-1912*

Street pitched in the early years of the 19th century, so the pub was probably adapted from a pair of artisan's cottages. An 'old accustomed public house' when for sale in 1881. The name is sometimes demonstrably heraldic, but in Derbyshire, only the Topliss family of Wirksworth sported such emblems at that time, and no connection with the area is known; alternatively, the bee hive is a common symbol for industry or, in the case of a pub, indicative of a busy house.

BEECH TREE

60-61 East Street (Bag Lane)   *by 1833-1912*

On the south side of the street, between Albion Street and Morledge, destroyed after a period of closure by the Derby

Co-operative Society to build their handsome 1926 extension. Its founding was undoubtedly too late for its name to be explained in terms of a surviving tree. Listed twice as the *Birch Tree* (1874, 1895). Previously the *Woodman's Stroke*, the sign (according to John Ward) depicting a woodman in the act of felling a (Beech) tree. The landlord, in 1862, was the improbably named Patrick Litchfield [*sic*].

BEER BARREL

See BARREL OF BEER, FOOTBALL

BELL*

Bridge Gate   *before 1740*

In 1740, 'a new house in Bridge Gate' was offered for sale – 'being late the sign of the Bell' – as a result of the death of the proprietor, James Stables. It does not reappear, so was either renamed or reverted to use as a private residence. The name, so common in these Isles, is said to derive from the Bellarmine jar, universally employed to hold drink in the 15th century and which took its name from its resemblance to Cardinal Bellarmine in profile, an ecclesiastic much hated in the Low Countries. Later versions were actually made with caricature masks on to rub home the point. They are said to have been hung up as a sign at inns run by Flemings in this country who had fled the baleful attentions of the portly Cardinal. The sign these days, is usually of a church bell, and is sometimes heraldic, too. *DM 17/7/1740.*

(OLD) BELL*

53 Sadler Gate   *by 1691-1988; 1990*

One of Derby's classic coaching inns, founded for that purpose, probably around 1680, and the last to serve as such. A large brick-built inn on the south side of the street of three storeys and attics with a four-gabled façade and central carriage entrance once leading to coach houses and stables. From the lobby, leading from the right of the carriage entrance, is a particularly fine contemporary staircase in oak, the best of its date in Derby. It seems to have been started by George Meynell – eighth son of Godfrey Meynell of Yeaveley, Willington and Anslow, Staffs. (d. 1667) – whose uncle Francis traded as an apothecary around the corner in the Market Place. By 1770 it was in the hands of Henry Tillotson, whose

Old Bell Hotel: Entrance to old bar.

Old Bell Hotel, Sadler Gate c 1930: Main entrance.

tenant since 1774, John Campion, a member of an old Derby family (several of whose members held inns, and an account of which will be found under the *Rising Sun*) who had made his fortune as a West India merchant. Tillotson sold it to Thomas Brentnall, and departed to start a rival inn a few doors down the street (*qv Bell & Castle*). On Brentnall's bankruptcy in 1780 the freehold was acquired by Campion. His initials and the date 1774 appeared on a pump in the yard (which mysteriously vanished during alterations in 1991).

He also added a very fine ballroom on the back (later divided and then partly redone and opened up again) and took over a Carlisle-London coach, called the *Cornwallis* from the proprietor of the *Swan With Two Necks* St James's Lane, in 1806. It went daily to the *Swan with Two Necks*, Lad Lane, London (hence the name of the Derby inn) at 4pm, fares being £1 11s 6d (inside) and 18s (outside). A year later he managed to persuade the proprietor of the *Defiance* coach to switch allegiance from the *George*, too. These services, however were lost to the *King's Head* only a year later. Campion's descendants owned it for over a century. In the 1790s, Hon John Byng stayed, commenting in his acerbic way: 'Roast fowl and asparagus served by females who ran about like rabbits; five of them are not

Old Bell Hotel: Two views of the Tudor Bar, showing original decor and furnishings.

equal to one man waiter... the landlord is fat, stupid and splay-footed'. Whilst the coming of the railways from 1839 had forced increasing numbers of coach services to the wall, the most successful proprietor of them, the Wallis family of the *New Inn,* astutely off-loaded them onto others, and several, including the once-famous *Derby Diligence* ('The Derby Dilly'), were taken over by Campion's grandson, John (1799-1864). Indeed, on 5 November 1855 the Dilly, which plied from London to Manchester, called there for the last time; the truncated service from Derby to Manchester ended 6 October 1858, thus bringing to an end the coaching era.

On 1 April 1842, during one of Derby's most memorable floods, the nine-year-old grandson of John Campion II was 'launched in a wash-tub in the cellars..., to save some rare old wines laid down in the previous century by the lad's great-grandfather, John Campion (I).

John Campion III died in 1864, after which the inn was sold to J.F. King. On its sale by him 17 years later a most useful description of the *Bell* as it then was appeared:

'A gateway divides the culinary and domestic offices from the body of the house, which (on the right hand side of the entrance) contains a spacious hall, large bar overlooking the front yard, smoke room, commercial room, coffee room, and private sitting room; on the first floor an excellent dining room, with store room, pantries, lavatories, closets, 7 excellent bedrooms and 2 family sitting rooms. The second floor contains 13 commodious bedrooms and

there are also two other good bedrooms, five servants' rooms, storerooms, lavatories, housemaids' closets, etc.

On the left of the entrance are box and luggage rooms, excellent kitchen, scullery, larders, servants' hall, good billiard room, laundry, two large commercial stock rooms and other offices. There is also a back yard covered over, with separate gateway from the main street, for the accommodation of carriages; stabling for 28 horses and saddle room, with a communication to the front yard and chief entrance.

The principal balls, dinners and other large gatherings have been supplied from this hotel, and the most important rent audits dinners of the district are held half-yearly; it is also a well-known mart for sales of freehold property and estates...'

The purchaser in 1881 was F. Rayner who issued a zinc 4d pub check. It eventually was acquired by St James's Hotels Ltd. In 1929 they set about refurbishing it extensively, refronting it with bogus half-timbering and built the (then) men-only Tudor Bar, all executed and designed by Messrs Ford & Weston, who used material rescued from demolished buildings, hence the meaningless dates on the rainwater goods. The Tudor Bar was full of ancient arms

Rear elevation of the Old Bell, drawn by Charles G. Harper c.1920, and showing the vanished pump.

and armour from the Earl of Bessborough's collections and had a very fine ebonised octagonal dial tavern clock; most was stolen in 1969, the rest vanished when St James's successors, Bass, sold out to a property company in 1988, when the establishment closed. On the reopening in 1931, Ernest Townsend was commissioned to paint the proprietors and their guests gathered in the Tudor Bar, with the barmaid, the unforgettable Alice Alsop, youthfully gliding amongst them with a tray. She remained in charge there until her tragic death in a street accident in the 1970s. Numerous prints of this excellent and atmospheric painting were made by Bemrose's, so that each participant could have one, and they still crop up in local sales from time to time.

The intention of the purchasers in 1988, Arkwright Investments, was to divide it up as retail units, which would have destroyed Campion's stuccoed ballroom and led to the removal of the 17th-century staircase. Mercifully, listed building consent was not forthcoming and it was sold, shorn of its two end parts (since converted into shops), to the Thompson family of Ingleby, already proprietors of the *Vines* and the *Shakespeare* nearby. Subject in October 2002 to a planning application from J.D. Wetherspoon for a full restoration.
Davison (1906) 210n; *DM* 28/5/1779; 5/6/1806; 24/10/1807; 22/6/1865 & 29/6/1881.

(OLD) BELL**

Willow Row   *1784-1801*
Probably of not very old foundation as implied by a notice to let in 1784 'lately occupied as a public house.' It may have been difficult to make a good return here, for it was for sale thrice more until 1801 when no more is heard of it; probably it closed and reverted to being a house or shop.
DM 1/4/1784; 21/7/1796; 28/1/1800 & 19/3/1801.

BELL

See also BLUE BELL

BELL & CASTLE*

86-92 Burton Road   *1801*
This listed Grade II building is a substantial brick two-and-a-half-storey one of *c.*1800, which may well be the date the inn was established, for it was to let and 'newly built' in 1801. The terraced row consisted of four houses, the end ones of a single bay each, the centre pair double-fronted. The inn began in the east end unit, but has since expanded into all but the westerly house, which remains a newspaper shop. The rear elevations have a long weavers' window with north light right across, suggesting that the development was associated with Thomas Madeley's nearby Haarlem Mill at Little City, on the edge of which the inn stands. From 1851 to 1860 run by John Allen, father of

Isaac, founder of Allenton; the former, whose brother Thomas ran the brewery, thereafter moved to the *Rutland Arms*. Offiler's in 1930s, then Bass.
DM 12/2/1801; Longdon (2000) 16

BELL & CASTLE*

Sadler Gate   *1774-1791*
In May 1774 it was announced that 'Henry Tillotson late of the Bell Hotel has removed from the Old Bell to his house a little lower in the same street, now the *Bell & Castle* and solicits the favour of his former customers' – perhaps without much success, for few mentions of it are to be found after 1791, when it was taken over by a businessman, Vicesimus Bradshaw (one of the numerous descendants of the prolific 16th century gentleman Anthony Bradshaw of Makeney Old Hall). He probably closed it and converted it into a shop.
DM 27/5/l774; 1/9/1775; 13/11/1788; 19/2/1789 & 11/8/1791.

BELPER ARMS
See LORD BELPER

BERLIN'S*

Becket Street   *1987*
Opened as a 'fun-pub' in 1987 in the former headquarters of the Derby Poor Law Guardians and later the County Education offices, which had lain derelict since 1974. The building was erected in 1865 to the designs of Messrs Giles and Brookhouse with a majestically enriched ashlar façade and was extended in brick in matching but more sober style by R. Ernest Ryley in 1894. The chief loss in the conversion was the magnificent staircase, above which soared a stained-glass window with allegorical figures, beneath which was the legend: 'Blessed is he who Careth for the Poor'. The window now ensigns the main bar area, where conspicuous teenage consumption is rampant: a bizarre juxtaposition indeed! Nice Victorian-style railings were installed along the street frontage to replace those removed in 1942. Renamed *Aruba* (an island in the West Indies) in 2001.

BIG SHIP

London Road   *–c.1875–*
Known only from a spirit bottle of the era thus marked.

BIRCH TREE
See BEECH TREE

BIRD*

1 Jury Street (corner of Willow Row)   *by 1818-1912*
Three-bay two-storey inn tucked away in an angle where

Bird Inn, Jury Street, 1912.

Jury Street (the mediaeval Jewry Street) and Willow Row met, opposite the lower end of Walker Lane. Offered to let in 1860 and for sale in 1878. Demolished in the summer of 1912 to widen the road.
DM 18/1/1860 & 8/5/1878.

BIRD IN HAND

Morledge   *by 1827-1842*

Named, no doubt, from the well-known proverb: 'A bird in the hand is worth two in the bush'; *ie* it is better to keep hold of what you have than gamble on doubling it in a risky venture. Usually the depiction of a bird of prey on a hawking glove, and thus falconry may provide an alternative derivation. A coronation dinner was held here in 1838. To be let in 1842 and not heard of again, so either closed or renamed.
DM 4/7/1838, 20/7 & 3/8/1842.

BISHOP BLAZE

Cornmarket   *–1761–*

One of the watering-holes where one could drink at Sir Harry Harpur's expense during the 1761 election, cf. *Bell*, St Peter's Parish and numerous others; £5 was deposited with the landlord of each inn. The information comes from a 10½in by 7½in broadsheet of the period now in the Derby Local Studies Library and published by Museum Curator F. Williamson in the local paper. The name is a corruption of that of St Blasius, Bishop of Sebaste, in Armenia, martyred by the Prefect Agricolaus on the orders of the Emperor Licinius I *c.*AD 316. He was said to have been put to death by being torn with wool combs before being beheaded, hence he is the patron saint of woolcombers, and a common pub name in market towns before this trade died out. Also the patron saint of people suffering with throat ailments. Saint's day: 3 February. His cult was brought back to this country during the Crusades.
DA 20/5/1938

BISHOP BLAZE**

Queen Street   *by 1822-1824*

A 'well accustomed public house' for sale. *DM* 9/1/1822, when J. Heath, landlord in 1824 may have acquired it.

BISHOP BLAZE

See (RISING) SUN/WHITE HORSE

BISHOP BLAZE*

St Mary's Gate   *by 1749-1822*

Situated in 'the middle of St Mary's Gate' according to an advert in the *Derby Mercury* (2 June 1749). To let in 1819, reduced to a beerhouse after 1830 and probably replaced by the Probate Court of 1859, designed by George Bridgart. *DM* 23/3/1819

BLACKAMOOR'S HEAD*

Market Place   *by 1745-1824*

The venue for a display by 'Furmston, the modern living Colossus' in 1752, and well known for its freak shows. Taken down by Joseph Pickford's workmen when preparing the site for the building of the new Assembly Rooms, 1763. The name derives in this instance from the crest of the Shirley family of Shirley, Brailsford and Staunton Harold, Earls Ferrers; *A Saracen's head in profile, couped at the shoulders proper wreathed about the temples or and azure.* It was probably no coincidence that Earl Ferrers designed the building that was to take the place of the inn, which his family may well have owned. Families using this crest almost always derived it from participation in the Crusades. Before 1763 it moved to new premises built beside the Assembly Rooms, erected that year, the old inn having been demolished on 18 February 1763 to make way for them. This inn closed shortly after 1824 to make way for the pitching of Derwent Street.
DM 29/9/1752; Saunders (1993) 62

BLACK BEAR

Unidentified location   *before 1822-1867*

The name derived from the arms of the Beresford family of Beresford Hall (Staffs) and Fenny Bentley: *Argent a bear rampant sable muzzled, collared and chained or.* Mentioned once in 1822 without a location, a situation repeated by Jewitt.

BLACK BOY*

St Peter's Street   *1761-1817*

An inn where Sir Harry Harpur hoped to ingratiate himself with the electorate. Somehow acquired as part of the Wallis empire, Alderman John Wallis selling it in 1817. Black servants, often very young, were brought to England from the 17th century to work in great houses and many inns derived their name therefrom. Dr Johnson's black servant, Francis Barber, as with many of his ilk, did well on his master's death, being left sufficient to set himself up as a tradesman in Stoke-on-Trent, where he left many descendants.

BLACK BOY
See ALBION

Sadler Gate, the former Black Boy, 2002.

BLACK BOY*

(6/7) Sadler Gate   *by 1755-1862*
The building may still survive, but when it was for sale in 1755 – being described as 'a good brick house, sashed, with brewhouse, stable and other conv[enience]s' – it was in premises which were later incorporated into the ballroom of the *George*. The inn was then relocated a few doors further down the street. The landlord, Richard Salt, went to the *Three Stags' Heads* in St James' Lane.
DM 25/7/1755.

BLACK BULL*

Canal Street   *by 1833-1846*
Nothing known of this inn, listed in 1846 as an anonymous

beerhouse. It possibly changed its name to *Canal Tavern.* Sign is heraldic, deriving from the badge of the mediaeval Dukes of Clarence and the House of York.

BLACK BULL**

Walker Lane   *–1790–*
An 'old accustomed public house' to let.
DM 9/9/1790.

BLACK COW**

Uncertain location   *before 1867*
Jewitt.

BLACK HORSE

1 Nuns' Street (corner Parker Street)   *by 1827-1925*
The name probably derives from the crest of the local banking family of Crompton, Samuel Crompton III being intimately associated with the Improvement Commissioners whose 1792 Nuns' Green Act created the West End. In the 1840s it was run by Benjamin Newbold, founder of a notable dynasty (see introduction) and later of the *Dove*. He held a sheep roast here to celebrate the 1856 Crimean War peace and sold it in 1862 as an 'old established' house. Zachary Smith's in the early 1920s, closing soon afterwards. Mr Ken Motley says that 'Old Dodger Birks went to live there after closure and opened a café on the other side of the street'.
DM 21/5/1856 & 28/5/1862

BLACK HORSE
See also BLACK'S HEAD

BLACK PRINCE
See MERLIN

BLACK'S HEAD*

30 Devonshire Street   *by 1843-1893*
The name is analogous the *Blackamoor's Head*. Sold twice at auction in the 1840s. It also appears to have been called – if briefly – the *Black Horse* listed at this address in 1850-2. It was probably again renamed the *Oatsheaf* as recorded in 1893 and subsequently closed.
DM 8/2/1843 & 1/1/1847.

(OLD) BLACK SWAN*

72 London Road (Street)   *by 1791-1857*
London and Osmaston Roads within the Borough boundary were, until 1879 called London Street and Osmaston Street respectively. The name derives from the badge of the mediaeval Bohuns, Earls of Hereford, who had no serious Derby connection. Listed only as an anonymous beer house in 1850 and 1857, so clearly well in decline. The 'Old' was

presumably added after *c*.1822 when the inn following was established.

BLACK SWAN*

49 (15) Siddals Road (corner Borough's Walk & Rivett Street)   *by 1822-1965*

Borough's Walk ran past the third side of the pub, which still brewed its own beer until March 1928. In the 1930s it was owned by Pountain's, but passed to Ind Coope after World War Two. Swept away when the area was flattened in the late 1960s. Derby Museum has a 19th-century Staffordshire half-pint mug with the name and a black swan on it from here.

BLACK SWAN**

Morledge   *by 1818-1824*

Recorded for so brief a period that the likelihood is that it was renamed as above for only a brief period.

BLESSINGTON CARRIAGE*

Chapel Street   *1977*

Converted from a pair of 19th-century buildings, one of which had many years previously been the *Old Crown & Cushion,* by Tom Glancz and Tony Suthers, who were already running a pub of the same name in Nottingham. The Blessington Carriage had been a Nottingham stage coach, taking its name from the 18th-century Irish peer of that name, whose countess was a famous society hostess.

(BLUE) BELL*

St Peter's Parish   *by 1761-1791*

Almost certainly the *Bell* mentioned in Sir Harry Harpur's 1761 list and last occurring in the *Universal British Directory* [UBD] of 1791. Probably renamed. *DM* 6/9/1776.

Blue Bell, Upper South Street, 1936.

BLUE BELL

78 Upper South Street   *by 1854-1972*

Upper South Street was a curt extension to South Street which lay in line with the latter across Uttoxeter Old Road;

this inn stood on the north-west corner opposite the *Earl Grey.* It was owned by Altons in the 1930s, by 1936 Ind Coope & Allsopp. Demolished 1972.

BLUE BOAR

Nuns' Green (Friar Gate)   *–1776–*

Nuns' Green was that part of today's Friar Gate which ran alongside the former Nuns' Green between Ford Street and Brick Street in the 18th century, when the one reference to this inn occurs. This sign is an heraldic one, but not local. *DM* 19/4/1776

BLUE DOG

See SHAKESPEARE

BLUE LION

See ODDFELLOWS' ARMS

BLUE STOOPS

Market Place   *by 1764-1772*

Recorded over eight years, during which successive unsuccessful attempts were made to sell it; it may have closed and reverted to retail use as a result. The stoops of its title were the posts in the Cornmarket on which containers were placed for measuring the grain when the market was in progress, so the inn must have been at the south end of the Market Place. A strong candidate for the inn subsequently renamed the *(Admiral) Rodney.*

BOAR'S HEAD*

21 King Street (Duffield Road)   *by 1843-1876*

Stood one house away from the end of Lodge Lane. It took its name from the crest of the Evans family of Darley Abbey: *on a charger a boar's head erased argent,* granted in 1815. The proprietor in 1855 was James Alton (brother of William, who founded the brewery, and formerly of the *Seven Stars,* King Street and the *Brown Bear* Lodge Lane), and he organised a sheep roast to celebrate the 1856 peace but left the year after to run the *Castlefields,* Siddal's Lane. Knocked down to make way for the GNR's line in 1876. *DM* 26/12/1855, 11/3/1857 & 26/71876.

BOAT*

3 Lodge Lane   *by 1874-1878*

No obvious reason for the name, being a reasonable distance from both canal and river. The freehold was for sale as the *Boot* in 1877 and it was taken by Frederick Flower. Also listed in 1878 as the *Boot* – perhaps, if correct – an association with the footwear pioneered by the Duke of Wellington. Presumably closed, as no other establishment in the street obtrudes as a likely renaming. *DM* 25/7/1877

(OLD) BOAT*

34 Morledge/32 Cockpit Hill   *by 1761-1927*

This tall, narrow, brick building stood at the south end of Cockpit Hill (despite the confusing address) and when the Derby Canal was first built, boats were able to reach it by a navigable arm, hence the name (*Reminiscences* of Mr Johnson, 1893). For sale in 1814, and to let 30 years later. By 1895 it was reduced to a beerhouse, and closed around 1930. It was sold in 1935 on behalf of the Nottingham Brewery by Arthur George Petts, then the landlord of the *Cock* and later at the *Chestnut Tree* (father-in-law of Alfred Whitehurst of the *Sir Robert Peel*) to Mr & Mrs Richard Kearney as a fish and chip shop. Their daughter, Mrs Kate Stokes later ran it until demolition to make way for the baleful Eagle Centre.

John Ward's *Notes of Reminiscences of Old Derby*, 15/3/1893 III.vi, Derby Museum; *DM* 8/9/1814 & 10/5/1844; *DET Bygones Suppl.* 3/11/1998 pp.24-5.

BOAT*

Nottingham Road   *by 1822-1852*

Probably built at about the time the Erewash arm of the canal was opened in 1796. It stood on the south side of the road, squeezed in beside the cut, and during its existence, the Cockpit Hill establishment took the additional title 'Old'. It appears on the 1852 Board of Health Map, but not thereafter – perhaps renamed.

BOATER'S BAR

16 Friar Gate   *1986-2000*

Formerly a restaurant - the *French Revolution* - and set in the best surviving 'Jacobean' house in Derby, built during the Civil War by the Parliamentary governor of the town, Sir John Gell, Bt, of Hopton Hall and listed Grade II. Later renamed *Outa Mongolia* [sic] and subsequently extended to become *Tony Roma's* (a bar restaurant) and then *Zizzi*, a restaurant.

BOOM

See FORTY SECOND STREET

BOOT

See BOAT

BOROUGH ARMS*

Upper Carrington Street   *1852-1853*

'Newly erected' when for sale in 1853 and listed the previous year, too. Probably renamed the *Carrington Arms*. The name represents the arms of the Borough family of Castlefields, across whose parkland Upper Carrington Street was pitched, rather than those of the municipality. Their very unusual arms are: *Argent on a mount vert in base the*

trunk of an oak tree sprouting out two branches proper hanging thereon the shield of Pallas or fastened by a belt gules; crest: *an eagle proper holding in its talons the shield of Pallas or*; motto: '*Virtute et Robore*'.
DM 9/3/1853

BOWLING GREEN*

Nottingham Road   *-1833-*

Only known from the somewhat unreliable 1833 list. The title may well be the suffix of one of the other pubs of this period along the Nottingham road having a bowling green. On the (admittedly later) 1852 Board of Health Map, a bowling green is shown behind the *Seven Stars* in this thoroughfare, so the reference may refer to this pub.

BOWLING GREEN & MAFEKING HOTEL

See MAFEKING

BOWRING'S VAULTS

See IRONGATES

BRANNIGAN'S

See MOLLY MAGOO'S

BRENTNALL'S WINE VAULTS

See WINE VAULTS

BRICK & TILE*

1 Brick Street   *before 1750*

One of the plethora of inns built to serve the beast markets when they were held at the west end of Nuns' Green. As the building is early 17th century - once little altered, two-storey, brick with some surviving mullioned windows and later sashes, now quite ruined by the brewery's successive 'improvements' - it is tempting to think that it may have been an inn throughout that period, perhaps under a different name, thus explaining its absence from earlier records. Its pre-1792 address would have been just Nuns' Green, so this is quite probable. Its present name derives from the brick yard on Nuns' Green which flourished in the 18th century and probably earlier, too. This was owned by Richard Roe and his family from the 1720s but, by the 1770s was in the hands of the architect Joseph Pickford (1734-1782), whose home and building yard were nearby. It supplied him with bricks, and, of course, tiles. It is possible that the inn could have been part of the same leasehold property. The brick pits were swept away by the development following the 1792 Nuns' Green Act, but this inn remained, being for sale in 1854. Strettons in the 1930s, later Ind Coope, then Ansell's, and now Burtonwood.

Derby Poll Books; DLSL, Mayor's Account Book 1731; Deeds of 41 and 45 Friar Gate; *DM* 15/2/1854

BRICK CART

Bag Lane   *–1761–*

One of the inns where Sir Harry Harpur hoped to ingratiate himself with his electors in the election of 1761. Only known mention. Could there have been a brick works as well as a pot works on Cockpit Hill to inspire the sign? Bag Lane became East Street in the 1870s.

BRICKLAYERS' ARMS

See LEATHER BOTTLE

BRICKMAKERS' ARMS*

1 (71) Fowler Street (corner Ashbourne Road)   *by 1850-1945*

The arms are as spurious as those of the Bricklayers', above; brickmaking was practised on Nuns' Green close by in the 18th century, however, see the note under *Brick & Tile*. The inn was established by 1850, but does not appear in the 1857 directory, so probably a low-level beer house. For sale in 1874 as an 'old licensed public house'. Later a Stretton's house, then Allsopp's; closed after World War Two.

DM 30/12/1874

BRICKMAKERS' ARMS**

33 Nuns' Street   *–1852–*

Situated a couple of doors up from the Dove but only listed once. There appear to be no candidates for its having been renamed, so probably ephemeral.

Bridge Inn, Mansfield Road, 1909. Note the poster advertising Derby Regatta.

BRIDGE INN*

2-3 Mansfield Road   *by 1857*

Established between 1852 and 1857 in a large former private house, of brick and stucco, dating from the 1790s, but with an earlier and quirky paired window on the south front, itself a portion of the building probably of earlier date and incorporated when William Forester was at work preparing the abutments of the new bridge in 1789-91. He probably designed and built the building itself too, embel-lishing it with busy quoins, a feature even extended to the window surrounds. It has subsequently been rendered. It was once equipped with a boat house, and was popular on Derby Regatta days. In the first half of the 20th century one wall was decorated by a suspended Ordinary Bicycle (a penny-farthing) for many years. Gutted internally and reconstructed 1989. Named after St Mary's Bridge, by which it stands. It was to let in 1857 as a 'well-accustomed and old public house' which might suggest that it was in being well before its first directory appearance, unless it was renamed then. The *Jolly Colliers* might be a candidate for its previous incarnation, or even the *Navigation*. In 1863 was advertised again 'near to the new goods railway station, Chester Road' in 1863. An Alton's pub at one time but Carlsberg-Tetley in 1994.

DM 14/2 & 9/12/1857; 1/7/1863

BRIDGE

1 Osborne Street (corner Barlow Street)   *by 1874-1977*

A plain stuccoed Regency house of three stuccoed bays and three storeys adapted as an inn, facing London Road, facing which it had paired tripartite windows either side of the entrance all with entablatures on brackets, a feature carried on the fenestration above, too, although the side elevation to Barlow Street was plain with a side door; nevertheless the address in 1878 was 80 Barlow Street, made even more bizarre because there were no other build-ings in that thoroughfare at the time! It took its name from the bridge carrying the London Road over the former Birmingham & Derby Junction Railway (later Midland Railway) line a few yards away. Closed in 1977 and demol-ished May 1979.

BRITANNIA*

4 River Street (opposite Bath Street)   *1827-1933*

River Street was laid out near the Britannia foundry of Weatherhead, Glover & Co of Duke Street, founded in 1819 and stood on an estate of building club housing of contem-porary date. The name reflects the adjacent iron foundry. 'Newly built' and for sale in 1827, it was bought and run by Joseph Bloor, younger brother of Robert, with whom he took over the China Factory from Michael Kean in 1811. He seems to have let his role in the Nottingham Road factory go after Robert's first nervous breakdown in 1828, and he also acquired a chemist's shop at 45 Queen Street. Joseph ran the pub until his death the same year as his brother in 1846, after which his son, also Joseph, well ensconced as a chemist, let it in 1847. The younger Bloor still owned it in 1867. Closed at the end of 1933 and the licence transferred to the *Sir Frederick Roberts*, 6 March 1934, and the pub demolished.

DM 3/3/1827 & 6/10/1847.

(OLD) BRITANNIA*

19 River Street (corner of Duke Street)   by 1827-1877

As if one *Britannia* was not enough for one street, this inn carried the same name, but by 1849 was calling itself the *Old Britannia*, doubtless from 1827 when Bloor had also cheekily named his new pub after the foundry; little doubt about the clientele they were aiming for! In 1856 the landlord was fined £5 (with costs) for being open during divine service on a Sunday.

It was for sale (as the *Old Britannia* Duke St) in 1877 prior to demolition to make way for a siding from the GNR laid to serve what had by then become Handyside's Britannia Foundry.

DM 13/12/1856 & 12/9/1877

BRITISH ARMS

49 (46) Bridge Gate   by 1833-1912

One of many inns in Bridge Gate, possibly renamed thus after the Napoleonic War, and of older origin as licensed premises; certainly in a much older building, demolished in c.1931. Stood on the north side, opposite the *White Hart*.

BRITISH GRENADIER**

Unknown location   before 1867

Jewitt. Named after the famous guards regiment.

BRITISH LION

24 Siddals Road   by 1874-1895

For sale in 1878; renamed or de-pubbed around the turn of the century. The lion features on the shield of the royal arms as well as on the crest and as the dexter supporter, hence the name. Possibly previously *Cook's Temperance Hotel* of 1852; the addresses almost match.

BRITISH OAK*

25 Carrington Street   by 1857-1895

Little information available about this inn, listed anonymously at this address in 1857 and 1862. The name refers to the oak-built 'wooden wall' warships of the Napoleonic era, since the 1850s being replaced by iron-clad and then iron ships.

BRITISH QUEEN*

26 (58) Lower Brook Street   1869-1919

Owned by Abell's iron foundry, and latterly tied to Alton's, but after World War One, a shop. Named after Queen Victoria or, possibly, Boadicaea (more correctly Boudicca these days).

BROADWAY HOTEL*

Duffield Road   1933

A once elegant slightly Italianate two-storey house built of

Broadway, Duffield Road, 1938.

brick in the 1870s as 'Tresilian' and latterly known as 'Darley Lodge'. It was put up or later acquired by the Evanses, of the Boar's Head Mill, in Darley Abbey, as a manager's residence. Lived in by John Peacock (1850-1930) the manager who took the mills over in 1903. Purchased by William Haddon Williamson, who was forced to relinquish his previous house, Abbott's Hill, Babington Lane, due to redevelopment, in 1926. He moved to The Leylands in 1933, mainly because the building of the Derby arterial road (the ring road), which was extended to meet Duffield Road in that year, deprived him of most of his gardens (not to mention his neighbours' house!). The new road, at this point called Broadway, came to within three yards of his study window. He thus sold the house, to Stretton's and they added a low extension with two canted bays to the north and opened it as *The Broadway Hotel*, subsequently much altered and extended. The licence was transferred from the *Wheatsheaf*, Walker Lane, by the brewer, Stretton. It has been refurbished and extended twice since 1980, to no good effect. It is now an Ember Inn.

BROWN BEAR*

20 Green Lane   by 1617-1878

Either an heraldic sign of uncertain connotation, a reflection of the now long defunct pastime of bear-bating, or of the performing bears brought to the Borough from time to time. Occurs in deeds 1617-1656 (DLSL) in the earliest of which it is merely the *Bear*. There was a stock & contents sale in 1779 (usually presaging a rebuilding) and it was for sale in 1864 and 1876. A sheep roast was held here in 1856 to celebrate the peace treaty with Russia. Closed after 1878, either to make way for a new building, or for conversion to a shop.

DM 16/4/1779, 21/5/1856, 5/10/1864 & 23/8/1876

BROWN BEAR*

55 (4) Lodge Lane   *by 1831-1925*

Situated on the south side next to Brown's steam mill. In 1839 it was bought by James Alton who left in 1846 for the *Seven Stars*, King Street, later moving along to the *Boar's Head* and ending up at the *Castlefields* Inn. His father, George (born in Heage in 1783) had also been a brewer. He and his successors – one of whom, from 1888, was Edmund, son of Benjamin Newbold, later of the *Hollybush* – brewed on the premises until closure. In about 1925 it was purchased by James King, a coal dealer at no. 61 and successor to his father, John, who converted the brew-house into stabling for his horses. By 1932, James's son Harry had turned the business into a cattle-moving one. The buildings were cleared in 1972.

DM 18/11/1839.

Brunswick Inn, Railway Terrace in the late 1970s before restoration.

BRUNSWICK INN*

1 Railway Terrace (Railway Parade)   *1842-1974; 1987*

Designed by the North Midland Railway's architect, Francis Thompson, to serve his triangle of railway housing to the south on a 'flat-iron' site. A stylish building with gauged brick lintels, low parapet and a tripartite wrap-around window on the Calvert Street corner, the contractor was Thomas Jackson of Pimlico. It was originally called 'The Brunswick Railway and Commercial Inn', the first purpose-built railway inn, and was leased out from the start, Miss Singleton taking a seven year lease @ £230 per annum and Jackson undertaking the finishing. It opened on 27th June, 1842. In the event, it was owned by the successive railway companies for 105 years before being bought by Hardy Hansons from the LMS in 1947. A spirit licence application was made in 1874 by landlord John Elliott. His successor but one was Benjamin Gardner (1849-1912), where he was assisted by his wife, daughter Nellie (Mrs Greatorex) and niece Beatrice. The late John Greatorex – born at the

One of Francis Thompson's chaste classic door-cases at the Brunswick Inn, 2002.

Brunswick in 1902 and Gardner's grandson – recalled:

'It was very hectic, especially on Thursdays, when all the railwaymen were paid at mid-day. Every available room was occupied and forms were placed all the way down the passage and the overflow even went into the yard. Almost every man had his work-basket with him in which he carried his lunch... quite a few pints were downed on those occasions [the beer] was home brewed and very strong. It was helped down by large trays of noggins of bread and cheese, supplied free... The inn was quite large, there were nine or ten bedrooms reached via a large curved staircase. Along the passage was the smoke room. I recall that in there was a rack with a large number of old white clay pipes which most of the smokers used at that time. A little further along was a large kitchen with a huge range over which hung the hams. This room was the one we mostly used. I remember the old grandfather clock standing in the corner with a picture of Nelson on the dial.'

Mrs Gardner kept the pub on until ill-health forced her retirement during World War One. A local resident can also recall being sent to the *Brunswick* as a child for barm for baking – presumably recovered from the casks.

Latterly it was a Hardy Hanson's pub, but closed in the early 1970s, when the Borough Council proposed to flatten the area to extend the Inner Ring Road. It lay derelict until 1983, when, at the urging of the Derby Civic Society, the Derbyshire Historic Buildings Trust acquired it and the Railway Cottages, got them all spot-listed Grade II and, having obliged the Council to adjust the Ring Road scheme (by then long a dead duck anyway), began restoration. This

Brunswick, Railway Terrace, 2002, prior to the sale to Everards.

was completed in 1984, but due to various factors, a buyer was not found to take it on and refit it until 1987. It was acquired by Trevor Harris, who reopened it as a free house on 3 October 1987. It later established its own brewery in 1991, Mr Harris pulling his first pint on 11 June that year. Nationally renowned for its beers, the pub has won numerous national awards and in 2001 was voted UK Beer Pub of the Year. In August 2002 the pub was sold, complete with its brewery, to Everards.

DM 26/8/1874; Information courtesy the late John Greatorex; NMR Board minutes 6/6/1843 and other information courtesy Peter Billson, Esq.

BUCK-IN-THE-PARK*

Copeland Street   *by 1849-50*

Took its name from the motif of *a buck couchant enclosed by park pales proper* of the 1446 Borough seal, later incorporated into the Borough's coat of arms. An ephemeral inn; nothing further known, perhaps renamed, cf. *Garibaldi.*

Buck In The Park, Curzon Street, March 2002.

BUCK IN THE PARK*

68 Curzon St/123 Friar Gate   *by 1818*

Established 1815 (if the Regency building, now stuccoed, is anything to go by) and possibly on the site of the *Crown* and in the 1930s owned by Zachary Smith's brewery. Gutted and refurbished 1990 by Marston. To let, October 2002.

BUCK IN THE PARK

St Mary's Gate   *–1761–*

Known from a single *Derby Mercury* reference; perhaps later renamed, cf. *Bunker's Hill.*

BUCK IN THE PARK

See also TOWN ARMS

BULL'S HEAD*

9 Queen Street   *by 1637-1939*

Henry Mellor of Idridgehay was the first man to hold office as Mayor of Derby under the 1637 Charter, but died in

Bulls Head, Queen Street, showing the inn sign, now in Derby Museum c.1919.

office the same year. His will establishes his ownership of the inn, but it may have been in his family for some time before. The Mellor family crest was: *A bull's head erased sable gorged with an eastern coronet and holding in its mouth the upper end of a broken lance or,* granted in 1719, but in use merely as a black bull's head from at least a century before; thus it would seem that in this case, the inn took its name from the crest of its owner. The building was early 17th century, with an early 18th-century wrought-iron sign, not by Robert Bakewell, but a vernacular, pretty, affair by a less refined contemporary. It is now in Derby Museum. A pub-based friendly society was based here in the 1820s. In the Regency period the inn was stuccoed over with the ground floor deeply grooved and the whole re-fenestrated. A façia board was added above the ground floor windows in the form of a deep cornice, arched over the entrance on brackets, all very vernacular and jolly. Run from 1823 until 1864 by Sampson King, his widow, and his son John Francis (known to contemporaries as 'JFK'!). A Coronation supper was held here in July 1838. Closed in 1939, being demolished in order to widen Full Street, November 1940. The shadow of its roof line is still visible on the south wall of St Michael's Church House.

DM 10/9/1828; 4/7/1838, 14/7/1855 (with long description) & 6/8/1855; Glover (1831/33) II. 539

(NEW) BULL'S HEAD*

34 Willow Row   *by 1846-1874*

A beerhouse situated close to the *Windmill* on one side and the *Chequers* on the other but which seems to have ceased to exist even as a building (along with nos. 33, 35-6) by 1878. Possibly the *Goat's Head* renamed; an anonymous beer house was listed at no. 33 in 1846 and 1862 which may be the same establishment with a typically imprecise address given.

(BUNCH OF) GRAPES*

13 Green Lane   *by 1791-1961*

Already 'very old' in 1833, so perhaps 17th century in

Grapes, Green Lane in 1912. A pony and trap is positioned in front of the inn.

Burley's, Duckworth Square, in the throes of closure, August 2002. The end cannot come soon enough for the white elephant of a shopping mall.

origin. Known just as the *Grapes* from c.1846, having come into new ownership in January 1840. After the building of the Hippodrome further up the street in 1913, the inn became a haunt of variety artistes, including Fred Barnes, Dan Leno Jr, Sabrina and Terry Dene. Closed by Offiler's (who had acquired it from Pountain's) on 8 August 1961, although by this date it had been refronted, probably in the 1920s, in a dignified classical style. It stood empty for a long time before being pulled down in November 1976. *DM* 18/12/1839.

BUNCH OF GRAPES**

Market Place   - 1785 -

Probably renamed more than once, the only reference is to its having been the venue for the first meeting of the newly-formed Derby Freemasons – calling themselves the Tyrian Lodge (still extant) – 17 March 1785.
Lee (1926) 8

BUNKER'S HILL

St Mary's Gate   *after 1775-1780*

Only known from an advertisement in the *Derby Mercury*, when it was offered to let. Named after the Battle of Bunker Hill in Boston, Mass., the first British victory in the American War of Independence, 1775, probably in a fit of euphoria (although the British casualties of 1,000 against the Americans' 400 made it a somewhat pyrrhic victory). Possibly a renaming of a pub known by another name (eg *Buck in the Park*) and, no doubt, renamed again after the final British defeat in 1781.

BUONAPARTE

See NAPOLEON

BURLEY'S**

1-2 Duckworth Square   *c.1995*

Practically the only shop unit in the locale still, in 2002, functioning, and situated beneath the former *Merlin* (*qv*).

Origin of the name quite unclear, perhaps a mistaken spelling for *Birley's*, Lady Annabel Birley (now Lady Goldsmith) having given her name to the famous London club, *Annabel's*, found by her first husband, Mark Birley; or perhaps a proprietorial name.

BURTON INN*

112 Burton Road (corner Gerard Street)   *by 1874-1895*

A beerhouse, taking its name from the next town down the road upon which it stood, cf. *Nottingham Castle*. It later became a Philosophist meeting room (at which period it acquired a tondo on the wall of an angel, still in situ) before assuming the humbler but more useful role of chip shop, after a spell as Barker's butchers shop.

BURTON BREWERY VAULTS**

Cornmarket   *–1849–*

Possibly a name for Cox & Malin's vintner's cf. (*Admiral*) *Rodney*, and thus not a pub but a rather grand form of off-licence.

BUTCHERS' ARMS

See MARQUESS OF ANGLESEY

BUXTON HOTEL*

12 Boyer Street (corner Warner Street)   *by 1891*

Built c.1890 in a style which can only be described as clumsily jolly, with an irregular roofline, handled with unexpected gaucheness at the corner, coloured brick bands, odd glazing bars to the ground floor windows and a couple of Gothic lancets on the Warner Street elevation, all in a street laid out from around 1873. Presumably named after the Peak District spa town, rather than the family of that name who, by 1890, spelled their name Buckston, but caution needs to be expressed, for note the presence in the

George Cross, formerly the Buxton, Boyer Street, 2002.

street of Rowland and Charles Buxton, respectively a bricklayer and a bootmaker from 1878 to the 1890s: it could be that they owned the plot, Rowland actually built the pub (it looks as if it could have been the work of an enthusiastic if over-ambitious brickie) and the name was cooked up in acknowledgement. Stretton's in the 1930s. Sold to Sycamore Inns and on 1 August 1998 renamed the *George Cross* due to the licensee's patriotism for the English flag.

BYRON HOTEL

Byron Street/80 Lower Dale Road   *by 1877*

This very modest 'hotel' bears the name of the Lords Byron, a Nottinghamshire family with local connections; the intention may have been to commemorate the poet. But note that neither Byron Street nor Lower Dale Road really existed in 1877, when there was a sale of stock on the premises, and an inaugural meeting of the local rate-payers' association, implying that the inn was then in existence. Indeed, in 1878 it was the only building in the street. It appears to have undergone a fairly thorough renovation in the Edwardian period. Ind Coope & Allsopp in the 1930s.
Harrison (c.1952) 30

CALEDONIA HOTEL

18 Midland Road
–1883–

First known from an official survey of 1883; stood next door to the *Clarendon* and was later absorbed by it. By 1898 it was, however, a Temperance establishment. Named after a well-known synonym for Scotland.

CAMBRIDGE HOTEL

86 Dairy House Road   *1892*

Built and dated 1892 and undoubtedly designed by James Wright, as the sponsors were Pountain's, and he designed their offices on the site of the Virgin's Inn, Market Place. Originally very respectable and luxurious and bounded by fine cast iron railings with stone gatepiers topped by vast lanterns. One of its landlords, Jos Holmes, was for 30 years the secretary of the Derbyshire Football Association. Renamed the *Windmill*, 1987, it has been boarded up for some time now.

CANAL TAVERN*

52-53 Canal Street (corner Park Street)   *1850-1965*

Named due to the proximity of the nearby arm of the Derby Canal, but listed anonymously in 1850. Area cleared of housing in the late 1960s-early 1970s for the benighted Inner Ring Road extension which was never built, cf. *Brunswick Inn*.

CANAL TAVERN

10 Cockpit Hill   *1800-1969*

On 5 April 1800, Benjamin Porter obtained a 60-year lease from the Corporation (at 10s per annum) and commenced to build the tall brick inn which was finally demolished for the Eagle Centre development in 1972. It was for sale in 1825 and again in 1861, after which it had a spirit licence granted in 1869. It was later sold to Hansons, who in 1899 were required by the local authority to 'renew the wood-block floors, add a kitchen and renew certain windows'. Sometime between the early 1850s and c.1870 the landlord Samuel Tetley issued a brass 1½d pub check.
DM 25/5/1825; 27/3/1861 & 26/8/1869.

Canal Tavern, Cockpit Hill.

CANNON**

Queen Street   1786-1794

Only known from advertisements offering it for sale on these dates. Named after the familiar piece of ordnance, then at the cutting edge of technological research!
DM 7/2/1786 & 26/5/1794

CAPTAIN BLAKE

See GOLDEN EAGLE

CARLTON BAR

26 Osmaston Road   *1922-1941*

An Offiler's property which masqueraded as a club.

CARLTON HOTEL

116 (58) London Road   *by 1935-1990*

The pretty late Regency house is of 2½/storeys and three bays, with a segmental headed window over the entrance which has a neat portico supported on cast-iron columns. The ground floor windows either side were once tripartite sashes, and those above have entablatures on brackets like those of the *Bridge Inn* nearby. It was built in the 1830s, and from 1861 until his death in 1908 it was the home and surgery of physician Dr Thomas Laurie Gentles. On his death it became the *Carlton Temperance Hotel*, run successively by Mrs A.M. Langford, Mrs Jane Knowles and A. Knowles. They presumably named it from the Carlton House Terrace, London, built on the site of George IV's neat palace Carlton House, designed by Henry Holland. It took its name, in turn, from the Elizabeth diplomat and historian Sir Dudley Carlton, Viscount Dorchester. Basically, the name had cachet. Between 1932 and 1935 a licence was obtained, and it was run as a small hotel with a public bar until closure in 1990. After four years lying abandoned it was incorporated into the building to the south, gutted behind the façade (the interiors were attractive, original but by then very derelict) and turned into an hostel.

CARPENTERS' ARMS*

10 Clifton Street   *by 1862-1874*

Named after the armorial bearings of the 26th oldest livery company. Listed anonymously at this address in 1862.

CARRINGTON ARMS*

5 Carrington Street   *by 1849-1895*

Like many inns in Derby, the street gave its name to the inn. The former was laid out in the 1840s, so the Carrington involved must have been Robert Smith (d.1838), president of the Board of Agriculture 1800-3, created 1st Lord Carrington (in the Irish Peerage) 1796 and Lord Carrington of Upton, Nottinghamshire, in the peerage of Great Britain in 1797.

He was the third son of the Nottingham banker Abel Smith (with a branch in Derby) and great-great-grandfather of the present Lord Carrington. The concordance in the street numbers informs us that it had started out by 1849 as the *Who Can Tell?* then run by George Lomas who doubled as a builder; perhaps he built the inn, who can tell? It was renamed after 1852. For sale in 1882, it was closed by 1898.
DM 9/8/1853 & 24/5/1882

CASTLE & FALCON*

1 Cockpit Hill (corner of East Street)   *1819-1970; 1974*

The origins of the name are unclear, despite many theories. It is the arms of Bedford, the Cornish family of Lanyon or the crest of the Bownes; none really relevant in the local context. It was for sale '...with a large family pew in St Peter's Church... the house newly erected' in 1819, and was being offered for sale again in 1824 (still 'newly built') and 1838. It was cosmetically rebuilt *c.*1870. It might have replaced the *(Lower) Green Man.* It was tied to Cox's in the later 19th century, but they sold it in 1879. Later, tied to Bass in succession to Offiler's, it was closed *c.*1970 and demolished to accommodate the Eagle Centre (taking its

Castle and Falcon, the replacement of 1975, before the market was extended and rebuilt 1993.

Castle and Falcon, Cockpit Hill, c.1970.

name from Eagle Street of c.1810 nearby), but replaced by a hideous modernist inn of the same name incorporated as part of the development on more or less the same site, but bereft of all charm.

DM 30/9/1819; 14/7/1824; 24/1/1838 & 4/6/1879.

CASTLE FIELDS INN*

19 (9, 14) Siddals Road (Lane) (corner Traffic Street) by 1827-1912

Named after the fields in which it lay, themselves leased to the Borough family in 1712 to build their house and estate of that name, the land being sold off in parcels from 1803 to 1856. Listed anonymously in 1846 and 1862, but for sale three times 1843-67 and to let in 1854 and 1861. Run from 1861 to 1867 by James Alton formerly of the *Boar's Head, Seven Stars* and *Brown Bear*. His daughter Hannah later married William James Platts, also a publican. Closed about the time of World War One and later demolished for road widening.

DM 10/4/1843; 12/7/1854; 19/2/1856/ 27/10/1861 & 19/8/1867.

CASTLE

See BELL & CASTLE

CASTLE*

40 Castle Street
by 1895-1963

Still home brewing when it lost its free house status on sale to Offilers' 1942, and thereafter up until closure, according to Mr Motley, who describes the beer as a 'rich, reddish, tinted brew'.

A beerhouse until granted a full licence on 9 February 1950. Closed after 1962 – probably the following year – and cleared by 1965. The name of the street is taken from the half-remembered site of a castle built by the Earl of Chester around Cockpit Hill, c.1141.

CASTLE

See CHEQUERS

CASTLE*

Thorntree Lane   *by 1857-1958*

Originally situated in a very ancient building with an 18th-century exterior to let in 1864, but demolished and rebuilt on an adjacent site (21 Albert Street) when the bank (now the Hong Kong & Shanghai Banking Company) was built in 1871. It was then endowed with a music hall. A free house when renamed *Mayfair Wine Vaults* c.1937. 'An unlikely name, you might think, for a pub in Albert Street, or anywhere else in Derby for that matter', Reg Newcombe recalls. 'The interior lighting was not bright, which seemed to suit certain of the female clientele...the place was not unlike the *Bell* inside, though how much of the paneling and timberwork was genuine I couldn't say.' The interior was indeed latterly fitted out in an attempt to replicate the sophistication required of an establishment named after London's most up-market residential area. On 16 August 1958 it was sold to the Midland Bank (the HSBC's predecessor), but this time was closed and pulled down not long afterwards.

DM 28/12/1864; DLC 12/1993 pp. 44-45.

Castle (later Mayfair Wine Vaults) on right, with Central to extreme left.

CASTLE
See CHEQUERS

The Smithfield, formerly Cattle Market Hotel, April 2002, showing (left) the arch from the former Sisters of Mercy Convent, Nottingham Road.

(CATTLE) MARKET HOTEL*

Meadow Road/Cattle Market Bridge   *by 1855*

Opened as the *Market Hotel* in an attractive building with a curving façade built in very traditional style probably around 1840. Renamed the *Smithfield* in July 1982. To let as 'A most complete beer house in the Smithfield Market, Derby' in 1855 and two years later described as an 'old licensed public house in Smithfield Market'. In 1863, the short-lived Convent of the sisters of Mercy on Nottingham Road – allegedly designed by A.W.N. Pugin – was taken down, and one of its gates incorporated into the inn. This survives rather incongruously as a gothic brick arch with stone dressings, bricked up and stuccoed over, the vast oak and iron furnished gates themselves surviving behind. It was let again in 1870 to John Meyer who was also a horse dealer. By this time the rather *ad hoc* beast market in the area outside the inn (intended to draw dealers away from the west end of Friar Gate), had been drastically remodelled for the Corporation by H.I. Stevens and Edwin Thompson to form the 'New Cattle Market', which survived until the coming of the Inner Ring Road. It was taken over by the first of a remarkable pub dynasty between 1926 and 1984. Martin Conneely was landlord 1926-49; his brother Percy William Conneely from 1953-78 and his son John (latterly with his own daughter Dianne) from 1978-84. Percy's wife was from the Harrison family, long landlords of the *Railway Tavern*, Canal Street. Bass from 1965, previously Offiler. Clientele changed from farmers in 1968 to journalists from 1981, the new *Evening Telegraph* offices having opened nearby. Since then it has become rather quiet, journalists being these days actively discouraged

from drinking during working hours. Owned by the Headless Pub chain of John Evans (see *Flower Pot*) since 1996.
DM 28/4/1855; 24/6/1857 & 12/1/1870.

Cavendish Hotel, Walbrook Road.

CAVENDISH

Walbrook Road (corner Upper Dale Road)   *1898*

Large brick public house, dated 1898, bowed around the acute angle at an intersection between five thoroughfares and today, inevitably, facing a roundabout. Gave its name to the immediate area of New Normanton and derived it from the family name of the Dukes of Devonshire.

CAVERN**

Queen Street   *–1780–*

Stood on the corner of St Michael's Lane, in the days when there was space between old St Michael's and the road. Once the church was rebuilt, the room was taken up and the old building removed, although there seems to be little sign it was then still a pub, although it might have been renamed. The name is, mercifully, 180 years before the club in which the Beatles made their early appearances, and was probably called after the appearance of what would have been low, mean rooms in an ancient building.

CENTRAL (VAULTS)*

2 Albert Street   *by 1852-1989; 1992*

This inn was founded on this site by 1852, and had probably been built with the street in 1848, especially as it had originally belonged to Jefferson's, on the corner of Cornmarket next door. In all probability it represented a migration from Cornmarket of an earlier inn called the *George and Dragon* notable for having been taken by 1765 by George Fritche (1726-1799), 'a former trumpeter of The

Blues', although he had moved on to the *Green Man,* St Peter's Church Yard in 1767. The likelihood is that the inn had to be demolished to form Albert Street in 1847-8, and was rebuilt round the corner at 2, Albert Street. George Fritche was the progenitor of a notable musical family, his son George Christopher (1769-1835) succeeding Charles Denby as organist of All Saints' (now the Cathedral) and his son George (1800-1890) succeeded him. Another grandson of the ex-trumpeter and a great grandson were also musicians.

It closed in 1857 and reopened with the original building refronted in bravura brick brick façade of ornamental classicism in 1861 designed by Giles and Brookhouse, still as the *George & Dragon,* owned and run by Edward Stamford Huggins, one of the entrepreneurial sons of Francis Huggins, long the landlord of the *King's Head.* In 1872, on the closure of the *King's Head,* Huggins, a brother of Charles, proprietor of the *Royal Hotel,* attempted to keep alive some of the *King's Head's* good will by renaming it as the *King's Head.* He was rapidly succeeded by his son, Richard Stamford Huggins, who died in 1878, when it was described as a 'well established hotel' and was for sale. They had from the start also dealt in wines and spirits from the premises, and were consequently taken over by Cox & Garrard, wine merchants (cf. *(Admiral) Rodney).* They renamed the inn *The Central* although it was from time to time also called the *Central Vaults.* By 1908 the firm had been taken over by Samuel Allsopp, and the dual arrangement continued under them. In the 1930s it was owned by Samuel Allsopp's, later Ind Coope & Allsopp. Renamed again *George and Dragon* in 1939, incorporating the next-door building at the same time. Closed 1989, granted listed building consent for demolition to be replaced by shops (this in a conservation area) but thanks to the recession, survived to be reopened as – once again – the *Central Vaults* in 1992 under the ownership of Banks's. Not so content, it became the *Tap House* in the late 1990s and is currently (2002) called the *Metro.*
DM 3/7/ & 9/10/1878

CENTRAL COMMERCIAL HOTEL*
21 Market Place   *by 1894-1896*
What in 1891 was the Central Restaurant, next to Pountain's on the north side of the Market Place, was acquired between then and 1895 by W. Pollicott and licensed as an hotel. It cannot have been viable, for by 1898 Pollicott is once again running the Central Restaurant.

CHEQUERS*
Cockpit Hill   *by 1761-1838*
Mentioned in Sir Harry Harpur's 'hospitality' list, 1761,

then spelt 'Checkers'. A new lease of 99 years was probably sold in 1794, for in 1814 it was to let with 79 years left to run. When sold in 1838 it was advertised as 'at the bottom of Eagle Street'. It is not heard of thereafter (although it is possible it is to be identified with the *Cock)* and was probably pulled down and replaced by commercial premises.
DM 17/4/1772; 4/8/1814 & 20/6/1838.

CHEQUERS*
43 Eagle Street (corner London Road)   *by 1814-1898*
Established before 1814 (but not that long, the street having only been built a decade before) as the *Castle* when William Mellor took over and described in the advertisement as being situated at the 'top of Eagle Street at the entrance to London Road.' He announced his intention of running a comprehensive off-sales department there too. Possibly the *Spread Eagle* revived. A beerhouse by the time it was listed anonymously in 1846/50 and 1862, and when for sale in 1873 and 1879.
DM 22/11/1814; 4/6/1873 & 21/5/1879.

CHEQUERS*
Nuns' Green/35 St Helen's Street/ 58 (41) Willow Row   *by 1761-1965*
Stood originally on the corner of Willow Row and Lodge Lane, part of Nuns' Green in the 18th century, and first appears on Sir Harry Harpur's list. It was for sale in 1791. In 1818 the landlord of the *Spotted horse* in St Helen's Street sold a 'substantial dwelling house' next door which sounds very much as if it, too, had been a pub at one time. It had a friendly society in the 1820s. For sale again in 1867 when it was bought by Long's, dyers, who later sold it to Offiler's between the wars. A spirit licence application was unsuccessfully made in 1874, after which it once again migrated to Willow Row (corner of Lodge Lane); the evidence seems to preclude there having been two pubs so close of this name for they are never listed simultaneously. Eventually a full licence was granted in 1950, but its existence was ended by plans for the Inner Ring Road. The sign derives usually from the checkered board used in mediaeval times (in association with counters or *jetons)* for computing accounts.

Some inn signs of this name derive from the arms of the mediaeval de Warrennes, Earls of Surrey, especially in the south: *chequy argent and azure.* The sign even exists on a tavern in ancient Pompeii, and is alluded to in Chaucer's *Canterbury Tales* (Ludgate's continuation). Closed and demolished 1965 and now the site of English Life Publications' offices.
DM 27/1/1791; 23/4/1818 (new location); 5/6/1867 & 26/8/1874; Glover (1831/33) II. 539; Palmer (1997) 7.

CHERRY TREE

See NAG'S HEAD

CHESHIRE CHEESE*

105 (41) St Peter's Street (corner Bloom Street) by 1818-1975

A tall narrow 18th-century inn latterly with false timber framing to the street, and entered from Bloom Street under an arch. Owned by Alton's from 1897. To let in 1851 and still brewing on the premises in 1935. Its small upstairs bar – which did not serve pints, only halves – was known as the Mousetrap. Closed in spring 1975 and converted into a shop. The cheese has been known from around Nantwich since 1100 and is justly celebrated. It is possible that it was briefly renamed the *Marquess of Anglesey* in 1841-2. *DM* 1/1/1851.

(LORD) CHESTERFIELD (ARMS)*

74 Nottingham Road   by 1857-1950

Situated on the south side of the street with the canal beyond. A beerhouse throughout its existence. Named after the arms of Philip Dormer Stanhope, 4th Earl of Chesterfield the 18th-century statesman and man of letters, whose seat was Bretby Park and who twice refused a dukedom. Between the wars, indeed, it was called the *Lord Chesterfield*. In 1857 it had been for many years run by John Wheeldon, nephew of William Billingsley of the *Sir John Flastaff*. His nephew, who inherited it, was Alderman George Wheeldon, who by that time was proprietor of the brewing and malting concern opposite the *Old Seven Stars* nearby. In 1914 Wheeldon's sold to Zachary Smith's and they sold in 1932 to Stretton's. The very early two-storey 19th century building had a cranked string course over its

Chesterfield Arms, Nottingham Road, 1937.

ground floor windows and door and was stuccoed and grooved to resemble ashlar.

CHESTNUT TREE*

Portland Street (corner of Peartree Crescent)   1940

Built and opened 6 March 1940 by Pountain's utilising the licence from the closed *Star & Garter*, St Mary's Gate. Origin of name unclear; possibly from a local landmark – no doubt felled to erect this largish pub. The first landlord was Arthur George Petts who came with the licence from the *Star & Garter* and formerly of the *Cock*. He was the father-in-law of Alfred Whitehurst of the *Sir Robert Peel*.

CHINA PUNCH BOWL*

Navigation Row (Nottingham Road)   by 1818-1824

Navigation Row was at the west end of Nottingham Road sandwiched between that thoroughfare and the China Works/Darley arm of Derby Canal; the inn took its name from a product of the nearby porcelain factory. It was for sale in 1824. Possibly to be identified with the *Punch Bowl* (*qv*), allowing for the imprecision of Regency addresses.

(OLD) CITY (OF LONDON) ARMS*

25 (17) Osmaston Road (Osmaston Street) by 1822-1862

Named after the arms of the capital city – *Agent a cross gules in the first quarter a dagger, point downwards* – and standing on the road (then Osmaston Street, at the north end) which, before the turnpiking of the present London Road, was the route to London, cf. *Burton Arms* (Burton Road) and *Nottingham Castle* (St Michael's Lane). Thus, it may have pre-dated 1756. For sale as a going concern in 1822 and 1824 and the venue for various sales until a sale of contents in 1861 which may have presaged its final closure less than a year later. Referred to by 'Old Mr Johnson' in reminiscences collected by John Ward, FSA as the *Old City Arms*. *DM* 14/8/1822; 7/4/1824 & 28/8/1861.

(GARDEN) CITY (TAVERN)*

New Chester Road (corner Vivian Street)   1850

Built as an early element of the final expansion of Little Chester, by John Thornhill in 1850 and named after the Roman settlement of Little Chester (Derventio), an ancient 'city', hence also City Road nearby. Thornhill's son, Thomas (landlord 1874), was a forebear of the late Clifford Burton. His family ran an attached draper's shop and bakery there, too. Acquired by Home Ales and rebuilt in

City Tavern, on the corner of Vivian Street and New Chester Street, 1911 looking towards St Mary's Goods Yard.

their 'house' style in 1930, being renamed the Garden City Hotel, probably as a tribute to the fame of such places as Letchworth and Welwyn, in Hertfordshire.

CITY INN
See (CORN) EXCHANGE, MELBOURNE ARMS

CLARENDON HOTEL*

15 Midland Road   *by 1874-1991*

Hotel to cater for railway travellers opened in a neat four-bay three-storey classical building c.1868, designed by Giles & Brookhouse. Later expanded into two adjoining premises, giving a less unified appearance, which became highly nondescript in recent years, making its retention almost impossible to advocate to planners and councillors, who in 1991, took the questionable decision to allow Conservation Area Consent to demolish so that the then proprietor of the Midland Hotel could replace it on a grand scale. It was made clear to the committee that if permission was not granted, the applicant would retire to another city and build there. Not having the confidence that another proprietor would undoubtedly fill the vacuum, permission was eagerly granted; in this manner are conservation areas

eroded. Demolition began in May 1992, and in 1995 the *European Hotel,* a 'no frills' establishment, was opened. The original name reflected perhaps the fame of Charles II's first Secretary of state, the Earl of Clarendon, author of a famous *History of England.*

(CLOCK &) MONKEY
See MONKEY

CLOISTERS

London Terrace, 115 London Road   *by 1965-1991*

London Terrace was built in 1825 by William Smith and Robert Bromley in a dignified classical style: a real Regency terrace of spacious houses. The southernmost unit was turned into a guest house which ultimately became a licenced hotel first called The *Kerrance,* but renamed the *Cloisters* c.1986. It closed in July 1991, later becoming an Italian restaurant.

CLOVELLY HOTEL*

Broadway (corner Kedleston Road)   *1952*

Opened in 1952 in a villa built as 'Cloverley' to designs by Arthur Eaton in 1892-3 which became a nursing home

between the wars and then a guest house. It later expanded into adjoining properties. Derelict for a time in the 1970s. Part was separated (under the same management) as a pub and named *Sobers* after Sir Garfield Sobers, the famous West Indian cricketer, in 1994, no doubt reflecting the interest of the owner, Roger Pearman, a former Middlesex cricketer and chief executive of Derbyshire County Cricket Club.
BBA no. 7171 of 1/3/1892

COACH & HORSES

15 King Street   *by 1846-1857*
The name is the classic coaching inn title, occurring from the later 17th century. Yet it frequently was employed to lend status to inns of little consequence; to gild the lily, as in this case.

COACH & HORSES*

3 Morledge   *by 1850-1878*
Stood on the west side of Morledge beside the Markeaton Brook and Tenant Bridge. Cleared for the culverting of the brook on this side.

COACH & HORSES

1 Old Chester Road / Mansfield Road   *by 1719*
An inn appears on William Stukeley's Little Chester Map of 1719-21 (published in his *Itinerarium Curiosum*) on this site called the *Crown*; by c.1750 it was the *Coach & Horses*, and performing at least a local coaching function. It was then a lowish vernacular brick building with a thatched roof and perhaps with a timber-framed core. It belonged at first to the Corporation (as did most of Little Chester), but by 1871 was in the hands of the Church Commissioners, who sold it to maltster Alderman Thomas Clarke (Mayor 1862). In the later 19th century it boasted a 25-member cricket club. In

1905 Clarke's heirs sold to Charrington's, who rebuilt it in typical Arts-and-Crafts Edwardian style with a bowling green to its south overlooked by a verandah from which the clientele could watch the games. Inevitably, this is now a car park. Sold in 1926 to Offiler's. An extension was added in 1981.

Former Coach and Horses, Sadler Gate, 2002, now converted to a shop.

COACH & HORSES*

9 Sadler Gate   *by 1818-1905*
Situated on the north side of the street nearer to the Irongate end, opposite the *Bell*, more recently Silvio's restaurant and bakery. For sale in 1845 and 1863.
DM 6/8/1845 & 25/2/1863.

(OLD) COACH & HORSES

2 St James' Lane   *by 1761-1867*
Once a genuine coaching inn, appearing on Sir Henry Harpur's list, but later declined due to the inconvenience of the site and competition from newer establishments, like the *New Inn* and swept away when the street was widened in 1867. Occasionally *Old Coach and Horses*.

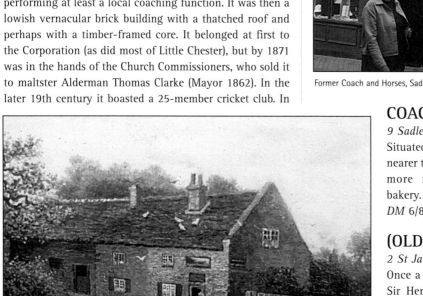

Coach and Horses, Mansfield Road, Little Chester.

COBBLERS' REST**

(34) Willow Row   *by 1769-1778 (?1861)*

According to an autobiographical note by his grandson, the china painter and author John Keys (1821-1897), Thomas Keys built this inn, presumably before his marriage to Sarah Smith at St Mary, Nottingham in December 1769, when he is described as an 'innkeeper'. We do not know when he died, but he is recorded in the Poll Book for 1778. He may have been the son of a cobbler (for he himself was a builder), and his younger son, William certainly was, so hence, in all probability, the name, reading the pun 'rest' for the more common 'last'. Interestingly, another descendant, Clement Keys, was a Willow Row publican 'and dealer in pots' who is recorded in the paper as being an insolvent debtor in 1848, 1850 and 1861. His address in 1852 is given as 34 Willow Row, but with no pub name attached; could the Cobblers' Rest have survived as an anonymous beer house? Note also John James Keys, landlord of the *Rising Sun* Osmaston Road in 1869: conceivably a son or other close kinsman.

DM 27/12/1848, 3/7/1850 & 9/1/1861; Keys (1895) 112-113, 131

COBDEN ARMS*

45 Cobden Street (corner Morley Street)   *by 1878-1977*

Named after the non-existent armorial bearings of Richard Cobden (1804-1865) the radical reformer, immensely popular in his day; note how the convention of having pub names ending with the word 'Arms' endowed both non-armigerous corporate bodies with arms as well as here, people. Called, more correctly, the *Cobden Inn* at first. Street pitched and inn built within a decade of the statesman's death. Pountain's house from 1901, and beer still brewed on the premises in 1931. In the 1890s the landlord was Thomas Spriggs; by 1915 until at least 1922 the joint landladies were the Misses Edith and Louisa Spriggs, perhaps daughters of the previous incumbent. In the years leading up to World War Two, Matthew Mather kept the inn.

COCK*

38 (18) Cockpit Hill (corner Eagle Street)   *1842-1948*

Granted a licence in 1842, but possibly older, the name conceivably deriving from the crest of Alderman Francis Cokayne (1652-1739), Mayor of Derby in 1703, 1711 and 1721, who came from the Chaddesden branch of that distinguished family. It is possibly to be identified with the 18th century *Chequers* although there appears to be a gap of 75 years between the two. In 1879 it was for sale as an 'old licensed public house' and the sign was associated with cock-fighting, sometimes taken to indicate that such activities went on there. Belonged to the Nottingham Brewery in 1930s, when Arthur Petts was the landlord, who later went to the *Star & Garter* and thence to the *Chestnut Tree*. It was

declared redundant in 1939, but spared by the war, lingering on for some years thereafter. Site cleared for redevelopment in the 1960s.

DM 23/4/1879.

COCKATRICE

Unknown location   *-1745-*

Mentioned only in a *Derby Mercury* advertisement. Named after the crest of the family of Curzon of Croxall Hall, also used occasionally by Lord Scarsdale's branch of the family. As the former family became extinct in the Jacobean period, the inn could have been very ancient.

DM 7/6/1745

COCK PITT*

Osmaston Road (corner Leopold Street)   *1988-1994*

A so-called 'fun pub' opened in January 1988 in a former villa, once of a stylish Italianate design, but previously retail premises; brighter exterior than interior, apparently. It is now an Indian restaurant.

CO-CO LOUNGE

See ARKWRIGHT'S

COLISEUM*

London Road   *1982-*

A modern brick public house built close to Main Centre and named (as a result of a competition) by the brewers, William Younger & Co, after the cinema of that name which stood nearby on the Traffic Street corner; the *Bonnie Prince Charlie* was the running-up entry. The cinema itself was an adaptation by T.H. Thorpe of a very fine stuccoed classical Congregational Chapel built to designs of Henry Isaac Stevens of Derby in 1846, and which was pulled down 20 years before the pub which commemorated it was erected, due to road widening. Opened 1 September 1982. The Colosseum in Rome (the Flavian amphitheatre) which inspired the name of both, is thus spelt. Renamed *Baroque* in 2000, although any building less overtly Baroque would be hard to imagine; perhaps the name refers to the behaviour of the clientele! Due to close for demolition and redevelopment as part of a large scheme to replace the awful Main Centre in 2003, granted consent in March 2002.

COLVILLE ARMS*

63 Colville Street   *by 1914-1947*

This establishment is anomalous and is only included because its name might suggest that it was an inn; in fact, it was only ever a beer off-licence. A weaver's house in 1878, it was an off-licence by 1891 and so continued, unnamed until 1908, when it was named, perhaps to honour the death of Major-General Sir Henry Edward

Colvile (sic) of Lullington Hall (1852-1907) a minor (local) hero of the South African War. The street name would have established the connection, and itself derives from General Colvile's grandfather, Colonel Sir Charles Colvile. The use changed in 1947.

COMMERCIAL HOTEL
See CROWN VAULTS

COMMERCIAL INN*

St Peter's Street   *1838-1846*

Little known of this establishment. The inns thus called were primarily for the convenience of commercial travellers, then commonly called 'bagmen'. However, a ball to celebrate Queen Victoria's coronation was held here in July 1838, which might suggest that the name was actually an appendage of another, well-documented, inn.
DM 4/7/1838

CONFETTI'S
See TIFFANY'S

COOK'S TEMPERANCE HOTEL

25/6 Siddals Lane   *-1852-*

Possibly later the *British Lion*, qv, for the addresses almost conform, and hence it must qualify for inclusion.

COOPERS' ARMS*

83 Litchurch Street   *by 1850-1898*

Started off as the *Vine* listed in 1852 without a street number and in 1850 anonymously. Renamed by 1874, taking its name from the Worshipful Company of Coopers' arms, granted 27 September 1509; the company was formed by 1396 and first incorporated on 29 April 1501. A common trade in Derby, bearing in mind it was a leading brewing town until Burton-upon-Trent overtook it, in renown, at least, in the earlier 19th century. After 1895 this beerhouse became a beer off-licence and relinquished its name.

COPELAND ARMS*

18 (37) Copeland Street
                                      by 1846-1963

This beerhouse, listed anonymously between 1846 and 1862, was named after the street which stood on land purchased from the Castlefield estate for £22,000 by Mr Copeland of

Lincoln, 13 April 1824. He was a cousin of William Taylor Copeland, MP (1797-1868) Lord Mayor of London (1835) and Stoke porcelain manufacturer, whose Parian statuettes were extremely popular in the mid-19th century, and whose descendant, Spencer Copeland died in April 2002. The arms were granted to W. T. Copeland's father on 28 July 1819. The inn was taken over by Sarah Johnson, formerly of the *Cossack* in 1919, and she was succeeded by her daughter Mrs Annie Winter in 1935/6, who brewed her own beer as late as 1963, when she retired, selling the freehold to Offiler's. Annie Winter was treasurer of the Derby Ladies' LVA when it was dominated by Alice Baker and Flo Liversage (cf. *White Horse, Neptune*). However, it closed soon afterwards; previously a free house.

(CORN) EXCHANGE
See EXCHANGE

CORPORATION HOTEL*

Cattle Market   *1868-1970*

Built in 1861-2 as part of the new Cattle Market, designed by H.I. Stevens and George Thompson, and opened seven years later in 1868. Tall Italianate building of three bays and angle pilasters in brick with stone dressings, the fenestration consisting of paired sashes either side of the central bay superimposed over tripartite segmental headed ones, with single segmental window over the entrance and large stone clock face above with movement by Smiths of Derby. The central bay broke slightly forwards and there were decorative bands between the storeys. It operated under a

Corporation Hotel, Cattle Market in its heyday, on a brisk market day.

Corporation Hotel, after closure in 1970.

market licence, and tenders to run it were invited by the Corporation in April 1868 and the civic opening dinner held there early in the November. When the market was replaced by the present one on The Meadows (to make way for the Inner Ring Road) in 1968, the inn's days were numbered: it closed on 30 May 1970 and was demolished in the following month. A free house owned by the Corporation. Once a popular venue for jazz.
DM 29/4 & 4/11/1868

COSSACK (ARMS) INN*

25 (17) Morledge — *by 1719-1919*
There was always an inn here from at least 1719, and it is clear from the deeds that *Cossack* was not the inn's name between that date and 1874, although from at least 1827 it was the *Noah's Ark* and probably always had been. The new name almost certainly represents a migration of the *(Don) Cossack* in East Street in the former year. Owned by the Melland family of Youlgreave for many generations, and latterly leased to Offiler's. It was rebuilt and enlarged in 1893. From 1874 run by London-born Joseph Parker (1839-1902), previously of the *Magnet*, who left to run a pub in Skegness. His daughter Alice (1870-1908) married John Renshaw of the *Queen's Head*, Victoria Street. Parker was succeeded by Frank Johnson, whose widow left for the *Copeland Arms* in 1919, when it closed and was demolished to allow for the rebuilding of the *White Horse*, which stood next to it. See also *Noah's Ark*.
Deeds, Private collection.

COSSACK
See also (DON) COSSACK

COUNTY HOTEL
See KING'S ARMS

COURT HOUSE
See WHITE HORSE

COURTYARD
See PYMMS

COX'S ARMS*
Unknown locale — *-1867-*
Named after the arms of the Cox family of Brailsford, prominent as lead merchants and vintners, and perhaps to be identified with *Cox's Wine Vaults* another name for the former *Rodney Inn*.
Reliquary VIII (1867) 169

CRANE*
Market Place — *by 1739-1745*
Stood 'behind the Town Hall in the Market Place' (ie in Breadleaps, later Leather Lane) and was offered for sale in 1745 with coach house and stable in Morledge. It must have been virtually (if not actually) next door to the *Dog & Partridge*. The sign is heraldic, perhaps representing the crest of Sir John Shore – a notable Market Place resident in the later 17th century and a well-known doctor which, although blazoned as a stork, is frequently shown as a crane. Shore was great-grandfather of 1st Lord Teignmouth. But note the fable of the crane as a clever drinker, dropping stones into a vessel until the liquid was sufficiently displaced to be consumed; in Lord Teignmouth's crest the crane is holding a pebble to echo the tale. It seems likely that it was renamed the *Nottingham Post* and eventually the *Vine*.
DM 7/6/1745

CRESCENT
Shaftesbury Crescent (corner of Malcolm Street)
by 1895-1981
Typical back-street pub taking its name, almost certainly, from the street's suffix, and not from the heraldry of some vaunted local family like the Cokes. *Crescent Inn* for the early part of its life, but *Crescent Vaults* in the 1930s, when it displayed the Alton's sign. The street, of course, took its name from the great Victorian reformer, Lord Shaftesbury.

CRESCENT
83 Wild Street (corner Campion Street) — *by 1895*
Almost certainly named after the arms of the Chandos-Pole family of Radburne Hall: *argent a chevron between three crescents gules,* on whose former land this western edge of the area known as New Zealand lay. Although only a beer-house until 1952, a gold medallion is known, dated 1909 bearing the legend 'Crescent Vaults', possibly a sporting item. A Stretton's pub in the 1930s.

CRICKETERS' ARMS**

Unknown location   *before 1867*

Possibly in Nottingham Road, and founded when cricket first started on the Racecourse in 1863 or, perhaps more likely, in Siddal's Lane by The Holmes, on which the Derby Town Cricket Club played before the building of the new Cattle Market forced them to relocate to the Racecourse in 1863.

CRISPIN**

Sadler Gate Bridge   *by 1818-20*

Only mentioned in Pigot 1818/20 and possibly a renaming of the *Five Alls* and shortly to become the *Flying Horse*. The name (also found at Litton and, more famously, at Ashover in Derbyshire) derives from the noble Roman brothers Crispinus and Crispinianus, martyred by the Emperor Diocletian early in his reign. They were converts, working incognito as shoemakers, mainly in order to avoid their having to take alms from the faithful, and their relics were translated to Soissons in Gaul in the 5th century, which became the centre of their cult. However, their cult also became rooted in Faversham (Kent) at an early date, and they were the patron saints of shoemakers, cobblers and leather-workers. Quite possibly in this case the landlord was (or had been) a cobbler. Their day was 25 October, on which the Battle of Agincourt was fought; hence the references to St Crispin's Day in Shakespeare's *Henry V*.

CRITERION VAULTS
See GREYHOUND

CROMPTON TAVERN
See QUEEN'S HOTEL

CROSS KEYS*

75 (72) Brook Street (corner of Ford Street)by 1842-1874

Closed and returned to domestic use by 1878. Beer brewed on premises.

CROSS KEYS*

45 Cornmarket   *by 1742-1862*

An ancient low and thatched market inn adjacent to the Guildhall, rebuilt with a delightful brick double-bowed façade in high Regency fashion *c.*1829 out of necessity when the Guildhall was built. Closed as a result of the end of the coaching trade and became the offices of the *Derbyshire Advertiser,* which firm later placed an attic storey in bright pink brick above the cornice, paying no respect to the shape of the façade. Now shops. The first known landlord was William Handford (d.1757), who was succeeded by William Pratt (there in 1754), a staymaker. He was succeeded by his son, Samuel (1733-1808) who also

doubled as a staymaker, but who was celebrated in his day amongst the artisans of the Borough for having founded the Union Dividend Friendly Society *c.*1764, which met at the inn. Indeed, by the 1820s it has split into a No.1 and No.2 branch both of which met here. He was prosperous enough to have sent his eldest son Thomas to Derby School, and his daughter Jane married in 1819 brickmaker John Harpur. A Coronation supper was held here in 1838. It was to let in 1845 and 1862. Note that the 1952 *Derby Directory* lists a *Cross Keys Inn,* in the Market Place; this seems to be an error and may refer to Belper, several pubs in which town are mixed in with those of Derby in the work; all very confusing. The sign is an old one, the crossed keys of St Peter being the heraldic arms of the See of Rome, but more importantly, of the Province of York, in which Derby lies. The sign, being a religious one, might suggest a pre-Reformation origin for the inn.

DM 11/1/1754, 4/7/1838, 24/9/1845 & 5/3/1862; Glover (1831-33) II.539

Crown Inn, Curzon Street during the days of Offilers Ales, c.1948.

CROWN*

58 Curzon Street   *by 1874*

In 1819-20 the Sowter family established a new mill for their malting and baking business, erected on Dayson Lane (later Curzon Street). This building, a handsome stuccoed three-storey building with a profusion of York sliding sashes, became empty after having been vacated by Messrs Bowmer & Kirkland and, against the wishes of the Council, permission was granted to demolish it for a new office block. English Heritage refused, inexplicably, to list it, and after losing a public enquiry, the Council was obliged to allow this to happen in 1994. No new building has been put up to replace it – a scandal. Behind it was a small square of workers' housing, demolished as unfit in 1935, and adjoining to its west was the manager's residence, a nice three-bay Regency house with a hipped roof. In the early 1870s it was sold, and turned into the *Crown*, the ground floor being extended as a six-bay ashlar arcade into the front garden to expand accommodation, probably to the designs of the ubiquitous Giles & Brookhouse. Purchased by Offiler's in 1913. Latterly Bass.

CROWN (VAULTS)*

51 London Road (62 London Street)   *by 1868-1902*
Stood on the east side of London Road, a couple of doors down from the corner of Castle Street. Clearly a going concern before 1868 when it was advertised with 'a magnificent 50ft by 19ft room just completed'. Its effect cannot have been an unqualified success, as it had been converted into a bottling store by 1874. Almost certainly that listed in 1883 and 1902 as the *Commercial Hotel*. A house furnishers after 1902.
DM 13/8/1868

(OLD) CROWN*

22 Morledge   *by 1818-1930*
Stood next to the *Durham Heifer* on the west side of Morledge. Probably of 18th-century origin and endowed with a traditional name much employed in the wake of the Restoration of Charles II in 1660. For sale as a going concern in 1823. Issued a token in brass with a face value of 2d in the third quarter of the 19th century. *Old Crown* in 1883, no doubt because of the coming of the London Road inn; closed 1930, and demolished to widen the road three years later.
DM 25/6/1823

CROWN

Nuns' Green   *by 1655-1732*
Probably on the west side of Friar Gate near the West End where the beast markets were held. The notorious whoremonger, adultress and murderer, Ellen Beare, was associated with this inn according to the Press accounts; Hutton says she was the landlady of the *White Horse*. Not heard of after 1732; possibly renamed.

CROWN

See COACH & HORSES

CROWN TAVERN*

21 Oxford Street   *by 1857-1930*
Listed anonymously at this address in 1857. Owned, at the time of closure, c.1930, by Home Ales. In 1908 it had become for a while merely an off-licence and its post-1930 role was similar.

CROWN*

30 St Mary's Gate   *by 1862-1898*
Two doors up the street from the *Marlborough's Head*, on the south-east side of the street; listed anonymously in 1862, and again in 1898, but retailing beer on-licence. By 1908 it was an architects' office: George Yates Mills & Sons. Demolished 1910 to make way for the County Offices.

CROWN*

St Mary's Bridge/Bridge Gate   *by 1550-1668*
Situated adjacent to the Bridge on the north side, opposite the Bridge Chapel. Owned by Roger More and left in his will (1577) to his son William. Almost certainly the same inn as that alluded to by the crown depicted on the 1668 token of George Blagreave (1623-1677) who also doubled as parish clerk of All Saints' from 1654. Probably subsequently renamed, conceivably as the *Sir John Falstaff*.

CROWN

Wardwick   *by 1761-1770*
Stood opposite St Werburgh's Church, probably on the site either of the *Lord Nelson* or the *Buck in the Park*, but the gap between them is probably too long to claim continuity. A great centre for cockfights on race days; all the entries in the *Derby Mercury* are advertisements for such.
DM 15 August 1766-24 August 1770

(CROWN &) ANCHOR*

63 St Peter's Street   *1761-1877*
It first comes to notice in 1761 when the landlord was George, brother of John Campion who took over the *Bell* in 1774. His cousin, Robert, was at this time landlord of the nearby *(Old) Swan*. Naval origin to sign, being the well-known naval officer's cap badge. In 1787 (contents sale) the address was given merely as 'St Peter's Parish'. It was for sale four times in the 50 years from the beginning of the 19th century. Landlord T. Hardy in the mid-19th century issued a 3d pub check in brass. By the 1820s it was usually referred to merely as the *Anchor*. Closed 1877 and demolished during the second phase of the widening of the street, 1878-9, having been built on the east side next to the *Nag's Head* and two doors up from the *White Swan*.
DM 15/2/1761, 28/6/1787; 14/5/1801; 23/3/1818; 20/2/1828 & 31/1/1849; Derby Local Studies Library [DLSL] deed D16.

(CROWN &) ANCHOR*

Cornmarket   *by 1732-1837*

Situated on the west side of the street adjacent to Markeaton Brook and, like the *Red Lion* and *White Lion* demolished for the culverting of the Brook. In 1732 the *Anchor* – an ancient Christian symbol of hope – but by 1827 'Crown' had been added in a spirit of patriotism, but this must have been confusing with a homonymous inn so close (see above).

DM 1732.

CROWN & CUSHION*

5 Chapel Street   *by 1850-1907*

The name is usually associated with coronations, wherein the crown is presented to the monarch on a silk tasselled cushion. Listed anonymously at this address as a beer house in 1850/7 and 1862. In 1871 it had been run since 1860 as tenant by Archibald Loates (1822-1898); when his landlord sold it in 1873 (and his brother Charles took over to 1898 and was succeeded by his widow Fanny, nee Cooper) it was described as 'old established'. Loates was also later tenant of the *Oddfellows' Arms* King Street. His seventh child (and third son) was the celebrated jockey Tom Loates (1867-1909), who rode for most of his highly successful career for the Duke of Portland.

Tom Loates rode his first winner in 1883 when attached to Joseph Cannon's stable and then weighing a remarkable four stone. In 1889 he was champion jockey with 167 winners, including the Derby on Donovan, repeating the achievement in 1893 on Isinglass, on which mount he also won the St Leger and the 2,000 Guineas, and the 1,000 Guineas on Siffleuse in the same year, in which he was again champion jockey with 222 victories, the highest total since Fred Archer. He won the 1,000 Guineas again three years later on St Frusquin, too. His brothers John (1846-1868), Charles (1853-1922) and Sam (born 1865) were also successful jockeys. Apart from John, who died at 22 of a 'diseased heart', Charles was the least successful, although he introduced the American style of riding – short leathers, forward seat, etc. – and Sam won seven classics between 1884 and 1900 and was champion jockey in 1899 with 160 winners. He also won the 1884 and 1885 Derbys, the former with a dramatic dead heat on Harvester and the latter on Sir Visto.

All three finished in the 1885 Derby, with Charles 7th on Chibiadus and Tom 10th on Raconteur. The brothers' nephew Sam Heapy was also a jockey, making a career for himself in Belgium and being interned by the Germans in 1914 with Steve Bloomer (see *Great Northern*, Junction Street).

The pub closed due to pressure from Mrs Henry Boden and the Temperance Society on the licensing Bench in 1907 and the building was much later incorporated into the *Blessington Carriage*.

DM 30/7/1873; Craven (1998) 135.

CROWN & CUSHION

Cornmarket   *by 1737-1742*

This inn acquired a new landlord, William Sherrin, who had 'lately kept the White Horse, on Rotten Row' in 1737 and he promptly transferred the name to this inn, which henceforth became the *White Horse*, being listed as such again in 1739 and 1742, when it was kept by Thomas Trimmer, draper. There is a possibility that the Rotten Row name was actually *White House*, but this could have easily have been a misprint; it would have been a most unusual name for its age. Probably later renamed again.

DM 20/10/1737

CROWN & CUSHION (HOTEL)*

1 Midland Road (10 London Road)   *1853*

Built in 1853 (dated on the fabric) and for sale only two years later – probably the time of its actual opening. Run in the Edwardian age by Arthur Cecil Felix (1878-1954), grandfather of the contemporary entrepreneur and Bonnie Prince Charlie enthusiast, Richard. His brother J.E. Felix was the landlord of both the *Shakespeare* and *Old Dolphin*. A 9in glass bottle in the Museum's collections bears the name of both the inn and A.C. Felix. A Bass house in the 1930s, subsequently sold to Mansfield Brewery.

DM 24/10/1855

CROWN & MITRE

See MITRE

CRÙ

See GREEN LANE HOUSE

CRYER

Market Place   *-1761-*

Only known from Sir Harry Harpur's hospitality list; named after the town's cryer, an office which lapsed early in 1902 and was revived 1989.

CRYSTAL PALACE*

42 Rose Hill Street (corner Madeley Street)

by 1878-1993; 1994

Named after the large glass conservatory built in the Arboretum in the 1860s and which was sufficient a wonder to the town to be vulgarly named the Crystal Palace after the London prototype, designed in 1851 by Sir Joseph Paxton. The Derby version was built by J. & G. Haywood, but it is unclear who designed it. It was demolished in the earlier part of the 20th century. The inn, open as a beer retailership, on licence and grocery by 1878, brewed its own ale until c.1967 and was an Offiler's house from 1924. Beerhouse until 1950. Inexplicably renamed the *New Inn* around 1990, when it had a relaxed tie and also sold Mansfield Ales. Closed in 1993 to be reopened in June the year following, as the *Crystal Palace* once more.

CURRIERS' ARMS**

Morledge   *by 1818-1820*

Occurs only in Pigot 1818/20, so probably ephemerally renamed. The nearby presence, in Tenant Street of the currier John Gadsby may have provided the inspiration for the change; perhaps landlord William Preston had a connection with his firm. The arms of the Worshipful Company of Curriers (dressers and colourists of tanned leather, also often vendors of finished products too) were granted 8/8/1583 and are: *azure a cross engrailed or between eight shaving knives in saltire argent handled of the second; crest: out of clouds two arms proper vested in shirt sleeves folded beneath the elbow argent hands holding a shaving knife of the last handled or; supporters: dexter an elk proper horned and hooved or, sinister a goat argent flashed sable; motto: 'Spes Nostra Deus'.*

CURZON ARMS*

18 Abbey Street (corner Monk Street)   *by 1857-1929*

A beerhouse listed anonymously in 1857 and 1862, which took its name from the Curzons (the Lords Scarsdales') armorial bearings: *argent on a bend sable three popinjays or collared gules.* Brass check issued by landlord J. Jackson with face value of 1½d, possibly before 1874, when the name was archaically spelt 'Curson'. Closed 1929 by Marston's and later demolished.

(KING) DAVID & THE HARP

Full Street   *1747-1763*

Situated at the Market Place end of Full Street, probably on the south-east side of the latter as it swept round into the former. For sale on 10 April 1747; later, having failed to sell, to let. The word 'King' in the title only used on one occasion. The inn was probably cleared in 1763 to make way for the catering establishment adjacent to the new Assembly Rooms. (cf. *Ramsden's*)

DEER

St Mary's Gate   *–1772–*

Situated opposite the Shire Hall, according to the only mention; probably on the site of the *Crown*, almost next door to the *Marlborough's Head*, which was similarly situated. Sign probably derives from the device on the Borough's coat of arms.

DM 15/5/1772

DEPOT TAVERN

27 Rose Hill Street   *by 1874-1890*

Probably on the corner of Depot Street; in 1898 long vacant. Took its name from the ordnance depot nearby in Normanton Road, built by James Wyatt in 1806, and which, but a decade after the first record of this inn, became Offiler's Brewery.

DERBY ARMS**

Unknown location   *before 1865*

Jewitt. Probably an alternative name for one of the pubs called the *Buck in the Park*.

DERBY PRIDE*

Cockpitt   *1975-1997*

Formerly the *Windmill* club, situated in what had been Tinkler and Hudson's premises in Bridgewater Buildings (once facing the Cattle Market), which gained a full licence in September 1975, when still called the *Windmill*; the name changed April 1976; it was said to derive from that of a scratch football team raised 1918-23, artfully presaging the name given to the 'Special Status' development area designated by the government in 1993 and later developed as Pride Park. Renamed the *Island Rock* in 1991. Closed and demolished 1997 to make way for one of the ugliest multi-storey car parks in the region.

DET 10/2/1992

DERBY STEAM BAR

See THOMAS-À-BECKET

DERBY TEMPERANCE HOTEL

Agard Street   *1845-1876*

Opened 1845 by one Dan O'Connor, an Irishman who had taken 'the pledge'. It is not clear when it closed, but the premises were sacrificed to the inexorable westward passage of the Great Northern Railway.

DERBY VOLUNTEER

10 (14) Hope Street   *by 1874-1912*

A beerhouse that took its name from the revival of the Derbyshire Yeomanry Cavalry in 1864 to counter a chimerical French threat; their barracks were close by in Siddal's Road. In the early years of the 20th century its landlord was Frank Rowley, great-grandfather of Derby author Nicola Rippon, whose forebears also ran the *Stag & Pheasant* (Brook Street) and the *Rising Sun* (Friar Gate).

DERBY VOLUNTEER

Litchurch Lane   *–1874–*

The name probably originated like that immediately

preceding, and was probably swept away not so long afterwards by the spread of the Midland Railway's carriage works or signalling stores.

DERBYSHIRE YEOMAN

Kingsway (corner Ashbourne Road)   *1959-1991*

A modern hotel which opened in time for Christmas 1959 to serve part of the Mackworth Estate (for the other pubs thereon, see suburban section). Named after the Derbyshire Yeomanry Cavalry, a unit revived in 1864 and amalgamated with the Leicestershire Yeomanry in 1956, subsequently in a rather nominal existence as part of a much larger territorial unit, but in the 1990s re-granted its autonomy. A popular place with a large meeting room – for some years it was the weekly venue for Derby Rotary Club – much frequented by organisations, antique fairs, etc, owned by Ind Coope and Allsopp (later Allied Breweries). They sold it to Home Brewery and in 1990 it was again sold to Marstons who, no doubt seeking a swift profit, re-sold to McDonald's, the burger chain. The closure took place in 1991 and McDonald's proposed to demolish it. However, the council (despite an astounding claim by McDonald's that tacit approval had already been given) refused, and the building was radically altered instead.

DERWENT HOTEL*

13 (15) London Street (Road)/Spot (corner Devonshire Street)   *by 1871-1970*

Some 40 years later, a parade passes the Derwent.

A very stylish late Regency building with tripartite windows, situated close to the New Jerusalem Chapel in London Street (as it was then called); it looks as though it was built *c.*1840, although it does not appear as a pub until 1871, when it was 'recently enlarged... bankrupt and to be sold'. This implies its earlier existence, so it may have indeed been built as an hotel and may have changed its name. Presumably the owners in 1871 had bankrupted themselves in enlarging it, having amongst other things rebuilt the frontage with a triple arcade on the left side of its façade which ruined its chaste symmetry. Bass pub in 1930s; closed 22 March 1970 to make way for a new shopping development associated with the Eagle Centre.
DM 20 & 27/9/1871

Derwent, London Road, 1906, decorated for the royal visit of Edward VII.

DEVONSHIRE ARMS

27 Devonshire Street   *by 1827-1955*

Built in the early 1820s, and named after the arms of the hereditary High Steward of the Borough, the Duke of Devonshire: *Sable three stags' heads caboshed argent attired or.* An Offiler's house in 1930s and and then brewing on the premises, it apparently closed quite 15 years before the street was finally cleared in advance of the building of the Eagle Centre.

DEVONSHIRE ARMS*

Queen Street   *by 1817-1854*

This inn could well have existed for some considerable time before 1817, when it was described as 'old established' and for sale. It was for sale again three years later by auction, when it was also described as 'well built' and 'in full business' with 'three good cellars, brewhouse, pump, houseplace and parlour, dining room, three lodging rooms', along with two tenements adjoining. Also to let in 1844. A contents sale a decade later probably marked the end of its existence as an inn.

DET 14/12/1817; 3,10 & 16/5, 23/8, 15 & 22/11/1820.

DIAL BAR*

Willow Row (corner of Walker Lane)   *by 1987*

Set in the redundant works of the former Derby Printing Company, a wildly art-deco brick building of c.1930. Acquired by the University of Derby Students' Union in 1996 and renamed the *Union Bar.*

DIVAS

See THOMAS-À-BECKET

DOG & DUCK

34 (13) Haarlem Street, Little City

by 1827-1926

Little City was built c.1816-21, and this small pub, tucked away on the corner of Cannon Street, may date from that time. In 1855 it was an unlikely acquisition of James Dimock (see *(Old) Spot(ted Horse)*)but he was offering it to let three years later. It was closed in 1926 by Marston's, when the licence was transferred to the *Mitre*, Osmaston Road.

DM 11/7/1855 & 21/7/1858

DOG & DUCK**

Union Street   *1850*

Only listed in one directory, thus an ephemeral domestic beerhouse without doubt. A shop by 1878.

DOG & PARTRIDGE*

55 Bedford Street (corner Crosby Street)   *by 1874*

Originally a beerhouse, and quite small; for sale as a going concern in 1874 and probably opened in former domestic premises in the 1860s. Owned by Pountain's in the 1930s. Brewed its own beer until January 1929, although Mr Motley informs us that Harold Brooks was still keeping this tradition alive as late as 1967. Full licence granted c.1951. Later expanded into adjoining property.

DM 29/7/1874

DOG & PARTRIDGE*

61 (27) Copeland Street (corner Liversage Street)

by 1846-1928

The name derives from the imagery of shooting and goes back to the 17th century. Listed anonymously at this address in 1846/50 and 1862. Although closed, it was still marked on a 1957 OS map revision.

DOG & PARTRIDGE*

Market Place (Cornmarket; Leather Lane)   *by 1737-1829*

This inn was situated approximately where the present Guildhall stands and must have stood cheek-by-jowl with the *Crane.* The address is variously given as Leather Lane (formerly Breadleaps) – the portion of the Market Place between the 1732 Guildhall and the south side of the square – Cornmarket (always deemed to extend round the corner into Market Place as far as the Guildhall) and Market Place. Indeed, it first appears as being 'near the Town Hall', address: Market Place. It appears as Leather Lane in 1749 and 1774. Described as 'at the back of the town hall' in 1791, at which date the Town Hall (Guild Hall) was still the free standing structure of 1731 erected in front of the site

Dog and Partridge, Bedford Street, 2002.

of the present Guild Hall. Headquarters of the Independent Oddfellows' Lodge in 1823/4. After a contents sale in the March of 1828 it too was demolished to make way for Matthew Habershon's Guildhall of that date, although appears in the *Pigot Directory* for 1829 due to the time lapse between compiling and printing such directories. DM 11/8/1737; 17/3/1749; 11/2/1774; 15/4/1790; 25/2/1812 & 12/3/1828.

DOG & PARTRIDGE*

Tenant Street   *by 1756-1848*

Situated on the east side of Tenant Street, the *Thorntree* took it over in 1848, according to John Ward's *Notes of Reminiscences of Old Derby*, IV. This is probably the *Dog & Partridge* at which a Coronation Supper was held in 1838 and the second anniversary dinner of the Derby Rose of Sharon Lodge of the Druids' Friendly Society the year before. DM 9/8/1837, 4/7/1838

Old Dolphin, Queen Street, 1900, with painted half-timbering on the stucco.

(OLD) DOLPHIN*

6-7 Queen Street

by 1610

A fine timber-framed structure clearly built in the mid-17th century, although the establishment claims to have been founded in 1530, which is unsubstanti-ated, but its religious name (the dolphin being a potent Christian symbol in mediaeval iconography) strongly suggests a pre-Reformation foundation, which accords well with the supposed date of establishment. The Derby Mercers' Company met here from at least 1670 and it was known for its 'Best Derby nappy ale' in the 18th century. About 1810 it was stuccoed over, which covering was removed in 1905, where-

upon the ancient timbers, exposed to the air for the first time for a century, rapidly deteriorated. Seven years later it was extensively rebuilt, with the result that much of the external timbering is today of early 20th century date. For sale in 1872, it was purchased by Offiler's in 1927 (later Bass), when Councillor John Edward Felix (1876-1951) was still brewing on the premises; he had formerly been at the *Shakespeare*. For 20 years a councillor, he was deputy mayor at his death in May 1951, a week from becoming chief citizen. He was succeeded as landlord by his sister, Mrs K. Tomlinson. From 24 October 1984 to 1995 the inn was taken over Nigel Barker, who was subsequently to build up quite a portfolio of local pubs, including the *Baseball*, *Silk Mill* and *Greyhound*, Normanton.

(DON) COSSACK**

55 Bag Lane (East Street)   *by 1843-62*

Why this inn should have been named after the Cossacks, at that period inhabiting the Don basin, it is difficult to see. Just the *Cossack* in 1862, and probably the anonymous beerhouse listed at no. 55 in 1846 and 1857. Probably a landlord, perhaps Joseph Parker, moved to the *Noah's Ark* with the name before 1874, and it was probably renamed the *New Market* whose address is usually given as no. 54.

DOUGLAS BAR

206 (185) Normanton Road   *by 1935*

Between the wars, a beer retailing business obtained a licence to operate as a beerhouse under aegis of Offiler's. It had originally been a restaurant called the 'Refreshment Bar' which flourished from at least 1889. It obtained a full licence in 1950. The name may derive from the same source as Douglas Street: Alderman Archibald Douglas, who owned much land in the area around 1800. However, the passage of time would seem to militate against remem-

Old Dolphin, Queen Street.

bering so obscure a character, even if one of his daughters did marry a Strutt! For many years the pub was known simply as 'Harry Leonard's', after the landlord, a Derby County footballer of the 1920s.

(OLD) DOVE*

1 William Street (corner Nuns' Street)   *by 1835-1933*

One of a great number of small 'corner' pubs in the former West End. In truth, it was one of the more spacious ones, having a well-proportioned four-bay frontage to William Street, brick, of two storeys with glazing bar sash windows under plain stone lintels, forming the end of a short terrace of similar design. The Nuns' Street side was of two bays, those nearest to the angle being blind, and at some later date, the upper storey over the second bay was removed and replaced by a lean-to roof. The name is of heraldic origin, deriving from the crest either of the Alsops of Alsop-en-le-Dale (members of which family were active in Derby in the late 17th and early 18th century), or of the Columbells of Darley Dale; the latter is probably more likely, as a cadet branch settled in Derby and by the second and third quarters of the 19th century were prosperous tailors with property on the west side of Duffield Road and the West End. Situated next door to the *Tanners' Arms*, and probably previously the *Vine* (recorded as an anonymous beerhouse in 1835 and named without a street number in 1850), it is first recorded under this name in 1857. It was for sale two years later, when it was acquired by Benjamin Newbold, formerly of the *Black Horse*, Nuns' Street and founder of a prolific dynasty of West End beerhouse keepers (see Introduction). In 1871 he went to the *Three Nuns* nearby, and took the name *Dove* with him, and Mr Johnson, who had taken over this pub, accordingly had little option but to rename it the *Old Dove*. When Newbold's son John eventually left the former *Three Nuns'* around 1880, Thomas Randall was then at liberty to allow the *Old Dove* to revert to the *Dove* once more, and the former resumed its original name. Home-brewed ale in 1925; acquired by Samuel Allsopp's brewery between 1919 and 1923, when it was run by George Leech. It closed on 31 December 1933 and became a lodging house.

DET Bygones 19/2/2002; DM 30/3/1859 & 5/4/1871

DRILL HALL VAULTS*

1 (2) Newland Street   *1869*

The Drill Hall was built in Becket Street adjacent to house the newly raised Derbyshire Yeomanry (as reformed 1864) in 1869, and the need for an adjacent hostelry was no doubt felt immediately, and an inn was duly built the same year, at first called the *New Vaults* being renamed the *Royal Drill Hall Vaults* following the Hall's use for a review by the Prince of Wales in 1872 by its enthusiastic landlord, John Bancroft. The 'Royal' was later dropped and, indeed,

it was advertised for sale as the *Newlands Inn* in 1876, although the new name seems not to have stuck. Completely rebuilt in the mid-1920s in brick with Stanton Stone dressings by Ind Coope to include the plot next door, in a regular two-storey style with paired fenestration and variegated brickwork. Today the Drill Hall has gone, to be replaced by the 1960s Modernist-Brutalist dole offices, whilst adjacent to the inn the Irish Club has been built on the corner. This might have been thought to have sounded the commercial death knell for the inn, but in fact it, too, has acquired an authentic Hibernian air and continues to thrive. Marston's by 1994.

DM 18/10/1876

DRUIDS' ARMS

39 Traffic Street   *by 1840-1928*

This inn was to let in 1857, the advertisement stating that the departing landlord had been there for 17 years, taking its establishment back to at least 1840. It was for sale in 1872 and was eventually closed for road alterations. The name derives from the entirely unauthorised armorial bearings of a leading friendly society: The Ancient Order of Druids. Roughly opposite the *Mazeppa*.

DRUIDS' RETREAT*

31 Mundy Street   *by 1846-1862*

This beer house was listed anonymously in 1846 and 1862, but named in 1855. Almost certainly named after members' gathering place of the same friendly society as mentioned above. It seems to have closed, the address becoming a house. Yet by 1874 it had been reinvented as the *Mundy Arms* (qv).

DUKE OF CAMBRIDGE*

34 Whitecross Street   *by 1857-1965*

Probably opened (or renamed) shortly after the death in 1850 of the 7th son of George III: Adolphus Frederick, 1st Duke of Cambridge, KG. A sheep roast was held here to celebrate the peace treaty with Russia in 1856 and an auction was held in 1859. It was brewing on the premises until 1952 although owned by Pountain's by the 1930s, when it was run by Charles Roberts, father of the redoubtable Flo Liversage of the *Neptune*. It was swept away in the rebuilding of the West End in the late 1960s, having been the subject of a CPO in 1961.

DM 21/5/1856 & 24/5/1859

DUKE OF CLARENCE*

87 (22) Mansfield Road (Chester Place) (corner Mansfield Street)   *by 1827*

Admiral HRH Prince William, 1st Duke of Clarence and St Andrew's (1765-1837), succeeded as William IV after this

pub was named after him. Indeed, its name was briefly altered to the *William IV* on his accession, but apparently failed to stick. William was the third son of George III. It was probably Little Chester's third pub, after the *Coach and Horses* and the *Duke's Head*. It was to let (as *William IV*) in 1832. The pub still occupies its original building, but has spread into a narrow adjoining house. Mansfield Street was called Chester Place when the inn was new. Owned by Hansons (now Hardy Hansons) from the 1930s.
DM 27/9/1832.

DUKE OF DEVONSHIRE*

55 Goodwin Street (corner Wright Street)   by 1827-1959
Named after William Cavendish KG, 6th Duke of Devonshire ('The Bachelor Duke'). Goodwin Street was one of the worst slums in Derby by the end of World War Two and was cleared in the 1950s; this inn closed in 1959, the licence being transferred to the *Derbyshire Yeoman*. It belonged to Pountain's in 1937 and beer was brewed on the premises until at least 1932.

(DUKE OF) MARLBOROUGH'S HEAD*

26 St Mary's Gate   by 1762-1915
This inn undoubtedly took its name from John Churchill, 1st Duke of Marlborough and Prince of Mindelheim KG (1650-1722), the famous general of Queen Anne's reign, and was probably built either at the time of his fame (he fell from grace in 1711) or at the time of his death. In 1808, the inn, which stood on the north side of the street, was demolished to make way for the building of the Judges' Lodgings, and a replacement built opposite the Shire Hall. After it closed it became offices, latterly a probation and Coroner's office, and is now part of the Derby City Education Service's offices.
DM 5/11/1762

(DUKE OF) WELLINGTON*

60 (16) Brook Street (Lower Brook Street)   by 1827-1908
Named sometime after the elevation of Field Marshall Sir Arthur Wellesley in 1814 to be Duke of Wellington; in fact the inn was probably built sometime in the period 1815-19. Wellington (1769-1852) acquired something of a cachet in drinking circles for his passing, as Prime Minister in 1830, of the Beerhouses Act to which most beerhouses subsequently owed their existence, allowing any premises to sell beer (but not wine or spirits) on purchase of a two guinea (£2.10) excise licence. In 1850 it was listed as being in Court No. 8, Lower Brook Street. To let in 1868 merely as the *Wellington*. Re-named around 1880 the *Great Northern Bridge Inn* (after the then newly erected GNR viaduct, spanning the street adjacent); a free house. Mr Motley tells us that it was latterly known as 'the blood tub of the West End'! It was closed

through Temperance Society pressure in 1908, and became a marine supplies store, later demolished by one Benny Robshaw and the site used for his rag and bone yard.
DM 24/6/1868

DUKE OF YORK*

17 (56, 3) Burton Road   by 1827
At first situated at No.56, near the *Tailors' Arms* but later relocated across the road next to Christ Church Mission Room at No.3. Named after the 'Grand Old Duke of York', Field Marshall HRH Prince Frederick, 1st Duke of York and Albany (1753-1827), who was also, by a bizarre coincidence, (lay) Prince-Bishop of Osnabrück, today Derby's twin town. Built and named either around the end of the Napoleonic Wars (1814-15) or at his death in 1827. In the 1920s it was acquired by Pountain's, who in 1937 closed and demolished it, building a fresh pub bearing the same name on the adjoining site, which opened on 15 September 1938, the initial landlord being Reg Woodyet, formerly of the *Reindeer,* and father of Tony Woodyet, later of the *Malt Shovel,* Spondon. Closed in 1992, refurbished rather brashly and reopened by Sycamore Inns 10 September 1993 as *Sergeant Pepper's* (as of Beatles fame).
DET 7/9/1993; DET Bygones 12/3/2002

DUKE'S HEAD**

Old Chester Road   -1719-
Marked by William Stukeley on his map of Little Chester published in his *Itinerarium Curiosum*. It is not known how long it had then been there, nor how long it survived. The duke in question must have been Devonshire who, as Hereditary High Steward of the Borough, enjoyed a lease of the Corporation's estates here for many years.

DUN COW*

21 Bold Lane   by 1835-1883
The sign of this inn, which first appears in directories anonymously in 1835, was a large whale's scapula, which hung horizontally outside, and was labelled on one side 'Ye Derby Ram'; and on the other, 'Ye Spade bone of ye Dun Cow 1606'. No inn is recorded as the *Derby Ram* (which is surprising indeed) except the *Ram*, Brook Street. The puzzle is the early date on the sign: could it be the date of this inn's foundation? The sign is now in the collections of Derby Museum. In 1849 the landlord, George Hodgkinson, also practised as a plumber and glazier. By the end of the century the building was one of several lodging houses owned in the area by Joseph Bate. The sign derives from the feat of Guy (de Beauchamp), Earl of Warwick, in slaying the Dun Cow on Dunmore Heath, commemorated in a ballad in which is mentioned that the Dun Cow was 'bigger than an elephant': some elephant; some cow!

DUNKIRK TAVERN

98 King Alfred Street (corner Bakewell Street)   *by 1895*
The enclave at the south-east corner of St Luke's was historically called Dunkirk, probably after a farm which once stood there, its name commemorating the loss of that last outpost of Britain in France in Queen Mary's reign. Stretton's house in 1937, in 1994 Pubmaster.

DURHAM HEIFER

23 Morledge (corner East Street)   *by 1846-1904*
Situated on the north-west corner with East Street opposite the *Castle & Falcon* and next to the *(Old) Crown*. Demolished and site empty for many years.

DURHAM OX*

124 (110) Burton Road (corner Gerard Street)   *by 1863*
The building would seem to pre-date the inn; it consists of three artisans' cottages all amalgamated into one at some unknown period prior to the 1939, when it was modernised, stuccoed, re-roofed and given Crittall (steel) windows by Alton's (by then a sub-division of Ind Coope). Named after the prodigious ox born in 1796 and reared by Charles Collings of Ketton, County Durham. By 1802 it was 11ft from nose to tail-tip; at 10 years it weighed 34cwt and was nationally famous. The landlord in 1863 became bankrupt, and it was for sale a decade later, too. Albert Foss was landlord here from before 1926 until he retired at the time of the rebuilding in 1939. The licence was taken over by his son-in-law Arthur Barr, who had married his daughter Elsie, and he ran it for a further decade before opting for a quieter life running Chellaston Post Office. Elsie later worked for Alice Baker at the *White Horse*. Their second son, Neville Barr recalled his boyhood there, including a visit from the diminutive comedian Jimmy Clitheroe whilst he was appearing at the Hippodrome. Apparently, Mr Barr's mother failed to recognise him, and refused to serve a minor! Mercifully, his companions pointed out the truth of the matter and all ended happily. It was also recalled that the police took a far more relaxed view of after hours drinking in the war years, even down to some pubs having a small shelf mounted discreetly on an outside wall where a pint could be left for the patrolling policeman. Closed in 2001 but reopened in August 2002.
DM 22/4/1863 & 23/7/1873; *DET Bygones Supplement* 29/1/2002 p.21.

DURHAM OX*

57 St Peter's Street   *by 1791-1877*
Built some time before 1791 as the *Woolpack*, but renamed between 1821 and 1822. The earlier name would pay homage to the woolstapling trade and its associated occupations, by the Regency period in terminal decline. The inn was demolished for street widening, like the *(Crown &) Anchor* close by and the remaining site purchased, along with other property either side, by Sir Edwin Ann, to build his great achievement: Derby's first independent department store, the Midland Drapery. Numbered variously 56½ and 57½ St Peter's Street, numbers with ½ added in Derby traditionally indicate a yard or other premises behind the whole numbered property. The original sign derives from the arms of the Worshipful Company of Woolmen, granted 19 November 1954: *gules a woolpack argent*. It would appear to have been completely rebuilt in 1821, when it was offered to let as a 'newly built public house' – probably the occasion of its renaming. For sale frequently thereafter, between 1824 and 1850. In 1845 it was to let '...with a butcher's shop to the front' (ie. 57 St Peter's Street itself) and in 1856 as 'recently altered'.
UBD 1791; *DM* 30/5/1821; 24/11/1824; 9/1/1828; 9/2/1831; 5/3/1845; 27/2/1850 & 2/4/1856.

(OLD DUSTY) MILLER*

33 Cockpit Hill   *by 1791-1868*
First recorded in the *Universal British Directory* (*UBD*) 1791 merely as the *Miller*. It stood next door to the *Boat* but was 'about to be pulled down' in 1868. Being close to a handful of watermills which once graced the Derwent at this point (but which had been long gone by 1822) it may have had a much longer existence than records would suggest; this is supported by the soubriquet 'Old' which it bore even in the 1820s. Millers were traditionally covered in white flour as a consequence of their trade; hence the sign which, in the case of this inn, showed the miller drinking with some jovial companions.
UBD 1791; *DM* 25/5/1825 & 29/4/1868

DYERS' ARMS

See ROYAL ALBERT

EAGLE (TAVERN)*

20 (6) Green Street   *by 1846-1963*
The name may be a recognition of the crest of the Borough family of Castlefields, owners of much property in Derby, but not perhaps in the West End. The Cottons, Montgomerys and Ropers, who also displayed eagles were, perhaps, too early in date. Thus the Russian Imperial Eagle suggests itself, in view of the fact that the Crimean War had not long been ended. Commemorating one's enemies on pub signs seems to have been remarkably common, cf. *Napoleon*. A beerhouse which was formed out of the amalgamation of two remarkably small cottages, one of two and one of three storeys, cosmetically united by a 1920s facelift, courtesy of Shipstones, and listed anonymously in 1846 and 1850 at this address. It brewed its own ale until

1952. Closed in advance of the Green Street Compulsory Purchase Order (CPO), 1963 and cleared soon afterwards.

EAGLE

St Peter's Church Yard   *by 1833-1866*
A very modest establishment in a tiny mediaeval building; perhaps of long foundation, just not mentioned in the sources, or possibly subject to a name-change. The Borough family crest seems a much more likely inspiration for the name in this locale. Known in 1866 through a photograph of the landlord's family, but gone as a pub by 1874 and cleared as a building in 1878, when it had been added to the *Green Man*.

EAGLE

See also SPREAD EAGLE

EAGLE & CHILD*

1 St Alkmund's Church Yard   *by 1732-1967*
Situated on the south-east side of Derby's only Georgian Square, by the entrance from Queen Street, and unlike the remainder of the square, in an un-refronted building of 17th-century origin, and one which bore all the signs of having been actually built as an inn. The sign commemorated the crest of the Stanley family, Earls of Derby (who derived it from the Lathoms of Lathom, Lancs), although that great Lancastrian dynasty had little to do with Derbyshire and had no holdings in the town. For sale in 1825 and 1828 and for £2,500 in 1877; still home brewing in 1964, having been sold to Offiler's in 1941. Closed and demolished when the entire area was sacrificed to build the ring road in 1967. Known to its habitués as the 'Bird and Bastard (or, Baby)' – a far cry from the quaint legend of the stolen royal child from which the device is said to derive! DM 12/10/1732; 30/11/17825 & 16/4/1828.

Earl Grey, Upper South Street, 1938.

EARL GREY

77 Upper South Street (corner Uttoxeter Old Road)
                                            by 1833-1972
Probably built and named *c*.1832-3 when Charles Grey, 2nd Earl Grey, KG (1764-1845) managed to force the

Reform Bill through the Lords; he was Prime Minister 1830-1834. The proximity to the 1826 County Gaol, broken into during the reform riot of October 1831 points up the appropriateness of the name. This inn faced across the mouth of Upper South Street towards the *Blue Bell*, with a rather attractive timber corner window with a bold cornice. The building was stuccoed over with Brookhouse's Roman Cement and grooved to resemble ashlar. It was an Ind Coope (Stretton's) pub in 1937. Demolished June 1972.

ELEPHANT & CASTLE*

30 Bold Lane   *by 1850-1870*
Nothing known of this inn, except for a beer house listed at this address anonymously in 1850, until it was extended in July 1864, and again when it was affected by Sir Abraham Woodiwiss's culverting of Markeaton Brook to form the Strand. We know it stood adjacent to Sadler Gate Bridge, so the works may have led to its demise, although no. 30 is missing from all directories from 1874, so it could have been demolished before that date. The name derives from the crest of the Worshipful Company of Cutlers, granted 10 May 1622: *an elephant argent armed and harnessed or bearing on the back a castle thereon two pennons displayed the dexter argent a cross gules the sinister a pennon of the arms of the Company*. This device derives, in its turn from the Indian howdah, and, indeed, the Cutlers Company had used a similar device as far back as 1445. Perhaps renamed the *Alexandra Vaults*.
DM 6/7/1864.

ELEPHANT & CASTLE

Cornmarket   *by 1741-1777*
Advertised to let in 1741, with brewhouse and stables, also a garden all lying near Gaol (St Peter's) Bridge, although on which side of the street is unclear; the east seems the more likely.
DM 6/8/1741 & 28/2/1772.

ELM TREE

25 (14) Borough' Walk (corner Union Street) by 1850-1969
Beerhouse, listed anonymously in 1850 and a freehouse in 1937, still brewing on the premises until the death of landlady Mary Reynolds in 1950, when sold to Offiler's. Cleared with the rest of the area to make way for the Main Centre extension and Eagle Centre, 1969. The Elm Tree (with shield of Pallas hanging from it) was the Borough family coat of arms, the inn being built on part of their former Castlefields parkland.

ELM TREE*

11 (14) Watson Street   *by 1846-1963*
Listed anonymously between 1846 and 1862, it was for sale

as a 'well accustomed public house' in 1870 and again in 1881, following a spirit licence application in 1874. Owned by Offiler's from 1928, and cleared under the Watson Street CPO of 1963. Beer brewed on the premises until at least 1955, when a photograph shows the legend, painted in large capitals between the floors: 'Home Brewed Ales'. Perhaps took its name from a once-prominent local landmark, as was possibly the substantial house nearby at Five Lamps, The Elms, built 1800 (see *White Stoup*).
DM 21/9/1870; 26/8/1874 & 1/6/1881; Palmer (1996) (i)

ENGINE TAVERN
See UNION OF HEARTS

EUROPEAN HOTEL
See CLARENDON

City Inn, formerly the Exchange Hotel, Albert Street, 2002.

(CORN) EXCHANGE*

12 Albert Street   *by 1863*
Built at the same time as the Corn Exchange, next door, to the designs of Benjamin Wilson in 1861. Not listed in 1862, but quite possibly opened within months, and probably to Wilson's designs also, although the building has been somewhat abused since, including the imposition of the thick coat of render. The application for a spirit licence at

Exchange, before the demolition of the Shot Tower in 1931.

the business, 'late Sarah Eyre' in 1863 (where it was called the *Corn Exchange*) suggests that it had been up-and-running for a while, at least. Sarah Eyre was probably a member of the Eyres of the Ashbourne Road brewery (see Introduction). Needless to say, it took its name from the Exchange whose customers it no doubt served. Purchased by Offiler's in 1920 and subsequently Bass. Refurbished and renamed *Mongolia* in 1997 and currently called the *City Inn*.

EXETER ARMS*

13 Exeter Place (corner Exeter Street)   *by 1818*
The Regency building, put up with most of the rest of the area around 1816, was plainly intended for an inn, and took its name from the Cecil family, Marquesses and Earls of Exeter, whose Exeter House (demolished 1854) stood nearby, and on the gardens of which the place was built, as were both streets. Brownlow Cecil, 8th Earl of Exeter, acquired Exeter House by marrying Miss Chambers, a local heiress. They gave some fine plate to All Saints' Church. A

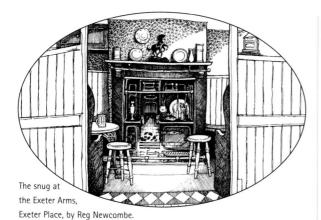

The snug at
the Exeter Arms,
Exeter Place, by Reg Newcombe.

spirit licence application was lodged in 1874. The pub was extended into no.32 Exeter Street in the early part of the 20th century. A free house with brewing on the premises in 1937, and was the last inn to do so in Derby when the latter activity ended in 1970 with the retirement of Winifred Jackson. Acquired by Bass, who sold it to Marston's in 1980. Interior, like that of the Dolphin, moderately well preserved at the time of writing, including some original settles and a very fine locally cast range. Unfortunately the sign erroneously illustrates the arms of the City of Exeter – an unforgivable solecism.
DM 26/8/1874

FALSTAFF*

74 Silver Hill Road (corner Society Place)   *by 1895*
A very bravura piece of exotic classicism in brick, and no small pub, either. Built around 1890 by Pountain's, possibly to the design of Alexander MacPherson. It is of two high storeys, with fenestration (sashes with glazing bars over plate glass) offset between the floors, the pilaster strips dividing the bays on the upper rising eccentrically from the prominent keyblocks of those below and all sitting on a moulded brick band. The upper windows also have shaped aprons in rubbed brick, also an element of the gauged brick lintels generally. The end bay has a large pediment like that which once graced MacPherson's Childrens' Hospital, North Street (of 1883) and there is a smaller, open one beside it, decorated with ball finials. Named after the well-known character by Shakespeare. Run for over 30 years from the earlier 1920s by Horace and Mary Scotton, and by Mr Scotton's father before him; the latter, who died in harness, was apparently laid out for three days on the tap room table so that his friends and customers could pay their respects.

The former's daughter Betty married Tony Woodyet of the *Malt Shovel*, Spondon. A micro-brewery founded here by Messrs Parkes in August 1999. It was mothballed in 2000.
DET Bygones 23/3/2002

FALSTAFF
See also SIR JOHN FALSTAFF

FARMERS' ARMS**

Unknown location   *before 1867*
Jewitt. The name would suggest a market pub, so it is likely that this inn would have been in or near the upper end of Friar Gate, the Market Place or possibly even the Morledge.

FAT CAT

18 Friar Gate   *by 1998*
Behind the obviously spurious 'half-timbered' façade, this Grade II listed building is indeed timber-framed and, as the entire structure was found in 1990 to be relying on No.16 (of *c*.1641) for support, we may assign it to the period of the Restoration.

A century ago it underwent a change from farriery to bike shop and thence to a motor car showroom, eventually becoming Peveril Motors. The entire ground floor was gutted in the process, making it an attractive proposition for conversion into a café bar in the 1990s, after many years of lying empty. The name is perhaps a whimsical reflection on the popular press's comments on the rewards for captains of industry! The establishment is part of a chain which also has bars of the same name in Nottingham and Leicester.

FEATHERS*

88 Park Street   *by 1855-1895*
A beerhouse, probably named in honour of the Prince of Wales (later Edward VII) whose badge was the well-known device of *three ostrich feathers issuant from a coronet* with the motto *Ich Dien* ('I serve'). He was born in November 1841 and created Prince of Wales a month later. Clearly in existence for long enough, in 1855, for the owner to go bust, there having been a contents sale that year. Closed before 1898 when it was a tripe dresser's shop and reportedly the residence of a retired pox doctor in the 1920s! Possibly previously the *Forester's Arms*.
DET Bygones 28/5/2002; *DM* 28/3/1855

FIVE ALLS

Bridge Gate   *by 1756-1761*
The sign, a well-known humourous one, depicted the King (I rule all), the Soldier (I fight for all), the Farmer (I work for all), the Parson (I pray for all) and the Devil (I take all)! The last element was often rendered elsewhere (mainly as a 19th-century refinement) as a working man ('I pay for all!'), but Jewitt confirms the diabolical version in the case of the two Derby inns of this name.
DM 31/12/1756.

FIVE ALLS

Sadler Gate Bridge   *by 1747-1756*

Advertised for sale in 1747 as 'a new-built brick house (being the sign of the Five Alls) with beerhouse'. It was 'near to Sadler Gate Bridge', which in terms of streets was that piece of road between the lower end of George Yard, Sadler Gate and Bold Lane, today occupied mainly by Messrs Prince's shop, formerly Bristol Street Motors. 'Near' suggests that it was away from the street somehow. Not heard of after 1756. Perhaps it became the *Flying Horse*.

DM 27/3/1747

FIVE LAMPS

See ST HELEN'S

FLAMINGO & FIRKIN*

127 Becket Street   *1985*

Originally opened in 1985 as *Liberty's*, a Home Ales bar. Extended and in November 1988, in Atkey's former motor-garage with a cast-iron awning outside next door to the auction rooms, became *Flamingo & Firkin*; extremely spacious but soulless interior. The company which promoted it was originally a London outfit with premises of this name, the landlord being Grand Metropolitan, who refused to sell it to Carlsberg-Tetley who had taken over the remainder of the chain, all suffixed with '& Firkin'. The *Flamingo & Firkin* was thereupon transferred to Derby complete with micro-brewery and installed in Becket Street. Sold to Midsummer Leisure in 1990. Beer was brewed on the premises until late 1990s. Closed for refurbishment at the end of 2001 and reopened as a 1970s-themed bar, with a late licence, called *Flares* in May 2002. Name purely whimsical; cf. *Foal & Firkin* sub *White Horse*.

FLARES

See FLAMINGO & FIRKIN

FLEET (STREET) TAVERN*

3 (1) Fleet Street   *by 1866*

A beerhouse, taking its name from the street which, like Cheapside and The Strand would seem to have been inspired (for no very good reason) by the London original. 'Known for some time past as a public house... by the sign of the Fleet Street Tavern' according to an advertisement for its sale in 1867, so probably established some time before. Owned by Ind Coope & Allsopp in 1937 in succession to Alton's (later Stretton's) by which firm acquired in 1903. The former endowed this very modest former artisan's cottage in the 1930s with a new steel ground floor windows, ceramic tiles arranged into Art Deco stripes and a black façia with stainless steel titulature. Samuel Bailey,

who brewed on the premises until 1953, was granted a full licence in 1951.

DM 16/1/1867

FLORENCE NIGHTINGALE

See NOTTINGHAM ARMS

(NEW) FLOWER POT*

40 King Street   *by 1818*

Opened in a pretty three-storey three-bay house of *c.*1800 with Derby windows either side of the entrance, today with plate glass instead of glazing bars, although these survive on the floor above. Named after an object associated with the flower shows held nearby in the Cherry Street Drill Hall, originally built for the Volunteers in 1822. A sale was held here in 1843 and both this inn and the one following held rival sheep roasts to celebrate the peace treaty with Russia in 1856. In 1903 there was still stabling for 10 horses and room for 10 waggons, which by this date had almost ceased to ply from the inn to surrounding villages on a scheduled basis. A free house in 1937, later Bass. Now a free house again, run by John Evans's Headless Pub chain, since 1993. Expanded into the Victorian building next door to the east, previously a car tyre centre; building colour-washed in a very horrible hue, 1980s.

DM 21/5/1856

(OLD) FLOWER POT*

9 King Street   *by 1791-1907*

Built and named for the same reasons as the inn above, although the venue for the flower shows was different at this earlier date. Stood on the east side of King Street, but later closed due to pressure on the Licensing Bench and converted into a shop, itself demolished for road widening, 1913. Changed hands four times between 1811 and 1871, after which it was run to *c.*1895 by Henry Renshaw, whose brother much later ran the *Queen's Head* after a spell in Skegness.

UBD 1791; DM 21/10/1811; 4/1/1824; 12/4/1854, 21/5/1856 & 31/5/1871.

FLYING HORSE*

Bold Lane (Sadler Gate Bridge, Court No. 2)by 1822-1850

Little known of this inn; perhaps originally the *Five Alls* and then possibly, if briefly, the *Crispin*. Flying Horse Yard, however, kept its name until at least 31/8/1850 (in which year the inn is listed as an anonymous beer house), when the Borough Surveyor, Samuel Harpur, referred to a Mr Roper being responsible for a vault there (probably James T. Roper, contractor for scavengers' manure, of Orchard Street in 1849). Named after the Pegasus of myth, a name later applied to a famous stagecoach.

FOAL & FIRKIN
See WHITE HORSE

FOOBAA**

Old Blacksmith's Yard   *2000*
Opened by Foobaa Ltd in 2000 with the avowed intention to attract the 'younger drinker' (where, in central Derby, is this not the case, one might ask?). Operated by the same partnership as Wardwick's *Susumi*. Heated outdoor seating – a handy innovation. Name inexplicable but setting is the late 18th- and early 19th-century complex established by Hugh Atherstone for his veterinary practice and run by his son, also Hugh, until the 1850s, when the Cartlich family took over. By 1878, Samuel Palfree had taken it over as a farriery. His daughter, who retired around 1980, practised as an unqualified vet and later ran an animal hospital there, in what had become known as Palfree's Yard. The area was developed by David M. Adams as a shopping precinct, and the 15th-century timber-framed merchant's house from the Market Place was retrieved from museum storage and re-erected there, albeit in emasculated form.

FOOTBALL*

13-14 East Street   *by 1887-1898*
In existence in 1887 when it was knocked down by the proprietor of the Midland Drapery (Alderman Sir Edwin Ann) and moved a few doors down the (north) side of the street to No.13-14, the proprietor then being William Cross. This move probably prompted a name-change, probably from the *Plumbers' Arms* (qv). Closed c.1900 and became a shop. Named after the game played through the streets of the Borough from time immemorial until 1846.

FOOTBALL (TAVERN)*

273-275 Osmaston Road   *by. 1898-1993*
A beerhouse which came into the hands of Stretton's in 1926 and which that firm reconstructed with an ornamental façade of ceramic tiling and odd paired windows in stone surrounds with tiled aprons in 1928. Full licence 1950. Named after the sport which displaced baseball at the nearby Baseball Ground in the 1890s. Known to many as the Football Tavern, a name it gave to its own pub soccer team. Closed since September 1993. It was repainted, fitted with lanterns and the old signage briefly restored, before reopening in August 2002 as the *Beer Barrel*, regrettably, despite the name, without any traditional beer. Its connection with the nearby Baseball Ground is now lost.

FORESTERS' ARMS**

Park Street (Park Lane)   *by 1835*
Listed anonymously, one of two beer houses so itemised at unspecified addresses in Park Lane, in 1835 and to let as a going concern in 1843, perhaps subsequently renamed, cf. *Feathers* or *Melancthon's Head*. Named, not after the well-known regiment (45th Nottinghamshire) but after the well-known friendly society, the Ancient Order of Foresters, strong in Derby.
DM 29/11/1843

FORESTERS' ARMS
See OLD VAULTS

FORTY-SECOND STREET

Sadler Gate   *by 1985*
Bar in Sadler Gate, named after well-known New York Street (or the song). Originally *Rio's* (1985) and later *Boom*.

FOUNTAIN*

83 (57) Osmaston Road (Street) (corner Upper Hill Street)   *by 1827-1963*
It is unclear whence this inn took its name, unless from a feature in the former park of Castlefields (on which Hill Street, then Ossian Street; was laid out c.1810). In 1827 the address was grandly given as 'High Park Terrace, Osmaston Road' which rather confirms the supposition. It was for sale that year, with full brewing paraphernalia, a 700-gallon cistern and stabling for 14 horses, also in 1865 and 1871. Nevertheless, around the latter date it was renamed the *Prince Leopold*, probably to commemorate Queen Victoria's fourth son, HRH Prince Leopold, 1st Duke of Albany (1853-1884). It was acquired in the 1920s by the Nottingham Brewery and closed in December 1963, being cleared some time later for site redevelopment.
DM 31/1/1827; 8/3/1865 & 22/11/1871

FOX & GOOSE

11 Friar Gate   *by 1833-1930*
A pleasant timber-framed building of early 17th or even late 16th-century date with two gables to the road, subsequently stuccoed over and in the 1880s given fancy barge-boards, a hung tile upper storey and a heavy ground floor cornice bowed up and open over the entrance. Closed 1930 by Marston's and the licence transferred to the *Mitre*, Allenton. The premises were then gutted at ground-floor level and was an antique shop (latterly by far and away the best in Derby) for many years. This was driven out of business, no doubt by a greedy landlord hoping to make a much higher rent from a café-bar, only to lie empty for five years. Traditional name.

(FOX &) GRAPES*

21 Castle Street   *by 1843-1908*
In its earliest manifestations, the name is the *Grapes* only,

Fox and Owl, Bridge Gate.

but was probably always intended to be the combination of Aesop's well-known fable. Two houses were knocked together to form the pub. The first landlord was John Woodward (1793-1852) probably brother to Frank (*Arboretum Tavern)* and George (*George IV*). Sold in 1863, when the licensee was Repton-born Mrs Edith Gell, who also ran a millinery business, and whose daughter married Timothy Pitman, one of the family connected with the King Street Marble works. She brewed her own ale on the premises. Sold again in 1878 and closed about 1910.
DM 29/12/1852, 15/4/1863 & 7/8/1878; Information courtesy Mrs M. Mack

FOX & HOUNDS*

Dog Kennel Lane   *by 1857-1876*
Probably in existence longer than the directories would suggest (it appears anonymously as a beerhouse in 1857) and undoubtedly named, like the street, after the presence of the kennels of the Borough's pack nearby, whence they had been moved following the sale for building of Nuns' Green (their previous home) 1768-1792. When the Great

Northern Railway was built, the houses on the north-east side of the street (mainly workers' cottages relating to the Rowditch brickworks) were demolished to make way for the civil engineering works. The inn shared the same fate. The street was thereupon renamed Great Northern Road.

FOX & OWL*

61 (43) Bridge Gate   *by 1716-1969*
Originally a handsome two-storey brick inn with extremely bold moulded brick cornicing and other features which suggest that it was built in the immediate Post-Restoration period by the same mason as the façade of the *Green Man* St Peter's Church Yard. Scene of the suicide (by poison) of a young soldier on furlough in summer 1745. In 1808 it was let to Robert Leach, 'late butler to Francis Noel Clarke Mundy' of Markeaton Hall for 12 years. For sale in 1817, when it had been 'occupied as an inn and an extensive business had been carried on there for over a century' and known as 'one of the best inns on Bridge Gate' in the 1830s, according to John Ward's *Notes of Reminiscences of Old Derby,* (I.vii). To let again in 1849, and in 1856 a sheep

roast was held to celebrate the peace treaty of 1856. In 1886 it was rebuilt in brick with a five-bay two-storey façade and a central, rather steep, pediment to a design by Arthur Eaton and with a dormered roof. Stretton's in 1937. Closed by Ind Coope 31/12/1969 after the death of the last landlady, Alice Flounders (who was also the last landlady of the *Lord Belper*) – the last occupied building on Bridge Gate, and cleared very soon afterwards.
DM 17/5/1733; 13/4/1808; 18/12/1817, 7/2/1849 & 21/5/1856; *BBA* No. 4093 of 1886

FREDDIE'S
See REFRESHMENT HOUSE

FREEHOLD TAVERN*
64 Franchise Street (corner Freehold Street)by 1857-1962
Franchise Street was named after the Reform Act, which widened the franchise to all property owners, around 1852. Freehold Street (and that just mentioned) were built up by one of the many building clubs, set up to enable artisans to acquire their own freeholds through a kind of hire-purchase. Hence the inn was named from the street and was probably in business by 1857/62 when it appears to be listed as an anonymous beer house here. Later a Stretton's house, but failed to get a full licence and closed, becoming a corner shop.

(FREE) MASONS' ARMS*
9 Albion Street (corner Bloom Street)   by 1823-1925
Conceivably a migration of the similarly named inn in Morledge, but no evidence for this obtrudes. In 1827 and 1843 its name was given merely as the *Masons' Arms*. It stood next to the *Albion* and was for sale (with the title in full) in 1865. In the 20th century it again became the *Masons' Arms*, having been named after the arms of the United Grand Lodge of Ancient Free and Accepted Masons of England, used for many years before a regular grant was made on 13 June 1919. Although a freemasonic lodge existed in Derby from the 1730s (based at the *Virgin's Inn*) it folded in the 1770s, and it was not until 1785 that the Tyrian lodge, still flourishing today, was founded by Dr. John Hollis Pigot, from Southwell.
DM 13/12/1865

FREEMASONS' ARMS
Morledge
by 1761-1767
Listed as one of Sir Harry Harpur's

favoured hostelries at the election of 1761, and for sale six years later. It could possibly have migrated a few hundred yards into the then newly-pitched Albion Street *c.*1816. Neither this inn, nor that itemised above had a Freemasonic lodge meeting there.
DM 19/6/1767

FREEMASONS' ARMS
See also MASONS' ARMS

FREE TRADE HOUSE**
201 Abbey Street   by 1857-1878
Listed anonymously in 1857 and 1862, it stood mid-way between Wilson Street and Spa Lane, and was later a furniture dealership. Obviously named by a landlord with a (popular) political axe to grind!

FRIAR GATE, THE
See RISING SUN

FRIAR GATE HOTEL
See HOWARD HOTEL

FRIAR GATE STATION
Station Approach   1878-1942
The buffet on the Great Northern Railway's station at Derby (Friar Gate) was licenced in 1878, shortly after opening, but the facility was allowed to lapse in 1942. Station closed 1965.

FRIARY HOTEL*
Friar Gate   1922
Mary Shuttleworth Boden, widow of Henry Boden, sold the Friary – the family home since around 1873 – in 1922 to

Friary Hotel, Friar Gate, 1994.

Friary Hotel, Friar Gate, c.1869.

The interior of the Friary.

the Whitaker family, who opened it shortly afterwards as a licenced hotel, a fact that was reported to have grieved Mrs Boden exceedingly, for she and her husband had been tireless workers for temperance! Indeed, it was her unrelenting pressure on the Licensing Bench in the early years of the century that led to not a few of the closures recorded in these pages. The fine Grade II* listed building, put up in 1730 for Samuel Crompton to a design probably by Richard Jackson, was extended in 1760, 1875, 1955 and again more recently. Thomas Roome brewed on the premises after leaving the Seven Stars 1962-8 under Rowland Hadfield, and his brewing copper went to the Bass Museum at Burton upon Trent in July 1988. Hadfield had succeeded the Whitakers, and had made his fortune running the family firm, Hadfield's Dairies 1959-72. By the late 1980s, after several fleeting ownerships, it was purchased by Clandean Hotels, who promptly ripped out some of the fine 17th century paneling, only to fall foul of the City's Conservation Officer, George Rennie. However, the Planning Committee allowed them to get away with several extremely unsympathetic alterations for which they had failed to seek listed building consent, including the masking of the very fine oak staircase from the entrance by

interpolating a bar. Poetic justice being what it is, this outfit swiftly went bankrupt, pitching *The Friary* and the *Howard Hotel* into a prolonged receivership. The former was eventually acquired by Bass, and the hotel turned into a training facility. The ground floor was converted into a 'fun pub' and opened in 1997 with the name *It's a Scream* the sign being derived from Edvard Munch's *The Scream* – tasteless, tactless and a total affront to culture.
DET 16/6/1980; Craven (1987) 56-59.

FURNACE (ARMS)*

9 Duke Street   *by 1846*
Originally a beerhouse on the Bridge Gate/Duke Street corner, as listed anonymously in 1846/50 and 1862, but as *The Furnace* in 1852. It took over its present premises (a house of c.1819 once part of the Handyside (previously Weatherhead, Glover & Co) Britannia Foundry complex, hence the name) around 1895. In 1937 it was in the ownership of Hanson's (now Hardy Hansons) and gained a full licence after World War Two.

GABLES HOTEL*

119 London Road   *1952*
The former vicarage of St George's church (later Holy Trinity) London Road was built to the designs of Joseph Botham of Leeds in 1838. The retrenchment in urban Church of England parishes led to its being placed on the market in 1951, and it was eventually purchased and opened in December 1952 as an hotel, the *Regent*, renamed *The Gables* in 1958 after a prominent feature of the Jacobean revival building. Unfortunately for the appearance of the original building, a not unpleasing one, it has subsequently been extended on several occasions, most recently in 1990-1, so that the original house constitutes but a quarter of the total. In 1991 it was renamed the *Periquito* (parakeet) after the chain which had then acquired it. However, in 1995 it was again renamed the *Royal Stuart* no doubt after Bonnie Prince Charlie, Derby being the most southerly town that he reached during his ultimately unsuccessful bid to regain the throne for the legitimate dynasty, 4 to 6 December 1745.

GALLANT HUSSAR (ARMS)*

110 Ashbourne Road (corner Noel Street)   *by 1852*
An Offiler's pub from 1925 which started out as the *Hope & Anchor* by 1852 and thereafter was known as the *Hussar* before taking its present title. Its first name is traditional and religious; its later name may be a throw-back to the earliest volunteer militia, raised in the late 18th century, disbanded 1827 and finally revived in 1864. The Chaddesden troop was of hussars, as were one or two others based further afield in the county. It was for sale as

a going concern in 1870, and eight years later was called the *Hussar Arms* thus proving that in those days one could add the word 'arms' to almost any name or everyday noun and create a name for a pub. Brewing on the premises until at least 1932.

GARDEN CITY
See CITY TAVERN

GARDENERS' ARMS*
Whitecross Street (junction of Upper Brook Street) – 1869 –
Sign was a shield of arms: *on a chevron a spade and a rake between two roses in chief and in base an apple tree.* Very ephemeral: a contents sale was advertised in 1869 and it had become a tailor's by 1874.
DM 6/10/1869; Reliquary IX (1869) 225.

GARIBALDI*
9 Copeland Street   *by 1869-1925*
A beer house named after Guiseppe Garibaldi (1807-1882), the romantic revolutionary figure, who in 1860 played a seminal role in the unification of Italy. The darling of the radicals of the age, he appeared in England to a tumultuous welcome in 1864, and the inn may therefore date from that time. Possibly a renaming of the *Buck in the Park*.

GARRICK HOTEL
See WHEEL

GARRICK
Osmaston Road   *by 1965-1977*
No information regarding this establishment.

GASLIGHT BAR
3 Friar Gate   *by 1989-c.1995*
Opened in the former premises of the Derby Gas, Light & Coke Company – hence the name. The building, the first in Derby with an iron frame, was designed by Naylor & Sale of Derby and completed in 1892, the showroom at the rear incorporating the dome from old St Werburgh's Church nearby at the instigation of the company's chairman, Capt Basil Mallender, a noted rescuer of the architectural relics of old Derby. When British Gas closed the premises in 1979, part became a casino, and part a pool saloon. The latter closed and a new canted bay was provided during the conversion, which boasts the best modern pointing in the city. It has now became a late-night venue with restricted admission.

GEORGE INN*
Iron Gate   *by 1648-1814*
One of the two truly classic coaching inns in Derby, the

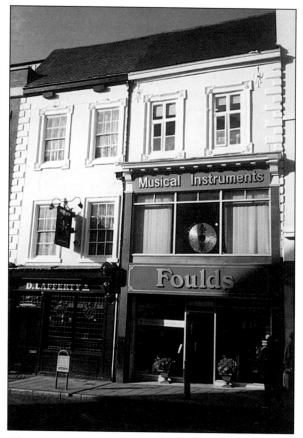

Alderman Samuel Heathcote's 1693 façade of the George, with Lafferty's (formerly the George, Mr Jorrocks and the Globe) to the left-hand portion of it, April 2002.

George is first mentioned in a deed granting the lease to Edward Osborne, Gentleman, of 1648. The present façade (now split between *Lafferty's* and Fould's music shop) was built in 1693, in which year Alderman Samuel Heathcote the elder was obliged to take a 999-year lease on a piece of land on Irongate 40ft long and 6½in wide, on which his newly-built façade had encroached the public highway! The interior still betrays signs of its earlier (timber-framed) fabric, and the building probably had 16th-century origins.

The Whig faction in Derby, under the leadership of the Duke of Devonshire, met here in the lead-up to the 1745 Rebellion (ironically, in view of its ownership by the Jacobite and Tory Heathcotes), and from here Alderman Stamford's horse was commandeered by the Scots advance guard at 11am on 4 December that year. From 1735 the London/Nottingham stage coach ran from the *George* making the journey in three days each way under the proprietorship of John Needham and Thomas Smith. In 1766 the post office was run from the inn, and not long afterwards an assembly room was built at first-floor level along the Sadler Gate frontage (behind the building now known as Lloyd's Bank).

This necessitated the purchase by the proprietor, Edward Chamberlain (who was also postmaster), of the *Black Boy*, which was relocated further down the street, and the *Sun*, both of which were pulled down. In about 1790, Hon. John Byng (later Viscount Torrington) visited Derbyshire and stayed at the *George* (as well as the *Bell*). He wrote: 'A bad dinner and a bad wine. Salmon peas and lamb; drank beer, wine, brandy and malt liquor.' He was not the only distinguished visitor, either, for in 1768 King Christian VII of Denmark and his Chancellor were guests.

In 1784 a tragedy was narrowly averted when the sign, then carried, like that presently at the *Green Man & Black's Head* at Ashbourne, on a timber gantry across Iron Gate, suddenly collapsed just as a chaise was travelling beneath it. In the event it was the poor old horse that suffered the fatal consequences, not the distinguished passengers!

Although, from the later 1760s, George Wallis of the *New Inn* was capturing (or generating) most of the coaching trade in the region, the *George* managed in 1802 to franchise from his son the daily post coach, probably because the former hostelry was unable to take the pressure of extra services. It was, however, not enough to halt its

The same building, in the 1990s. (See Globe)

decline, for it was offered for sale in May 1814, and was 'now discontinued as an inn' 11 months later, having been 'broken up and sold in lots' in July 1814 with further sales taking place in November 1818. Later still, in 1823, the local paper announced 'All that part of the former George Inn on the north side of the gateway is to be sold as retail shops'. One of these, in the event, was opened within a very few years as the *Globe*, ensuring some form of continuity of hospitality after an interruption of only a decade or so.

The business and most of the goodwill went, with the penultimate landlord, George Woodward, to the *Talbot* in 1804, and that inn was renamed the *George & Talbot* accordingly. However, in 1815, the *King's Head* came onto the market, and Woodward outbid the sitting tenant, John Hoare, for it. Woodward therefore abandoned the *Talbot* and renamed his new charge the *George & King's Head*. Hoare, meanwhile, decamped across the road in a huff to found a rival establishment, the *Hotel & King's Head*.

To the rear of the inn, in George Yard, a balconied extension was built for patrons to watch cock fights and similar sports; the balustrade was in the Rococo Chinoiserie style, even today often called 'cockpen' by auctioneers. There were also three three-storey dwelling houses there, once part of the inn, a gateway into Sadler Gate (still extant), carriage sheds and enormous stables. In one of the hay-lofts adjoining, in 1849-50, Thomas Rushton Brown and Amos Scotton (father of the Midland Railway's first official photographer) and 10 others founded a Co-operative Society on the lines of that of the Rochdale Pioneers of five years' before. They had the encouragement of their employer, William Mansfield Cooper, architect and builder, and £2.

This pioneering organisation went on to great success, but the sale, in June 1855, of these premises in severalties caused them to remove to other premises and they fetched up in Victoria Street by 1858.

The grand assembly room, 56ft by 19ft, latterly a billiard room, was taken over not so long afterwards by William Bemrose, the printer, as a printing works (1848); he had previously acquired the present Lloyd's Bank on the Iron Gate/Sadler Gate corner as his headquarters. The *George* had been kept from the 1730s to the 1780s by two generations of Matthew Hows, both aldermen and both mayors, and, by coincidence, ancestors of the Bemroses. DM 3/4/1735, 5/9/1768, 8/7/1784; 18/11/1802; 25/10/1804; 5/5, 23/6 & 19/7/1814; 6/4, & 5/5/1815; 15/9 & 24/11/1818; 23/7/1823 & 6/6/1855; Eardley Simpson (1933) 131-142; Holyoake & Scotton (1900) 23-30; Jeayes (1904) III.4.88)

GEORGE*

13-15 Midland Road (corner Carrington Street)   by 1853
One of many inns established on what was originally

Station Street to serve the needs of railway travellers. The name was a traditional one, deriving (like that above) from St George, England's patron saint, although it must be borne in mind that this 3rd-century hero-martyr was a Georgian, and is thought by some never to have existed! It first appears on record when a sale was held there in 1853. Rare surviving Offiler's windows.
DM 9/3/1853

GEORGE
See KING'S HEAD

GEORGE & DRAGON**
Cornmarket   *by1765-1847*
First noticed in 1765 when kept by George Fritche (1720-1799) a former trumpeter with The Blues, who had moved on to the *Green Man* St Peter's Church Yard by 1767. Probably renamed and later reverted to *George & Dragon* before, in all probability, being demolished for the culverting of the Brook and the creation of Albert Street in 1847-8. A new *George & Dragon* was founded around the corner at no. 2 in the new street by 1852. (see *Central*).
All Saint's parish register 1765; Cox & Hope (1881) 47, 196; *DM 28/8/1767*

GEORGE & DRAGON
See also CENTRAL, LONDON TAVERN

(OLD) GEORGE & DRAGON*
43 Walker Lane (corner Jury Street)   *by 1805-1895*
A small inn situated in a jettied timber-framed building of 16th-century origin. To be let in 1805 and advertised as 'old established' three years later. 'Old' added to its titulature after the opening of the establishment in Albert Street. A spirit licence application was made in 1874, but it closed about 1897 to make way for widening Jury Street. Named after the central emblem of the Order of the Garter, which shows St George slaying his (mythical) dragon. The order was founded in the 14th century and the name flourished from that time.
DM 10/10/1805; 28/1/1808 & 26/8/1874

GEORGE & TALBOT
See TALBOT

GEORGE CROSS
See BUXTON

GEORGE WINE VAULTS
37 Cornmarket   *by 1874-1898*
Opened by Messrs Cox & Gerrard in Lock Up Yard, in the rear of the very fine building by Joseph Pickford of Derby

– the former *Tiger Inn* – which spans the entrance. It continued for many years as a retailership of wines, beers and spirits, but was de-named around 1898 and had its licence changed to off.

GEORGE THE FOURTH
36 Leonard Street   *1827-1946*
Probably built around 1827 and advertised as 'newly built and well accustomed' in 1829 when it was for sale. Named to commemorate the death of the portly monarch who died in that year. Leonard Street (named after a former leper hospital dedicated to St Leonard which existed in the area in mediaeval times), had been built by a housing club around that time. To let in 1856 when George Woodward – probably brother to Frank (*Arboretum Tavern*) and John (*Fox & Grapes*) – left and for sale in 1872; it belonged to Shipstones in 1937. Closed after World War Two and the entire street has now vanished.
DM 18/3/1829; 24/12/1856 & 12/6/1872

Mr Grundy's, Ashbourne Road, 2002.

GEORGIAN HOUSE HOTEL*
32-34 Ashbourne Road   *by 1967*
A modest hotel established in a delightful Regency stuccoed house of c.1815 by 1967 but recently extended. A separate pub portion was formed (in a way detrimental to the building's fabric, it has to be said), as at the *Clovelly*, and named (for no known reason) *Mr Grundy's* in May 1996.

GISBORNE ARMS*
17-19 (7-9) Franchise Street   *by 1852*
There is some evidence that in the 1870s, this inn moved one house along the street. It is named after Henry

Franceys Gisborne (1807–1887), Mayor of Derby 1856-7, suggesting a building date of 1857, but the 1852 Board of Health map shows it already built and named, the only building then in the street, which was laid out and pitched, according to Borough Surveyor Samuel Harpur's Journal, the year before. Owned by Pountains in 1937.

George, Iron Gate, as Mr Jorrocks, 1980s.

GLOBE (WINE VAULTS)*

41 (34) Irongate   1823

The 17th-century classical façade, which once graced the *George,* of which this inn is almost a surviving remnant, is complemented by really good carved pilaster brackets on the façade, currently picked out in authentic Victorian manner in bright naturalistic colours. It first appears listed in 1823 as the *Globe Wine Vaults* but never thereafter. Owned by Hanson's 1937, but closed, sold, refurbished and reopened under Allied Breweries 18 May 1967 as the *Mr Jorrocks,* after R.S. Surtees' celebrated character who, needless to say, has no local connections at all; neither had his creator, born in County Durham! In 1991 it was embel-

lished by an iron plaque commemorating the *George's* role in the 'Forty-Five' and after some pressure (from the first edition of this book, its author and Mr Felix) the brewery, Carlsberg-Tetley agreed to rename it the *George* being refurbished and reopened as such in 1994. The owners then became Allied-Domecq and in 1997 proposed, in the teeth of furious opposition, to turn it into an irish theme pub bearing the name *Lafferty's.* It again reopened in August 1997; the Irish theme, it must be said, lacks conviction.

GLOBE INN*

49 (43-45) Sacheverel Street   *by 1844-1979*

This inn first appears on record 'new licensed' in 1844 when it was advertised to let as the *Prince of Wales.* It may well have been founded then, if not a year or two before, the Prince having been so created in December 1841, when a month old. However, in 1849, it was listed as the *Town Hall Cellars,* which makes one wonder whether the landlord had bought some fire or water-damaged stock from the Corporation after the Guildhall fire of 21 October 1841. In 1856 when a sale was held there, it had become the *Globe.* A modest beerhouse, so modest, in fact, that in the 1890s and 1900s, it is consistently listed as an unnamed on-licence beer-retailership (but was not that unusual in this). Belonged to Hanson's in 1937, became theatrical from 1948 through the establishment of the nearby Derby Playhouse, but closed and cleared with most of the rest of the street under a 1973 CPO in July 1979. The site still appears to be derelict, which suggests the usual planning botch, sheltering behind the mythical Ring Road extension. The name, an ancient one, is taken to imply universality.

DM 14/8/1844 & 27/8/1856

GLOBE

36 Kensington Street   *by 1874-1895*

A beerhouse, only two doors away from the *Green Man,* and thus closed and operating as an off licence by 1898.

GOAT'S HEAD*

Willow Row   *by 1833-1862*

The name is heraldic, but to which family it may refer is unclear: the Whites of Duffield were long gone by 1833, the Bagots of Blithfield too distant, and the Jacksons of Clay Cross did not receive their grant of a goat's head until 1869. Most likely the sign derives from the arms of the Worshipful Company of Cordwainers: *a chevron between three goats' heads.* Possibly renamed, the *Bull's Head* being the only likely candidate. 'Old established when for sale in 1852 and sold again five years later and finally in 1862.

DM 5/5/1852; 19/8/1857 & 27/8/1862

GOLDEN BALL

24 Willow Row   *by 1833-1862*

Possibly named after the chief motif on the arms of the Cox family of Derby, prominent vintners and lead merchants – *per chevron gules and azure a bezant between in chief two roses and in base as many cocks respectant argent* – which were, nevertheless, unauthorised. Note also that silk mercers anciently used a golden ball as a shop sign, derived from the gold orb of Royal Authority first introduced by Emperor Constantine the Great. This later developed into an inn sign. This inn had become a private house of Henry Collins, pavior, by the 1870s.

GOLDEN CROSS**

Unknown location   *before 1867*

Jewitt. The sign may be religious or reflect the arms of the local families of Ward (Derby) or Willoughby.

Captain Blake, Agard Street, 2000.

GOLDEN EAGLE*

55 (27) Agard Street   *by 1835*

First recorded in 1835, and for sale in the year following, so must have had an existence beforehand. The golden eagle may refer to the family of Greaves, prominent in the fashionable Derby society of the late 18th century, and seated at Aston-on-Trent and Ingleby. Note also that the sign derives from the insignia of the Holy Roman Empire. In 1856 a sheep roast was held here to celebrate the peace treaty with Russia. Beer brewed on premises in 1925, but later an Offiler's house. In the early 1980s the inn was sold off by Bass, and was briefly renamed *Pizza and Pasta* (1980). In 1983 it was acquired by a Nottingham firm which prefixed all its pubs with the title 'Knight' (it was owned by the same person who ran the *Fallen Knight* in Ashby-de-la-Zouch) and they renamed it again *Knight Fall*, being a licenced restaurant for a short time, before Ward's Ales returned it to its original name by 1994. In 1997 it was

refurbished and yet again renamed the *Captain Blake* opening again 12 October 1998. Walter James Blake (died 1948) was an LMS official (who actually lived at Harrington House, Pear Tree) appointed to be Army Welfare Officer for Derby during the years of World War Two. In the 1930s and most especially in the war, he worked tirelessly amongst the poor lads of the West End, founding a boys' club in Agard Street in 1942, organising football teams and boxing matches, and generally raising the self esteem of boys in an impossibly tough community at a time of national crisis when their fathers were largely away on active service. Although one might regret the loss of a traditional name, this move, unusually, represented an inspired piece of renaming.

DET 8/10/1998; DM 21/5/1856; Goodhead (1983) 61-62.

GOLDEN FLEECE**

10 South Street   *by 1827-1869*

Probably built as a speculation by Thomas Cooper, mason and building contractor, along with most of the lesser cottages on South Street, a fact revealed by the deeds of one a few houses further along. To let in 1832 and again in March 1869, yet a month later it was for sale, and may well have become a house, for such it was by 1876, when Henry Redgate lived there. Demolished by the GNR to build their Friar Gate Station, bonded warehouse, locomotive depot and sidings, the same year. The sign, although the Greek hero Jason springs to mind, may represent either the Habsburg Order of the Golden Fleece, founded in the 15th century and second only in prestige to the Order of the Garter, or the arms of Leeds: *Azure a fleece or on a chief sable three mullets argent.*

GOLDEN HART*

Sadler Gate   *–1744–*

Nothing known of this inn. The sign is heraldic, the (unauthorised) arms of Lowe, at that time Derby brewers and hijacked, with a change of tincture of the hart from *argent* to *or,* from the Lowes of Denby. For sale in 1744.

GOLDEN LION**

London Road   *1851*

A single mention of this beer house which was probably subject to some renaming; without a precise address, it is difficult to suggest its alternative identities (if any).

GOLDEN LION*

5/6 Bridge Gate (12 St Alkmund's Church Yard) by 1833-1908

Although the chief component of the royal arms of England, in a local context, the sign might represent the arms of the Talbot family, Earls of Shrewsbury, once all-

Golden Lion, St Alkmund's Church Yard.

powerful in Derbyshire; George, 6th Earl of Shrewsbury was Mary, Queen of Scots' gaoler for 25 years under Elizabeth I. Alternatively the powerful local family of Gisborne sported one, too. Proprietor from 1844 until he advertised for a tenant in 1862, was William Alton, who founded the Wardwick Brewery, whose father, Heage-born George Alton, had also been a brewer. A private house by World War One, having been closed due to pressure on the Bench by the Derby Temperance Society.
DM 25/9/1844 & 26/3/1862.

GOWER'S ARMS

(?) Gower Street/Babington Lane   –1869–
Named (like the street, formerly Blood Lane) from William Leveson Gower, who sat as one of the two MPs for Derby 1847-52. Thus founded after 1847 but closed (or renamed) by 1874.

GRANDSTAND (HOTEL)*

Nottingham Road (previously Siddal's Lane)   1832-1998
In 1832, William Abbott 'late of the Royal Oak, Market Place, resumed superintendence of the catering at the Racecourse Grandstand, which will be kept open for the accommodation of parties during the summer season'

which implies that he had been so occupied at a previous period. Racing moved to the Holmes in 1804 from Sinfin Moor, and thus there may have been a licensed facility there from that date. The coming of the Railway to the adjoining Siddals, however dried out the racetrack so badly that all racing stopped in 1844, and the meetings transferred to the present Racecourse in 1848.

A licenced bar was incorporated in Henry Duesbury's new grandstand on the Derby Racecourse from its building in 1853, but was refused a licence in 1854; the inn portion itself was 'newly erected' and for sale in January 1860, and again in 1861, so the Justices must have relented. In 1878 it was called the *Stand Hotel* but 1911 the entire grandstand complex was demolished and replaced by the kernel of the later edifice which was much extended subsequently. Tennant Bros had it on lease from the Derby Recreation Company in 1929. The bar and restaurant were much frequented by visitors to the adjacent Derbyshire County Cricket ground – the rear of the Grandstand served as a watching area – but the cricket club incorporated their own members' bar in a new pavilion erected in 1982.

The *Grandstand* was memorably kept in the 1950s and '60s by Fred and Margot Apthorpe, Fred being a scion of an old innkeeping family from Cambridge which once

Grandstand Hotel. The end of the line as photographer Eric Streets captures the demolition of the pub in December 2001.

owned a brewery there. Mrs Apthorpe was one of a long line of 'Grande Dame' landladies, whose son Keith was for many years landlord of the *Bridge Inn*, Duffield. An amusing incident, long remembered afterwards, was when the Apthorpes, having some old stables available acquired some livestock including some pigs. Unfortunately, the day after they arrived, they managed to break into a store of hops from the brewery. Having consumed all they could, they then managed to blunder out onto the hallowed turf of the County Ground, staggering and reeling from the effects of the hops. Keith Apthorpe recalled, 'We were racing everywhere trying to catch them. Some were virtually unconscious, falling over and lying on their backs with their legs in the air... Walter Goodyear, Derbyshire's head groundsman was going mad in case they got on to the square. It took ages to clear them off and they next day they were off to market and sold.' The Apthorpes also opened a ballroom there in 1952, which attracted a number of prestigious events including the Shire Horse Society's shows. Pigs departed, the old stabling, originally provided for the runners on racedays, came into its own on this event.

Latterly owned by Banks's, it was sold to the Derbyshire County Cricket Club on 12 June 1998, having closed for the last time at 11.00pm the previous night. It was all demolished in December 2001.
DET Bygones 23/4/2002

GRANGE HOTEL

1 Malcolm Street   *by 1874*
Stood close to the corner of Grange Street, once the drive to Normanton Grange, the seat of the local family of Goodale and later of Midland Railway engineer Matthew Kirtley and his family. Landlord Murrow issued a brass PA token in the 1880s. Later a Stretton's pub.

Grange Hotel, Malcolm Street.

GRAPES
See BUNCH OF GRAPES; FOX & GRAPES

GRASSHOPPER**

Cornmarket   *–1791–*
Mentioned only for 1791; the sign is most famous as that of Martin's Bank, but 1791 would be premature for Derby in this context. In mediaeval times the grasshopper was a good luck sign; it was later the crest of Sir Thomas Gresham and was adopted as a sign by tea-dealers.

GREAT NORTHERN

28-30 (10-11) Henry Street   *1878-1977*
Built by the Great Northern Railway in 1878, to replace the *Park Fountain Inn*, demolished to enable the railway to be built three years before. Now cleared for new housing. In the 1920s owned by Nottingham Breweries, but sold by them to Tennant's before 1937.

GREAT NORTHERN*

17-19 (6) Junction Street   *by 1874*
Built before 1874 when it was the *Jolly Soldier*, named after the presence of the Rowditch Barracks, built in 1859 nearby to house the Derbyshire Volunteer Rifle Corps. These closed in 1877, and the following year the pub was renamed the *Great Northern* after the Railway Company whose line, also nearby, had just been completed. The street, despite its name, was pitched by 1869 (cf. *Junction Tavern*). In 1883 it had a small home-spun music hall going, according to *The Magnet*, a contemporary organ devoted to such things. An Alton's house in the 1930s.
DLC 12/1993 pp.44-45

(GREAT NORTHERN) REFRESHMENT HOUSE*

101 Curzon Street (corner of Talbot Street)
by 1898
Set up in the 1890s in a brick villa of 1860s type, as refreshment rooms with beer available on licence and in 1898 run by the evocatively named Ernest Grudgeings. Gradually became a beer retailer and ultimately an ordinary pub. The Great Northern part of the title was gradually dropped (it stands opposite the gates to the former Great Northern Railway's goods depot), and officially so from 1 January 1923, when that railway company ceased to exist. Owned by Offilers' by 1937. Renamed *Freddie's* March 1993 after the pop star Freddie Mercury of Queen, who had recently died of AIDS, and a free house.
Derby Drinker XLV (4/1993)

GREEN DRAGON*

Cornmarket   *by 1738-1801*

Situated 'at the lower end of Cornmarket' according to an advertisement of 1738. Landlord George Fritche (1726-1799) let the inn in 1767 and removed to the *Green Man*, Bag Lane (also of the *Tiger*, Cornmarket and a 'former trumpeter of The Blues'). He was the founder of a remarkable dynasty of musicians: his son George Christopher (1769-1835) was organist of All Saints' for 42 years, being succeeded by his own son, also George Christopher (1800-1890). The latter's younger son was a musician and teacher, as was Christopher Froude Fritche, his uncle. George Fritche the younger sold the inn in 1801, after which we hear no more of it. In 1793, Fritche had managed to capture the business of the Newcastle coach, possibly franchised out by George Wallis of the *New Inn*. It is possible that this inn relocated to St Peter's Street (see below) due to building works in Cornmarket.

DM 12/10/1738; 2/11/1793; 12 & 26/11/1801; *UBD* 1791

GREEN DRAGON*

36 (35(A)) St Peter's Street   *by 1818-1969*

A three-bay three-storey brick building of *c.*1800 on the

Green Dragon, The Spot.

east side of the street near The Spot, owned by Ind Coope in the early 1930s and refronted in a mild art-deco style. Possibly newly erected after 1801 by whoever purchased the inn of the same name in Cornmarket of G.C. Fritche (see above). Alterations and additions were made to designs by George Bridgart and executed by his builder brother, Robert in 1872. Purchased for demolition on 2 December 1969, when it closed. Pulled down 1970. Named after a Tudor royal heraldic beast, echoing that dynasty's Welsh origins.

BBA 1872.

Green Dragon, St Peter's Street in July 1905, with people viewing from every vantage point as a lifeboat procession goes by.

Ranby's in February 2002. The former Green Lane House occupied the right-hand portion.

GREEN LANE HOUSE*

12 Green Lane   *by 1857-1981; 1983*

Modest beerhouse in a brick building of *c*.1800, subject of a spirit licence application in 1874, before which it had been listed here as an anonymous beer house in 1857 and 1862. Owned by Offiler's in 1937 and granted a full licence only in 1951. Suffered the same fate as the *Queen's Head*, which was swallowed up by Ranby's store, except that the store had become Debenham's when this fate befell the *Green Lane House*. Closed and incorporated into the store for a while, before being reopened in 1983 as a café-bar and named *Jelly Roll's* – presumably after the legendary New Orleans jazz-band leader and pianist Jelly Roll Morton (1885-1941), although the connection seems elusive, and the sound of inter-war New Orleans never seemed to emanate from the establishment! Sold by Bass in 1991, closed in January 1992 and reopened 10 February following as *Ranby's* by Nigel Barker. Thereafter it was acquired by Enterprise Inns by 1994. Renamed *Crù* in 2002.
DM 26/8/1874

GREEN MAN

32 Kensington Street   *by 1833-1965*

A modest inn a few doors from the *Globe*, long a free house brewing on the premises and to let in 1855. Declared unfit

by the Council, July 1959; made subject to a CPO on 25 February 1960, but still listed in 1965 when W.E. Dawes was still brewing on the premises. Closed and cleared soon after.
DM 10/1/1855

(LOWER) GREEN MAN

Bag Lane (corner of Morledge)   *by 1732-1799*

Advertised as being in 'St Peter's Parish on the corner of Bag Lane next the Morledge' in 1732. Taken over by George Fritche (formerly of the *Green Dragon* and the *Tiger*) in 1767, who remained there until his death in 1799. Probably renamed the *Castle and Falcon* shortly afterwards. Named after the Jack-o-Th'-Green figure of ancient custom; probably a Celtic throwback, although it may not be without significance that the arms of the Kingdom of Denmark are supported by two *woodwoses* or wild men, invariably shown as 'green men'.
DM 9/11/1732 & 28/8/1767

GREEN MAN**

Osmaston Road (Street)   *by 1818-1820*

Probably a renaming of an existing house, perhaps even by a landlord of one of the other *Green Man* inns taking the name with him to a new place. The consequences were confusing, causing the old *Upper Green Man* St Peter's Church Yard, to be renamed, on topographical grounds, the *Lower Green Man* (*qv*)! Not listed by 1822, and probably (and sensibly) renamed.

Green Man, St Peter's Church Yard, extreme right. Richard Keene photograph, 1882.

(UPPER) (OLD) GREEN MAN*

17 St Peter's Street (St Peter's Church Yard)   *1671*

A delightful listed Grade II brick building with a proper Dutch gable and once with timber cross windows, allegedly dated 1671. The bold moulded brick cornicing and banding, with mini-pediments over the windows, are reminiscent of the *Fox & Owl*, Bridge Gate before rebuilding in the 1880s. If it was built as an inn, then this fixes its date; if not, the first mention is in an advertisement of 1732 and again in 1734, where it is stated that the inn was situated 'at the upper end of St Peter's Parish'. It was for sale in 1817, and in 1818 was listed – most confusingly – as the *Lower Green Man*, because someone had renamed an inn in Osmaston Street the *Green Man*, palpably further 'up the hill'.

This seems to have been rationalised by 1823 and 1827 more sensibly as the *Old Green Man*, later photographic evidence suggesting that it had expanded into the former *Eagle* next door by 1878. This part was demolished due to road widening (contents sale 1882) and replaced very tactfully to designs by Arthur Eaton in 1886. It was in the hands of Offiler's in 1936, in which year it was gutted by fire on 26 May, destroying the original Restoration interiors, wainscot etc. Subsequent rebuildings have given it a sterile interior; it also lost its original fenestration and a brick parapet was erected behind the picturesque Dutch gable (weakened by the collapse of the roof) which has obfuscated its distinctive outline. It was sold off by Bass in 1994 and refurbished, reopening with an Irish theme – somewhat more authentic than *O'Neill's* or *Lafferty's* (cf. *Saracen's Head, Globe*) – as *Ryan's Bar* in October 1995.

BBA 3785 of 1886; *DM* 15/8/1734, 28/8/1767, 18/9/1817 & 19/4/1882; *Illustrated Carpenter & Builder* 5/11/1887 p. 36

GREYHOUND*

75-76 Friar Gate   by 1774

A pleasant vernacular brick building probably originally of late 17th-century date and once thatched, but gutted of original features within, and its original windows replaced by timber casements. Many people believe that this inn took its name from the stadium in nearby Vernon Street, but the early date – when landlord Joshua Simmonds was selling stocking frames – unequivocally belies this. One of only two survivors of the plethora of pubs which once existed at this end of Friar Gate which served the markets. A sheep roast was held here to celebrate the 1856 peace treaty with Russia. A free house prior to purchase by Offiler's c.1923/28 and subsequently Bass. Today it has been deprived of its carriage arch and ancilliary accommodation by separate sale, and extended rearwards in several stages, the pool table area occupying the area of the old brewhouse, where beer was brewed on the premises until 1928. For the name, see also below.

DM 19/2/1774 & 21/5/1856

GREYHOUND (VAULTS)*

5 (4) Market Head (Rotten Row)   by 1761-1908

A good market and (alleged) coaching inn in a handsome brick 18th-century building which, after the demise of coaching, was completely rebuilt behind the façade, being

Greyhound, Friar Gate.

advertised in consequence as 'newly built' and 'old estab-lished' in 1836 when it was for sale. In 1838 a Coronation supper was held here. It thereafter shrank steadily until sold in 1879, when it lost its street frontage to a shop, and was merely a series of bars behind No.4. Indeed, between 1883 and 1904 it was renamed *Criterion Vaults*, but reverted to *Greyhound Vaults* for the last few years of its existence. Its licence may have been suppressed as a result of Temperance Society pressure. The greyhound was a badge of Edward IV and, by inheritance through Elizabeth of York, of the Tudor monarchs. In a Derby context it is worth noting that it was also the crest of the Blackwalls of Blackwall and more especially of Sir John Gell of Hopton, 1st Bart, Parliamentary Governor of Derby during the Civil War; his posterity held property in the town and had a town-house in Friar Gate until *c*.1852. It was probably called the *Hare and Hounds* prior to 1761.
DM 14/9/1836, 4/7/1838 & 23/4/1879

GRINDING YOUNG

Unknown locale   *before 1867*
Listed by Jewitt and named after the ancient (and exces-sively quaint) *Ballad of the Miller's Maid Grinding Old Men Young Again*, in which a girl turns the handle of a large hand mill with a funnel, into which various ancients, glasses of ale in hands, jump, to emerge head first below as young *beaux*. Such machines were apparently shown at fairs by strolling mountebanks up to *c*.1810 – except that they were not capable of delivering! A picture of one is known on a Cockpit Hill teapot.
Reliquary IX (1868-69) 86-87

GROVE INN*

5 Darley Lane   *by 1835-1908*
A small beerhouse, listed anonymously as being in Darley Lane, in 1835, at the North Parade end of the Lane, and named after Darley Grove, of which Darley Lane and North Parade formed a part after realignment and building up from 1819. To let as a going concern in 1856 and for sale in 1865. Probably closed by the Bench under pressure from the Derby Temperance Society, as were a number of pubs in this area in 1907-8. Later a shop, but cleared after World War Two.
DM 24/12/1856 & 18/10/1865

HALF MOON*

30 Sadler Gate   *by 1791-1963*
A three-storey three-bay brick building embellished with rusticated pilasters with (as usual in Sadler Gate) an earlier rear, probably refronted *c*.1790, which may be the date the inn was opened. On the other hand it might just as easily be the *White Horse* 'near to Sadler Gate Bridge' of 1765

The former Half Moon Inn, Sadler Gate, pictured in 2002.

Half Moon, Sadler Gate, 1932.

renamed. It was for sale with a brewhouse attached in 1808 and to let in 1863. In 1937 owned by Tennant Bros, but closed November 1963 and sold, de-licenced, as retail premises 24 January 1964. Now a shop and colour-washed in a ghastly grey colour.
DM 3/3/1808 & 4/3/1863; *UBD* 1791

HALLAM'S VAULTS*

51 Queen Street   *by 1878-1883*
Presumably founded by the same man as that following, but established long enough to have acquired a new land-lord (Henry Parker) in 1878. It may well have migrated with its owner to the West End and closed, therefore, in 1883 the year that the following establishment is first recorded. Premises subsequently absorbed by Samuel Gilbert's drapery shop next door.

HALLAM'S VAULTS

20 (51) Green Street (corner Bridge Street) by 1883-1922
Named after the first proprietor who probably transferred from Queen Street (previous), and demolished in 1922. Free house.

HARE & (GREY)HOUNDS*

26 Erasmus Street   by 1827-1961
Probably opened around 1826 in an area slowly built up from 1796 when the Derby Canal came. Erasmus Street was named after Erasmus Darwin, on whose garden – reached from his house at 3 Full Street by a hand-operated ferry of his own devising – it was pitched; he died in 1802, which fixes the street's *terminus post quem*. The first landlord was Minshall Birchall, followed by his son Thomas in 1835 when the pub was called the *Hare & Greyhounds*, the name being associated with the politically incorrect country sport of hare coursing. Birchall, senior was the son of Minshall Birchall (1762-1811) a Bridge Gate clockmaker, and he doubled as a farmer and coal merchant. It was to pursue the latter activity that he made the pub over to Thomas (1785-1856) on whose death (his son having migrated to the USA) it passed to his nephew William who put in a tenant and sold it in 1871. Thomas's grandson was the marine artist William M. Birchall (born 1884) of Cedar Rapids, Iowa, later of Hastings. By the 1930s it was owned by Pountain's, but on 8 September 1961 its licence was not renewed and it closed, being demolished with the rest of this area, once called Canary Island, in advance of the building of the inner ring road in 1966.   *DM 17/5/1871*

HARE & HOUNDS*

Rotten Row   by 1737-1761
Situated at the Irongate end of Rotten Row, presumably on the east side, fronting the butchery. First mentioned in 1737 and run by Henry Campion in March 1761. A good old name again associated with field sports. Not heard of subsequently and probably renamed the *Greyhound*.
DM 25/5/1737 & 15/3/1761

HARE & SETTER

King Street   by 1827-1829
Nothing known of this apparently very short-lived inn; interesting variation of the hare coursing traditional name.

HARVESTER**

Pride Park   1998
Vernacular-style 'family' pub set up in Pride Park, although it was initially closed on match afternoons. Grim Post-Modernist offices blocks currently arising all round it seem set to further deaden the setting.

THE HAUS**

Wardwick   July 2002
In the summer of 2002 *The Haus* café-bar and restaurant opened in the Jacobean House, an enigmatic 17th-century building which lost three of its original five gables, and much more besides, when Becket Street was put through in 1855. Originally belonging to the Gisbornes, then to the Heathcotes, to Alderman Francis Jessop (mayor in 1840), and to John Huish of Smalley Hall. For much of the 20th century it was the Jacobean Café until becoming an estate agents.

HAWK & BUCKLE*

Bradshaw Street   by 1833-1843
The date evidence would suggest that it became the *Ring O'Bells*. The sign is the crest of the family of Cotton of Etwall Hall and Combermere Abbey in Cheshire; a *Hawk & Buckle* still remains at Etwall opposite the site of the Hall. The Combermere Cottons produced a Peninsular War hero, Field Marshall Sir Stapleton Cotton, 6th Bart, GCB, GCH, KCSI, created 1814 1st Lord Combermere and in 1827 Viscount Combermere of Bhurtpore. He was born in 1773 and died in 1865, and married a daughter of 3rd Duke of Newcastle. It is probably this man whom the inn sign commemorated, suggesting that the establishment could have gone back to c.1820: about the time the street was pitched across Bradshaw Hay, a former Borough open field.

HEARTY GOOD FELLOW

27 Nottingham Road   by 1827-1862
Situated on the north-east side of the street not far from the *Punch Bowl*. It was after about 1835 universally known as the *Jolly Toper* (ie. when for sale in 1838 and 1840) and is so listed in the majority of directories. In 1851 it was also called in error the *Jolly Trooper*. Nevertheless the reason for the name seems self-evident, somehow!
DM 28/2/1838, 5/2/1840 & 9/3/1857

(OLD) HEN & CHICKENS*

26 Walker Lane   by 1790-1930
Situated on the north side of the street between Court No.7 and Workhouse Yard. A typically bucolic name, it was for sale early in 1791 and 1878 and twice to let between those dates. Closed about 1928-9 to make way for the building of Queen Street Baths, and the licence was in 1930 transferred to the *Osmaston Park Hotel*. The design of the ground-glass window of the baths' boiler house was intended by the architect, C.H. Aslin, to reflect the sign of the former pub.
DM 27/1/1791, 2/9/1846, 6/1/1864 7 11/12/1878

HENLY'S

See IRON GATES

HENRY'S
See IRON GATES

HICKORY'S
See THOMAS-À-BECKET

HIGGS CAFÉ BAR
96 St Peter's Street 1999
Opened in a striking Art Deco building with a stone front built in 1935 for Ratcliffe & Co's famous Derby toy shop. perhaps to a design by George Morley Eaton. Use of the genitive case in the title suggest it is named after its proprietor.

High Street Tavern, High Street 1965.

HIGH STREET TAVERN
33 High Street *by 1862-1965*
Drastically refronted by George Bridgart about 1860 from one of the larger Regency house in this insignificant street with a grand-sounding name. Possibly renamed from the *White Horse*. It was for sale in 1872. Stretton's by 1937, closed and cleared for the Derbyshire Royal Infirmary extensions.
DM 19/7/1872

HILTON ARMS*
256-258 Osmaston Road *by 1891-1975*
A beerhouse, established by 1891 in no. 256, but expanded into No.258 as well by 1898; there seems no clear reason reason for the name of the adjacent houses (and thus of the inn) – Hilton Villas, extant by 1874, the Hiltons being of very much later renown in Derbyshire. Offilers' by 1937, full licence granted in 1950 and closed in the 1970s.

HOLE IN THE WALL
St James' Lane *by 1819-1852*
The name sounds highly colloquial and may well refer to another inn bearing a name recorded elsewhere or lost –

there were several to choose from. The reference is from John Ward FSA. Probably demolished 1866-7 to make way for the St James' Street Improvement Scheme.
Ward, J. *Notes of Reminiscences of Old Derby*, I. Vi.

HOLLY BUSH*
142 (96) Bridge Street *by 1818-1972*
Built probably when Bridge Street was pitched (1792) or within a decade. From before 1893 until World War One it was run by Edmund Newbold, formerly of the *Brown Bear*, Lodge Lane. Brewed on the premises until 30 March 1937, when it became one of Offilers' pubs. Closed 19/12/1972 the last landlord being Mark Gargaro.

HOLY FRIAR*
69 Upper Brook Street *by 1850-1862*
Named due to the fact that Brook Street was pitched across Nuns' Green, and the pre-Reformation presence of the nuns of St Mary de Pratis (King's Mead) no doubt added to the jollity of the nearby Friary's Dominican friars! Although only recorded in 1850, and anonymously as a beer house in 1862 at this address, an advertisement of the former year describes it as 'well accustomed' so it must have been in existence for a little while before that date if only to build up the said custom! Having been let in July, it was for sale within the month 'on the death of the owner'. It later became a shop.
DM 24/7 & 14/8/1850

HOPE & ANCHOR
See GALLANT HUSSAR

HORATIO'S
See LORD NELSON

HORSE & GROOM*
48 Elms Street *by 1850*
This inn is one of the few West End survivors and may have been older than the reference to 1850 implies, in view of the Willow Row establishment of this name prefixing itself with 'Old' as early as 1818, but there is no other testimony to its existence between the two dates. A Bass house in 1937 with a common traditional name. Either this house or the one following was the venue of a sheep roast to celebrate the peace treaty with Russia in 1856. Of the 18 inns which held similar festivities, the vast preponderance were situated in the West End – probably because most of the soldiers involved were from poor families living in this area.
DM 21/5/1856

(OLD) HORSE & GROOM*
11 Willow Row *by 1818-1871*
On its earliest mention its name is prefaced with 'Old', but

this is not repeated; it implies that there was another, unrecorded pub of this name or that the establishment in Elms Street was then newly opened. In 1849 it, was described as 'old licenced and well accustomed' when for sale, and it was offered again in 1869 and 1871, after which it appears to have closed. Possibly of quite old foundation, but turned into a shop in the early 1870s. The name is usually more associated with racing than travel.
DM 21/5/1849, 14/7/1869 & 15/3/1871

Former Horse and Jockey, Sadler Gate, 2002. Note the re-fronting:the façade has been raised an extra storey to include two gables and their attic windows, hence only two windows now on top floor. The quoins only go as high as the original façade.

HORSE & JOCKEY

21 Sadler Gate   *1791-1912*

Two doors down from Palfree's Yard (now Old Blacksmith's Yard), the 17th-century building with its later façade survives, now a shop. Name probably inspired by the frenetic conviviality which went on in town during race weeks in the 18th and 19th centuries. It was for sale in 1827 ('eligibly situated') and 1877.
DM 19/12/1827 & 18/4/1877

(OLD) HORSE & TRUMPET*

44 Full Street   *by 1761-1967*

One of a range of four elegant early 18th-century gabled

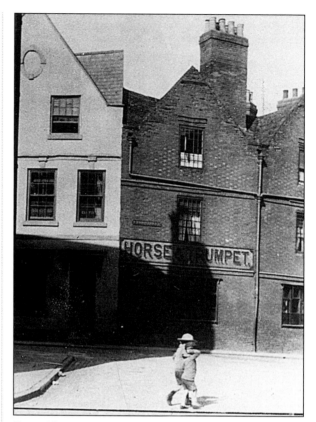

Horse and Trumpet, Full Street, 1714, County Assembly Rooms to left.

three-storey brick buildings, and until 1764 situated beside the County Assembly Rooms, built 1714; it therefore follows that the *Horse and Trumpet* was probably built about the same date, possibly to supply catering to the Assemblies. The name is redolent of coaching days, although this inn was never claimed as a coaching inn. It was for sale in 1859 and again two decades later. In 1926 the landlord was Ludlam Ramsden, whose Huddersfield-born father, Horace, had come to Derby in 1886 after a stint as chef to the Mosleys at Rolleston Hall, Staffs, setting up as a confectioner and restauranteur at 111 St Peter's Street and later at 35 Cornmarket. He shortly afterwards sold it to Pountain's (their offices were just around the corner) and took over the Assembly Rooms restaurant (see *Ramsden's Tavern*). Pountain's later re-sold it to Offilers'. That firm committed an intolerable sin and in 1939 demolished the twin-gabled, delightfully vernacular late 17th-century building. It retained its eight-light mullioned and transomed windows on the ground floor those above and in the left bay latterly having very early 19th century cast iron 30-pane casements. They replaced it with a dreary exercise in false half-timbering in their house style. Known to its customers as the 'Whore and Strumpet', the pub was closed in 1967 and the entire building was swept away to build the new Assembly Rooms and car park in 1970.
DM 29/6/1859 & 20/8/1879; DET 22/1/1993

Horse and Trumpet, Full Street, c.1960.

Devonshire House (Hotel & King's Head), 1901, Cornmarket, later to become Ramsden's Tavern and – briefly – the Knotted Snake, in the 1980s.

HOTEL & KING'S HEAD**

[35-36] Cornmarket   *1815-1823*

Having been pipped at auction at which the *King's Head* was put up for sale by George Woodward, formerly of the *George*, John Hoare, up to that point landlord of the former,

took himself and much of his custom and good will across the street to new premises, where he opened up as the *Hotel & King's Head*, starting off with an inaugural dinner for all his 'friends' (customers) on 12 May 1815. So successful was it, that another had to be arranged for two weeks later. Poetic justice thereafter intervened, and the Woodwards were declared bankrupt in December 1822, and Hoare was able to purchase the *King's Head* more or less on his own terms, closing his new establishment in 1823 and resuming at the former as if nothing had happened. It is not clear exactly which building this hotel was in, but the evidence suggests that it was the former Devonshire house, built by the Duke of Devonshire as a town house in 1755 and sold off at about the time the *Hotel* was established, the Bachelor Duke thereafter exercising his privilege as Lord Lieutenant of the County and using the Judges' Lodgings thereafter. Part of it was later to become *Ramsden's* and then – briefly – the *Knotted Snake*.

DM 6/4/1815; 8/5/1815; 25/12/1822 & 5/2/1823.

HOWARD HOTEL*

50 Friar Gate   *by 1926-1991*

Adapted from the centre unit of a most elegant range of ashlar faced houses built 1841-2 to designs of Thomas

Howard Hotel, Friar Gate, late 1970s.

INTERNATIONAL HOTEL

288 Burton Road 1970
Started in a large villa of *c.*1880 built for Alderman Cornelius Boam, Mayor, 1903-4, since vastly rebuilt, and gradually took over adjoining houses, now totalling five, thus creating quite a large three-star hotel united behind a brash façade. Previously Hargrave House School.

IRISH HARP

Unknown locale *before 1870*
Jewitt. He supposes it was founded by an Irishman 'to call his countrymen around him'. It has long been a quartering on the Royal Standard, however, and part of the insignia of the 19th-century Order of St Patrick.
Reliquary XI (1869-70) 92.

Cooper, set on the underworks (including cells) of the former County Gaol, built by William Horne in 1754, and rightly listed Grade II*. The cells below were adapted in the 1960s into *Judge Jefferies' Bar* (later *JJ's*), named rather speculatively, as Jefferies never held his courts in Derby and had he done so, it would have been 75 years before the site was made a gaol! The building was taken over as an hotel as the *Friar Gate Commercial Hotel* after World War One, under Fred German, although in 1932 it was being run by Fred Stamford and shortly thereafter renamed the *Stamford Hotel.* Oddly, by 1935 it was back with the other Fred (German), and one is inclined to speculate that both Freds were in reality the same man. After the war it was again renamed the *Howard* (after yet another proprietor) and this name stuck. The main bar, in the former drawing room, off the spacious top-lit staircase hall on the left, was latterly given a fibre-glass 'cave interior' effect (without listed building consent), whilst *JJ's* numerous ill-lit former prison cells – liberally scrawled with contemporary graffiti – were the delight both of courting couples and confirmed inebriates alike. It was renamed the *Secret Place* in the 1970s. Taken over by Clandean Hotels in 1988 and run with the Friary, but the firm went bankrupt in 1991 and the Receivers closed the *Howard* at the end of that year after failing to find a buyer, at £600,000. The price was reduced to £450,000 by May 1992, while it was run as an accommodation annexe to the Friary, being operated by the Receiver. Later converted for use as office accommodation.

HURLEY'S
See MELBOURNE ARMS

HUSSAR
See GALLANT HUSSAR

Cox and Bowring wines and spirits merchants, 1906, later Irongates Tavern etc.

IRONGATES HOTEL

12-14 Irongate 1877
A substantial five-bay three-storey building with a central carriage arch (now blocked); slightly concave façade with pilasters. Built as offices and bottling facilities for Messrs Cox & Bowring, one of three firms of vintners and drinks merchants which grew out of Henry Cox's original foundation, this one in partnership with Sir Clement Bowring, an attorney and Conservative Party magnate. It was

designed by Frederick J. Robinson and built about 1876. It was adapted to provide accommodation, eating and drinking on the premises, and this aspect was called *Bowring's Vaults*. It was taken over by Offiler's 1933 and run on a six-day licence; latterly a Berni Inn (from 1968), when it obtained a full licence and sported a German-style *bierkeller*. The new owners, Whitbread, converted it to a 'fun pub' and renamed it *Henry's* (after Henry Cox?) in December 1991. However, in 1993 its title was altered slightly to *Henly's (Vaults)*, wags assuming it was to make its previous name more intelligible to the visiting executives of the then new Toyota Car Plant at Burnaston! There is no explanation for the name, for both the Oxfordshire town and the head of the Eden family both bear it spelt 'Henley'. However, in spring 1995 it was again renamed, this time *P.J. Pepper's*. Inevitably, so ephemeral a name turned out to be unacceptable to the brewery's marketing team, and in 1998 it was renamed for the sixth time in a decade *Casa* (Italian for 'house'). Since 1993 the cellar bar has been run separately, as *The Vaults*.

ISLAND EXCHANGE
See RHODE ISLAND

ISLAND ROCK
See DERBY PRIDE

IT'S A SCREAM
See FRIARY HOTEL

JACKIE STAMPS**

4-6 Market Place   *1998-2001; 2002*
Opened in the former Cantor's furniture store (incorporating part of the former *Greyhound*) with seating outside on a pavement-side dais. Part of a chain of pubs called *Jack Stamps*. By a remarkable coincidence, one of Derby County's greatest players was Yorkshire-born John David

Walkabout, formerly Jackie Stamps, Market Place, 2002.

'Jackie' Stamps (1918-1991) who joined Derby County from New Brighton in 1939 and played for the Rams until 1953. A heroic figure in the old-fashioned bustling centre-forward mould, Stamps scored twice in the 1946 FA Cup Final – the only time Derby County have ever won the Cup – and altogether scored 100 Football League goals for the Rams. The name seemed appropriate enough and the inn sign showed Stamps in his Derby County kit, but in 2001 it closed and was extensively refurbished, reopening 7 June 2002 as an Australian theme pub called *Walkabout* (perhaps they intended to remove all the seating!) – another marketing triumph for a distant charmless chain.

JELLY ROLL'S
See GREEN LANE HOUSE

JERRY LEE'S
See THOMAS-A-BECKET

JEW'S HARP**

Uncertain location   *before 1867*
Jewitt. Named after a simple and very ancient musical instrument, much played amongst the poorer classes in bygone eras.

JIMMY'S
See ST JAMES' HOTEL

JOHN WILKES

Morledge   *1773*
Advertised to let in 1773, and then probably but recently renamed after the radical hero and reformer John Wilkes (1727-1797). A change in public taste may have led to a further renaming.

JOINERS' ARMS*

102 (143) (Lower) Parliament Street   *by 1857-1975*
Built before 1857, when it was listed anonymously. First named by 1862 after the arms of the Worshipful Company of Joiners, founded 1401 and incorporated 14 April 1571. The arms were granted 10 August 1571: *Gules a chevron argent between in chief two compasses extended points downwards and in base a globe or; on a chief of the second a pale azure between two roses of the field enclosing an escallop also of the second.* It was sold in July 1874 and the new owner immediately applied for a spirit licence. It was renamed the *Prince Arthur* between 1878 and 1883 after HRH Prince Arthur, 1st Duke of Connaught (1850-1942), probably at the time of his marriage to HRH Princess Louise of Prussia in 1879. The inn survived until 1975 when it was a casualty of the St Luke's redevelopment scheme. The last landlord was William Henry Lenney.

JOINERS' ARMS
See OLD VAULTS

JOLLEY'S TAP HOUSE
See TAP HOUSE

JOLLY BOATMAN
See PLUMBERS' ARMS

JOLLY COLLIERS**
St Mary's Bridge (Navigation Row)   *by 1823-1825*
'Next to St Mary's Bridge, St Alkmund's Parish' when for sale in 1824, and 'near Derby Canal' in an advertisement the following year. In 1823 it is listed after the *Three Crowns* which rather suggests that it was initially the *Three Jolly Colliers*. Possibly a later name for the *Trent Boat* or, more likely, in view of the fact that both were sold with five cottages adjoining, the *Navigation*.
DM 18/4/1824 & 26/4/1825

JOLLY DOGS
See ALEXANDRA VAULTS

JOLLY SOLDIER
See GREAT NORTHERN

JOLLY TOPER
See HEARTY GOOD FELLOW

JONTY FARMER
Kedleston Road   *1989*
Built on the site of a much-loved small holding belonging to a family called Cope which a developer cleared after allowing it to rot away despite Council and Civic Society opposition. Opened July 1989, by Banks's, and named (after a competition) after a local character associated with the area.

JUBILEE CITY
See BARLEY MOW

JUNCTION TAVERN
12 Junction Street   *by 1869*
Despite the obvious connection of both pub and street with railways, the street was pitched and the inn founded by 1869, eight years before the building of the adjacent Great Northern Railway. The name probably

Junction Tavern, Junction Street in 1922, as a Junction Street Sunday School outing is set to depart.

refers to the junction between the Roman Uttoxeter Old Road and the 1819 turnpike called Uttoxeter New Road, a few hundred yards away. A beerhouse, for sale in 1879, which obtained a full licence in 1950. Owned by Zachary Smith's brewery (Shardlow) in 1937, but later Marston's. Given ridiculous false timber framing in 1979.
DM 26/11/1879

KENSINGTON TAVERN*
22 Talbot Street (30 Drewry Lane)   *by 1846*
In 1869 and 1874 the address is given as Kensington Street, hence no doubt, the name, and it was listed anonymously

Jonty Farmer, Kedleston Road, undergoing a revamp and coat of white paint, August 2002.

here in 1846, 1850 and 1862. Before 1883 it appears to have migrated to its present (Regency) building. It is not wholly clear how the street got its name, and hence the tavern. Sold to James Eadie & Co of Burton-upon-Trent in the 1920s, and beer was brewed on the premises until at least 1928. A beerhouse until 1951.

KERRANCE
See CLOISTERS

KING DAVID & THE HARP
See DAVID & THE HARP

KING OF PRUSSIA
Morledge   *by 1761-1772*
Mentioned in Sir Harry Harpur's list, and to let in 1772; nothing more is heard of it; possibly its name was changed after the death of the monarch in question. Frederick II (the Great) of Prussia was born in 1712 and death took him from the European stage, which he had so successfully dominated in 1786, after a reign of 46 years. Britain was his chief ally during the Seven Years War (1756-63) and it must have been at the beginning of this conflict that the name was bestowed.
DM 18/8/1772.

KING'S ARMS COUNTY HOTEL*
20 St Mary's Gate   *1798-1934*
This listed Grade II inn, which also has a long Bold Lane

King's Arms County Hotel, c.1920.

frontage, is a two-and-a-half-storey brick building with a parapet making much use of conjoined ('Derby') sash windows. It was originally of five bays to the Shire Hall courtyard and three very widely spaced ones facing Jury Street. It was built as an element of the Shire Hall buildings, closing the courtyard off to the south-west. The promoters were the County Hall Improvement Committee, looming over which, even then, was the powerful figure of William Strutt, Chairman of the Derby Improvement Commission, whose architect, Charles Finney (1773-1828) probably designed it. The Committee advertised it on completion as 'A new and commodious inn'. The intention was to provide refreshment and accommodation for lawyers, witnesses, plaintiffs and others connected with the Assizes, which were held in the County Hall until 1971, after which it became a Crown Court. Its main façade faced the slightly later (1811) Judges' Lodgings. The stucco sign shows the arms of George III after 1816: England with the Kingdom of Hanover in pretence, and the sign remains on the short street front, above the long since blocked up doorway, nearly 70 years after it closed and was turned into the County Library. The first advertisement read: 'The convenient situation of this house to jurors, witnesses & others who may have occasion to attend in business of the County Hall is too obvious to need any explanation.'

The first proprietor was sheriff's officer, John Webster, who renewed his lease in 1813 and who probably retired in 1828, when there was a sale of contents, before the inn was extended with two extra bays in exactly matching style, stretching the building so that it actually touched the south-west angle of the County Hall, and adding a long office and stabling range with large coach house on the Walker Lane corner.

It was described after rebuilding as having '2 bars, 8 sitting rooms, a very large and commodious dining room, large kitchens, pantry, and larders, 20 bedrooms, 2 billiard

King's Arms County Hotel, St Mary's Gate, c.1875

Commercial Inn and County Hotel, St Mary's Gate, advertisement, 1852.

King's Head, Cornmarket, c.1866 prior to demolition for the widening of St James Lane.

Cornmarket, from the Market Place, photographed in 1872. The closed down King's Head has a group standing in front of it.

rooms, large brew house and laundry over. A large yard at the back, partly covered over, with harness room, several good [loose] boxes and stabling for 20 horses.' It also had a news-room by 1826.

It was taken over by John Dodgson in 1870, who probably rebuilt the parapet advertising it in 1876 as 'recently repaired' and it finally closed in 1934.

The county library inserted an extra window on the second floor and lowered two others, ruining the symmetry of the very spare façade. Around 1967 it became a divisional police station for the Derbyshire Constabulary, which it remained, partly gutted within, shabby and neglected until this closed in 1994. From that date the entire complex – one of the finest classical legal ones in central England – was planned to be converted into magistrates' courts, but all the plans envisaged demolition of the inn. However, a long and bruising campaign by the Derby Civic Society, backed by the National Amenity Societies, ensured that both schemes put forward were scrapped. Finally a third scheme, much more enlightened, envisaged the conversion of the inn, and at the time of writing it is undergoing extensive renovation to turn it into administrative offices. *DM* 6/4/1798, 14/10/1813, 27/2 & 23/4/1828, 10/3/1870 & 13/12/1876; Simpson (1826) II. 515

KING'S ARMS**

Walker Lane   *1798*

To let in 1798. Either an inaccurate address for the then new *King's Arms County Hotel* or a previous establishment in the street behind, from which the new one took its name, and as a result looking for a new owner who would have been expected, without doubt, to rename it. It may well have become one of the other pubs listed as in that street. *DM* 8/11/1798

KING'S HEAD (& GEORGE) INN*

Cornmarket   *by 1665-1872*

One of the classic coaching inns of Derby and the favourite meeting point of the Tory faction in the town; they met there frequently during the 'Forty-Five' and later, in 1777, Daniel Parker Coke, MP, chaired a dinner of the True Blue Club at the inn, although this association was not long afterwards persuaded to transfer to the *New Inn* by George Wallis. It was rebuilt in the mid-18th century with the sort of detailing associated with the style of Joseph Pickford: tall, three storeys and three bays with a rusticated archway leading into a spacious courtyard behind, all topped with a pyramidal roof carrying a prominent weathervane. In 1665 it had been owned by Henry Hayward, a vintner (died 1681) who issued a token in that year depicting Charles II's head; Hayward may, indeed, have founded the inn, or his like-named father, after the Restoration – hence its name. Not long after issuing his token it was in the hands of Henry Corden (who also issued a similar token, albeit undated). He was a vintner, too, and may have been related to his predecessor. The inn also occurs in the account book of Hon Anchitell Grey of Risley Hall, who laid out 2s 6d on drink there, 21 October 1681. In 1807, the *Defiance* and *Cornwallis* coaches transferred here from the *Bell*, probably all under franchise from the Wallises at the *New Inn* who actually owned the services. In 1814 the inn was run by John Hoare, as tenant and it was put up for sale. Coincidentally, in that year the *George* closed down, and a former proprietor of that inn – long regarded as the *King's Head's* chief rival – George Woodward, who for a decade had been running the *Talbot* (to which he had added the name *George*) outbid Hoare for the *King's Head*. Hoare thereupon moved across to the recently vacated Devonshire House and founded therein the *Hotel & King's Head* (*qv*) which opened in 1815. Indeed, the two establishments placed side-by-side advertisements on the front page of the local paper on 13 April that year! From 1814 until 1823 Woodward renamed the inn the (*Old) George and King's Head*. In late 1822, Woodward (who died in 1844) went bankrupt, having overstretched himself adding a new portion of 24ft by 18ft 'on each side of the gateway which, with the attached buildings, are capable of being converted at small expense into very commodious shops and dwelling houses.' At a sale held in February the following year, Hoare bought the inn back and restored the name as the *King's Head*. Hoare (1760-1834) had first taken over the tenancy of the inn in 1789, and by 1826 was living at Litchurch Cottage, now Litchurch Lodge, on Osmaston Road, recently restored. On his death on 20 February 1834, his widow, Joanna, remarried George Wallis of the *New Inn*. She and her step-daughters catered for the Assembly Rooms' Hunt Balls and other prestigious functions in the 1830s and '40s. The Hoares' eldest son had died in India in 1824 when a lieutenant in the Indian Native Infantry, and the younger son, Philip was active as the Derby agent for Allsopp & Co's ales, later for Bass, so that Wallis himself took the *King's Head* over.

Wallis was acute enough to see the writing on the wall, not only for his extensive coach services, but also for his inns, with the coming of the railways to Derby, and he began to wind both down, and began to diversify, a Coronation dinner being held here in 1838. As a result he advertised it to let in 1843, and it was taken on by Francis Huggins, born in Middlesex in 1798 and until 1838 a surgeon with S. Davenport in Queen Street. In 1854, he made 'extensive alterations' to adapt the inn, which had lost much trade after the end of the coaching era. He diversified by running an extensive catering business and attracting major events and important groups, like the County Club, who were meeting there regularly in 1861. He was the beneficiary of a complimentary dinner from his customers in 1859, and died in November 1862, by then long also the owner of the *Royal Hotel*, being succeeded by his son Francis Whitton Huggins, also a wine merchant with his brother Edward Stamford Huggins, whilst their other brother, Charles, took over the *Royal*. The St James' Street development and widening scheme which finally got off the ground in 1867 sounded its death knell, as part of it was affected by the promoters' plans. It finally closed in September 1872, and F.W. Huggins moved the business to the *George & Dragon*, Albert Street, which he duly renamed the *King's Head Hotel* (*qv*).

DM 22/10/1807, 6 & 13/4/1815, 25/12/1822, 5/2/1823, 15/4/1824, 20/2/1834, 28/1/1835, 25/1/1837, 4/7/1838, 18/1/1843, 25/9/1844, 16/12/1846, 20/3/1851, 29/3/1854, 1/7/1857, 26/1/1859, 5/6/1861, 26/11/1862, 1/9/1872

KING'S HEAD
See also CENTRAL

KING'S HIGHWAY
Kingsway   *1990*
Built near the gates to the Kingsway Hospital but, more to the point, close to a branch of Sainsbury's, and named after the road, itself built in 1930 as part of the Derby Arterial Road (the Ring Road) and named Kingsway after George V. Neo-Edwardian building, lowish and with barge-boarded gables. Spacious but characterless interior. Opened August 1990. In 2000 part of its most attractive feature, its spreading lawns, were taken over for the building of a 'Travelodge' overnight no frills hotel.

KNIGHT FALL
See GOLDEN EAGLE

KNIGHTS
See ST JAMES'S HOTEL

KNOTTED SNAKE
36 Cornmarket   *1984-1990*
Installed in the premises vacated by *Ramsden's Tavern* in the northerly four bays (all that survives) of the former Devonshire House (Grade II), built for the Duke of Devonshire in 1755, and largely destroyed by Messrs Littlewood in 1969. Named because of this by Davenport's, at the suggestion of the author, and opened by disc jockey Dixie Peach on 12 December 1984. Closed through loss of trade 1990 and, for more than a year before conversion into an amusement arcade, derelict. The name, of course, referred to the crest of the Cavendish family (Dukes of Devonshire): *a snake nowed [ie. Knotted] proper.*

LAFFERTY'S
See GEORGE INN, GLOBE

LAMB
Nuns' Green   *by 1744-1761*
A brick built inn (according to an advertisement), which survived to be included on Sir Harry Harpur's list; thereafter nothing further is heard of it. If it was at the market end of Friar Gate, it may have survived to be renamed. The name derives from the Paschal Lamb (also manifest as the Lamb and Flag in other locales), and is one of those religious signs which survived from the monastic period,

although the presence of the beast market may here have influenced the choice of name. Nevertheless, it is indeed possible that this house originated in that way, perhaps belonging to the nuns of King's Mead Priory, in view of its position on what had been their estate.
DM 7/12/1744

LAMB

84 (60) Park Street (corner John Street)   *by 1833-1966*
A typical back-street corner pub, which was for sale in 1839. Beer was brewed on the premises until closure (for slum clearance) in 1966, despite having been purchased by Offilers' on 3 February 1926. Sign discovered in a Normanton Road builder's yard in 1984.
DM 7/8/1839

LAMB*

11 St Alkmund's Church Yard   *by 1835-1967*
A small pub in a late mediaeval building of the east side of Derby's only Georgian square, but with a vernacular 18th-century façade. It was listed anonymously in 1835 and 1850. A sheep roast was held here to celebrate the 1856 peace treaty with Russia. Taken over in 1897 from R.A. Carey by Thomas Keenan, who was succeeded by his daughter Margaret by 1925, and ran the pub until well after World War Two. Her brother ran a bakery at no.16 from 1912 for over 30 years and his wife had a sweet shop in the mediaeval timber-framed building on the corner of Bridge Gate. Sold by Pountain's to Offilers' before 1937, but the signage does not fit one that turned up in Normanton Road in 1984. Closed and demolished (with the rest of the square) in 1967. Beer brewed on the premises in 1925.
DM 21/5/1856

LAST INN**

Unknown location   *before 1867*
Jewitt. An example of a whimsical pub name.

OLD LEATHER(N) BOTTLE*

The Spot (1 Osmaston Street (Road))   *by 1822-1857*
Situated 'at the bottom of Osmaston Street', and thus cannot have been far from the *Neptune*, although listed in St Peter's Street in 1823/4. The name is pub-related, if archaic, referring to the leather bottles or 'black jacks' used from early mediaeval times until the early 18th century. Jewitt quotes a ballad of 11 stanzas in praise of the leather bottle! From 1829 to 1850 it is listed as the *Bricklayers' Arms*, yet another non-existent livery company, and a name more associated with, perhaps, a railway junction in south London, but by 1852 was again the *Old Leather Bottle*.
Reliquary XI (1870-71) 94-96

LEOPARD*

59 (29) Agard Street   *by 1857-1898*
A Stretton's inn, two doors down from the *Golden Eagle* on the other side of Searle Street. Listed anonymously in 1857 and 1862, and frequently as a nameless beer-retailership on licence thereafter, although first named in a reference of 1864. An off-licence by 1908. Now long demolished.

LEOPARD

Brook Street   *-1895-*
Little known about this inn; probably retailed beer without a name for many years. The sign began as the badge of Anne Boleyn, Henry VIII's second wife, and mother of Elizabeth I, although it should be noted that the *lions passant guardant* on the royal coat of arms are properly blazoned *leopards*.

LEOPARD

Full Street   *by 1850-1852*
Quite possibly of old foundation under another name, and demolished shortly after 1852 to make way for the first Corporation Swimming Baths, designed by H.I. Stevens and opened in 1856. Conceivably this was the original name of the *Bath*, however.

Leopard Inn, Grove Street, 1937.

LEOPARD*

19 (16) Grove Street (corner Poplar Street) *by 1835-1974*
Built as the *Tiger* before 1835 (the interchangeability of these two animals seems to have been endemic), and renamed the *Arboretum* probably in 1840, when Britain's first public park was opened in September that year. The landlord in 1850 was Frank Woodward, probably brother to George (*George IV*) and John (*Fox & Grapes*); could they have been kin to the George Woodward who in 1814 went from the *George* to the *King's Head* with such unfortunate consequences, one wonders? Some time after 1867, when it

was to let in its former guise and probably as a result of the opening of the establishment following, it was renamed the *Leopard*. It was a fairly commodious building stuccoed and grooved to resemble ashlar but, oddly, only on the Grove Street frontage; the effect shut off suddenly four feet on to the Poplar Street side. Later a Stretton's pub, then Ind Coope, it was cleared under a CPO in 1974.

LEOPARD
See TIGER

LEVIATHAN*

110 (61) London Road (corner Litchurch Street)
by 1862-1939

The Leviathan was the whale of the Old Testament, popularised in Victorian poetry, and which gave its name to an early and famous steamship. The landlord in 1861 moved here from the *Rutland Arms* and it was the venue of an inquest in 1873. It was for sale six years later. A Stretton's house, it stood on the opposite corner to the *Nottingham Arms* and was rebuilt by them in the 1890s in ashlar, brick and half-timbering. Closed on 9 February 1939 and sold to the Governors of the Derbyshire Royal Infirmary for expansion plans. Whilst empty, it was damaged by a bomb in 1941, but thanks to the intervention of hostilities, still standing 5 March 1952, although it was pulled down soon afterwards. The upper rooms were once used by Olympic weight-lifter Fred Attenborough and his partner, who later performed on the halls as the Serge Brothers. Original licence to the *Coronation*, Baker Street.
DET 28/3/1984

LIBERTY'S
See FLAMINGO & FIRKIN

LIFEBOAT*

30 Wilson Street
1840-1980

A remarkably small and intimate beer house – latterly at least, Derby's smallest pub – allegedly founded in 1840 but in fact first listed by name in 1895. Since at least the 1860s, Derby people had subscribed towards a lifeboat, usually one stationed on the east coast; hence the name. The inn seated 12 people comfortably, the seating latterly being provided by some former Barton's Bus seats. Legend has it that comedian Tommy Cooper once walked in for a pint whilst looking for a chip shop, when appearing at the *Talk of the Midlands*, Mill Street – he must have wandered fruitlessly in his quest for quite a way! Pigeons were also kept there in its later years. It was for sale in 1881. Full licence 1950. Demolition of the surrounding housing in the later 1970s for the still unbuilt Inner Ring Road extension led to a drastic diminution of trade, nearby pubs the *Marquess of*

Granby and the *Pelican* closing in 1978/9. The last licensees were Gordon and Violet Vickerstaff, and in 1980 the owners, Bass, announced closure in the February. Mrs Vickerstaff told the local paper, 'Two years ago this pub was packed but we are now lucky to get seven people in at a weekend. I took only £34 last Saturday' her husband adding, 'Bass don't want to know, they are making all their pubs into managed houses and at 54 they think I'm too old to be a manager.' Despite a campaign to save it, the inn closed in April 1980 and was demolished in 1984 because it stood on the course of the inner ring road extension.
DM 17/8/1881; Derby Drinker 2001

LION & TIGER*

Bradshaw Street
by 1848-1849

If it were not for the fact that this inn appears alongside the one following in *Glover's Directory* of 1849, one could be forgiven for thinking that they were one and the same; yet they were not, but it is the only place the reference occurs. The landlord, James Barker, doubled as a joiner. He was the successor of the future brewer, William Alton, who departed in 1848 for the *Golden Lion* Bridge Gate.

LION & TIGRESS*

30 (42) Bradshaw Street
by 1833-1925

Three doors down from the *Ring O'Bells*. Puzzling sign, the combination of animals suggesting that it was non-heraldic. To let 1848 as 'old licensed and well accustomed' and sold to Home Brewery between 1904 and 1928, Henry Thornhill brewing on the premises in 1925, about the time it finally closed. Mr Tranter remembers it as being a thriving Home Guard Club in 1955.
DM 22/3/1848; E. Tranter, pers. comm. 30/4/2002

Litchurch Inn, Russell Street, 1912.

LITCHURCH INN (TAVERN)

44 Russell Street (corner Cotton Lane)
by 1857-2001

Earlier Victorian stuccoed inn with more spaciousness than

might be expected, and situated right in the middle of the town's foundry area. The pavements on this corner must have been put in after the pub was built, for a wagon clearance chamfer was provided at ground floor level. Named after the township of Litchurch, the existence of which goes back to the time of *Domesday Book*. In the mid-19th century, Litchurch had a completely separate local government from the rest of Derby, a sort of town within a town. Landlord in 1878, John Sherwin, was a cousin of Stephen, landlord of the *Sir Charles Napier* and of china painter William Hill. J. H. Hiley took over 29/9/1931. Known locally as 'Top House' (cf. *Barley Mow* – 'Bottom House' and the *New Inn* 'Middle House') Stretton's in 1937. For sale in September 1993, but closed 2001 and again for sale by auction as 'suitable for conversion to residential accommodation in the form of flats' at a miserley £30,000 guide price in February 2002. In the September, permission was sought for change of use to convert it into five apartments.
DET 21/2/2002

LIVE & LET LIVE**

Unknown location   *before 1867*
Jewitt. Elsewhere, the sign usually depicts a cat and mouse co-existing in apparent amity – very whimsical.

LIVERSAGE ARMS*

63 (18) Nottingham Road (corner of Alice Street) by 1850
Built and owned by the Trustees of the Liversage Charity, set up under the will of Robert Liversage, dyer, Bailiff of Derby in 1515 and 1524, and who died in 1529. His arms appear, from the terracotta image on the fabric of the inn (rebuilt in a debased Arts and Crafts style as part of a terrace at about the end of the 19th century to designs of Alexander MacPherson), to have been retrospectively invented: they are unlikely enough in all conscience. Yet in the 1860s the arms given on the previous sign were *a chevron between three leopards' heads jessant-de-lys*. A sale was held here in 1857, and it was tied to Stretton's by 1903. It was a free house in the early 1930s, but soon after leased to Marston's. It was extensively refurbished in 1999-2000 not long after the locale was made a Conservation Area. Closed in 2002, awaiting further developments.
DM 4/3/1857; Liversage Trust MSS.

LLOYD'S
See SPOTTED HORSE

LOCOMOTIVE*

154 London Road (corner High Street)   by 1874-1977
Named, no doubt, under the inspiration of the works of the Midland Railway nearby, but probably the *Railway Inn* previously, recorded 1844, 1856 and 1857 without a street number. In 1856 it was offered for sale with 1-3 Litchurch Street. A stock sale was held here in 1878. Later owned by Pountain's, but demolished in the early 1980s.
DM 24/4/1844, 30/4/1856 & 11/12/1878

LOFT
See WHEREHOUSE

LONDON TAVERN*

32 Hope Street   by 1852-1878
Appears anonymously in 1857 and 1862, but listed in 1852 as the *St George & Dragon;* after 1878 listed as a private house. First name taken from the 'Great George' portion of the decoration of the Order of the Garter – St George slaying the dragon – and latterly named after the capital.

LORD BELPER*

245 (255) Abbey Street (corner Spa Lane) by 1857-1962
Built on an acute corner as a beerhouse and demolished 1962, after having been closed on 31 January that year without seemingly ever having received a full licence – perhaps the last beerhouse in Derby. Named after Edward Strutt, MP (1801-1880), who sat in Parliament for Derby for 20 years to 1848 and was elevated to the peerage in 1856 as Lord Belper. He was son of William, FRS, of St Helen's House, and grandson of the spinning pioneer Jedediah. Probably, therefore, named in or immediately after 1856, but listed anonymously as a beer house in 1857, and named in a notice of the following year. Referred to as the *Belper*

Lord Belper, Abbey Street, 1948.

Arms in 1867. In 1926 it was merely listed as an off-licence, so may have endured a period as such before re-acquiring its 'on' licence. The last landlady, Alice Flounders, moved to the *Fox and Owl*, where she was also the last landlady.
DM 16/10/1867

LORD BYRON

7 Sadler Gate Bridge (7 Bold Lane)   *by 1833-1912*
Stood one property from the commencement of Bold Lane, and may have been renamed from the *Flying Horse*. The impetus for such a change was undoubtedly the fame of George Gordon, 6th Lord Byron, the poet, revolutionary and rake (1788-1824), perhaps more for his heroic contribution to the liberation of modern Greece from the Turkish Empire than for his poetry or libido.

LORD CHESTERFIELD

See CHESTERFIELD ARMS

LORD HILL*

2 Short Street   *by 1818-1876*
Named after General Sir Rowland Hill GCB (1772-1842), another Peninsular War hero, created in 1814 1st Lord Hill of Almaraz. In 1828 he was appointed C-in-C and raised to a Viscountcy on his retirement in 1842. Thus founded after 1814, for sale in 1858 but demolished to make way for the Great Northern Railway in 1876. The last landlord was a maltster called George Smith, consequently, no doubt, a free house.
DM 13/1/1858

LORD MACCLESFIELD**

Unknown location   *before 1867*
Jewitt. Named after a famous Derbeian, Thomas Parker, 1st Earl of Macclesfield, an early 18th-century Lord Chancellor who was forced to resign through his sleazy dealings. He came to Derby as a young lawyer, and was MP for the Borough 1705-10. Note the eminent lawyer's connection, however, with the *Three Crowns* Bridge Gate; could this house be identified with it, allowing for Lord Macclesfield's fame and the proximity of his lodgings?

LORD NAPIER

2 Milton Street   *by 1874*
A beerhouse granted a full licence in 1951; owned by Bass in 1937. Built between 1868 and 1874 and named after Field Marshall Sir Robert Napier, GCB, GCSI (1810-1890) the victor of Magdala, Ethiopia, being created 1st Lord Napier of Magdala. In 1880, the landlord, Robert Stevens, was fined for allowing illegal gaming. In 2002, after being closed for about year, its owners, Punch Pub Company, quite vicariously planned to alter the name to the *Penny Black* after

Lord Napier, Milton Street, 2002.

Rowland Hill's pioneering 1d postage stamp introduced in 1840.
DM 30/6/1880

(OLD) LORD NELSON*

11 Wardwick (corner Curzon Street)   *by 1814*
Named after the victor of Trafalgar (21 October 1805), Admiral Horatio Nelson (1758-1805) created 1798 1st Lord Nelson of The Nile and in 1801 Viscount Nelson and Duke of Brontë. He was posthumously created (in favour of his brother William) 1st Earl Nelson. It might represent a renaming of the *Crown* (but see also the *Buck in the Park*). It had plainly been going for some time when for sale in 1814, and a spirit licence application was made in 1874, along with numerous other beerhouses. The inn became the property of Pountain's by c.1890, and they rebuilt it in an inconveniently long narrow footprint in Jacobethan style and a shaped attic gable on the angle, now butchered. The architect was probably James Wright. 'Old' added to title – quite unnecessarily by Ansell's in 1990. Sold to Tetley's and in 1997 refurbished and renamed *Horatio's*. By 2002 owned by Punch Taverns and for sale as a going concern.

LORD RAGLAN*

38 Clover Street   *by 1857-1965*
Perhaps established shortly after Lord Raglan's death in the Crimea, where he was commanding British forces, in 1855, although as the inn is not listed with a name until 1874; previously, in 1857 and 1862 it appears at this address anonymously. Field Marshal Lord FitzRoy Somerset GCB (1788-1855) was youngest son of 5th Duke of Beaufort and lost an arm at Waterloo. He was created in 1852 1st Lord Raglan. Home Brewery from around 1928, and beer brewed on the premises to 1940, but in the hands of Offilers' by 1945. Closed and cleared 1965.

LOUDON ARMS
See ROSE HILL TAVERN

(LOUIS) NAPOLEON*

23 London Road (Street)   *by 1858-1884*

Louis Napoleon was the only son of Louis, King of Holland, the next brother of Napoleon I, and was born in 1808. In 1848 he took the newly-declared French Second Republic by surprise by being elected President, later styling himself 'Prince-President.' In 1852 he declared the Republic an Empire with himself as Emperor Napoleon III (his father being the notional Napoleon II). He was deposed in at the revolution which followed the defeat of his army by the Prussians at the Battle of Sedan in 1870 and died in England in 1873. Thus it may have been founded and named as early as 1848; a beer house appears anonymously at no. 25 in 1850 and may be intended for this house. The inn represented a triumph for temperance, being purchased by the Methodist New Connexion and demolished in 1884 to make way for their London Road chapel.

(LOWER) GREEN MAN
See GREEN MAN

LYNDHURST BAR*

264 (185) Normanton Road (corner Lyndhurst Street)

by 1903

By 1890, a Miss Charlotte Bryan was running a confectionery business at this address, but within five years she had opened 'refreshment rooms' on the premises, which were granted a licence as a beerhouse by 1903 when her successor was being supplied by Buntings of Uttoxeter. It spread over time into adjacent properties both in Normanton Road and Lyndhurst Street – all, however part of the same building – and a full licence was granted in 1951. It was named after the street, itself called after Sir John Copley (1772-1863) judge, statesman and orator, who thrice served as Lord Chancellor, in 1827-30, 1834-5 and 1841-5. In 1827 he was created 1st Lord Lyndhurst. Later Offiler's (their brewery was close by) and latterly Bass.

(BOWLING GREEN &) MAFEKING HOTEL*

129 Porter Road (corner Belvoir Street)   *1900*

Founded as part of the Porter Road development in Normanton, undertaken by a Spondon builder, Joseph Porter. The largish brick two-storey building, turning the corner under a small Dutch gable below which is the stone date plaque, is dated 1900 and the name (at first planned to be called merely the *Bowling Green Inn* to draw attention to a particular facility, which still exists and is the only bowling green in Derby still attached to a pub), commemorates the raising of the Siege of Mafeking in 1900, during the South African War. The crown bowling green, which measures 824 square yards, is still well patronised, having once survived a plan to convert it to a car park. In 2000 the bowling club won the South Derbyshire Men's Division Six Bowls League, winning promotion and teams from the pub have also flourished in other games, winning the Sunday Lunch Pool League, the Thursday Evening Derby City Pool League and the Ladies Darts team were 2000 runners-up in their league, too. In the 1930s the pub passed from James Eadie & Co to Bass and in 1998 to Punch Taverns PLC. Unusually, there were only seven landlords in the pub's first century of existence, starting with a Mr Parkinson, then, from 1909, Henry Ellis, followed between the wars by Francis Lewsley and, from 1940, three generations of the Morris family: Ron Morris succeeding his brother in 1947 and being followed, in his turn, by his son, Peter, in 1972, who served until October 1997. The Morrises were followed by Mr & Mrs Richardson.

MAGNET*

159 (51) Siddals Road (corner John Street)

by 1846-1962

A beerhouse, for sale as a going concern in 1870, which found inspiration for its name from the works of Sir Walter Scott. It (or the *Arms of the Isle of Man & Moira, qv*) was probably the anonymous beer house listed here in 1846 and 1862; they may well have been one and the same, although it is possible that they stood contemporaneously for a time in the 1850s on opposite corners of John Street. It was run by former engine-fitter Joseph Parker (1839-1902) from 1871 to 1874 when he went to the *Cossack* in Bag Lane and transferred the name to the

Mafeking Hotel, Porter Road. Drawing by Reg Newcombe.

Morledge. It was sold in 1882. It was granted a full licence in 1951, and owned by Pountain's in 1937. Closed on 1 February 1962 and cleared shortly afterwards.
Census 1871; *DM* 19/10/1870 & 28/6/1882

MAGPIE**

Unknown location   *before 1867*
Jewitt.

MALIN (WINE VAULTS)*

205 Normanton Road   *by 1967*
At the turn of the 19th century, 205-207 Normanton Road was the premises of a surgeon; by 1908 Cox & Malin Ltd had opened a wine and spirit store there. In the 1960s this was converted into a pub with a rather frightful new façade, pulling together no less then three former dwellings, but for which permission was sought for alterations – which will hopefully result in an aesthetic improvement – in May 2002. It was opened under the aegis of Mansfield Brewery, and named after the Malin half of the old vintner's business. William Malin took over the running of Mr Mott's vintner's business in Cornmarket in the 1830s (see *Rodney*); his son, another William, of Overdale, Whittaker Road, was also a co-founder of Messrs Thurman and Malin, St Peter's Street, a draper's and millinery store. Renamed the *Malin Wine Vaults*, 1997.

MALLARD**

Uttoxeter Road   *1995*
A large modern 'family' pub, constructed in brick and of no particular style, on part of the site of the demolished Union Workhouse, later Manor Hospital. Named after the London & North Eastern Railway's celebrated A4 Pacific locomotive which achieved the still-standing world speed record for steam in 1938, a local connection in that the engine was designed by the aristocratic Derbyshire-born engineer Sir Nigel Gresley (1876-1941).

MALT SHOVEL

44 Kedleston Street (corner Garden Street) by 1847-1965
From 1880 this inn was kept by William Newbold, a member of a notable dynasty of beerhouse licensees (see introduction). Owned by Pountains in 1937 and beer brewed on the premises until at least 1938. Closed by 1965 for clearance under a CPO. The implement from which it took its name is a large wooden spatula used to turn and spread the barley in malting, a notable Derby trade.
DM 4/8/1880

MARKET TAVERN

4-6 Derwent Street   *by 1874-1929*
Opened in a good Regency three-bay, three-storey house,

stuccoed, with quoins, rusticated lintels and a first floor sill band, next to the bridge on the south side of the street, for sale in 1878. Latterly owned by Alton's, but closed 1929 or 1930 to facilitate the rebuilding of Exeter Bridge and (ultimately) to make way for the new Council House. Standing, but boarded up, in October 1931. Licence transferred to *Osmaston Park Hotel*.
DM 3/4/1878

MARKET HOTEL
See CATTLE MARKET HOTEL

MARKET VAULTS
See NEW MARKET

MARLBOROUGH'S HEAD
See (DUKE OF) MARLBOROUGH'S HEAD

MARQUESS OF ANGLESEY*

10 Cheapside   *by 1827-1857*
Opened in an oldish building standing in front of part of St Werburgh's Church Yard before 1827 (the street only being laid out in *c*.1800) and at first named the *Butchers' Arms* after another non-existent livery company. Later renamed after yet another Peninsular War hero, Field Marshall Henry William Paget, 2nd Earl of Uxbridge, KG, GCB, GCH (1768-1854) created in 1815 1st Marquess of Anglesey. He lost a leg at Waterloo, lived at Beaudesert, near Rugeley, and owned much of Burton upon Trent. The building was cleared around 1860 as part of an improvement made to St Werburgh's Church after a flood had weakened it (and the inn).

MARQUESS OF ANGLESEY**

St Peter's Street   *by 1835-1843*
An 'old accustomed and well established public house' when for sale in 1841, which rather suggests no great antiquity, but of some years' standing. Thus its foundation might go back to the days of the good Marquess's heroism in 1815 or just afterwards. The sale included two cottages in Bloom Street, which suggests that it stood close by. It is possible, therefore, that it is the *Cheshire Cheese* briefly renamed.
DM 14/3/1841

MARQUIS OF GRANBY*

84 (124) Gerard Street   *by 1857-1978*
Stood immediately south of the Board School in Gerard Street and was owned by Alton in 1937. Listed anonymously in 1857, but named after General the Marquess of Granby (English Marquesses should always be thus spelt), C-in-C during the Seven Years War in Germany, when he

covered himself with glory and earned the admiration of his men. Born in 1721, he died in the lifetime of his father, 3rd Duke of Rutland, in 1770. He was thus a member of the family of Manners of Haddon Hall (and Belvoir Castle) and so a local notable as well. Mr and Mrs McLocklin moved here from the *Old Spa* in 1947, and brewed on the premises. Inn cleared in 1978, due to falling income and its position on the course of the supposed ring road extension. Among the landlords in its later years were Billy Metcalfe, and Harry Farmer, who later ran a butcher's stall in the Market Hall.
DET Bygones 19/2/2002

MARQUIS OF GRANBY*

Osmaston Road (Street)   *by 1810-1857*
For sale as a going concern in 1810 (its last named mention), and perhaps dating back to Lord Granby's death in 1770, but subsequently may have been renamed. It may have 'soldiered' on until 1857, as one of two anonymous beer houses listed in this part of Osmaston Road between 1835 and 1857.
DM 21/6/1810

MARQUIS OF GRANBY

Walker Lane   *by 1772-1775*
Probably named shortly after the late Marquess triumphs, c.1763 or on his premature death, 1770. It was for sale in 1772 and gets a single further mention later. Probably renamed, the *King's Arms* being a possibility.
DM 18/9/1772 7 2/6/1775

MARQUIS OF HASTINGS

21 (1) Parliament Street   *by 1874-1956*
Although it might be tempting to think that this inn was named after the last Marquess of Hastings, who died in penury in 1868 after losing all on the Derby, it probably commemorated another Napoleonic War hero: Sir John Rawdon Hastings, 2nd Earl of Moira and 1st Marquees of Hastings, KG, GCB (1754-1826), who was raised to his Marquessate after a stint as Governor-General of India in 1816. His seat was nearby Donington Hall. Derby Museum has a portrait of the landlord, David Buckler, outside the inn, dated 1896 and painted by W.F. Austin. Sold by Nottingham Brewery to Tennant Bros in the mid-1930s. Closed by 1960, and later demolished.

MASONS' ARMS*

2 (6) Edward Street (corner Arthur Street)
                    by 1862-1996; 1997
Opened some time after 1857 in a three-bay two-and-a-half-storey Regency stuccoed house, still retaining its glazing bars in all but the ground floor windows, and oddly

colour-washed. Owned by Pountain's in 1937. Conceivably named after the Worshipful Company of Masons, incorporated 1414, whose arms were *Azure on a chevron between three castles argent, a pair of compasses extended of the field,* but the site owner, William Strutt, was not only an amateur architect but also a keen freemason. For sale by Carlsberg-Tetley in September 1993, closed and boarded up in 1996, but reopened under new ownership 14 August 1997 as *Montague's*. Subsequently renamed the *Strawberry Tree*.

MASONS' ARMS
See also (FREE)MASONS' ARMS

MASTER LOCKSMITH**

Meteor Centre, Alfreton Road, Little Chester   *1993*
A modern, amorphously styled brick 'family' pub opposite the utilitarian spreading ugliness of the Meteor Centre, an out-of-town shopping mall. Named after a trade which still, mercifully, flourishes, possibly due to a local association with the site. Part of the Tom Cobleigh chain.

MAYFAIR
See CASTLE

MAYPOLE

42-44 (47) Brook Street   *by 1863*
To let as a going concern in 1863, so probably established in the 1850s. Owned by Home Ales since at least 1937 but now by Scottish & Newcastle. The is name traditional, and most UK pubs so named are associated with the site of one; did Derbeians course around a maypole on Nuns' Green in the 18th century?

MAYPOLE**

Friar Gate   *-1853-*
Only known from a contents sale – perhaps here indicative of closure – of 1853. It is possible that an old established Friar Gate pub was purchased for redevelopment and the proprietor took premises close by in Brook Street and continued the business there. 8-9 Friar Gate is the only building which springs to mind of approximately this date, and so the inn may have been close to St Werburgh's; where was the maypole once erected?
DM 24/8/1853

MAYPOLL

Cornmarket   *18th century*
No firm date is available for this inn, which was situated, apparently, in a yard behind the buildings on the east side of the street. Perhaps later renamed the (*Admiral*) *Rodney*, or *Rose and Crown*? Note the early 20th-century Maypole

Dairy also situated on the east side of Cornmarket; perhaps a conscious revival of the name (originally spelt as above) read in the deeds.

MAZEPPA*

65 (58) Traffic Street (junction with Hope Street)
by 1846-1935

Named after a 17th-century Polish nobleman, Count Ivan Stepanovich Mazeppa (1644-1709) who, due to the discovery of an illicit alliance with a married lady, was tied naked to a horse and galloped east. He ended up in the Ukraine, where, by dint of personality and ability, he became *Hetman* (elective ruler) of the Kosakhs (Cossacks) in 1687, leading them to glory until he unwisely backed Charles XII of Sweden against Peter the Great, was discarded by his peers and died in exile in Turkey. The tale was much aped by a notable circus act and was immortalised by Byron's poem of 1819; he doubtless saw something of himself in the dashing Pole! Listed anonymously in 1846, but named and for sale as a going concern in 1850 and again in 1873. Home-brewed ale until closure in 1935, at which time there were a number of full-sized billiard tables upstairs, and when the licence was transferred to the *Blue Pool* by Offilers', the owners.
DM 13/3/1850 & 19/2/1873

MEADOWS

Chequers Road, West Meadows   *1970*

A modernist pub built as part of the old Borough Council's new Cattle Market development on The Meadows, hence the name. Owned by the City Council and a free house. Burnt down 1976 and rebuilt.

MECHANICS' ARMS*

51 (30, 70) Bridge Street (corner of Brook Walk)
by 1849-1874

Another pub bearing the name of the arms of a completely non-existent London livery company. Served an area full of silk and narrow tapes mills, hence, undoubtedly the name; listed anonymously in 1850 at this address, situated next door to the *Woodlark* (Nos.70 & 71 in 1852) and today absorbed into the latter. A free house closed around 1874.

MECHANICS' ARMS**

King Street   *-1862-*

Possibly the *Shamrock* under a new name. If so, a greengrocery by 1874, and thus closed before that date.

MELANCTHON'S HEAD*

46 (80) Park Street   *by 1846-1908*

An extraordinary name for a pub; Philip Melancthon (1497-1560) of Wittenberg was a German theologian and an associate of Martin Luther; he wrote the *Augsburg Confession,* which set out the principles of Lutheranism. The inn was said to have been the only one so named in the UK. Later closed, from the date, probably during the Bench's Temperance Society inspired blitz and subsequently a private dwelling, close to F.E. Wood's depot. Possibly the *Foresters' Arms* renamed, but cf. *Feathers.*

MELBOURNE ARMS*

113 (94) Normanton Road (corner Melbourne Street)
by 1874

Takes its name from Melbourne Street, which has been in existence much longer than the inn, which evolved out of a confectionery business and refreshment rooms, much as the *Lyndhurst Bar* did. A spirit licence was applied for in 1874, so it must have been going by that date, although in 1898 it was still combined with Mr Robinson's confectionery and café business. Not named after 2nd Viscount Melbourne, Queen Victoria's first Prime Minister, but the local town, birthplace in 1801 of Alderman Robert Pegg, who in the 1860s built gloriously Gothic Melbourne House on Osmaston Road. After his death in 1870, the gardens were sold off by the next owner and Melbourne Street pitched across them to Normanton Road and houses built; hence both names. Refurbished and reopened in June 1996 as *Hurleys* not – as (once again) some might suspect, after the film star – but after the new proprietress, Mrs Hurley. By 2002 renamed the *City Inn.*
DM 26/8/1874

MELBOURNE ARMS

35 (11) Siddals Road   *by 1846-1961*

Probably built shortly after Lord Melbourne's term as Prime Minister, in the early 1840s. Still brewing on the premises in 1961, but closed on 31 May that year and demolished soon afterwards. At the time of closure beer was 1s 1d per pint, the home-brewed being a mild. The unbuilt ring road extension was to have gone through the site; 41 years on it still hasn't.

MERLIN

11 Duckworth Square   *1965-1991*

Part of the Duckworth Square development of 1962-4 which swept away Becket Well Lane and the historic well with its conical cover. The pub was situated over the entrance, being initially the *Merlin* since an aeroplane propeller adorned a bar wall, and thus named after the famous Rolls-Royce aero engine of Battle of Britain fame, which was manufactured in Derby. It then became the *Black Prince,* since it stood on the site of the *Black Prince* cinema. This opened as the Victoria Electric Theatre in 1910 and closed as the *Black Prince* (named after the 14th-century hero of the French Wars) in 1962. It then became, in quick succession, *Annie's Bar*, later *Roscoe's*. In December 1991 it closed and the entire complex gradually followed it into desuetude. In 2000 the council announced that it was a 'redevelopment opportunity' and marketed it, but at the time of writing, with no apparent success.

MERMAID**

Market Place   *1692*

Occurs in an unprovenanced deed; probably renamed. The sign is heraldic, and in this context probably derives from the mermaid used as the sinister supporter of the arms of the Worshipful Company of Fishmongers, the arms having been granted in 1512 and the supporters in 1575.

MERRY WIDOWS

See WRIGHT'S VAULTS

MIDLAND ARMS*

44 Midland Road (Station Street; corner of Nelson Street)
1853-1900

The Midland Railway did use arms, although unauthorised, from 1844 to 1923, consisting of the coats of arms of Birmingham, Derby, Bristol, Leicester, Lincoln and Leeds, quarterly of six. It was described as 'newly erected' and for sale in February 1854 and was for sale again in 1871, but was eventually demolished to make way for the GPO sorting office after a brief renaming as the *Vine*.

MIDLAND HOTEL (& POSTING HOUSE)*

Midland Road   *1841*

A very fine four-square brick building of two-and-a-half storeys for the main east block, with a two-storey extension (later lengthened c.1852) to the south, all in a stripped classical style by Francis Thompson, the accomplished North Midland Railway architect. A second parallel range, identical with the first, was added in 1842 with a low, recessed cross-wing incorporating a grand columned entrance topped by a stone Royal coat-of-arms, which may have been added after Queen Victoria stayed, en route for Balmoral via Chatsworth, 28 September 1849. This gave the accommodation 'upwards of 50 bedrooms'. As with the *Brunswick* the contractor was Thomas Jackson of Pimlico at whose sole expense it was erected, and it opened 1 June 1841, being 'franchised out' to John Cuff in the November.

Cuff was born in London in 1805, the son of John Jackson Cuff, and he married Elizabeth Collier of Horley in Surrey in 1826, and they went on to manage, with their brother-in-law, Robert Bacon, the *Freemason's Tavern,* in London's Great Queen Street. On taking the Midland, they settled at Hill House, Littleover, whilst Bacon went in 1846

Midland Hotel, Midland Road.

to take over the *Queen's Hotel* in Birmingham. The Cuffs had six sons and two daughters, one of the latter marrying a Scottish brewer. The whole of the rest of the family migrated to New Zealand in 1854, when Cuff sold the lease to Mrs Susan Chatfield.

The NMR minutes of July 1843 record the '...the proprietors of the Midland Hotel... and the licensees of the Brunswick Inn... shall have the exclusive privilege of sending porters on the station platform to solicit the custom of passengers to their respective premises... the parties to conduct themselves to conduct themselves with civility and propriety in all respects...'

In 1843 accommodation was charged @ 4s (20p) per night, doubles @ 5s (25p) with sitting room included, another 5s. A fire in one's

John Cuff (1805-1864), landlord of the Midland Hotel.

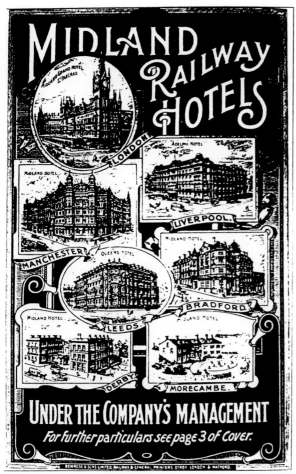

Advertisement of c.1910 for the Midland Railway's hotels; the Midland appears lower left.

bedroom cost 1s (5p) extra and a full breakfast 'with chops and eggs' was 3s (15p) as was (high) tea. The housekeeper was Mrs Susan Chadfield, the later manageress. Queen Victoria stayed again in September 1859, Edward, Prince of Wales (later King Edward VII) following in 1881, HRH Princess Mary of Cambridge in 1895 and on 16 February 1902 HRH Princess Louise, Duchess of Argyll and her husband, the Duke. On 23 March 1928 the hotel was –topically – host to TM King Amanullah and Queen Soriya of Afghanistan.

In 1859 Jackson went bankrupt and the Midland Railway (as the NMR had since 1844 become) took over the ownership, at first via trustees, but from 1862 directly, under legislation of 1861. The catering contract was then let to Spiers & Pond, but in 1871 the youthful Twyford blacksmith's son William Towle (1849-1929) was appointed manager. His family had been seven generations in Twyford. He steadily increased the Midland's catering and hotel empire, earning himself a knighthood in 1920, six years after his retirement, when

his sons Col. Sir Francis Towle (1876-1954) and Arthur Towle, CBE (1878-1948) succeeded him as joint managers of Midland Railway Hotels until 1922. It remained in railway ownership – Midland Railway to 1 January 1923, London Midland & Scottish Railway until 1 January 1948 and then British Railways, under which organisation it became part of British Transport Hotels. In the 1930s, the original entrance, from Midland Road into what is now the restaurant, was altered to the east where an existing secondary entrance was refashioned. It was sold off in 1982 to Mr T. Harris, who vastly improved it. A sympathetic porch was added, and a scheme to heighten the lower wing has undoubtedly detracted from the design of what was arguably the earliest railway hotel in the country. Three types of token were issued in the 1860s: a brass 1s 3d, a 6d and 4d in zinc.

An engaging character associated with the *Midland* was the late Harry ('Len') Watson (1904-2001). Barring six years during World War Two, he worked there for 49 years until his retirement in 1972, rising from shoe boy to *Maitre d'Hotel*. In his time he served such people as Sir Don Bradman in 1948, Arthur Askey, Wilfred Pickles Joe Loss and, during their early playing days with the club, Derby County stars Dave Mackay and Roy McFarland. 'We had a private dining room', Watson later said, 'for sports stars and celebrities, where they'd come and eat breakfast before going off for the day.' As a boy he slept 'in the rafters' and his working day was split into two shifts, 8am to 2pm and 5pm to 11pm.

Billson (1996) 82-87; *DM* 10/5/1854; *DET* 7/11/2001

MIDLAND RAILWAY STATION BUFFET*

Railway Station   1840

Situated today on both platforms 1 and 6. The refreshment rooms existed inside the entrance from very early, the original one opening 1 July 1840, that on platform 1/2 following in 1842 (licence) being built by the ubiquitous Thomas Jackson, leased by him in November 1841 and then sub-let to the Midland Hotel. Platform 3 in 1887 and platform 4 (now 4/6) in 1881. The full licence came later, at an undetermined date.

Billson (1996) 84.

MILLER

See DUSTY MILLER

MILTON'S HEAD

22 (18) Hill Street (Ossian Street)   *by 1827-1931*

Ossian Street was the original name for Hill Street; Upper Hill Street had been, by the same token, Fingal Street. The inn was named after the poet John Milton (1608-1674). A

notice concerning it appeared in 1854 and it was for sale in 1872. It closed in 1931.
DM 8/3/1854 & 9/10/1872

MINERS' ARMS*

St Mary's Gate   *by 1750-1784 (1849)*
No doubt part of a chain of multiple re-namings, so frequent in the 18th century. The name is quite fictional as a reflection of heraldry, as no such company as the Worshipful Company of Miners existed; it was a notable Derbyshire calling, however. It may well have survived, renamed, until 1849, as in 1784 there was an unexpired lease with 65 years remaining for sale. Assuming that this lease was for 99 years, the pub's existence can therefore be inferred back to 1750. Could it have been the *Roebuck* prior to this date? Its subsequent identity could, of course, be the *Star & Garter*.
DM 18/2/1780 & 25/3/1784

MINSTREL BOY*

1 Whitaker Street (corner Rose Hill Street)   *by 1878-1981*
The name reflects a popular poem written by the Irish poet, Thomas Moore, who lived for a time at Mayfield from 1813 and was a friend of the Strutts. Offiler's by 1936. A relatively recent loss, having been sold by Bass in 1981.

MINUTES VAULTS

See OLD VAULTS

MISTER GRUNDY'S

See GEORGIAN HOUSE HOTEL

MISTER JORROCKS

See GLOBE

(CROWN &) MITRE*

Amen Alley   *by 1779-1868*
First appearing in the will of the *stuccadore* Abraham Denstone who died in 1779, and left to his heir. He was the plasterer who worked with Joseph Pickford and who executed the plasterwork in the Assembly Rooms to Robert Adam's design in 1774. It boasted a 'new clubroom, lately erected' when for sale in 1824, then and in 1822 called the *Mitre*. It was to let as the *Crown & Mitre* in 1846, and as the *Mitre* with a 'concert room' (clearly the former club room) three years later. It was for sale in 1854 and when for sale to the developer in 1868 it was 'owned by the late John Sanders, Esq' – a former Mayor of Derby (1840-1) who lived at Parkfields Cedars. It stood on the corner with Iron Gate and was demolished in 1868 to allow for road widening.
DM 1/5/1822, 28/4/1824, 18/2/1846, 23/2/1848, 23/8/1854, 22/1/1862 & 26/2/1868.

(OLD) MITRE**

Full Street   *by 1791-1820*
Mentioned in *UBD* and could be almost any of the four inns with 'mitre' in their names, including that above, but the mention of an *Old Mitre* in Full Street in 1818/20 suggests that this may be one and the same, differentiating itself from that above. Possibly renamed the *Bath* in 1852, but what it was called in between 1820 and 1852 seems elusive.
UBD 1791

MOIRA (ARMS)

See ARMS OF THE ISLE OF MAN

MOLLY MAGOOS

Colyear Street   *by 1984*
A short-lived bar situated between the Pennine Hotel and the *Pink Coconut* nightclub. Subject subsequently to a bewildering plethora of rebrandings – *Branagans, Heroes, Dylans*. The author confesses himself to be completely defeated in attempting to explain the original name.

MONGOLIA

See (CORN) EXCHANGE

(CLOCK &) MONKEY*

Location unclear (?St James's Lane (Street)) date unknown
This house owes its inclusion to its mention in a poem contributed to the local paper in 1985; it has so far eluded research. The name must derive (in a local context) from the two baboons supporting a barrel, the rebus of the Babington family – baboon-tun – displayed both inside and outside Babington Hall, St Peter's Street, demolished 1811. Mr Motley has suggested *Clock & Monkey*, St James's Lane, but evidence for a house of this name is equally elusive; conceivably it was a colloquial name for a house listed elsewhere.
DET 21/6/1985

MONKS' TAVERN**

Unknown location   *before 1867*
Jewitt. A whimsical name which, if it bore any relation to a location on or near the site of one of the town's dissolved monastic houses, should have been in Abbey Street, Darley Abbey, St James's Lane, Friar Gate, King Street or Osmaston Road. Perhaps an ephemeral beerhouse.

MONTAGUE'S

See MASON'S ARMS

MOULDERS' ARMS*

31 Mansfield Street (corner City Road)   *1873-1898*
Yet another coat-of-arms ascribed to a non-existent livery company, but nevertheless appropriate, in view of the

number of foundries nearby; Cheetham and Hill, Fox, and Haslam's. The sign showed various tools of the iron-founder's trade. Its foundation goes back to a first licence application of 1873. By the 20th century it was an off-licence but originally a beerhouse.
DM 1/10/1873

MULBERRY TREE
See NEW INN

MUNDY ARMS*
56 Leaper Street (31 Mundy Street)   *by 1869-1910*
Founded in the same building as the rather more ephemeral *Druids' Retreat* only recorded two decades before, especially as it was advertised as 'old established' when for sale in 1869. Despite the name, it was actually in Leaper Street, and near a group of 10 tenements called Water Houses. A beerhouse, owned by Offilers' when last listed. Arms of the Mundys of Markeaton Hall, owners of much land in the West End.
DM 9/6/1869

NAG'S HEAD*
4 Exeter Street (corner Stuart Street)   *by 1872-1969*
Two Derbyshire families used what might be termed a Nag's Head in their arms: the Dethicks of Newhall and the Meynells of Langley. The latter acquired the emblem by marriage with an heiress of de la Warde of Lincolnshire in the 14th century and transmitted it to the Dethicks of Newhall in like fashion. Both families had close contacts in Derby, the Meynells especially, one of whom ran the *Bell* (Sadler Gate) in the later 17th century, and another was a prominent apothecary in the Market Place, later with interests in Little Chester. Nevertheless, this inn started out as the *Cherry Tree* before 1872, when a contents sale seems to have ushered in a new landlord who changed the name. The original name, as with the *Mulberry Tree* (cf. *New Inn*), probably marked a feature surviving from when this area was part of Erasmus Darwin's garden. In 1932 Zachary Smith's brewery sold this inn to Marston's. From 1919 until closure it was run by one family, being taken in that year by Robert Brown. He was followed in 1934 by his son, also Robert and his wife, Lavinia (1894-1974): 'Landlord Bob and Ma Brown'. Robert Brown II died in 1956 and 'Ma' Brown carried it on to closure (and her retirement) in 1969. It was consequently always known in its latter years as 'Ma Brown's', during which time it was reportedly unmatched for both its ale and its immaculate bar. Ma Brown's great-grand-daughter and her husband, Mr & Mrs V. Bednall, are currently licensees of the *York Tavern*. The area was cleared soon after closure to make way for the Inner Ring Road.
DET Bygones 26/3/2002, p. 23; DM 23/10/1872

NAG'S HEAD INN (VAULTS)*
64 St Peter's Street (Nag's Head Yard)   *by 1714-1959*
For most of the 18th century this important coaching inn was kept by the Oakes family, who were rich attorneys and who became richer by discovering oil shale on their newly-acquired estate at Riddings in 1818. They descend from Gilbert Oakes, a maltster, in 1649; his grandson James (1673-1714) seems to have built it, or been its first owner. It seems to have been run by younger sons for the most part. First mentioned in 1734. In 1779 Benjamin Oakes (1746-1785) – also a 'liquor merchant' – was declared bankrupt and it was all to be sold up, but it must have been kept within the family for his brother, Alderman James Oakes (1750-1828) – father of another James, first of the family to own the Riddings estate – was offering a lease of it two decades later. His sister Mary married Derby-born Charles Houghton, landlord of the *Black's Head* in Ashbourne. Oakes eventually sold it in 1822, and it was to let in 1828 with a newly erected dining or club room 30ft by 19ft and stabling for 50 horses – a time when the inn hosted a 99-member friendly society – following a contents sale. By 1833 it was in the hands of a Mr Mason, a coach proprietor, who ran the London to Manchester *Independent* from here. It was approached by a lane leading from St Peter's Street. In 1856 it was the venue for one of a number of sheep roasts to celebrate the peace treaty with Russia, and by the year following it had been renamed the 'Nag's Head and Commercial Inn, coach office and Nag's Head stores', which suggests a degree of diversification in the post-coaching era. Reduced in size in 1877 by losing its original façade to street widening and again much later by extensions to the Midland Drapery 1924-9, reducing it to little more than a beer house in size. In the 18th century, the Nag's Head was the inn for the registration of race-horses wishing to be entered for the Derby Races on Sinfin Moor, and the place of numerous bloodstock sales, so the sign in this case may have been associative. Sold to Marks and Spencer's in 1958 for an expansion project and closed on 28 January 1959, being demolished shortly afterwards.
DM 26/7/1733, 4/6/1779, 28/4/1785, 10/1/1799, 26/3/1822, 18/6 & 30/7/1828 & 21/5/1856; Glover (1831/33) II. 539

NAG'S HEAD*
Wardwick   *by 1761-1779*
Stood opposite St Werburgh's Church Yard, *ie* before the building and naming of Cheapside, when the name Wardwick covered a wider area. In 1774 it was 'a well accustomed public house' and was to let in 1779. Probably demolished by physician Francis Fox to build his house on that corner around 1784.
DM 22/5/1779

NAKED BOY**

Unknown location   *before 1867*
Jewitt.

NAPOLEON*

103 (99) Parker Street   *by 1844-1963*
Named after the French Emperor Napoleon I (1806-14/15). Beer brewed on premises in 1925; then a Stretton's House. Jewitt says of the sign: *A sign which shewed no good taste in adoption and one which cannot too soon be allowed to die out* – this, however, long after the unfortunate monarch's fall, as a result of defeat at the Battle of Waterloo; in the event, the sign outlived Jewitt's disapprobation by nearly a century! It was to let as a going concern and 'good accustomed' in 1845, and let again a decade later. Mr Motley adds that 'Cock' Cunningham was the brewer here when Ind Coope attempted to put their beer in, but 'it didn't sell'. Closed in 1963 and cleared in 1965. At some point referred to as *The Buonaparte*.
DM 1/2/1845 & 17/10/1855; *Reliquary* XIII (1872) 53

NAPOLEON

See LOUIS NAPOLEON

NAVIGATION**

Bridge Gate   *after 1796-1812*
Situated, according to the advertisement for its sale in 1812 when the owner and landlord was the gentleman, Edward Coke, of the Trusley family, 'in St Alkmund's Parish, near to St Mary's Bridge', which doesn't actually tell us on which side of the river (or the street) is meant. It could refer to either the *Bridge Inn*, the *Jolly Colliers* or the *Trent Boat*. The probability is that the two latter are both to be identified with this inn. In either case, the name cannot pre-date 1796 when the Derby Canal was opened, for it had an arm which diverged from the Erewash Branch, went along Nottingham Road and emerged into the Derwent immediately south of St Mary's Bridge. Note that the sale of 1812 included five cottages, and the same number were included in the 1825 sale of the *Jolly Colliers* which strongly suggests the name bestowed upon this inn within the following decade or so.
DM 24/4/1812

NELSON**

Midland Place (corner of Calvert Street (North Street)   *by 1845-1861*
Converted from a bakery and grocer's shop in one of the NMR's cottages in 1842, recorded as this combination in 1846 under the sign of the *Nelson Inn*. Recorded further in 1851, 1852 (as 25 Railway Terrace) and 1858 (and listed anonymously as a beer house in Midland Place in 1857),

but had reverted to a provision shop by 1861. The suggestion that it was a beer house in North Street (off Duffield Road) fails to stand up to the evidence of the directories. Furthermore, that North Street was then extremely 'respectable' and an unlikely place for a beerhouse. Named after Admiral Lord Nelson.
Peter Billson, *pers. Comm.; Census* 1861, 1871.

(OLD) NEPTUNE INN (HOTEL)

10 Osmaston Road (Street) (The Spot)   *by 1761*
This inn has had a continuous existence on the same site for at least 240 years which, in Derby in the early 21st century, is good going. It was first mentioned as one of the houses Sir Harry Harpur had earmarked for free drinks during the 1761 election. For sale in 1809. The building, however, is a much-butchered later 19th-century replacement for the original. Purchased by Offilers' from Zachary Smith's brewery in March 1928 and refronted in their inimitable style; later Bass. Named after the Roman God of the Sea and thus a surprising sign for a non-maritime county. It was run from the end of World War Two by Bill and Flo Liversage. He had been a bookmaker pre-war, and died in the 1950s, his wife taking over the licence. Her daughter-in-law wrote of her: 'In those days the landladies were often more outstanding than the landlords. [Flo] was like Hyacinth Bouquet, she could be really posh, but she could be the other way when it suited her.' If a problem arose in the pub, she was usually well equipped to cope. Her son added, 'But in the event of something serious, the men of the darts team would always make sure my mother was OK.' She was an ally of Alice Baker (of the *Royal Standard* and *White Horse*) working closely with her on the Derby Ladies' Licensed Victuallers Association. She was also the daughter of Mary and Charles Roberts, landlords of the *Rising Sun* and of the *Duke of Cambridge*.
DET Bygones 26/2/2002 p. 23; *DM* 6/12/1809

(NETHER) SHIP

See SHIP

NEVILL'S WINE VAULTS

Bridge Gate (corner King Street)   *–1768–*
Opened by Henry Nevill on the opposite corner to the *New Inn* some time before 1768, but probably removed by William Strutt *c.*1803 to improve the view from or of St Helen's House.
DM 1/4/1768

NEW BULL & BUSH

See BULL & BUSH

NEW BULL'S HEAD

See BULL'S HEAD

NEW FLOWER POT

See FLOWER POT

NEW INN*

93 Canal Street (corner Park Street)   *by 1841-1951*

An 'old licensed public house' when to let in 1855 and again the year following. Owned by Ind Coope & Allsopp in 1937. Closed around 1952. Almost certainly previously called the *Mulberry Tree.* The latter is recorded only in 1841, the advertisement for its sale as a going concern reading 'Castlefields, on the corner of John Street and Canal Street adjoining a branch of the canal'. As John and Canal Streets run parallel, the south-east angle of Canal Street and Park Street must be intended, in which case the two inns must be the same. Possibly, in 1841, with the Castlefields Estate still being broken up, the spot was still marked by a Mulberry Tree. Doubtless it was later felled or died as a result of the rapid build-up of adjacent ware-housing and dwellings, and ceased to have significance as a landmark and hence the change of name.

DM 29/12/1841, 12/12/1858 & 18/6/1856

NEW INN*

19 King Street (corner Bridge Gate)   *by 1766-1967*

One of the last of the celebrated coaching inns to be built, between 1761 and 1766, perhaps to the designs of Joseph Pickford, although stylistic confirmation is not possible due to a thorough rebuilding some time after 1873 when a part of it had been lost to street widening and a new façade was put on to the original two and a half-storey brick building – rather awkwardly, in fact, as its cornice stood forward of the roof eaves by a foot. The new King Street front, however, was handsome enough, the window openings almost certainly corresponding to those originally existing, although the sashes were of the upper leaf with glazing bars over plate glass type. Below the sills were rubbed brick shaped aprons which, with the playful interplay of string courses, banding and keyblocks evoked the style of the *Falstaff,* Silver Hill Road, suggesting the young Alexander MacPherson as the architect. The side elevation was also refenestrated at the same time, but within the old openings with their rusticated lintels. It was built for George Wallis, a relative of Joseph Wright and of the Gells of Hopton; Sir William Gell is known to have stayed there when in Derby in 1793.

The Wallises were probably the single most important inn-holding family in Derby's history, and the *New Inn* remained in their family three generations and four propri-etorships. George Wallis (1694-1780) was the son of a John Wallis, both blacksmiths in King Street, the site of their works being so occupied until the later 1960s. George's son, George Wallis I (1731-1786) was a born entrepreneur, and

probably had access to the funds he needed through his marriage in 1753 to Rebecca, daughter of John Clarke, a Nottingham Road maltster, whose family ran the Derby Brewery right through the 19th century. George had, though, been apprenticed to his father, becoming a freeman of the Borough in 1754, and initiated a series of stage coach and mail services from his new foundation from the start, buying up others and consolidating his hold both regionally and nationally in a remarkably short period of time. Notable amongst these was the *Derby Diligence* ('Dilly'). A service which, amongst others, he later 'fran-chised out' (to the *Bell* in this case) simply because the *New Inn* could not alone cope with the pressure of all the Wallis services running by the dawn of the following century. The 'Dilly' ran from Derby to Nottingham on Mondays, Wednesdays and Fridays at a fare for inside passengers of 4s 0d. Wallis also had, by 1773, a mourning coach and hearse for hire and did a roaring trade in funerals and wakes. His sister, Sarah married Dr Richard Wright, the painter's brother, in 1774, and on his death he was succeeded by his eldest son William Wallis I (1763-1791). His wife was a cousin of Alderman Samuel Rowland, the co-proprietor of the *Derby Mercury,* and his elder sister, Sarah married Alderman Dr Thomas Haden, Richard Wright's young partner, later father-in-law of Kirk Boott, the founder of Lowell, Massachusetts, USA. Although he died young, like his father, he left three children, of whom the only son, George Wallis II (1788-1834) was too young to succeed him at the *New Inn* but later married the widowed Mrs Hoare and through this astute move became the proprietor of the *King's Head.* One of William's daugh-ters, Sarah, became related by marriage to William Billingsley, the celebrated Derby China painter, and to William Wheeldon, another, whilst the other daughter, Anne, married one of Billingsley's former colleagues, the talented George Robertson.

In 1791, therefore, William Wallis's widow Felicia took the inn over, but was quickly supplanted by her brother-in-law Alderman John Wallis (1776-1821). He was a promi-nent Tory, the founder of the Derby True Blue Club (which, inevitably, met at the inn) and the All Saints' leader in the Derby Shrovetide football. He also ran the *Black Boy,* St Peter's Street, until 1817. In 1801 he married Sarah, the daughter of yet another China painter from the Derby factory, John Yates, himself a landlord, in retirement, of the *Seven Stars,* Nottingham Road. She died in 1821, leaving four sons and two daughters, and her husband, true to family precedent, also died relatively young in the October, when an advertisement appeared informing the public that the 'business [is] continuing for the benefit of the late Mr John Wallis's family.'

This left the 19-year-old eldest son, William (II) Wallace

Wallis (1802-1859) in charge. Fortunately, he was also endowed with talent, an acute business sense and boundless energy. He decided that he couldn't run both inn and the coaching business, so in 1829 he let the inn to one Isaac Spencer and retained the posting and coaching business. Spencer held a Coronation dinner here in 1838, and it became the venue for auctions. W.W. Wallis married twice, leaving children by both marriages, his first wife Sarah (*nee* Wightman) being painted on a Derby porcelain plaque by William Corden around 1830. In the event, Isaac Spencer soon handed over to William's brother George Wallis III, who also took the *King's Head* over from his homonymous uncle around 1846. W. W. Wallis's third brother, John (1809-1885) who was latterly of Gerard Street, was listed as a publican, but so far his pub has proved elusive. The fourth brother, Robert (1810-1871) became landlord of the *Green Man* at Ashbourne, where he was succeeded by three of his sons in succession to 1898. He was ancestor of the late but much liked Dick Wallis (1931-1984) of the *Derby Evening Telegraph*.

William Wallis II, however, was also shrewd enough to foresee the rapid decline of the coaching trade when the railways came, so he reinvented himself as the booking and freight consignment agent for the Midland Railway, and initiated an omnibus service from the new Trijunct Station to the Market Place from 1840. He also ran a large number of wagon services and was for a time landlord – of all unlikely inns – the *Milton's Head* in Ossian Street, conceivably connected with his omnibus enterprises. His second son, Percy succeeded him as the MR's agent, and his eldest son, Alfred (1833-1918) later became editor of the *Derby Mercury*. In the 1900s the inn was owned by James Eadie & Co, but leased to Zachary Smith's of Shardlow before Marston's took it on in 1922. Yet by 1929 it had been acquired by Offiler's and latterly, therefore, Bass. It was closed in 1967 and demolished the following year to make way for the Inner Ring Road in 1968.
DM 13 & 20/8/1773, 15/3/1776, 19/12/1777, 5/6/1817, 31/10/1821, 11/11/1829 & 4/7 & 25/10/1838.

NEW INN
28 Russell Street (corner Gilman Street)   by 1874-1964
An Offilers' pub by 1937; cleared, with the decline of the numerous foundries in the area, 1968, having closed in 1964.

NEW INN
See CRYSTAL PALACE; ST HELEN'S INN

NEWLANDS
See DRILL HALL VAULTS

New Market, Albert Street, 1972 awaiting demolition.

NEW MARKET VAULTS*

27, Albert Street (Tenant Street; Market Street)
by 1873-1971

Opened in a building very much in the style of G.H. Sheffield, in brick with a triple arcaded ground floor with twin round headed lights above and a muscular bracket cornice at the eaves, all with keyblocks and brackets richly carved, probably by Joseph Barlow Robinson of Derby, between 1862 and 1874 on 'Mill Ground' Albert Street as *Market Vaults*. Mill Ground was the name for the row of buildings on the north side of Strutt's 1793 'fireproof' calico mill, burnt down in 1852 and (finally) in 1876. It seems to have had a music hall, which was damaged by fire in 1873, when Samuel Spencer was licensee, but which was still going in 1888. It was renamed *Albert Vaults* by that year, becoming *Spencer's Vaults* (after Samuel) not long afterwards. By 1910, however, it had become – and remained – the *New Market Vaults* after the Market Hall, behind, completed in 1866. It backed on to Market Street, and was owned throughout by the corporation. Closed 1971 and demolished 1972; some fittings were rescued by the museum, most currently dressing up the Guildhall bar.
DM 25/5/1873

NEW MARKET*

54 East Street (corner Albion Street)
by 1874-1967

An adjoining cottage was added in 1939 to expand this free house opened to serve the new Corn Exchange, hence the name. Probably it was previously the *Don Cossack*, which inn was listed at no. 55, conceivably the usual compiler's inaccuracy, and where there was an anonymous beer house listed from 1846. Sold to Samuel Allsopp between 1910 and 1919 and brewing on the premises as late as 1928. It closed as a free house in April 1967 and was replaced by the *Trident*, Albion Street.

(NEW) STATION (ARMS) (INN)*

7 Clifton Street
by 1878-1945

A beerhouse owned in 1937 by Ind Coope & Allsopp's brewery. The name refers to the Midland Station, but the 'New', added after 1878 when it was merely the *Station Arms*, distinguishing it from the earlier *Station Inn*, Midland Road. Closed by 1952.

(NEW) STATION (HOTEL)*

123 (50) Nottingham Road (corner Clark Street)
by 1874

The Nottingham Road station (Midland Railway) was opened in 1856, and this inn was built about a decade later to serve it. By 1937 under the aegis of Ind Coope & Allsopp. Acquired in a very rundown state in 1994 by Sycamore Brewery and in June 1997 renamed *The Tavern*, on the whim of a new landlord, Derek Beaumont, who wanted to recreate the atmosphere of his previous pub, the *Sitwell Tavern*.

NEW VAULTS
See DRILL HALL VAULTS

NEW ZEALAND ARMS

2 Langley Street (corner Peel Street)
by 1860

The entire area to the south of Ashbourne Road at this point is known as New Zealand from the name of a farm on the former Markeaton estate, probably renamed in honour of the Treaty of Waitangi (1840) or earlier, after its discovery by Captain Cook. Thus the inn was named after the area which, strangely, lacks a New Zealand Street! Spirit licence refused in 1874, and for sale in 1877. A Stretton's House for very many years, appropriately so, for the brewery was situated nearby in Surrey Street. In the 1990s it was taken over by Festival Inns and Taverns, who also ran the *Wardwick Tavern* and the *White Swan* (Littleover).
DM 26/8/1874 & 30/5/1877

NOAH'S ARK**

25 (17) Morledge
by 1719-1919

The building was later 18th century, and the inn went back to 1719 as the deeds to the *Cossack* demonstrate. It may have been named after the publication of the tale of the

New Zealand Arms, Langley Street, 2002.

Noah's Ark, Morledge, 1970s.

coin-clipper and forger Noah Bullock, the Restoration forger of good birth who carried out his illicit trade on a houseboat tied up on the Derwent, and who was spared the gallows by Sir Simon Degge. However, as Bullock's children were all baptised in the wrong parish, it is likely that their floating home was moored nearer to St Mary's Bridge.

By 1827 it was run by James Bull, followed before 1843 by his son, Samuel. But in that year it is listed as one of two *Noah's Arks* adjacent, for another inn of this name was then being run by one William Tarr at No.16, an extraordinary situation which continued for no less than 30 years, until just before 1874, when this inn was renamed (probably by migration from East Street (see *(Don) Cossack*) of Joseph Parker, who renamed this the *Cossack* sometimes adding *Arms* and *Inn*. The newer *Noah's Ark* (called, no doubt for distinction, the *Old Noah's Ark* in 1852) thereupon continued, but this one, as the *Cossack*, survived only until 1919 when it closed to make way for the enlarged *White Horse* (see next entry).

For sale in 1818 with brew house, brewing equipment

and 150 gallons of fine strong ale and again in 1864-5, when it was advertised with 'a small brewery attached'. A sparring bout took place here in 1860, one of the contestants being someone called Posh Price – which sounds worryingly familiar! It was rebuilt and enlarged in 1893.
DM 23/4/1818, 22/5/1864 & 22/2/1865

(OLD) NOAH'S ARK**

23 (16) Morledge   *by 1843*
Between 1835 and 1843 this inn was established bearing exactly the same name as that adjacent (see above) and the two ran thus side by side until just prior to 1874 when the original *Noah's Ark* became the *Cossack*. However, one concession to pre-empt confusion was that this inn prefixed its name with 'Old' in 1852. In 1891 and again from 1908 it was merely listed as an unnamed beer retailership on licence, run by William Sewell and latterly by his widow Ellen. In 1919, the former *Bishop Blaze* (from 1875 *White Horse*) at no. 27 (18) was demolished, along with the *Cossack*, formerly the original *Noah's Ark*, by Pountains to build the present *White Horse (Court House)* and the second *Noah's Ark* survived to be acquired in 1926 by Home Ales, refronted with false half-timbering over dark green ceramic tiles. For most of the inter-war years, however, it was still listed as a beer-retailership on licence and rarely named, not obtaining a full licence until World War Two. The landlord from 1940 to 1945 was Arthur Trueman, formerly of the *Horse & Jockey* Somercotes; he was succeeded for the decade up to 1955 by his son-in-law Harold Read (1910-1999).
DET Bygones 20/4/2002

Normanton Hotel, Lower Dale Road, c.1904.

NORMANTON HOTEL*

1 Lower Dale Road (corner of Pear Tree Road)   *by 1878*
Large, rather forbidding corner hotel at a busy junction in a once salubrious part of town. Passed from Stretton's to Ind Coope, which latter firm had it on lease before the amalgamation. An elaborate five-branch street lamp standard, like that once at the Five Lamps and probably from the same local foundry, once stood in the road outside, now long since

vanished. In August 2002, after a police raid where several people were arrested on suspicion of offences against the immigration and drugs laws, the licence was revoked.

NORTHERN BRIDGE INN
See GREAT NORTHERN BRIDGE INN

NORTHERN STAR*

153 Bridge Street (corner (24) Lodge Lane) by 1822-1898
Behind this inn lay eight tenements called Star Yard, although the inn was never listed simply as the *Star*. In 1827 this address (24 Lodge Lane) was that of a pub called the *Old Windmill,* suggesting that it was renamed subsequently or revived. Such a name – the epithet 'old' clearly implying that it pre-dated the Willow Row establishment of that name – rather suggests that there may have been a windmill on the higher part of Nuns' Green here, bordering Duffield Road; no doubt when it was swept away, the pub, established (by inference) prior to 1822, was renamed after the celestial object. Latterly it was an Alton's House, but had become an off-licence by the Edwardian period, and was later still the home of Ernie Redfern.
Palmer (1996) (ii).

NOTTINGHAM ARMS*

58 (21) Bridge Gate (corner Court No.5) by 1818-1925
Situated halfway down the street on the south side, and quite possibly dating back to the mid-13th century when the thoroughfare was first pitched along the course of the former Town Ditch. There is a tradition that pubs on the road from one town to another take their name from the destination settlement. It cannot be without significance that on St Michael's Lane stood the *Nottingham Castle*, for that road was the route to Nottingham from Derby before the bridge was built and Bridge Gate made. However, an alternative suggestion is most persuasive. Up to 1847 (when he died) it was owned by William Billingsley's nephew William Wheeldon (1789-1847), also involved with the China Factory and a farmer and maltster on Nottingham Road. His son, George, founded the brewery there later, and his brother, John had owned the *Chesterfield Arms* also on Nottingham Road. The Billingsley connection raises the possibility that this inn was the former *Sir John Falstaff* renamed by the Nottingham-Road-dwelling Wheeldons. Rebuilt many times and closed about 1930. The arms of Nottingham are: *gules a cross raguly vert between three crowns or* – a classic example of arms breaching the heraldic laws of tincture.

NOTTINGHAM ARMS*

111 London Road (corner of (109) Litchurch Street) 1854
Tom Wheeldon was granted a licence here in 1854, and this beerhouse latterly (1937) was owned by Offilers' and which obtained a full licence in 1950. In February 1990, after extensive alterations (*ie* total gutting) it reopened as the *Florence Nightingale*, the name inspired by the proximity of the Derbyshire Royal Infirmary, in front of which stands Countess Feodora v. Gleichen's statue of the great lady. The original name may have arisen like that of the inn in Bridge Gate, for by 1874 the Midland Station was the 'gateway' to the next town to the east. If the name is revived again it should be by the bus station!
DM 13/9/1854

NOTTINGHAM CARRIER
See NOTTINGHAM POST

Nottingham Castle Inn, St Michael's Lane, c.1947.

NOTTINGHAM CASTLE

12 Queen Street (corner St Michael's Lane) by 1550-1962
The earliest fabric of the inn lay in St Michael's Lane, a timber-framed range of 16th-century date (borne out by a deed of c.1550) incorporating even earlier parts, including a pair of baseless crucks. The establishment of the inn may go back to before the mid-13th century (see above,

Nottingham Castle, St Michael's Lane.

Nottingham Arms), when the lane was connected to the old Nottingham Road via a ford called the Causey. In the late 17th century or early 18th, another range was erected facing Queen Street, in brick, and it was in this portion in which the public rooms latterly lay, the older part becoming a store, brewhouse and offices. In 1781, Henry Tomlinson put its lease up for sale, announcing that he was moving to the *Tiger* – presumably that in the same street. A freehouse, which brewed on the premises until sold by the executors of Harry Groome, who took over from his father, John, in 1941 and who died in 1959; his brother, Alfred, was the brewer. It closed in 1962 and was demolished almost two years later, for no apparent reason: the site remained empty until 1988.

NOTTINGHAM CASTLE*

(12) Wellington Street, Litchurch   *by 1857-1868*
Listed anonymously in 1857 and 1862 as a beer house but for sale and so named as a going concern in 1868. Later converted into a residence, lived in for three generations of the Bradshaw family from around 1900.

NOTTINGHAM HOUSE
See TALBOT

NOTTINGHAM POST

Leather Lane (Market Place)   *by 1749-1778*
Known in 1761 as the *Nottingham Carrier*, and possibly a place from which fly-wagons departed for Nottingham. Sold by James Holme in 1751. Possibly the *Crane* renamed and later the *Vine*; the dates dovetail well.
DM 16/2/1751

NUNS' INN
See THREE NUNS'

OAK
See BRITISH OAK, OLD OAK

OAK & ACORN

Unknown location   *1791*
Listed in the *Universal British Directory* 1791, but without a locale, and nowhere else; no doubt renamed.

OAST HOUSE

Foresters' Park Centre, Sinfin Lane   *1989*
New pub/hotel opened in 1989 and designed by Michael Sassoon to incorporate a pair of oast towers with typical conical tops: looks bizarrely like a piece of Herefordshire or Kent plonked down in the middle of the Foresters' Park, the site of the former Sinfin Lane Barracks, headquarters of the Sherwood Foresters Regiment (45th/95th).

OATSHEAF
See BLACK'S HEAD

ODDFELLOWS' ARMS**

8 East Street (Bag Lane)   *by 1850-1852*
No doubt one of the other inns with no recorded street number in this street, probably renamed when a meeting place of a local lodge of the Oddfellows friendly society. Recorded anonymously at this address in 1850.

ODDFELLOWS' ARMS*

13 (18) King Street   *by 1833-1907*
Named after another friendly society, the Grand United Order of Oddfellows, whose arms were, as usual with these institutions, unauthorised. In *Reliquary*, Jewitt contemptuously remarks of the arms: "They... are the most absurd concoction conceivable and are worthy of no other name." True to its name, the Oddfellows' actually met here; the Anniversary of the Good Intent Lodge of Oddfellows being held here in 1837. For sale in 1868, it was run from 1873 by Archibald Loates, formerly of the *Crown & Cushion*,

Chapel Street (where his extraordinary family are described) and he remained there until 1888, when his son Rowland – appropriately an ex-brewer's apprentice – took over for a while. It was closed after pressure from the Temperance Society in 1907 and the building gobbled up by a new Co-op store shortly afterwards.
DM 6/9/1837

[OLD
prefix: if not listed below, see under next word of title]

OLDE AVESBURY
See ARBORETUM

OLD ENGLISH GENTLEMAN*
62 (59) Grove Street (corner Normanton Road)
by 1840-1965
A separate pub called by this name existed at 59 Leonard Street in 1857, in which year the Grove Street address was not given; it is possible that the premises migrated and later moved back. Owned by Pountain's in 1937, but closed around 1938, only to be reprieved by the outbreak of World War Two. Headquarters of the Derby Anglers' Association post-war and previously of the Boer War Veterans' Association. The separate brewhouse survived as a shop until 10 January 1986, and the inn was still standing in the December of that year. In 1868 human remains were found on the site during alterations *(DM 22 July 1868)*, probably a burial associated with the Lazar Hospital of St Leonard which flourished in the 14th century nearby. The name comes from the traditional song *The Fine Old English Gentleman* – allegedly sung outside the house at the opening of the Arboretum of Joseph Strutt – and the sign in the 1870s depicted Strutt (1765-1844) the munificent donor. A doubt arises, because the song was not current before 1841, when its composer, Henry Russell (1812-1900) – as Ivor Clissold perceptively pointed out – returned to England. Thus there would seem no doubt that the inn was renamed immediately following his death, not in 1840.
DET 24/9/1948 & 3/9/1986

OLD HOUSE AT HOME
73 (12) Large's Street   *by 1874-1897*
Traditionally-named inn about which little is known except that Joseph Collumbell was the landlord in 1878 and that it closed in 1897.

OLD INSTITUTE**
Wardwick   *2000*
Established in the former Mechanics' Institute by Hobgoblin Inns, for which the Derby Civic Society gave them a Highly Commended award in their annual George

Old Institute, Wardwick, 2002

Old Institute, Wardwick, 2000.

Larkin/ABCD Awards for their refurbishment. The building (listed Grade II) was erected to the designs of William Mansfield Cooper in 1836 in a bold Greek revival style, with a stone façade. Inside was a spectacular lecture/exhibition hall, with a barrel-vaulted ceiling below which was a copy in stucco of the Pan-Athenaic frieze from the Parthenon around the cornice, itself supported on Ionic pilasters. The east end was lit with a large Diocletian window, and that side – since 1878 overlooking The Strand – was stuccoed. The Institute was founded by a group of philanthropic Derby gentlemen in the 1820s – William and Joseph Strutt, Douglas Fox and Richard Forester French – to help give the working man and artisans a chance of self-improvement. In 1879-82, the widening of the Wardwick caused that front to be demolished and replaced with a new façade in Victorian classical, again in stone, by George Henry Sheffield and Arthur Coke-Hill. It lost its pre-eminence with the 1870 Education Act, and after World War Two, the lecture hall was penetrated from end to end by a gloomy shopping arcade called the Haymarket. The restoration was therefore comprehensive and has restored to the city one of its finest interior spaces.
DM 10/11/1859; Glover (1831/33) II 458

OLD OAK (TREE)*

29 (16) Agard Street   *by 1833-1912*
The name in 1843 was merely the *Old Oak*, in 1850 the *Oak* and a single mention of an Agard Street pub called the *Royal Oak* almost certainly refers to this house. Latterly owned by Home Ales, but not listed after World War One. Traditional, rather than a local toponym, coming from the poem *A Song to the Oak, the Brave Old Oak*.
DM 1/10/1873

OLD VAULTS*

18 (4) St Helen's Street   *by 1846-1964*
Allegedly founded in 1842 but not listed until 1846 when it appears as an unnamed beer house. Owned by Alderman W.H. Marsden (Mayor 1892) at the turn of the century but sold by his executors to Nottingham Brewery Co. In the 1920s it was known as *Minute's Vaults*, a corruption of the name of a 19th century landlord, Thomas A. Minnitt, who replaced the previous name, the *Joiners' Arms* (before that it had been since 1846, the *Foresters' Arms*) with his own as *Minnitt's Old Vaults*, 1862. In 1873 he was also of the *Queen's Hotel*, Crompton Street, 'wine and spirit merchant, and brewer' and he was still the proprietor in

1878. At closure in 1964, when Sam & Florrie Sharpe were licensees, it still had a six-day licence. It was then full of repositioned 17th-century panelling (some of which survives in situ) and was whitewashed all over. Thereafter it was absorbed into the works of Messrs Batterby & Hefford, who occupied the former marble works adjacent. Due for demolition in 2002.
DET 13/9/1983, *DM* 15/10/1873 & 27/6/1877

O'NEILL'S
See SARACEN'S HEAD

(NEW) ORANGE TREE*

70 (1) Burton Road   *by 1818-1874*
Only known with this name from 1874 and thus possibly renamed, but an unnamed beer house listed at the address from 1835. Most inns of this name derive from the adoption of this symbol and colour by the supporters of King William III (William of Orange), not in those days confined to Ulster. 'New' no doubt because, despite the paucity of record, the inn of this name in Bridge Gate pre-dated it. It was called the *Ordnance Arms* previously – so recorded between 1818 and 1834, when it was for sale – from its proximity to James Wyatt's spectacular Ordnance Depot of 1806. This was de-commissioned in the 1820s, becoming a silk mill, hence, ultimately no doubt, the change of name. The Depot, of course, was latterly (and appropriately in this context) Offiler's Brewery. Demolished, we are told, to make way for Christ Church School playground.
DM 12/3/1834

An 1874 detail of the Old Vaults, St Helen's Street and Queen's Vaults, Crompton Street.

(OLD) ORANGE TREE*

10 Bridge Gate   *by 1835-1898*

The name may derive as above or more likely be a misunderstanding of the badge of Chesterfield: *a pomegranate tree*; Bridge Gate was also the route to Chesterfield. Probably long established before its appearance on record. Listed anonymously in 1850, it was part of a large grocery business as a beer retailership on licence by 1898 and was closed down shortly afterwards.

ORDNANCE ARMS

See (NEW) ORANGE TREE

OSTRICH

See SHAKESPEARE

OSTRICH

St Peter's Parish   *by 1763-1770*

Situated at 'the upper end of St Peter's Parish', presumably near The Spot. Nothing further known and probably renamed.

OUTA MONGOLIA

See BOATERS

PACK HORSE

Bridge Gate   *by 1748-1768*

Mentioned only twice; the name is redolent of the standard method of freight transport before the canal came.

DM 1/7/1748 & 8/5/1768

PALMERSTON ARMS*

14 Back Parker Street   *by 1855-1925*

The sign derives from the arms of Sir Henry Temple, KG, GCB, PC, MP, 3rd Viscount Palmerston (in the Irish Peerage) MP 1807-65, and Prime Minister 1855-8 and 1859-65. He was born in 1784 and died in office, a popular figure, and hence the establishment of the inn in his first year in power seems entirely likely. He was brother-in-law of Lord Melbourne, and lived in Derbyshire for some years. The inn was never more than a beerhouse, being to let as a going concern in 1855 for sale a decade later. The last landlord was Ernest Chambers in 1925, but it was an off-licence by the following year under William Wilkes.

DM 25/4/1855 & 6/10/1865

PARK FOUNTAIN*

1 Henry Street (corner North Street)   *by 1835-1876*

Probably named after a long-forgotten feature of St Helen's House's Park, on which the Strutt's Park estate (of which Henry Street is a part) was laid out, over the 80 years from 1819. The site of Edward Street lies across a sizable lake, and the fountain may have fed it, possibly via the hydraulic ram devised by John Whitehurst FRS, at the behest of William Emes, the landscaper. Listed anonymously in 1835, 1846 and 1850, the inn was destroyed to make way for the cutting, which carried the Great Northern Railway through the area. The *Great Northern Inn*, nearby, was probably built by the company as a replacement.

PARK TAVERN*

85 (38) Park Street (Park Lane)   *by 1846-1951*

Small inn named after the park of Castlefields, on which Park Street – originally Park Lane – was laid out. Listed anonymously in 1846 but for sale and named in 1848 as 'a substantial and well accustomed public house'. In Offilers' hands 1937, and closed in the 1950s.

DM 13/9/1848

PARLIAMENT HOUSE (INN)*

114 (37) Stockbrook Street (corner St Luke's Street)   *by 1857-1977*

A beerhouse which may have taken the inspiration for its name (as perhaps did nearby Parliament Street) from the passing of the 1867 Reform Act, although it was listed at this address anonymously in 1857; could it have had another name when first established? It was named and for sale in 1869, and was acquired by Ind Coope & Allsopp by 1935 when that firm did extensive interior alterations. Cleared in the late 1970s under the St Luke's clearance scheme. It was granted a full licence in 1951.

DM 24/11/1869

PEACOCK*

87 (34, 71) Nottingham Road (Navigation Row)   *by 1818*

Pretty little stone built inn of 18th-century date, although not recorded as an inn until 1818, when the address was given as Navigation Row. It has belonged to the Liversage Trustees since its sale in 1837, having been let six years before. There was a sale held there in 1878. In 1934 it was leased to Marston's, who still run it. The Peacock is the crest of the Manners, Dukes of Rutland, and was anciently associated with incorruptibility and has been, in consequence, a mediaeval symbol of the Resurrection.

DM 16/11/1831, 11/1/1837 & 9/10/1878

PEACOCK**

St Peter's Parish   *by 1775-1776*

Situated 'next door Mr William Squire'.

DM 1/1/1776

PEAR TREE (TAVERN)

193 Harrington Street   *by 1883*

Established on part of the former Pear Tree Farm,

Pear Tree Inn, St Thomas's Road.

Normanton, over which streets began to spread from 1865, in 1883. Originally only a beerhouse, but later extended to include a house with workshop and carriage entrance next door. Allsopp's were granted a full licence in 1939, which persuaded them to rebuild the ground floor of this two-storey stuccoed pub in a symmetrical form with three light mullioned windows either side of the entrance. It was previously in the hands of Stretton's. Since 1999, the *Apna Punjabi*.

PEAR TREE (INN)

155 St Thomas's Road (corner Rutland Street)   by 1883
Named, confusingly perhaps, for the same reason as that above. A purpose-built two-storey brick corner pub, originally Marston's. Later owned by Stretton's, who pulled it down and rebuilt it as a brand new pub in 1934 with a Art Deco stuccoed shell, with slightly turreted angle with vertical emphasis, tripartite steel-framed windows and horizontal stripes applied to the upper storey.

PELICAN*

174-178 Abbey Street (corner Stockbrook Street)by 1855-1979

A two-and-a-half-storey brick inn with glazing bars to its windows and rusticated keyblocks, built around 1825 and

Pelican Inn, Abbey Street, late 1940s.

opened between 1849 and 1857; it was for sale in 1855 merely as 'well accustomed' but not 'old established'. By 1864 a bowling alley had been added to its attractions and it was again for sale in 1870. It probably took its name from the arms of the Cantrell family of King's Newton and Alvaston Fields, who owned some property in this area: *Argent a pelican in her piety sable*. Anciently, the pelican pecking her breast to feed her starving young was a symbol of Our Lord's Ultimate Sacrifice. Later owned by Stretton's (later Ind Coope), who rebuilt it in 1929, the ground floor receiving paired windows separated by blank panels under a plain but bold cornice. Closed and demolished in 1979 due to its presence on the supposed course of the seemingly chimerical ring road extension.

DM 10/10/1855; 3/8/1864 & 19/10/1870

PELICAN

Full Street   *–1756–*

The only mention is in 1756, when it was to let, had a brewhouse and was owned by Cornelius Mousley, ancestor of the opulent attorney, Alderman William Eaton Mousley, last owner of Exeter House. It was situated somewhere between the *Horse & Trumpet* and the Market Place. Named after the crest of the Buxton (later Buckston) family of Bradbourne and Sutton-on-the-Hill, which had extensive interests in Derby in the early 18th century. George Buxton had a malting business in 1705, in Walker Lane and he was then owner of the *Bull's Head*, Queen Street.

DM 7/5/1756

PENNINE HOTEL

Macklin Street   *1966*

A not over-large, but tall and hideous modernist hotel set in an unenviable situation. Opened with high expectations and standards in December 1966, but now much favoured for coach tour stopovers, Rotarians' bashes and suchlike. Named after the mountains, the southern end of which lie in Derbyshire. Extensively refurbished in 1997, but with no appreciable effect on the ambience.

PENNY BLACK

See LORD NAPIER

PERIQUITO

See GABLES

PHEASANT**

Bridge Gate   *by 1829-1858*

A 'well accustomed' pub for sale in 1858, at which 12 years previously the Pheasant Friendly Society of 50 members sat down to their annual dinner, even in the 1820s it was the venue for this group. A lack of other references to this inn suggests that it was probably renamed at some stage.

DM 10/6/1846, 25/8/1858; Glover (1831/33) II. 539

(OLD) PHEASANT*

112 (82) Bridge Street   *by 1818-1961*

The house is one of those built shortly after the street was pitched by the Improvement Commission in 1793. It was certainly adapted as a pub before 1835 and probably before 1818, for the landlord of the unlocated *Ring o' Bells* in the same street was, in 1827, one Samuel Gaskell

The former Pheasant Inn, Bridge Street, pictured in February 2002.

– the same man who appears as landlord on the first mention of *The Pheasant* in 1835. Perhaps the colossal mill to its south blocked the sound of the bells of All Saints', prompting the name change! It was offered for sale in 1849, and in 1858 it was bought by Thomas Bridgett & Co., of the mills.

Although it was offered for sale again in 1869, it was in fact not sold until 1872, when Bridgett's disposed of it to a Mr Ryde for £660. Ryde's kinsman, William Hobson, had been the landlord since before 1862, and he and his family ran it until about the end of the century. The name is probably not heraldic, but bucolic or sporting. There was brewing on the premises and it was once tied to Zachary Smith's brewery, but by the 1930s to Offiler's. In 1961 it was purchased by Claude Lilley (then co-proprietor of the mills) and he closed it in October that year, converting it into offices and storage, which it has been ever since. With the mills' closure it stands a chance of being reconverted into a dwelling, possibly for students.

DM 24/10/1849, 25/8/1858 & 15/9/1869; Rykneld Tean MSS courtesy Peter Billson, Esq.

PHEASANT

57 (27) Traffic Street   *by 1857-1935*
Latterly owned by Ind Coope & Allsopp, but lost to street widening in 1935. The licence went (7 January 1936) to the *Blue Boy*, Chaddesden.

PHOENIX**

201 Normanton Road   *by 2001*
So named because the previous establishment, an Indian restaurant, was burnt. As the Phoenix it is an Indian restaurant and also bar, so presumably it falls within the remit of this work. A recent application (March 2002) to adapt it as a lap-dancing club may get approval which, if successful, would remove it from qualifying as a pub, however.

PIG & TRUFFLE
See SPOTTED HORSE

PIG OF LEAD

Unknown locale   *-1872-*
Mentioned in *Reliquary* XIII (1872) 55 as existing in Derby. Named after the staple diet of Cox's lead works which were opened in 1809, so possibly in Tenant Street or the Morledge.

PIZZA & PASTA
See GOLDEN EAGLE

P.J. PEPPER'S
See IRON GATES

PLAISTERERS' ARMS*

Queen Street   *-1755-*
In 1755, David Keane, a former London poulterer, kept it. It lay opposite St Michael's Church. Probably renamed. Named after the armorial bearings of the Worshipful Company of Plaisterers, incorporated by Charter 10 March 1500-1, and arms granted 20 January 1545-6. The blazon of the shield is: *Azure on a chevron engrailed argent a rose gules budded or stalked and leaved vert between two fleurs-de-lys of the field in chief a trowel fessewise between two plasterers' hammers palewise all of the second handled of the fourth in base a plasterer's brush of four knots tied of the second handled of the fourth.* Plaisterer is, of course, an archaic rendering of plasterer. The location suggests that it may be identifiable with the slightly later *Tiger*.
DM 13/6/1755.

PLASTERERS' ARMS*

19 Siddals Lane   *by 1827-1862*
Siddals Lane of course, later became Siddals Road but was originally a drift road which traversed The Siddals, a parcel of water meadows beside the Derwent. The inn was probably renamed, and was listed only as an anonymous beer house in 1846/50 and 1862.

PLOUGH

Cornmarket   *before 1744*
A shop 'formerly known as the sign of the *Plough*' was for sale 31 August 1744. A nicely authenticated example of a phenomenon to be seen increasingly in the later 19th and early 20th centuries.
DM 31/8/1744

(OLD) PLOUGH INN*

33 (71) London Street (Road)   *by 1823-1898*
This inn seems to be identical with a *Plough* in St Peter's Street, which has matching dates. It was separated from the *Louis Napoleon* only by one shop and the Methodist New Connexion chapel. For sale in 1824, but closed around 1900 to make way for the expansion of the Midland Furniture Store at No.31.

PLOUGH

44 Nottingham Road   *1846-1916*
An inn which long brewed on the premises and was a free house. Another account claims that it was opened 1868, refuted by the report into the unsolved murder of Spondon man, Enoch Stone, who left this inn on his fatal return journey home in June 1856. The deeds established that it closed in 1916 and became a house, which it still is. An early 19th-century stone building of some charm. A hearsay account has it remaining in business to 1922. Owned by the Liversage Trust.
DM 25/6/1856

PLOUGH**

Osmaston Street (Road)   *by 1835-1843*
A beerhouse recorded but twice; possibly later the *Queen's Vaults*.

PLOUGH
See also SEVEN STARS

PLUMBERS' ARMS*

32 (28) East Street (Bag Lane)   *by 1833-1885*
East Street had only just been so named when this inn was demolished in 1885 to make way for new shops; Bag Lane is the usual address. Named after the Worshipful Company of Plumbers, incorporated 12 April 1611 but granted arms 24 November 1588. These were: *or a chevron between in chief a Jacob's staff fessewise sable between two sounding leads proper and in base a water level of the second on the*

Plumber's Arms, Bag Lane (now East Street), 1885. The Barley Mow is also visible in the distance to the left.

chevron two soldering irons in saltire between a cutting knife on the dexter and a shaver on the sinister argent. In 1835 the inn at this address is listed as the *Jolly Boatman* – either an ephemeral renaming or a colloquial usage mistakenly accepted by the compiler of the directory (but *qv*). This inn was probably the one closed in 1887 and moved by Sir Edwin Ann, and thereafter renamed the *Football Inn.*

PLUME OF FEATHERS
Morledge   *–1761–*

Only mentioned in Sir Harry Harpur's 'hospitality' list. The name derived from the well-known emblem of the Prince of Wales, in this case, presumably, 'Poor Fred', who died in 1751 during the lifetime of his father George II. This probably establishes when the pub was named.

PORTLAND ARMS
89 Prince's Street (corner Pear Tree Street) by 1895-1977

A beerhouse, originally on the corner, but rebuilt by Home Ales in 1930 with full licence. The rebuilt edifice included an extra cottage on the Prince's Street side and no less than three in Pear Tree Street, all brought together behind a coat of stucco, ground floor tiling and heavy modillion top cornice with deep frieze below in which the name was set out also in stucco. Named after the armorial bearings of the Dukes of Portland, considerable Derbyshire landowners.

POST OFFICE HOTEL
See SPOTTED HORSE

PRINCE ALBERT
High Street   *–1862–*

Only listed in 1862, and named in memory of the Prince Consort (HSH Prince Albrecht v Saxe-Coburg und Gotha) who died in 1861. Quite possibly the same establishment as *The Allies* (*qv*), swiftly renamed thus. High Street seems

hardly likely to have been able to support three pubs, even in 1862!

PRINCE ARTHUR
See JOINERS' ARMS

PRINCE LEOPOLD
See FOUNTAIN

PRINCE OF WALES*
8 John Street   *by 1846-1903*

Named after Queen Victoria's eldest son, Edward (1841-1910), Prince of Wales from a month old, and later Edward VII. This beerhouse may thus go back to that year; before 1869 it was listed unnamed. It was for sale in 1872, was owned by Stretton's in 1903 but closed by 1908 when it became Mrs Sarah Ann Pymm's laundry, continuing for over 20 years.
DET Bygones 28/5/2002; DM 19/6/1872

PRINCE OF WALES
73 (5) London Road   *by 1874-1937*

A small beerhouse very close to the (*Royal*) *Telegraph*, and which was demolished in 1937 to allow for the setting back of the latter for road widening; then the property of Hanson's.

Prince of Wales, Whitecross Street, 1967.

PRINCE OF WALES*
97 Whitecross Street   *by 1862-1975*

Built as a tradesman's house and yard, with limited stabling reached through a carriage arch of gauged brick. The fan-lit front door windows with rusticated stone lintels and glazing bars, suggest a date in the 1820s. The arch was by 1910 blocked to form additional accommodation and the remaining ground floor window altered. Owned by Pountain's in 1937. Cleared in the late 1970s, it was the subject of a CPO as early as March 1967.

Prince Regent, Regent Street, 1938.

PRINCE REGENT*

57 Regent Street   *by 1857-1965*

As the inn was named after the Prince Regent, who became George IV in 1820, and the street was pitched between 1810 and 1820, it would seem logical that the inn dated from that time too, yet it is not listed until 1857, and then only as an unnamed beer-house. Most likely, therefore, it was so named after the street. Owned by Stretton's in 1937; beer brewed on the premises until 1949. Cleared in the late 1960s to accommodate plans to expand the Derbyshire Royal Infirmary.

PUBLIC HOUSE

See QUEEN'S (HEAD) HOTEL

PUNCH BOWL*

53 (13, 20) Nottingham Road   *1758-1908*

A delightful brick-built vernacular cottage built gable end to the street on the east side of Nottingham Road, built as an inn in 1758, no doubt to serve the workforce of the then newly-established china works. The name cleverly couples drinking with a particular sort of product of the factory. Conceivably to be identified with the *China Punch Bowl*, (although both are listed in 1823) but it is possible that the latter added the word 'China' to differentiate two separate establishments. Venue of the meetings of the Punch Bowl Dividend Society and the Hope Lodge of the Oddfellows (friendly societies) in the 1820s. Closed through pressure by the Derby Temperance Society upon the Licensing Magistrates in 1908 and became Punch Bowl Cottage, today a remarkable survival amidst the concrete of the inner ring road.

Glover (1831/33) II. 539

PUNCH BOWL

Sadler Gate   *by 1755-1777*

Name first occurs in a deed of 1755. Probably named for the same reasons as above and no doubt renamed. In the later 17th century, punch was the drink of the Whigs, 'sack, claret and canary [ale]' being that of the Tories. Pubs so named were thus originally favoured by local Whigs, although with the passage of time, the political significance of the name became lost.

DM 30/1/1756 & 14/11/1777

PYMM'S*

Clock Yard, Friar Gate   *1987-2000*

Opened in the yard of a mill, once Robert Bridgart & Co, builders, founded adjacent to the *Wheel's* bowling green in the late 18th century by the Denstone family (cf. *Mitre*) and ultimately Joseph Parker & Sons. The developer was local architect Derek Montague of 1 Vernon Street and it opened May 1987. James Pymm was a wheelwright working on the site in 1826; the celebrated drink is spelt with an 'I'. Sold to a new owner in 2000, and since subject of alterations, it became the *Courtyard*.

QUARN TAVERN*

34 Quarn Street (corner Parker Street)   *by 1857-1963*

A modest free house recorded as an anonymous beer house in 1857 and first mentioned by name two years later. By the 1930s, when Charles Henderson was brewing on the premises, it had been leased by John Hair & Son's Melbourne brewery. It was named after the old name for Quarndon, near Derby, rather than the village in Leicestershire, which is spelt differently. Closed and cleared under a CPO, 1963.   *DM* 28/9/1859

QUEEN ADELAIDE*

9-11 (2-3) Canal Street   *by 1846-1960s*

A beerhouse named after the then dowager Queen Adelaide (1792-1849), daughter of George I, Duke of Saxe-Meiningen and widow of William IV, who lived in retirement in Derbyshire. Opened between 1843 and 1846, when it was recorded as an anonymous beer house, the name first being recorded in 1849. It was in the hands of Offilers' from 1928, and brewing on the premises continued until 1942. It was granted a full licence in 1950 and apparently closed in the mid- 1960s, being demolished around the latter period.

QUEEN'S HEAD*

25 Victoria Street (Brookside)   *by 1667-1959*

A plain two-and-a-half-storey three-bay inn in a two-and-a-half-storey building of around 1800 on Brookside (as the street was then known) facing the Brook; probably an unmatched setting in its day. It was first mentioned in 1764

Queen's Head, Victoria Street, c.1930.

and then presumably occupied a previous building on the site. The inn was probably founded around the time of George III's wedding in 1761 to Sophia Carlotta (1744-1818) daughter of Charles I, Duke of Mecklenburg-Strelitz, but there is a possibility that it was an inn a century earlier, for there is a token known, issued in Derby 1667 by Edward Dentith (spelt Denty on his copper halfpenny) proclaiming him to be the landlord of the *Queen's Head* (at that date, of course, named after Catherine of Braganza, Charles II's wife); Dentith certainly lived in the correct parish. From 1928 to 1941 it was run by John Renshaw, who had previously run a chip shop at 3, Queen Street, and who was the widower of Alice, daughter of Joseph Parker, of the *Magnet* and *Cossack*. His widow (his second wife) carried it on until 1952, and his brother Henry had long before run the *Old Flower Pot*. Reg Newcombe recalls of it, 'The interior... was not the real thing, though it was smartly panelled and had beams. The ceiling was higher than you might think from outside, because you stepped down into it on entry, as you do in the *Wardwick* and presumably for the same reason.' Purchased post-war by Ranby's store, which by then had acquired all the surrounding property, closed 31 December 1959, and pulled down for the rebuilding of the store in 1961.

QUEEN'S (HEAD) HOTEL (VAULTS)*

46 (70) Crompton Street   *by 1869*

Originally the *Queen's Vaults*, when to let as a going concern in 1869. Thereafter the *Queen's Head* (in this case, of Queen Victoria), but by 1898 shortened to *Queen's Hotel*. The lessee in 1869 was none other than Thomas A. Minnitt, of the *Old Vaults* St Helen's Street, under whom it was still flourishing in 1874. Later owned by Alton's, but by 1983 it had been sold off and was briefly renamed the *Public House*, before again being renamed as the *Crompton Tavern* in 1984. The latter name was after that of the street, and that, in turn, was named after Alderman John Gilbert Crompton, early 19th century Mayor and member of a family which founded a bank in Derby as early as 1685.

DM 9/6/1869 & 15/10/1873

QUEEN'S VAULTS

13 Osmaston Road (Street)   *by 1874-1908*

A beerhouse on the east side of Osmaston Road not far from the Spot, doubtless, again, named in honour of Queen Victoria, possibly as early as her accession, for there are two beerhouses recorded in this road 1846/62, but without numbers, and this inn may well have been one of them. However, in 1835-43 the *Plough* may have preceded this inn on the site. Later became an off-licence, then a shop, before being pulled down and replaced between the wars.

QUIET WOMAN*

1 Brook Walk (8 Ford Street)   *by 1833-1878*

Traditional sign of a headless woman, nowadays doubtless considered chauvinistic and discriminatory! In 1857 called the *Silent Woman*. Marked on the 1883 licensed premises map, but absent from the 1878 directory, so closed somewhere about that time and the corner buildings here demolished.

RAFFLES BAR**

31 Normanton Road   *c.1995*

Converted from a former shop in the mid-1990s and named either after St Thomas Stamford Raffles HEICS, LLD, FRS (1781-1826), Lieutenant-governor of Java and later of Singapore (who gave his name to the world famous Raffles Hotel on that island), or from the fictional thief who bore his surname. Relaunched by Bish Wojick in July 2000, the venue has an international flavour and features bands.

RAILWAY*

2 (117) Canal Street (corner Siddals Road)   *by 1843-1972*

Canal Street was a very well-pubbed street: in 1898 there were seven inns, all but this one on one side. The name derives from the nearby Midland Railway's line. For sale in 1871, new landlord James Pegg doubling as a joiner at 58 Siddals Road. Owned by Pountain's 1937, and cleared between 1972 and 1977 after closure in the former year.

RAILWAY

See LOCOMOTIVE

RAINBOW

Green Street   *by 1849-1850*

Little known about this inn; it would be pleasant to think that it took its name from Joseph Wright's famous painting.

RAM*

82 (59, 72) Bridge Street (corner Brook Street)   *by 1827*

Undoubtedly named after the celebrated (and prodigious) Derby Ram, celebrated in a ballad first published in the 1730s; in the hands of Stretton's (previously Alton's, later

Ram, Bridge Street, 2002.

Ind Coope) by 1937 and brewing on the premises until at least 1940 in a brewhouse shared with the adjacent *Woodlark*. It was the scene of one of the 18 sheep roasts held in 1856 to celebrate the peace treaty with Russia. And it was to let as 'old established' in 1863. By 1994 in the hands of the Pubmaster chain.

RAMSDEN'S TAVERN*

Market Place/35 Cornmarket   *by 1924-1984*
In 1774 a building was put up, probably to a design by Joseph Pickford, beside the newly completed Assembly Rooms to provide suppers for the Assemblies, run by Brian Hodgson of Ashbourne's Grey House, and also proprietor of the *Bell,* Barnby Moor, Nottinghamshire, the *George* at Stamford, Lincs, (both on the Great North Road) and the *Old Hall Hotel,* Buxton. It remained in this role for well over half a century. Hodgson had been recruited by the 'Committee of Noblemen and Gentlemen' formed to raise money and build the Assembly Rooms especially for his catering expertise. Horace Ramsden, a Huddersfield-born confectioner, once chef to the Moselys at Rolleston Hall, Staffs, founded a restaurant in 1886 at 111 St Peter's Street. By 1908 he had also opened at 35 Cornmarket, and his eldest son, Ludlam, was in the 1920s landlord of the *Horse & Trumpet* before starting a bar and restaurant beside the Assembly Rooms in the same building (named after its proprietor). In 1946, Ramsden closed the establishment and moved back to 35 Cornmarket – the northern third of the former Devonshire House (listed Grade II, cf. *the Hotel & King's Head*), on a full licence. It was from the 1960s run by Luldam's elder son Kenneth jointly with Berni Inns but closed in 1984 to be replaced by the *Knotted Snake* (entered separately). The Market Place premises were demolished at the same time as the Assembly Rooms façade in 1971.
DET 22/1/1993

RANBY'S
See GREEN LANE HOUSE

RED BALL*

St Peter's Street (entrance to Oakes's Yard)   *1673-1761*
Recorded in a flood report in the Town Annals for 1673, and in 1726 the St Peter's parish register tells us that this inn was run by Robert Bainbrigge, member of a notable Derby family; it is also mentioned in the list of Sir Harry Harpur's 'hospitality'.

The name is obscure although heraldry suggests itself, notably the arms of Babington (whose town house in St Peter's Parish survived until 1811): *Argent ten torteaux (ie red balls) and a label azure.* The argument against this attribution is that the inn should have been called the Ten Red Balls! The ancient entrance to Oakes's Yard was at the north end of St Peter's Street on the west side, from whence it ran diagonally towards Green Lane; here Robert Bakewell had his workshop 1708-52.

RED LION*

74 (86) Bridge Street   *by 1846-1895*
Recorded in 1846, 1850 and 1857 at this address as an anonymous beer house and first named in 1862. Closed by Zachary Smith's brewery before 1898, when it became a shop. The name is remarkably common. On a national scale, a red lion was borne heraldically by William le Marechal, Earl of Pembroke (d.1219) and Richard Plantagenet, Earl of Cornwall and King of the Romans (second son of King John) (1209-1272); locally they had few connections so in this context it may derive from the red lion of the Kingdom of Léon, used as a badge by John of Gaunt who, as Duke of Lancaster, had great Derbyshire estates.

RED LION*

33 (14) Canal Street (corner New Street)   *by 1844-1912*
To let in 1844 as a going concern, and a contents sale was held in 1853. It was for sale again in 1883. Became a shop after World War One.
DM 25/9/1844, 28/12/1853 7 20/6/1883

RED LION*

Cornmarket   *by 1733-1836*
Situated at the south-west end of Cornmarket 'on Gaol Bridge' and separated from the immediately adjacent *White Lion* 'by a carriage arch'. In existence by 1733, when it was 'A large, commodious carriers' inn', sending a waggon to London every Monday, returning on Friday or Saturday, although this service later departed from the *White Hart.* Two years later the landlord was Thomas Tabberer, cousin of the architect, Samuel. It was sold in 1752 and 1779. In 1820 the *Bruce* coach stopped here to change horses and

for the passengers to be refreshed, a mere 15 minutes being allowed. It was for sale in 1835, and was eventually sold on 7 September 1836 (followed by a contents sale a month later) and thereupon demolished (along with the *White Lion*), to considerable public regret, to accommodate the culverting of the Markeaton Brook and the erection, by Robert Wallace, of the Derby and Derbyshire Bank.
DM 27/12/1733, 10/4/1735, 28/5/1779, 6/5/1835, 7/9 & 26/10/1836; Ward, J., *Notes of Reminiscences of Old Derby*, III.viii.

RED LION*

37 Mansfield Street   *1857-1925*
A beerhouse for which a licence application was made in 1873, although an anonymous beerhouse existed at this address in 1857 and 1862; presumably the licence had lapsed between 1862 and 1873. It closed around 1925.

RED LION

Nuns' Green   *by 1750-1761*
One of the list of inns where Sir Harry Harpur arranged hospitality for potential electors.

REFRESHMENT HOUSE

See (GREAT NORTHERN) REFRESHMENT HOUSE

REGENT HOTEL

See GABLES

REINDEER

Bridge Gate   *-1770-*
An alehouse doubtless renamed, rather than closed.
DM 13/7/1770

REINDEER*

24-25 Eagle Street (corner Earl Street)   *by 1846-1970*
The origin of the name is obscure; the date of the Bridge Gate inn of this name (*qv* above) rather precludes Father Christmas's sleigh team, a 19th century conceit. This vernacular brick two-storey cottage of c.1810 was the address of an anonymous beer house in 1846, 1850 and 1857, but clearly the same establishment. It was in the hands of Offilers' between the wars, and had the misfortune to be refused a licence renewal in March 1939, shortly after the departure for the *Duke of York* of Reg and Lucy Woodyet, parents of Tony Woodyet later for many years of the *Malt Shovel*, Spondon. The outbreak of war, however, swiftly rectified the situation, and it continued up until the clearance of the area to make way for the abominable shopping precinct, which bears the street's name.
DET Bygones 12/3/2002

Revolution, on the corner of The Strand and Victoria Street, 2002.

REVOLUTION**

1-2 Wardwick (corner of The Strand)   *2000*
An imposing 'flat-iron' building of three storeys and attics, built to house the Nottingham & District Bank Ltd in 1882 to designs by Giles & Brookhouse of Derby, later the Refuge Insurance Co, and finally a wool shop before being converted into Russian-themed vodka bar over two floors. Faced in fine ashlar, the building is in an enriched Classical style and has some surprisingly elaborate interiors. It is listed Grade II. The refurbishment was highly commended in the Civic Society/ABCD Awards in 2000.

(RHODE) ISLAND (DINER) (EXCHANGE)*

Queen Street   *1982*
Founded by Tetley's as a restaurant with a bar, called the *Baltimore Diner* and changed to the *Rhode Island* in the mid-1980s with pub licence. Named after the north-east American state. Ansell's, Tetley's sister company, were incensed about this intrusion of Allied Breweries' northern arm into their territory, so eventually the bar was transferred to Ansell's. Subsequently merely the *Island* to allow for the promotion of Texan/Mexican menus.

RICHARD COBDEN*

201 (191) Abbey Street   *by 1857-1895*
For the origin of the name, see above (*Cobden Arms*); this beerhouse was recorded in 1857 and 1862 anonymously at the address. It may have acquired its name on or after Cobden's death in 1865, but just as easily before, his fame going back to the late 1840s. For sale as 'old established' in 1880. It is said to have closed in 1918; it was certainly open in 1914. One source calls it the 'Sir' Richard Cobden, although that statesman was never knighted!
DM 16/6/1880

RING O' BELLS*

36 (27-28) Bradshaw Street   *by 1835-1925*
A beerhouse was listed anonymously at this address for

1835. Situated but three doors down from the *Lion & Tigress* and probably renamed from the *Hawk & Buckle*; closed between 1925 (when William Renshaw – perhaps an kinsman of John, of the *Queen's* Head – was brewing his own ale there) and 1935. There was a largish function-cum-dining room on the first floor at the front. It was subsequently let as furnished rooms. Mr E. Tranter moved in there to one of the two upstairs apartments with his wife and small son in 1955 when it was owned by Mrs Huffe of the *Welcome Arms,* who sold to Mr Dixon. It was whilst exploring the cellars that Mr Tranter discovered the original lamp-sign, which the landlord fortuitously presented to Derby Museum where it still is.
E. Tranter, Esq, *pers. comm.*30/4/02.

RING O'BELLS*

Bridge Street   *by 1818-1827*
The name is traditional, and perhaps originates from Derby's All Saints' church (since 1927 the Cathedral) having the oldest ring of ten bells in the country, doubtless once very clearly audible from Bridge Street. An exact location is uncorroborated but Samuel Gaskell is listed as landlord in 1827 and as landlord of *The Pheasant,* in the same street, by 1835. The likelihood is, then, that they are one and the same, and that a name change occurred c.1830.

RIO

See FORTY SECOND STREET

RISING SUN

Bridge Gate   *by 1736-1737*
For sale in 1736. The sign is traditional and Edward III used as his badge a rising sun, but note the crest of the Pegge family of Ashbourne, Osmaston, Yeldersley, Beauchief, etc, very prominent in 17th and early 18th century Derbyshire.
DM 20/1/1736

RISING SUN*

Cornmarket   *by 1673-1785*
Almost certainly the inn referred to as the *(Old) Sun,* described by Glover as '...in St Peter's Parish near Markeaton Brook': the parish actually includes part of Cornmarket. The suggestion is that it was on or near the south-east corner of the street by the Bridge. It was run by John Sandars, a descendant of the famous Parliamentary commander in the Civil War, to 1753 – ancestor of the last owner of the *Mitre* in Amen Alley – and after that by Robert Campion 1763-9, who must have moved there from the *Swan,* if this name is not an error (in the original source) for *Sun.* Campion (1716-1789) the son of a Robert (1683-1759), was the cousin of two brothers, sons of Thomas, of a local family going back to the late 16th century. One was George Campion, landlord of the *Anchor*

in St Peter's Street in 1761, whilst the other, John, started off in 1759 as a 'serving man' (no doubt learning his trade), became a successful merchant and later, in 1774, took over the *Bell.* In 1751 the *Rising Sun* is described as a 'large public house' – it could have been renamed after 1785 – perhaps as the *Red Lion* or *White Lion.*
DM 7/6/1751; Glover (1829/31) II.608

(RISING) SUN*

114 Friar Gate   *by 1600*
The present establishment was built, with 'extensive stabling', in 1887-8, having closed temporarily in the September of the previous year, to designs by Arthur Eaton of Derby. Yet it was a very ancient inn even then, the previous building being a low brick-clad timber-framed structure with tiny gables, probably once thatched. Referred to merely as the *Sun* in 1827 and 1833 and for sale in 1859. In 1841 its landlord was William Rowley, at the same time as his mother, Sarah, kept the *Stag and Pheasant.* The present building is quite a pleasant Victorian structure, and was owned by Stretton's between the wars. It was sold off by its last institutional owners, Ansell's in 1990, to Hoskins of Leicester and completely refurbished (after some years being exclusive to the gay community) and reopened under the name of the *Friargate (sic).* Whilst one appreciates the new proprietors' reasons for wishing to rename it, the move is, nevertheless, much to be regretted after almost four centuries as the *Rising Sun*; it must have been one of the oldest sites of a licensed house in Derby which has continued throughout under the same title. Sold by Hoskins in the mid-1990s to John Evans's Headless Pub Company and at the time of writing possibly about to be renamed the *Bishop Blaize* by a current owner, Tony Williams of the *Blessington Carriage.*
BBA No. 4106 of 1888; DM 28/9/1859

RISING SUN*

67 (63) Osmaston Road (Street)   *by 1850-1956*
Situated opposite the end of Wilmot Street, listed anonymously in 1850 and for sale as a going concern in 1871, probably on the departure of John James Keys (cf *Cobblers' Rest*). It was in the hands of Stretton's in 1937, in which year its licence was restored after a short lapse. It was kept during the 1930s by Charles and Mary Roberts (who brewed on the premises), formerly of the *Duke of Cambridge,* Whitecross Street and parents of the memorable Flo Liversage of the nearby *Neptune Hotel.* It closed in the later 1950s, and was demolished soon afterwards.
DM 9/8/1871

ROBIN HOOD (& LITTLE JOHN)*

38 Iron Gate   *by 1692-1950*
A coaching inn with a commodious yard off Iron Gate into

Robin Hood (far right of picture), Iron Gate, c.1857. The Globe is just to its left. The Greyhound is straight ahead.

which the institution retreated in the 20th century. Although reputed to have been in existence as early as 1692, it appears first in an advertisement of 1761 with its full title, but by 1770 this had been dropped. In his youth, Joseph Wright was said (on the evidence of his daughter) to have painted the sign, which would push its earliest date back to *c*.1744. It may be viewed (with the benefit of hindsight) as a tragedy that this sign was never preserved! If the anecdote is true (and as it was but a few doors from Wright's childhood home, we may be prepared to believe what the artist told his daughter), then it was probably a repainting. Further, the part which survived longest as an inn, up to demolition (a typical act of Derby vandalism of the period), the portion up the yard, was timber-framed, which might also suggest an early 17th-century date. *DM* 12/6/1761, 27/4/1770

ROBIN HOOD**

Osmaston Road (Street)   *by 1818-1824*

Osmaston Street (today's Osmaston Road from the Spot to Bradshaw Street (Way)) must have been crowded with inns; this one seems ephemeral, either through multiple re-namings or by being of itself short-lived.

(ADMIRAL) RODNEY (ARMS)*

30 Cornmarket   *by 1785-1836*

Named after a popular hero of the day, Admiral Sir George Rodney, KB, RN, 1st Bt, victor over the French at the Battle of Cape St Vincent in 1780 and again against Admiral Count de Grasse on 12 April 1782 ('The Glorious Twelfth of April') for which achievement he was raised to the peerage as 1st Lord Rodney of Rodney Stoke, Somerset, 10 June following. He contributed many inn-names and a new Christian names to our culture. The inn probably already flourished under another name – the *Blue Stoops* is a strong candidate – and it probably changed in 1782, and was first so recorded in 1785. It was situated in a yard beside the *Angel* and was for sale in 1796 (name in full), 1799, 1820 and 1836. It was the *Rodney Arms* in 1823/4.

Early in the year following we read: 'Julius Mott, wine merchant of Loughborough and Leicester has opened new premises erected on the site of the old Rodney Inn, Cornmarket, as an establishment for the sale of wines and spirits, wholesale and retail as the 'New Rodney Wine & Spirit Establishment'. This marked the end of the inn, although the elegant

stuccoed three-storey three-bay Regency building was designed and built by Joseph Goddard of Leicester. It ushered in, however, a century-plus as a wine merchant's. Within two years, however, Mott had departed, and an advertisement appeared to say that it had been 'Purchased by William Cox [of the lead refining family who built the shot tower in 1809] who has entered into partnership with W. Malin, Mott's manager'. This heralded the beginning of a firm which, despite occasional changes of name (Cox, Clarke & Co in the 1870s; Arthur John Cox & Co in the 1880s), flourished into the middle of the 20th century here, the building being known as Rodney Chambers. In 1910 it was called Cox's Wine Vaults, but did not have an 'on' licence. It was finally demolished to build Littlewoods ugly store in 1969. A music hall token of mid-19th century date noted in January 1999 remains a complete mystery. *DM* 15/3/1785, 7/4/1796, 30/5/1799, 3/5/1820, 6/4/1836, 11/1/1837 & 18/4/1838; Broadwood & Cherry (1990) 106.

ROEBUCK

1 Amy Street (corner of Stockbrook Road)   *by 1895*

The Roebuck features on the arms of the Blythe family, important in north Derbyshire but not particularly so in Derby. The *Roebuck*, Amy Street is a commodious corner establishment owned by Alton's between the wars, with a curving two-storey façade of brick with stone dressings in the 'Jacobethan' manner of Messrs Pountain's architect, James Wright.

The windows are mullioned and transomed, with an entablature and frieze between the floors, odd-looking pediment above the entrance – itself set between pilasters – and another over the secondary (Stockbrook Road) entrance, topped by an odd pyramid.

Roebuck, Amy Street, 1938.

ROEBUCK*

85 (35) Bridge Gate   *by 1818-1880*

Probably in existence a good time before 1818, although arguably under another identity. This supposition is reinforced by an advertisement for the sale of an unexpired 108-year portion of a lease on it in 1847. Assuming that the lease was, say for 150 years, the inn might well go back to 1805. The lease, though, never ran to 1955, for the inn was sold again in 1871 and for the last time as an inn in 1880, after which it seems to have become a shop. The building was eventually cleared in the 1960s. It is possible that in the 18th century, the buck in the city arms may have been envisaged as a roe, and hence the popularity of the name locally.

DM 31/3/1847, 3/5/1871 7 29/9/1880

ROEBUCK*

St Mary's Gate   *-1746-*

Mentioned only in 1746. Perhaps later the *Miner's Arms*.

DM 29/8//1746

ROSCOE'S

See MERLIN

ROSE & CROWN*

15 Cornmarket   *by 1725-1965*

A former coaching inn set in a yard on the west side of Cornmarket, and (if not renamed) in existence by about 1725. This date can be fixed by the beautiful 16ft-wide cambered wrought-iron overthrow by Robert Bakewell which once spanned the yard; it was centered by a very large drop-in lantern bearing the inn's name, a traditional one dating from the Tudor settlement of 1485, although the county coat of arms also consists of a (Tudor) rose surmounted by a crown. For sale in 1817 and to let a decade later; the *Rose & Crown* inn listed in Pigot's 1835 directory in Market Place is without doubt this inn inaccurately placed. This yard ran through to St James' Street via a right turn, and in 1909 the wrought iron smith Edwin Haslam made some very fine gates to close off the yard and to compliment the overthrow. The inn was owned by Stretton's in the 1930s, but was closed and swept away by redevelopment in 1965, being replaced on both streets by some particularly horrendous buildings. Mercifully, the wrought-iron overthrow was rescued (minus its lamp) and placed in the care of the Museum, yet despite its evidence, the inn is only recorded under this name from 1791: was it renamed?

DM 29/5/1817 & 14/11/1827; UBD 1791.

ROSE & THISTLE*

25 (8) Chapel Street (corner Orchard Street)by 1838-1915

For sale as a going concern in 1838 with 'a good parlour with dining room above, tap room, bar, brew house, yard, 4 lodging rooms, and a coach house for two carriages'. It was owned latterly by Hanson's, who lost their licence in 1915 due to Temperance Society pressure, after which it became a house, being demolished in the 1960s. The sign owes its origins to the union of the crowns of England (rose) and Scotland (thistle) at the accession of James I in 1603 or, possibly, the Act of Union of 1707.

DM 21/3 & 2/5/1838

ROSE HILL TAVERN*

4 Loudon Street   *by 1862*

Built with the street, which was named after John Claudius Loudon, the landscaper who laid out the adjacent Arboretum for Joseph Strutt in 1840. He was born in Scotland in 1783 and died in London, where he had his practice, in 1843. It is first recorded as an anonymous beer-house in 1862, but John Phillips, the landlord in 1878 operated as a wine merchant, too, emphasising the status of the area in those days. Between the wars it was an Alton's pub. Subsequently it had its name changed from one which echoed that of the area in which it lay to the *Loudon Arms*, after the street. This happened between 1966 and 1977. In reality, J.C. Loudon did not bear arms.

ROWDITCH*

246 Uttoxeter (New) Road, Rowditch   *by 1846*

Situated at the junction between Uttoxeter Old and New Roads, where lies a small settlement recorded since mediaeval times called Rowditch, which is a corruption for the Old English words meaning 'Rough Dyke'. The inn first appears named on the 1852 Board of Health map, although it is listed only as an anonymous beer house in 1846 and 1857. A double-fronted two-storey building, originally stuccoed and grooved to resemble ashlar and with quoined window surrounds.

Owned by Stretton's between the wars, then Ansells and now a free house. The former Roman road runs just beyond the original rear (NW) curtilage of the pub, an alignment tested by excavation in 1859.

ROYAL ALBERT*

107 (48) Canal Street   *by 1843-1908*

Situated, perhaps inconveniently, next to the *Barleycorn* which, in the long run, led to both going out of business before 1912, although this inn was probably closed through Temperance Society pressure. Originally the *Dyers' Arms*, it was later renamed, probably following his death in 1861, after HSH Albert v Saxe-Coburg und Gotha, the Prince Consort. Exactly when the change of name took place is difficult to determine, as it is recorded as a beer house anonymously in 1850, 1857 and 1862.

ROYAL DRILL HALL

See DRILL HALL VAULTS

ROYAL HOTEL*

1 Victoria Street (corner Cornmarket) *1839-1951*

The *Royal* was undoubtedly the finest hotel in Derby, and indeed, has yet to be surpassed. The company set up to create Victoria Street by culverting Markeaton Brook intended to develop the south-west corner of the new street and Cornmarket, and initiated a competition to build an hotel and Athenaeum club. This was very conveniently won (out of 52 entries) by the London architect then building the Derby and Derbyshire Bank next door in Cornmarket: Robert Wallace. The building was executed at a cost in excess of £20,000 in a Greek revival style and is a most imposing and dignified building, especially today, since the cleaning of its millstone grit sandstone quarried from Morley Moor, in 1990. The Cornmarket façade is 62ft long; that along Victoria Street, 98ft, and the entrance was originally on the angle with an aedicular portico of arresting simplicity, topped by a cast iron anthemion balustrade. The ground floor is treated as a plinth storey, the *piano nobile* effectively being the first and second storeys, embellished with a giant fluted Ionic Order supporting a massive frieze and entablature with an attic storey over, the royal arms once being set both between the columns and on the top parapet. Inside, the hall was hexagonal, from it rising a cantilevered stone staircase, since destroyed by adaptation as shops. The public rooms were also once very fine. The part to the north end of the range was built as the Post Office, but this was superseded in 1867 by the present GPO building, and became a shop. The exterior of the Athenaeum club was to have been graced with a Pan-Athenaic frieze at second-floor level (the saloon behind rising through two storeys with a gallery) carved by John Hemming the elder of London (1771-1851), but although it is shown on early engravings and lithographs of the building, there is some reason to doubt that it was ever executed. Hemming also carved the royal arms once over the entrance. To increase capacity and to obviate the results of sudden flooding, the stables were built on two levels – a great novelty. To build this impressive complex,

Royal Hotel, Victoria Street, c.1947.

The view from the same position in 2002.

the Derby Athenaeum Society (proprietors): Alderman Johnson, Joseph Strutt and his nephew Edward (later 1st Lord Belper) had to buy (from the Derby & Derbyshire Bank) and pull down the *Red Lion* and *White Lion* inns, and at least one other besides. They also undertook to culvert the brook, to form Victoria Street, work commencing in May 1837 and completed in 1839, the contractor being Thomas Cooper, designer of the block in which the former *Howard Hotel* once lay.

The first proprietor was Middlesex-born Francis Huggins (1798-1862) who came to Derby in 1823 and entered into partnership as a surgeon – of all things, in the light of subsequent events – with Samuel Davenport, practicing alone after 18 months. He married a granddaughter of Alderman Stamford whose horse had been commandeered by Bonnie Prince Charlie's vanguard from the *George* on 4 December 1745. He enjoyed the honour of a complimentary dinner as early as 1843, attended by his three sons. Later he also took on the *King's Head*, leaving the *Royal* in the charge of his eldest son Charles Whitton Huggins, also a wine merchant with his brother Francis – a business which went under in 1855, but was resurrected at the *George & Dragon*, Albert Street (another later family enterprise, *qv*) by the third brother Edward Stamford Huggins (1826-1875). Francis junior, after his father's death made a presentation to the Derby Licensed Victuallers' Association (of which the father had been a co-founder).

On Francis Huggins's death in 1862, the lease was sold to John Taylor, who held it into the 1880s, when it reverted to the company which owned the freehold, controlled by Alderman W.H. Marsden (1838-1899, Mayor 1892), a

vintner who, in 1892, put in Miss Lottie Frost (later Mrs Baker) as manageress. Around 1898 she married a kinsman of John Cuff, formerly of the *Midland Hotel* (who, perhaps significantly, had run a share-brokership in the Athenaeum building with Alderman Douglas Fox in the 1840s). He was Cambridgeshire-born Ambrose Otway Fuller (1867-1956), until then manager of the *Sherwood (Forester) Hotel*, Normanton. They ran it, later acquiring the freehold, their eldest son Eric Otway Fuller (1899-1984), succeeding them until 1939 (when the second son, Gerald Otway Fuller took over until 1945) and again from 1948 until closure in 1951.

The hotel underwent alterations in 1924, and two bars were converted into shops in February 1930, a new bar being built at the rear. After World War Two, the hotel began losing money and closed on 4 June 1951, being sold off to the Civil Service and became a Social Security office. In the 1980s, the DHSS, as it had then become, moved out and the accommodation, which had survived being turned into shops in the 1920s, was purchased by C.W. Clowes, who restored it, letting much as offices, part as a restaurant and the Athenaeum as the *Royal Suite*, which is not technically licensed as a pub, although anyone eating or attending a function there can obtain at least a flavour of the grandeur that has passed. It reopened in this guise in 1989.

DM 13/3/1855, 26/11/1862, 28/1/1863, 5/11/1876; Glover (1843) 56-7; Information courtesy Mrs P. Warrington.

ROYAL OAK

30 Market Place (corner Tenant Street)   by 1727-1920
First mentioned in 1732, and then probably newly established in the building which survived until 1890. The location of annual flower shows in the mid-18th century. The inn itself may have been established in the Restoration, the name being redolent of that happy event, commemorating, as it does, the King's sojourn in the branches of an oak at Boscobel, Salop, a house owned, in the 1800s, by the Derby bankers, the Evanses of Darley. It was to let in 1784 and again in 1843. In 1818, someone had been circulating rumours about the then landlord, W.H. Ingham, and he put a notice in the paper:

'W. H. Ingham, grateful for the past favours of his friends and the public in Derby and its vicinity most respectfully returns thanks for the same and begs leave to state, in contradiction to a report, industriously circulated (with an

Royal Oak, Market Place, as a solicitor's office, 2002.

apparent mischievous intention), that he intends to continue at the above Inn and most respectfully solicits a continuance of their future favours and support, which he will use every endeavour in his power to merit.'

A Coronation banquet was held here in 1838. In 1890 (date on gable) the 18th-century building was damaged by fire, demolished and replaced by James Eadie & Co of Burton with the surviving half-timbered effort with brick infill on a stone plinth and ornament. Its most engaging detail is the pargetted gable facing the Market Place, an unusual feature in Derby at any period. A range facing Tenant Street was retained, but the whole was compulsorily purchased by the Derby Urban Sanitary Authority at a sum of £14,100, agreed by arbitration, the Tenant Street range being demolished as unfit in 1892-3 and later replaced by a wing of the utmost banality which hardly complimented the 1890 build. But it was always a market pub and when the use of the Market Place for the purpose its 12th-century founders intended declined from the early years of the 20th century, the landlord was obliged to take a daytime job with newly-founded British Celanese at Spondon in 1916 to make ends meet. The *Royal Oak* closed in 1920, becoming council offices, later those of a solicitors' practice, which it still is. Most English of inns of this name – at least up until the end of the 19th century – used to hang out a branch of this tree on Oak Apple Day.
Derby City Council Estates Dept. Records, 22/6/1894; *DM* 19/12/1732, 8/10/1784, 4/7/1838, 29/11/1843

ROYAL OAK
See also OLD OAK

ROYAL STANDARD*

1 Derwent Street (corner Exeter Place)   1862
Originally on a much more restricted site, being 'newly

erected' and for sale in February 1864, this inn was amalgamated with two adjoining cottages and extensively rebuilt in the 1890s to use the whole corner, the impetus coming from its acquisition by Pountain's, so the architect was probably James Wright; later Ind Coope/Ansell's, then Mansfield Brewery, then Wolverhampton & Dudley. A successful spirit licence application was made in 1874. The sign was named after the Sovereign's personal flag, always flown when the King or Queen is personally present.

Sometime between 1908 and 1911, the licence was taken by William Parnell, formerly of the *Sir Robert Peel* and the *(Bunch of) Grapes*, Green Lane. His wife, Alice, was a memorable figure, who ran a soup kitchen for foundry workers in Cotton Lane before taking a fish shop at 198 Harrington Street before 1908. They had two sons and two daughters, and Parnell himself began a haulage business in a yard behind the inn, later taken over by his second son, William and expanded at premises in Alfreton Road, called the Standard Transport Co and the Standard Garage after the pub. The elder son, Reg (1911-1964), went on to become the celebrated Grand Prix motor-racing driver. The *Royal Standard* itself was taken over before 1925 by one of the daughters, Alice, who had married George R. Baker (universally known as 'the old Scholar') in 1915. She was as redoubtable as her mother, co-founding the Derby Ladies' Licensed Victuallers' Association because the male-dominated LVA would not then accept women members. She worked tirelessly as its secretary for years, in association with such colleagues as

Royal Standard, Derwent Street. The lounge in 1935 when George H. Baker was proprietor. It was known then as the 'Aquarium House' – at 8.30 each Sunday evening regulars would gather for the treat of watching the fish being fed!

The Telegraph, London Road, with the Prince of Wales, next door.

Florence Liversage of the *Neptune*. She and her husband later went to the *White Horse* in the Morledge, the *Royal Standard* being taken on by the third generation of the family in the person of her daughter, Doreen, Mrs Len Harfield, who was secretary of the Derby Ladies LVA in 1952. They later moved to Blackpool.

DET 21/12/1996, 3/11/1998, 8, 15 & 29/1, 12 & 19/2/2002 (*Bygones Suppl.*); *DM* 17/2/1864 & 26/8/1874

ROYAL STUART
See GABLES

(ROYAL) TELEGRAPH*

69 (1) London Road (corner Traffic Street)   *by 1823*

Originally a smallish inn, taking its name from a stage-coach which plied the London road from Manchester. A sheep roast was held here in 1856 to celebrate the peace treaty with Russia. It was for sale in 1878 and later acquired by Pountain's who took the opportunity of a road widening scheme in 1936 to buy out the nearby *Prince of Wales*,

demolish it and the two intervening shops, and to rebuild the inn with a long curving frontage and an entrance at either end, like a more expansive version of the *Star and Garter*. The 'Royal' part of the title was dropped early on, and the rebuilt *Telegraph Inn* was reopened 17 March 1937. In 1983, it was again rebuilt (internally) by Mansfield Ales and renamed *Trinian's*: a so-called 'fun pub'. Not content with its new soubriquet, the proprietors again renamed it, in October 1986, *Strutt's*: a rather back-handed compliment to Derby's most eminent Regency family!

DM 21/5/1856 & 1/9/1878

RUTLAND ARMS*

112 (32) Carrington Street (corner Nelson Street)

        by 1860-1996

Named in honour of the Manners family, Dukes of Rutland, owners of the Haddon Hall estate (served by the nearby Midland Railway) and one of the greatest 19th century Derbyshire landowning families. In 1861 John Allen, father of Isaac, founder of Allenton, moved here from the *Bell &*

Castle following a contents' sale. By 1878, John Allen had died and Isaac was running it, but he sold it in 1881, no doubt to help fund his Allenton enterprises. Owned by Hardy's Brewery in 1937, but closed around 1996 and still boarded up. The lowish two-storey late Regency building is a pleasant one, enlivened further by the presence of a pair of pedimented and fan-lit late 18th century door aedicules embellishing the two entrances. It would be a tragedy if this inn were to be demolished, although its situation is somewhat against it.

DM 26/1/1861 & 28/9/1881; Longdon (2000) 16

RYAN'S (BAR)
See GREEN MAN

SADDLE*

17 Hill Street   *1835-1857*

A short-lived inn, about which little is known except that it stood next door to the *Milton's Head* which later may well have expanded into it as no candidates exist to suggest a renaming. The origin of the name, which is only recorded in 1849 and '50, may relate to a neighbouring livery stable. Probably the anonymous beer house in this street listed in 1835 and 1857.

SADDLER'S

8-9 Sadler Gate   *1980*

One of many Wine Bars establishing themselves in Sadler Gate, and taking its name (perhaps a change from a surname of no obvious significance) from the street, itself first named in the 13th century after the trade most commonly pursued there. A free house.

ST GEORGE & DRAGON
See LONDON

ST HELEN'S*

25 Duffield Road (corner Kedleston Street)   *by 1850*

Although conceivably a migrated *White Stoup* this beer

St Helen's, Duffield Road c.1890.

house was more likely founded before 1850 as the *New Inn*, but by 1883 had changed its name to the *St Helen's* after Derby's first monastic foundation, established a little to the south on King Street c.1138. Beer brewed on the premises in 1925, when owned by Stretton's. Later bought by Home Ales, who immediately demolished it and built a stylish and well-proportioned new pub, of brick with a grooved tile-faced ground floor, an asymmetrical Classical centrepiece and brick parapet in 1928. In 2001 it was renamed the *Five Lamps* after the area in which it stands, itself taking its name from the heroically proportioned cast iron lamp standard moved here in the 1880s from outside the *Royal Hotel* and subsequently removed and scrapped.

St James's Hotel (now Sugaz), 2002.

ST JAMES'S HOTEL

13 St James's Street   *1871*

Founded and built as part of the widening scheme for the entire street and, although the entrance was relatively modest, the accommodation stretched along the upper floors right round into Cornmarket. There was (and still is) a fine top-lit dining room, later the main bar area) and at the rear was a large ballroom at first-floor level, later to become Messrs Richardson & Linnell's much-missed auction rooms. There were also extensive stables and offices framing a spacious courtyard at the rear, much of which survives. The architects were Messrs Giles and Brookhouse and it was advertised as 'shortly to be completed and to let' in 1870. The Derby County Club was also to have premises within the building, which covered some of the site of the *King's Head*, closed to extend the *St James's* in 1872. It never fulfilled expectations, and it was leased to Alton's in the 1920s and by 1926 it had ceased to be an hotel, becoming a licensed restaurant with bars, the ballroom being turned into an auction room, and the residential accommodation and many public rooms becoming offices. During World War Two and until 1948 it was run by the Fuller family from the *Royal Hotel*. Yet it continued to decline, its reputation with it, despite a sale (to Bass) in

St James's Hotel, St James's Street entrance, 1910.

The same establishment pictured from the Cornmarket, c.1905.

1958. It has been since the later 1980s a 'fun pub' called 'Jimmy's' (for many years the nickname of the hotel's bar) but in 2000 renamed *Knights* and more of a night club. The original name, of course, derived from that of the street, itself being named after a very early parish church, which became a cell of the Abbey of Bermondsey in the 12th century. In 2002 the premises were acquired by Clowes

Developments, and *Knights* let to Cathy McCoy (formerly landlady of the *Junction Tavern*) and Chris Mills. They renamed it *Sugaz* ('the name they were drawn to out of hundreds'!) and reopened it on 23 August 2002.
DET 20/8/2002 Business Supplement, p.1; *DM* 31/8/1870.

SALISBURY**

London Road   *1893*

The fame of Robert Gascoyne-Cecil, 3rd Marquess of Salisbury, KG, PC, GCVO (1830-1903) as a statesman was only matched by that of Palmerston and Disraeli, and this pub – undoubtedly already in existence – was probably renamed in his honour at the end of his second stint as Prime Minister (his first two terms being broken briefly by Gladstone). Doubtless a less Tory-minded landlord reverted to the original nomenclature shortly afterwards, for the name is absent from the 1895 *Directory*. Nevertheless, Salisbury served a successful third term from 1895-1902.

SALUTATION

Rotten Row   *–1768–*

Only known from a reference of 1768 offering the inn for sale. The name refers to the well-known New Testament incident, and dates to pre-Reformation times.
DM 5/2/1768

SARACEN'S HEAD*

St James's Lane   *by 1723-1868*

Built on what later became the site of the rear, lower, wing of the Post Office, added in 1869-70. First mentioned in 1723, but probably much older. In 1741, German Pole of Radburne Hall, setting a yardstick which was to be well surpassed by Sir Harry Harpur two decades later, received the following bill after the 1741 parliamentary election, during which, as a Tory, he had failed to be elected:

'By the first orier	£ 1 0s 0d
For 210 gallons of ale @ 16d per gall	£14 0s 0d
For eating, £2 & tobacco @ 10/-	£2 10s 0d
For wine & mead	£1 16s 0d
	£19 6s 0d'

It was a coaching inn, for sale in 1786 and 1831, and to let in 1804 (with a billiard room) and 1826, but it lost business rapidly after the end of that era, although a coronation dinner was held here in 1838. It was advertised for sale in 1858 as 'Suitable as shops or warehousing'. Nonetheless, it soldiered on under former *Coach & Horses* landlord William Hollis until December 1867, and it was offered for sale as a development site in January 1868, being purchased by the GPO and was pulled down in that year. The name derives from the crest of the Shirleys, Earls Ferrers of Staunton Harold (Leicestershire.) and of Shirley, which derives from their service in the Crusades in the 12th

century: *a saracen's head in profile couped at the shoulders proper wreathed about the temples or and azure.* Its demise may have led to the renaming of the *Turf* in Victoria Street, only a few yards away, as the *Saracen's Head*.
DCR 8/10/1858; DM 4/10/1739, 2/2/1776, 12/1/1786, 25/9/1804, 4/10/1826, 26/10/1831, 4/7/1838, 13/10/1858, 31/12/1867 (with inventory) & 22/1/1868

Saracen's Head, Victoria Street, 2002.

SARACEN'S HEAD*

12 Victoria Street by 1846
An 18th century building on an odd, wedge-shaped site, refronted in 1938 by Bass in a restrained style reflecting that of the original building: three storeys, three bays and top parapet, with the ground floor *in antis* embellished with two attached Doric columns. Originally named the *Turf Tavern* later adding and *Wine Vaults* to its name (in 1881 when it was advertised for sale as an 'old established public house'), no doubt as a reflection of Derby as a venue for race-meetings.

Between 1903 and 1908 James Eadie & Co acquired it and renamed it the *Saracen's Head*, perhaps as an echo of the old coaching inn, which once stood only a few yards away in St James's Lane and which had closed slightly less than 40 years before. Sold to Bass in 1937. In March, 1996, in search, no doubt, of a quick buck, Bass refurbished it as a 'themed' Irish bar, calling it *O'Neill's* after the great Irish princely house, but this purely cosmetic facelift failed to bring the expected rewards and in 1999 it was surprisingly renamed the *Victoria*, after the street. In 2001 it reverted to the *Saracen's Head*.
DM 2/3/1881

SAWYER'S ARMS*

See SIR HENRY WILMOT ARMS

SCARSDALE ARMS*

7 Brook Street   *by 1835-1876*
A reference to this inn occurs under 1858 in a list published in 1987. It may be the same as the anonymous beer house listed in 1835 at 6 Brook Street, bearing in mind the unreliability of addresses at this period. Landlord John Brentnall made a spirit licence application in 1874, but his free house was demolished to make way for the Great Northern Railway's Friar Gate extension in 1876-7. The arms are those of the Curzons, of Kedleston, created Lords Scarsdale in 1761: *argent on a bend sable three popinjays or collared gules.*
DM 26/8/1874; DT 13/2/1987

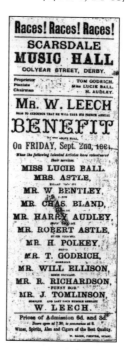

Scarsdale Arms, Colyear Street, music hall poster, 1881.

SCARSDALE ARMS*

9 Colyear Street by 1850-1965
Although listed in 1857 it appeared to have been unoccupied at that date; most of the housing in the area was fairly new then, however, having been put up on the former parkland of the Jacobean House from 1852, when that building was truncated in order to accommodate Becket Street. However this inn was up and running by 1850. By 1881, it had a rather home-spun music-hall attached. A poster of that year advertises an 11-act programme (all without doubt, part-timers), promoted by the landlord, Tom Goodrich, who also appeared as promoter and as a comedian, putting himself rather modestly as 7th on the bill. Goodrich was landlord from 1877 to his death in 1886 when his wife took over, and closed the entertainments. In the 1930s it was owned by James Eadie & Co Closed and demolished in 1965 to enable the completion of the Pennine Hotel (*qv*). The name probably is to be explained by the fact that Lord Scarsdale owned the site and, indeed, the majority of the land in the area.

SERGEANT PEPPER'S

See DUKE OF YORK

SEVEN STARS*

97 (23) King Street   *by 1775*
One of the best-known Derby inns, set in a vernacular Grade II* listed building dated 1680 but with an earlier

Three views of the Seven Stars, King Street, the first a very early representation, the second from the late 1970s.

Seven Stars, King Street.

core. Yet there is no proof that the inn was established there before 1775, when the sign was described as 'the *Seven Stars*, otherwise the *Plough'* and Hutton and the *UBD* also call it the *Plough*. The question thus arises: was this inn previously called the *Plough*? Unfortunately it has left no record as Jewitt, in his wisdom, thought it represented the 7th degree in freemasonry, and another suggestion has been that it was named after the celestial aureola of the Blessed Virgin. Unfortunately, inn signs rarely included a written element in the 18th century to lend certainty. It was for sale in 1814, when it was bought by John Yates, the china painter, whose daughter married Alderman John Wallis of the *New Inn*. Until World War Two the customers drank their beer out of Derby porcelain (King Street)

tankards, the works being virtually next door. The closure of those works in 1935 meant that the supply dried up, and only six remained by 1944, due to their having been taken as 'souvenirs' and to normal attrition. Unfortunately, not one appears to have survived. Run 1846-1856 by James Alton, formerly of the *Brown Bear* and brother of the brewer, William. It was in the hands of the Henry family from 1920 until 1962, and beer was brewed on the premises by Tom Roome from 1930 until the same date when in July of that year, Mr P.A. Henry retired for reasons of health and it was sold to Scottish & Newcastle (then their only pub in Derby) who, according to the local paper, 'assured him that they intended to preserve the atmosphere and unique features of the pub.' In 2002 its existence was threatened by a new road scheme.

DET 5/6, 15/6 & 10/7/1962; *DM* 24/8/1775 & 18/12/1814; Hutton (1791); Jewitt *Reliquary* IX (1868-9) 157; *UBD* 1791

SEVEN STARS*

13 Leaper Street (126 (33) Brook Street)   by 1833-1963
Scene of a celebrated incident during the 1833-4 'Silk Trades' Lock-out' when a group of strike-breakers had been drinking here on 18 February 1834. Joseph Brown, a striker, was seriously injured in a fight with Harry Ingram,

a 'black sheep' as the black-legs were then called. The latter was transported for life, Charles Howard Whitehurst QC having got him off a capital charge. Full licence by 1874 and an Offilers' pub by 1937, when Charles E. Rushton was landlord and it was the most popular local pub, according to Elsie Goodhead. Subject of a CPO 1961. Mr Motley adds that in 1955 'old Bluenose' was 'still brewing strongly' (on the premises) and that he handed over to Jack Cadman who served the last ale in 1963. Demolished shortly afterwards. Craven (1988) 159-160; Goodhead (1986) 13

(OLD) SEVEN STARS*

29 (1) Nottingham Road (Navigation Row; St Mary's Bridge) by 1777-1912

The fact that this inn was named (almost universally and from 1777) the *Old Seven Stars*, suggests that it was longer known by that name than the better-known establishment in King Street. It stood opposite the bridge, an iron *pissoir* in the road in front, and was very close to the old China Factory. A notable landlord was Thomas Tatlow, there from before 1818 until after 1835. He was another china painter, although his brother, Joseph, is rather better known, having been a friend of William Billingsley of the nearby *Sir John Falstaff*. Repton-educated Tatlow, nevertheless, was a flower painter of some repute and he and his brothers were great nephews of John Tatlow of Codnor (died 1763), a friend of John Whitehurst's and son-in-law of his great friend, the millionaire mine-promoter Anthony Tissington FRS. Tatlow was, by 1843, succeeded by a third china painter, in this case the relatively obscure William Hill. One is tempted to wonder if the *Old Seven Stars* had become a sort of unofficial pension fund for time-expired china painters! The pub thereafter soldiered on until about the time of World War One. It was reconstructed with a 125ft frontage (according to the sale advertisement of 1808) by William Forester when the bridge was replaced in 1792-4 and the approaches needed to be rebuilt and widened. It was for sale again in 1883 but was later pulled down; had it survived longer, the ring road would have accounted for it anyway. It conceivably had a short period bearing the name *Navigation*. It had a bowling green in 1852 and may well have added 'bowling green' to its title in 1833, *qv Bowling Green.*

DET 14/3/2002; DM 11& 15/2/1808, 1/8/1883

SEYMOURS

Cheapside (St Werburgh's Church Yard) 1988

On the closure of Ashley's, chemist's, in Cheapside in 1980, the whole of this rather ramshackle block of 18th century buildings, once with top-floor north light weavers' windows, became semi-derelict until this pub was opened,

Seymour's, St Werburgh's Church Yard, March 2002.

initially as a wine bar, with a first-floor restaurant. The latter later closed, but the inn is still in business.

SHAFTESBURY

16 Shaftesbury Street by 1898-1977

A beerhouse incorporated in a relatively new street laid out to accommodate workers at Ley's Foundry, and named after the reformer Sir Anthony Ashley-Cooper, KG, MP, 7th Earl of Shaftesbury (1801-1886). He was admired by Sir Francis Ley, and had just died when Ley developed the area. Shaftesbury married Lady Emily C.C.F. Cowper, a daughter of 5th Earl Cowper, of Melbourne Hall, which was a notable local connection. Full licence granted to Hardy's brewery in 1950, but closed and cleared two decades ago.

SHAKESPEARE**

Unknown location - 1736 -

Named as the venue for a duel between Lord Southwell and Hon. John Stanhope MP in June 1736. Sir Thomas Southwell MP for Leitrim in the Irish Parliament, succeeded his newly-ennobled father in 1720 as 2nd Lord Southwell of Castle Matress (Irish Peerage) and was Governor of Limerick, dying in 1766. His presence is explained by the fact that he was married to a daughter of Thomas Coke of Melbourne Hall. Stanhope, MP for Nottingham 1727-48, was the 3rd son of 3rd Earl of Chesterfield, of Bretby Hall, and brother of Derby MP Charles Stanhope, and also of the famous connoisseur and man of letters, Philip Dormer, 4th Lord Chesterfield. Both survived the encounter, so honour must have been satisfied. Neither of the other inns of this name were then in existence or so called, so this one must have been one of the more fashionable town centre ones, later renamed.

DM 24/6/1736

(OLD) SHAKESPEARE*

17 Bold Lane by 1778-1903

After the opening of the theatre in Bold Lane by James Whiteley in 1773, two inns came into being, called after our greatest poet; this one by 1778. That it was the first is attested by its use of the adjective 'Old' in its title. In fact, the building was very much older than the inn which occupied it, a not uncommon phenomenon, as the probable case of the *Seven Stars* attests. It was for sale in 1795 and 1864, when the closure of the theatre for conversion into a gospel hall by Alderman Wilkins probably threatened a drastic falling-off of trade. Indeed, from being a fashionable post-theatre venue, it declined into a beerhouse, being to let as such in 1869. By 1908 it had been purchased by Mrs Boden (a temperance fanatic) and was demolished by 1910 to make way for the small park she created on the south-west side of Bold Lane in memory of her late husband, Henry (died 1908): Boden's Pleasaunce, her testamentary intentions being later stretched to allow the building of a vast and hideous car park on the site.

DM 22/6/1795, 24/8/1864 & 13/10/1869

SHAKESPEARE*

16 Sadler Gate   *1737*

Advertised to let as the *Ostrich* and 'newly built' in 1737, the proprietor being George Bage (died 1766) a Darley Abbey paper manufacturer, and son of Stanton-by-Dale

Shakespeare, Sadler Gate, 2001.

born George, senior. The later story that he was a Quaker is quite unconfirmed by the sources. He was thrice married, his first wife being the sister of England's greatest native-born wrought iron-smith, Robert Bakewell (1682-1752). They had three children, of whom the youngest, Robert (1728-1801) of Elford Hall, Staffs, was, after Derbyshire-born Samuel Richardson, England's second great pioneer of the novel, his finest work being *Hermsprong or, Man as He is Not* of 1791. He was a friend of Erasmus Darwin, and his son Charles (1753-1822), of Shrewsbury, was an architect and engineer, friend of William Strutt, and designer of the first iron-framed fireproof mill, in Abbey Foregate, Shrewsbury. It is not known how long the Bage family held on to the freehold. It still appears under this name until at least 1791. The name represents the crest of Sir Thomas Coke of Holkham, Norfolk, and of Longford Hall, Derbyshire, who had been raised to the peerage as 1st Lord Lovell in 1728, later becoming Earl of Leicester, and he owned property in Derby. His heir, Wenman Roberts (later Coke) was a leading subscriber to the Assembly Rooms. The building is 16th or 17th century but with a late 18th or early 19th-century façade, and had extensive stabling even as late as 1936 (entered from George Yard, behind). It had been renamed the *Shakespeare* by 1822, and was to let in 1855 and for sale in 1873, when the Corporation of Derby bought the freehold. Beer brewed on the premises until 1925. Early in the 20th century the licensee was J.E. Felix, later of the *Old Dolphin*. Belonged to Pountain's in 1937. Around 1982 its carriage arch to the front was covered in to extend the accommodation: a great mistake visually. Until recently part of the Thompson dynasty, being held on lease in 1994 from Carlsberg-Tetley by one of the sons of John Thompson, of Ingleby; another was proprietor of the *Bell*. The *Vines* is also part of the family empire. John Thompson brews his own (very likable) beer at Ingleby. On 1 June 2002 this historic inn was renamed by its new proprietor, Simon Marriott, the *Blue Dog*, after his Staffordshire Terrier named Blue. There is another establishment, in Atherstone, Warwicks, similarly named after this dog.

DET 8/6/2002; DM 1737, 13/6/1855 & 27/8/1873; UBD 1791.

SHAMROCK*

59 Goodwin Street   *by 1857-1908*

Named almost certainly to encourage the colony of Irish families who in the early and mid-19th century lived (in some squalor, unfortunately) in this area, mainly in 'Rookeries' – grandish old houses split up by unscrupulous landlords. First recorded by name in 1874, but to be identified with the anonymous beerhouse listed at this address in 1857 and 1862. The name quite probably migrated with a landlord from King Street. Closed in 1908 after pressure from Mrs Boden and the Derby Temperance Association.

SHAMROCK**

34 King Street   *by 1850-1852*

Possibly later renamed the *Mechanics' Arms;* it seems not unlikely that the landlord took the name with him to Goodwin Street, first recorded by name only a few years later.

SHEARMAN'S ARMS

Bridge Gate   *1658-1691*

Established by Thomas Hutton (1616-1691) an ex-Northallerton shearman himself, in one of those 'three low houses' on the south side of Bridge Gate east of the church. It may have been a pub before Hutton took over and changed the name to that of a non-existent livery company's arms, and the *Life* of the landlord's great-grandson, the historian does not make it clear what happened when the old man died. Certainly not in the family by the historian's childhood (1730-40s), and probably renamed.

Hutton (1816), 6.

SHERWOOD (FORESTER)*

85 St Thomas's Road   *1890*

This large brick villa with stone dressings was built as a private house on part of the Normanton estate of the Edge family by Mr A. Taylor in 1885. Yet four years later it was sold to Ind Coope's brewery for conversion into an hotel, a job which was completed the following year, March (Cambs)-born Ambrose Otway Fuller being appointed manager. He later married Lottie Baker of the *Royal Hotel* for which more prestigious establishment he thereafter forsook this hotel. It took its name from the 45th/95th (Sherwood Foresters) Regiment, whose headquarters the nearby Normanton Barracks were. Later it declined from being an hotel to a (fully-licensed) pub. Post-war it was a much-favoured venue for wedding receptions and the like.

(NETHER) SHIP

Cornmarket   *by 1750-1772*

Situated at the 'lower end of Cornmarket' and sold up in 1770. It is referred to as the *Nether Ship* in 1772, when it was run by Withnall Clarke 'late servant to John Gisborne' (of St Helen's House). Also, inexplicably, called the *Upper Ship* in 1772. Could it have been a renaming of the *Angel*?

DM 4/5/1770, 3/1 & 20/3/1772.

(OLD) SHIP*

East Street   *1778-c.1870*

Although this appears in no directory, it was drawn by George Bailey of Derby *c.*1870, which shows it to have been

a very low little inn with an extravagantly shaped gable of *c.*1660, all done in brick. That, and the name, might imply that it perhaps dated from that period, but it may even have been long closed when Bailey drew and captioned it. In 1789 it boasted an assembly room.

DM 26/3/1789

SHIP*

48 (8) Ford Street (corner Friar Gate)   *by 1827-1846*

Stated to have been on the east corner with Friar Gate. This was a late 18th-century building, with a curved angle, which certainly looks as if it had been built as a pub, rather in the London style of the period. Thus the establishment may date back to *c.*1790 or so, and it may have closed around the date given. If so, it would have escaped notice in the unreliable *Pigot's Directory* of 1822, and have been one of a pair of anonymous beer houses listed (unnumbered) in Friar Gate in 1835 and 1846. Let to Thomas Briand in 1841. Apparently a free house.

DM 17/3/1841

SHIP

Alderman Hill (Full Street)   *1713-1827*

The Every papers reveal that this inn was built in 1713 'in Alderman Hill' (ie the north end of Full Street) by Sir Henry Every, 3rd Bt, for his cousin Henry, son of Francis, (3rd son of Sir Simon, 1st Bt) who, up to that date, had a rather chequered career. He, naturally, became the landlord, and also ran a chandlery business, which he handed on to his son, John (1725-1767) on his death, aged 64, in 1765. The family connection was severed when John's son, Edward, succeeded to the family baronetcy and the estate at Egginton in 1779 on the death of his kinsman, Revd Sir John Every, 7th Bt. One source claims that this inn came into existence when a landlord of the *Ship* in Cornmarket transferred the business to Full Street. The evidence of the Every papers and, indeed, all the independent corroboration, establish that this was not so. It appears to have finally closed (perhaps long after the Every estate sold it) between 1827 and 1835.

Every MSS, courtesy the late Sir John Every Bt.

(OLD) SHIP*

111 (45) Gerard Street   *by 1861-1912*

Probably consciously named *Old Ship*, it was to let following a contents sale in 1861, implying an existence of some time previous to that date. It was again for sale in 1864 and 1865. It closed during World War One and became a private dwelling until being demolished in the late 1970s as part of the clearance of the Gerard Street area, although the block of houses next to which it was built remains up as far as Webster Street.

DM 21/8/1861, 11/51864 7 20/9/1865

SHIP

St Michael's Lane   *–1906–*

Only recorded in a painting in Derby Museum's collections, depicting it in 1906. No other record of it appears to have come to light. The site is so close to Alderman Hill that this inn may represent a migration of the *Ship* built by the Every family. Possibly also long converted to another use when painted.

SHOULDER OF MUTTON

St Peter's Parish   *–1761–*

Occurs only in the list of inns in which Sir Harry Harpur left money for the wooing of potential voters; traditional name.

SILENT WOMAN
See QUIET WOMAN

(OLD) SILK MILL*

19 (21) Full Street (corner Silk Mill Lane)   *by 1862*

It may be that this small inn soldiered on for generations as an unrecorded beerhouse, for by the time it is first recorded by name in 1874, the silk industry had departed from Sir Thomas Lombe's historic Silk Mill nearby, and after which it had been named. The cottage in which it existed was undoubtedly one of those built by the Lombes for their workers in the years following the establishment of the mill in 1718. It was listed anonymously as a beerhouse in 1862 and later was acquired by the Nottingham Brewery, who sold it to Tennant Bros in the 1930s. By this time, the extension of the power station had necessitated the pitching of Sowter Road and the demolition of the old inn in 1924; it was replaced by a half-timbered and stone-based building by 1928 on a slightly different site, but adhering to the original alignment of the street. It passed to Whitbreads in the 1970s, and was by 1989 incorporated into Mr Nigel Barker's empire, now part of the Wibberly Inns chain, and refurbished, although still in the regrettable open-plan mode much favoured by all but the customers today. A

mural on the north-west wall, painted in 1986, depicts a view of the Silk Trades' Lockout of 1833-4 and was executed with indifferent perspective and a selective view of history.

SILVER LION
See WELLINGTON

SIR CHARLES COLVILE

Midland Road   *–1874–*

Possibly a renaming of the *Midland Arms*. Free house, named after the rather obscure local grandee Sir Charles Colvile of Duffield Hall (1759-1833), High Sheriff of

Old Silk Mill, Full Street, c.1920.

Derbyshire 1832. He was elder son of Robert Colvile of Newton Colville, Cambridgeshire, and came to Derbyshire by virtue of his marriage to the heiress of Thomas Porter Bonell of Duffield Hall (cf. *Colville Arms*).

SIR CHARLES NAPIER*

88 (92) (Upper) Brook Street   *by 1871-1908*

A free house, but had become a shop by 1908. Named after Admiral Sir Charles Napier, 1st Count of St Vincent, KCB, MP (1786-1860), who served in the Napoleonic Wars under locally educated Sir John Borlase Warren and commanded the Royal Portuguese Fleet in 1833. He was elder son of Hon Charles Napier and grandson of 6th Lord Napier. The establishment of the inn probably coincided with this man's death, thus ruling out the less likely possibility that it was named after Field Marshal Sir Charles James Napier (1782-1853) GCB, the conqueror of Sind and a cousin of the above. From 1877 to 1885 run by Stephen Sherwin, cousin of John (of the *Litchurch Inn*) and by marriage of China painter William Hill of the *Old Seven Stars*.

DLSL Conveyances, Deposit DL3d (ii) nos. 28 & 32 of 1877 and 1885.

Sir Frederick Roberts, Pear Tree Road, c.1930.

SIR FREDERICK ROBERTS*

131-133 (49) Pear Tree Road (corner Yates Street)   *by 1892-1991*

Corner pub converted from his corner shop by Thomas Richard Bird (father of the founders of Birds' bakery) after 1891 and before 1895, when first listed as a pub. Probably named immediately prior to the elevation, in 1892, of Field Marshal Sir Frederick Roberts, VC, KG, KP, GCB, GCSI, GCIE, OM, PC, VD, to the peerage as 1st Lord Roberts of Kandahar, or else it would have been called the *Lord Roberts*. He had won his VC at Lucknow in the Indian Mutiny, rather topically (at the time of writing) captured Khabul and relieved Kandahar in the Second Afghan War,

and was an even greater hero than Wolseley. He went on to become C-in-C 1901-4, being created in the former year 1st Earl Roberts and Viscount St Pierre. Even his son was a hero, receiving a posthumous VC in South Africa in 1899. Inn sold to Stretton's and granted a full licence in 1950. Known to locals as 'Dicky Birds' from the name of its first (and memorable) landlord, who remained in charge until after World War One. Ground floor rebuilt with a covering of decorative ceramic tiles in the 1920s. Closed by the magistrates on the recommendation of the constabulary in 1991, reputedly due to having become a centre for drug transactions and left empty, boarded-up and decaying until a demolition order was granted in October 1997 and acted upon before the year's end.

SIR HENRY WILMOT ARMS**

17/18 (Little) Castle Street (corner Union (Short) Street)   *by 1852-1874*

This beer house had, in 1852, a bowling alley and stables, entered from around the corner in Short Street; it would appear to have later become the *Sawyers' Arms*. Named as the next (below) and renamed after the non-existent arms of a non-existent livery company, the stimulus coming, no doubt, from Alderman Thomas Roe's nearby timber yard, later destroyed by fire. It is possible that the original name migrated with the landlord to Rivett Street, forcing his successor to think of something new.

(SIR HENRY) WILMOT('S) ARMS

50 (17) Rivett Street (corner Chetwynd Street)   *by 1857-1935*

Named after Colonel Sir Henry Wilmot's coat-of-arms. He was at the time the recently-succeeded head of the house of Wilmot of Chaddesden Hall, 5th Bt (1831-1901), who, like Sir Frederick Roberts, was also awarded the VC at Lucknow, and later sat as MP for Derbyshire. Listed in 1878 merely as the *Wilmot Arms*. Beer brewed on the premises as late as 1932. The licence was purchased by the Corporation so that the inn could be sacrificed for the widening of Traffic Street, and was transferred by further sale to the *Blue Peter*, Alvaston, 7 January 1935.

SIR JOHN FALSTAFF*

Bridge Gate   *by 1761-1791*

One of the inns used by Sir Henry Harpur to encourage the electors of Derby to vote for him in 1761, and possibly the former *Crown*. In 1767 it was for sale, 'Late William Billingsley'. This is an interesting reference to William Billingsley (d.1770), china painter at Duesbury's China Factory and button warehouse proprietor, who ran it for a number of years. He married Mary Dallison at St Werburgh's in 1757 and their eldest son was the celebrated

china painter and failed entrepreneur, William Billingsley (1758-1828), who also began his long career at the Derby factory. The elder Billingsley died in 1770 with the pub still unsold, and indeed, his illustrious son is listed as its proprietor in the *UBD* of 1791; between 1770 and his coming of age in 1780 it was probably run by his mother Mary. In 1796 he left Derby for Pinxton, never to return and the pub was probably sold and underwent a name change after its sale, losing the association with Shakespeare's flamboyant character, as modelled by the China factory in the elder Billingsley's day (c. 1765) as 'James Quinn in the role of Sir John Falstaff' – no doubt the sign's direct inspiration. Whilst it may have become the *Jolly Colliers* or the *Navigation*, the Billingsley connection strongly suggests that it was renamed the *Nottingham Arms*. Haslem tells us that Billingsley lived at no. 22, which was right next door to this inn, in Haslem's day no.21. The *Nottingham Arms* was, from the 1820s, run by Billingsley's nephew, William Wheeldon (1789-1847), sometime partner in the China factory, farmer and maltster of Nottingham Road. Whilst Billingsley clearly held on to his inn whilst in Derby, later financial disasters would have without doubt forced him to sell it, and to whom better to sell it than to his brother-in-law, William Wheeldon, or one of his sons, of whom the younger just happens to turn up towards the end of Billingsley's life running a pub on Bridge Gate?
DET 14/3/2002; Haslem (1876) 50,54; Jewitt (1883) ii.101; *UBD* 1791

SIR RICHARD COBDEN
See RICHARD COBDEN

SIR ROBERT PEEL*
45 (43) Wellington Street (corner Park Street)
by 1852-1995
Probably founded shortly after the death of Rt Hon Sir Robert Peel, PC, MP, 2nd Bt, (1788-1850), who served as Prime Minister in 1834 and 1841-6, being listed anonymously in 1857. Landlord Thomas Maundrell, shortly after 1862, issued brass 3d and 1½d checks made by Edwin Cottrill. By the 1930s it was an Alton's pub and in December 1938 it was reopened after having been replaced by a new edifice, tall, three storeys on the angle with a hipped pantiled roof, steel windows and a lower wing of two paired bays to Wellington Street, all united by light

---

The Sir Robert Peel
Commercial Inn & Chop House,
Corner of Wellington St., near the Railway Station, Derby.
Good and well-aired Beds, and first-rate accommodation for Railway Travellers, &c. JOSEPH DOLMAN, Proprietor.

Sir Robert Peel, Wellington Street, advertisement, 1852.

ceramic tiling at ground floor level and a bold string course above it. From 2nd December 1953 until his death in June 1994, the landlord was Alfred Whitehurst, when he was succeeded by his widow, Jean, until closure by Pubmaster in January 1995. She was the daughter of Arthur George Petts (1901-1953), landlord of the *Chestnut Tree* and previously of the *Cock*, Cockpit Hill, and the *Star & Garter,* St Mary's Gate. The inn had been up for sale in September 1993. Since 1995 the building has been licensed only as a railwaymen's club, inevitably losing its name, although it is still displayed above the entrance.
DET 29/3 & 13/7/1988, 7/9/1993 & 11/5/1994

SIR WALTER SCOTT
180 Osmaston Road
by 1874-1965
A beerhouse established next door to the former Litchurch Post Office and named after the celebrated author of the *Waverley Novels*, Sir Walter Scott of Abbotsford (1771-1832), created 1st Bt in 1820. In the 1930s it belonged to Ind Coope & Allsopp, and the rate assessor wrote in his book: 'Note after the war *(ie World War One)* many people in rooms around here have now got houses on Corporation estates, 23 November 1932.' Because of the serious decline in clientele, the landlord accordingly got a rate reduction; the phenomenon explains the demise of many a small inner-city pub. Nevertheless it lingered until the later 1960s, when it was closed and later demolished, to be replaced by Council flats.

SIR WALTER SCOTT**
Wardwick
by 1842-1843
There is no clue to the site of this inn.

SITWELL ARMS
51-53 Sacheverel Street
by 1833-1950
Built in a street which ran right across the grounds of Babington House (previously Sitwell Hall) then still standing, and named after the family whose town residence the house once was. The family had married an heiress of the Sacheverels, hence the name of the street. It was for sale in 1881 and in the 1930s it was owned by Offilers', but was closed 9 February 1950, when the licence was transferred to the *Kingsway Hotel*. It was eventually demolished.
DM 21/8/1881

SITWELL TAVERN*
21 Sitwell Street
by 1856
Named for the same reasons as the preceding, although why two such similarly named pubs should exist so close to each other is a mystery. It was a going concern in 1856 when a sheep roast was held here to celebrate the end of the war with Russia. A spirit licence application was made

in 1874. Brewing on the premises in 1926 but since the 1930s owned by Shipstone's Brewery, and now the only surviving building in the street, bar a mosque.
DM 21/5/1856 & 26/8/1874

SLOANES
See THOMAS-À-BECKET

SMITHFIELD
See (CATTLE) MARKET HOTEL

SODA BAR**
Friar Gate   *2001*
Named, presumably, after the now-unfashionable sparking drink additive rather than the chemical.

SOUGH, THE
See (OLD) WINE VAULTS

(OLD) SPA INN
204 (210) Abbey Street   *1832*
The early 18th-century gabled brick building, now largely stuccoed, is part of the spa complex built in 1733 by Dr William Chauncey around a mineral spring he found on the site. Chauncey 'put down a basin into the spring of it, to come out fresh: he built a cover over the spring which discharges itself by a grate (grating) and keeps the place always dry. About 20 yards below the spa he made a handsome cold bath and some rooms to it... two dressing rooms and with a large room over the whole and pleasure walks... at considerable expense'. This was nothing new, though, for the spot was known as a 'watering place' as early as 1611. Chauncey died in 1736, and it is by no means clear how long it flourished – as an intended rival to Buxton, which plan never really took off. It was let (probably by Chauncey's widow) to Samuel Greatorex who held it until at least 1759 and it occurs as a spa on a deed of 1764. It is even marked as a spa on Rogerson's map of Derby (1819) but this may merely mark the survival of the name, for advertisements in the local press suggest that by that date it was a private residence. In 1821 we find 'the Spa House in this town' was occupied by William Boothby Gent, and later that year it was to be sold by auction. Boothby was a member of a Nottingham family (not the Ashbourne Hall baronets) from which the late Lord Boothby descended. This having failed, it was in 1823 to be let 'as a respectable family residence'. Not long afterwards it was sold to a Mr Bentley and in 1832 was established as a simple inn, at the same time that the newly-pitched Abbey Street (about 1825) was being built up.

Ye Old Spa Inn, Abbey Street. **Three pictures here,** first from c.1940s, second 1977, third 2000.

'To be let and entered upon immediately, the Spa public house, situate within a short distance of Derby, containing brew house, good cellars and every convenience... together with three acres of land attached' – no doubt part of Dr Chauncey's original demesne. The advertisement ends '...the vendor Mr Bentley being on the premises'. Indeed, there were later three houses (198-200 Abbey Street) built on the street in front of it and court No.2 crammed in around it too, although these were cleared away to enlarge the car park in 1978. At or around the date of its conversion, the ancillary buildings were cleared away, and other parts added.

Traces of Chauncey's baths remain, however, for three blocked stoke-holes were noticed by Mrs Barbara Hutton and her team in surveying the fabric in 2001 visible in the cellars. Traces of what were interpreted as a sunken bath (but on a different alignment to the present cellar) were also found, suggesting that Chauncey based his system on Roman Baths and built a *calidarium* next to a plunge bath. The building itself, probably originally T-shaped, is not aligned upon the street (which long post-dated it) but upon some odd east-west field boundaries which may relate to the mediaeval headlands laid out for rent to townspeople by the canons of Darley who then owned the land, called the Newlands. The southern portion of the present building appears to have been a Regency addition, stuccoed and grooved to resemble ashlar, probably put on by Boothby to afford improved accommodation for his family.

It was sold as the *Spa Tavern* with a house adjoining in 1853, perhaps to Thomas Chapman, the licensee in 1862-4, and again with three acres – perhaps part of its original demesne – in 1882. Chapman was succeeded as licensee by 1871 by William Birks, and he held the licence until it was taken over by William Hollis either in 1878 or by his son Edward between 1891 and 1893 – there is uncertainty on the point. However, the Hollises descendants are clear that prior to Edward taking over, the Spa was actually owned by

his father, William, in which capacity he appears on the unreliable licensed houses list of 1861. However, this shows only the licensees, and the freeholder was sometimes a different person altogether. Edward's grandfather – another William – had been a country boy who rose from an ostler to become landlord of the *Coach & Horses,* St James's Lane, later crossing the street to run the *Saracen's Head.* Compensation paid to him for the loss of the latter may have enabled him to buy the freehold (or a reversion) of the *Spa* perhaps in 1868, later than the 1861 list (compiled from census returns, apparently), but it must be borne in mind that John Arguile has noted that Edward Hollis bought it from R. Lyon of Clay Cross (a person notably absent from the directories) as late as 1894. Edward's great uncle, Thomas, married a daughter of pioneer hydraulic and gas engineer Thomas Crump and took over the chemist shop in Queen Street run by the younger Joseph Bloor (*qv Britannia*) – can there have been a direct connection, one wonders? Edward Hollis (1869-1932) was a larger-than-life figure, businessman, property developer, golfer and generally flamboyant figure. Under him a Mr Wallace brewed on the premises, and there were 'several bars including a billiard room, and customers were served from a central circular counter.' Hollis sold most of the three acres of land to the Derby Co-operative Society for their transport depot in Woods Lane. His elder daughter and co-heiress had married ex-RR premium apprentice Reginald Arthur Newbold (son of Edmund, of *Hollybush* fame) and when he became ill, they took over, selling to Ind Coope (as Stretton's) on 26th May 1933 for £8,750, a year after his death. The new landlord was Harold Lakin, succeeded in 1938 by Albert McLocklin and his wife 'Biff' (another stalwart of the Derby Ladies' LVA) under whom beer continued to be brewed on the premises until December 1941. He, along with neighbouring landlord Arthur Barr (*Durham Ox*) and Jerry Shaw (*New Market*, East Street) were die-hard boxing enthusiasts, and in the winter of 1941/2, brewing having ceased, the brew-house was turned into a gymnasium which attracted young boxers of local repute. The 'resident' manager was Fred ('Bauble' or 'Bawbal') Harrison,

Ye Olde Spa, Abbey Street. Licensee Edward Hollis with straw boater on the lawn.

who ran a neighbouring chip shop, aided by Bob Kirkly, who had fought as Bob Curley. A few were of, or rose to, national repute, like Derby-based Bert Gilroy, the Scots middleweight champion. Memorable exhibition bouts were held in the rear yard on Sunday mornings. The departure of the McLocklins to the *Marquis of Granby* in 1947 led to this effective forcing house of pugilistic talent moving to Agard Street, where it became the Premier Boxing Club. The landlords from 1954 to 1968 were the father and son Bert and Ken Rawson, but in the latter year Derek Tranter took over. He was a former professional jockey, who still kept a racehorse in stables and served until 1983, when a refurbishment of the fabric of this Grade II listed building was undertaken by architect Keith Roberts.

In some ways it is a pity that this inn, opened out and refurbished by the brewery (Allied), not only in 1983-4 but in 2001, cannot be more imaginatively restored, taking better account of its history, and become an element on the itinerary of visitors: it is an important site. Nevertheless, it deservedly won CAMRA's top award for pub refurbishment in 1985.

DBR No. 252 of 3/4/2001; *DET* 26/6 & 21 & 24/8/2000, 19/3/2002; *DM* 10/10/1755; 16/1 & 14/3 & 22/8/1821, 21/3/1832, 9/8/1853 & 21/3/1882; 'J. O. King' in *Derby Drinker* 1985; *DAJ* XXXVI (1914) 93; Simpson (1826) II. 531-2.

SPENCER'S VAULTS
See NEW MARKET

SPOTTED BOAR
St Peter's Parish −1760−
Known only from an advertisement of 1760. Probably later renamed. Name agricultural (the Old Spot is a well-known breed of pig, now very rare) rather than heraldic.
DM 14/11/1760

(OLD) SPOT(TED HORSE)*
47 (26-7) St Helen's Street (corner Goodwin Street)   *by 1818-1912*
Started off as the *Spotted Horse* when owner Mr Cross offered for sale in 1818 'a substantial dwelling house in complete repair with brew house, yard, garden Etc, adjoining the *Chequers,* Willow Row' the tenant being William Adcock: this sounds like another ex-pub. Listed as the *Old Spot* between 1827 and 1843 when run by Thomas Dimock, later (after the defection of the landlord's son James Dimock to Victoria Street in 1841-2, perhaps taking the name with him, *qv*) the *Old Spotted Horse*, and colloquially thereafter (and formally in due course) merely *Old Spot*. This chopping and changing of the name between pig and horse might suggests that the *Spotted Boar* was its precursor, and existed all the while – from 1760 – in Willow Row, the snag being that Willow Row was never in St Peter's parish. It was re-let in 1855. Closed just after World War One by the then owners, Home Brewery, and much later (after 1956) demolished. Today the site lies beneath the east end of BBC Radio Derby.
DM 23/4/1818 & 7/11/1855

JAMES DIMOCK'S
WINE AND SPIRIT VAULTS,
SPOTTED HORSE INN, VICTORIA STREET, DERBY.
Dealer in London and Dublin Porter, in Casks and Bottles.

Spotted Horse, Victoria Street, advertisement, 1852.

SPOTTED HORSE*
5 Victoria Street.   *1842*
Founded by James Dimock, formerly of the *Spotted Horse*, St Helen's Street, who brought the name with him. It was listed as an unnamed beerhouse 1842-7, but appears as *Spotted Horse* thereafter. After he had transferred the inn to Victoria Street, Dimock in 1855 sold it to James Windsor and instead took over the *Dog & Duck*, Haarlem Street, Little City. However, he repurchased to the *Spotted Horse* in 1857, where he remained until 1860, a period during which he issued a 3d brass impressed pub check or token. In the 1850s the sign showed a white horse with black spots, with trees behind, and the name has been suggested to have stemmed from the fame of *The Tetrarch* which is eminently unlikely, as that celebrated thoroughbred, ever associated with jockey Steve Donoughue (died 1945), retired unbeaten well into the 20th century. In 1871-2 it was completely rebuilt with a 28ft frontage, in brick, of four storeys and five bays with stone dressings supported by an arcade at ground floor level, all in a rather feeble Lombardic style, probably to designs by George Henry Sheffield of Derby, butting up against the

new General Post Office (by J. Williams 1867), a much more distinguished stone building. It was accordingly renamed the *Post Office Hotel*. A spirit licence was accordingly applied for in 1874 and obtained. An Alton's pub at one time. In 1959, when the landlord was Joe Rostron, the retired boxer (see *Woodlark*) it closed for refurbishment, which entailed internal gutting, and the replacement of the arcade by a flat 1950s modernist façia of startling banality (replaced in 1983), by E.W. Edwards for Ind Coope, reopening 17 June 1960 once again as the *Spotted Horse*, a welcome revival of the ancient name. Rostron retired from it thereafter in 1963. A further refurbishment followed at the beginning of 1989, and this improved its appearance (whilst temporarily revealing the original façade in the process).

Unfortunately, as with the *Rising Sun*, the original name was (again) lost, and it became *Lloyd's*, part of a national chain of inns of that name. It was again renamed, as part of another nationwide 'branded' chain, the *Pig & Truffle* (not an activity carried out within these shores!) in December 1995 by Carlsberg-Tetley. Their PR department claimed that the new name generated the 'right mood signals': what (expensive) tosh!
DM 14/7/1855, 28/7/1858, 31/5/1871 & 26/8/1874

SPREAD EAGLE

Cornmarket   *by 1772-1791*
Mentioned in 1772, to let in 1787 as 'entirely rebuilt' and mentioned again in 1791, but nothing else known. The sign is generally taken to reflect one of the varying alliances with Prussia, Austria and Russia at various times in the 18th century, all of which states employed *eagles displayed* ('spread'). But note should be taken of local examples, *eg* the crests of the Boroughs of Castlefields, the Montgomerys of Cubley and the Cottons of Ridware and Derby.
DM 20/3/1772, 28/6 & 25/9/1787; *UBD* 1791.

SPREAD EAGLE*

53 (82) London Road (Street) (corner Eagle Street)
                                                        by 1756-1855
Probably the first inn one reached on the then new (1739) London Turnpike when coming from the south, and possibly established, with their help, on Borough family land at about the same time, hence the name, from their crest. In 1757 it was being run by William Brentnall (d.1775) father of Charles, who later ran the *Wine Vaults*. To let, confusingly, as 113 St Peter's Street, 'old licensed' in 1846 but plainly the same establishment, it is not heard of after being sold in 1855 and was probably pulled down and replaced by new buildings.
DM 21/1/1757, 9/9/1846 & 10/1/1855

SPREAD EAGLE*

47 Rivett Street (corner Chetwynd Street) by 1867-1898
A beer house, probably taking its name from the Borough family crest, Rivett Street having been laid out in the early 19th century on their former estate. It was certainly in existence in 1867, when a 'incident' of a criminal nature was reported as having occurred there, and for sale in 1879. Possibly a migration of the London Road pub of this name. Later a shop.
DM 14/8/1867 & 17/5/1879

STAG & PHEASANT*

25 (7) (Lower) Brook Street   by 1833-1875
A sporting sign for this beer house in the West End, built by 1833, and the scene of an attempted murder arising out of conflict between union and non-union labour a year later, like the incident at the *Seven Stars* nearby. To let in 1869, but sold and closed after 1874 and before 1887 when it was a barber's shop. Much later demolished to extend a mill complex. In the late 1830s the landlord was George Rowley, whose family had come here from Staffordshire, and in 1841 his widow, Sarah, had the inn; his son William Rowley (*Rising Sun*) and great-grandson, Frank Rowley (*Derby Volunteer*) were also local landlords.
DM 26/3/1834 & 16/9/1869.

STAG (& THORN)

109 (52) Traffic Street   by 1833-1912
Stood next to the rear of the Congregational Chapel and listed once or twice as the *Stag* but advertised for sale in 1873 under its full title. Later pulled down after a period as a shop.

STAMFORD HOTEL
See HOWARD HOTEL

STAND HOTEL
See GRANDSTAND

STANDING ORDER**

28-32, Iron Gate   1995
Opened 18 October, 1995 by J.D. Wetherspoon of London in the former NatWest Bank, and originally to have been called the *Banker's Draft*. The magnificent Grade II* listed building was erected for Crompton & Evans Union Bank to designs by J.A. Chatwin of Birmingham 1876-8 and is in Italian Palazzo revival style, with a rusticated ashlar ground floor, the two above being subtly detailed in stone around the fenestration but skinned over in plain brick giving the impression of lavishness. The banking hall itself, said to be the finest of any date in the Midlands, has been opened out and restored by the owners, and is most impressive.

STAR

See NEW MARKET, STAR & GARTER

STAR INN*

17 Gilman Street (corner Graham Street)   by 1874-1914
A beerhouse, turned into a shop and then cleared for works expansion after World War One. The name is a pre-Reformation religious one, probably reflecting the Star of Bethlehem, although one local family, the Ashtons of Castleton, Stoney Middleton and Killamarsh, bore *argent a mullet* (star) *sable* as their arms, and the Ropers of Turnditch and Heanor bore a shooting star as their crest. Perhaps more relevantly, the star is also the crest of the Worshipful Company of Innholders, and derives from the Star of Bethlehem as well. After 1914 the building was divided up as 'rooms' – today we would call them 'bed-sits' – and was demolished during the Cotton Lane clearance scheme in the 1960s.

STAR*

105 (27) Siddals Road (Siddals Lane)   by 1846-1935
Stood two doors down from the *British Lion*. Thrice for sale in the 19th century, in 1869, 1882 and 1884. Demolished for the slewing and widening of Traffic Street done in 1935, having become Gilman's motorcycle shop by then.
DM 24/3/1869, 22/2/1882 & 27/2/1884

STAR & GARTER*

21-22 St Mary's Gate (corner Bold Lane)   by 1800-1940
Said to have been a very old pub, even in the 19th century, so probably a renaming of one listed elsewhere – perhaps the *Miners' Arms*. The sign, which may have migrated with a landlord from the pub next listed, reflects the regalia of the Order of the Garter, founded in the 14th century by Edward III. When for sale as a going concern in 1800 it was known simply as the *Star,* and the *Old Star* in 1818/20 but correctly located at the corner of St Mary's Gate and Bold Lane. It may have been trying to differentiate itself from the *Star* in Siddals Lane, and gave up the struggle and added 'Garter' after 1827. In 1878 it was listed as 13 Bold Lane. A sheep roast was held here to celebrate the peace treaty with Russia in 1856. Acquired by Pountain's, who demolished it in 1934, replacing it by a larger building, following the curve of the street corner, and architecturally closely akin to the (*Royal*) *Telegraph* rebuilt by the same owners, and both undoubtedly by T.H. Thorpe. The last landlord, from 1 October 1939, was Arthur George Petts, formerly of the *Cock*. Commandeered because of the war and closed in February 1940 being in consequence transformed into County Council offices (since 1996 those of the City Council) and the licence – along with Mr & Mrs Petts – transferred to the *Chestnut Tree*.
DM 30/10/1800, 21/5/1856

Former Star and Garter, St Mary's Gate/Bold Lane corner, from Bold Lane car park 2001.

STAR & GARTER*

Walker Lane   by 1744-1791
Stood 'over against' (*ie* opposite) St Michael's Church when for sale in 1744. To let in 1769 by the owner, the *stuccadore* Abraham Denstone, who sought yet another tenant in 1775, but not owned by him by the time his will was proved in 1779 (cf. *Mitre*). It is possible that a later landlord transferred the name to the St Mary's Gate premises (above).
DM 12/10/1744, 24/2/1769, 3/3/1775; UBD 1791

Station, Midland Road, 1948.

STATION INN*

11 Midland Road (Station Street)   by 1854
Established by 1854 when there was a contents sale, it allegedly harboured a music hall in the 1870s and then known as 'Tyler's' – the name without doubt being peculiar to the music hall rather than the inn. It occupies two thirds of a row of three terraced houses of three storeys with sill bands and bracketed entablatures over the

windows, probably built in the 1840s. Purchased in 1926 from Charrington's, who rebuilt the ground floor with attractively decorative ceramic tiling, for £6,500 by Worthington's, later Bass, and by 1994 an Enterprise Inn.

STATION
See NEW STATION

STEAM BAR
See THOMAS-À-BECKET

STEAM MILL*
2 Ford Street (corner Willow Row)   *1857-1875*
Only known by name in the years either side of 1874, but the address appears as an anonymous beer house from 1857. Named after Brown's Steam Mill, Lodge Lane (cf. *Brown Bear*). Demolished to make way for All Saints' Mission Room, itself knocked down after World War Two.

STOCKBROOK TAVERN
110 Stockbrook Street   *by 1857-1935*
Named after the Stock Brook, the course of which (since culverted) is followed by the street, pitched around 1850. The inn fails to appear in the 1937 rate book, so presumably it closed in the later 1930s. Area cleared in the 1970s.

STORK*
54 (24) Macklin Street (corner Colyear Street) 1854-1965
A beer house which was granted a licence in 1854, and to let in 1868. The name may derive from Aesop's fable 'The Fox and the Stork' but more directly from the crest of the Derby Shores, and probably commemorates Sir John Shore, 1st Bt, later 1st Lord Teignmouth (1751-1834) – great-grandson of the celebrated Derby medico Sir John Shore – and Governor General of India 1792-7. The inn was later acquired by Pountain's who expanded it into two cottages in Colyear Street, later fitting steel windows and harling it. It was closed and demolished in the mid-1960s to make way for the Duckworth Square/Pennine Hotel 'improvement' scheme.

STRAWBERRY TREE
See MASON'S ARMS

STRUTT'S
See (ROYAL) TELEGRAPH

SUGAR LOAF**
Unknown location   *-1791-*
Listed without an address in 1791 [*UBD*] – doubtless the subject of various changes of name.

SUGAZ
See ST JAMES'S HOTEL

SUN
See RISING SUN

SUN (HOTEL) INN
34 Middleton Street (corner St Giles's Road)   *by 1898*
A common inn sign, and probably purely traditional, but NB the powerful Coke family of Trusley, Melbourne and Derby, who still flourish and bear for crest: *a sun in splendour or.* Built by Hardy's brewery as the *Sun Hotel* and retained by them as Hardy Hanson's.

SUN
Sadler Gate   *-1755-*
Taken over by Richard Woodhouse, 'late of the Barley Mow, Rotten Row' (*qv*) who transferred the latter name, allowing the previous one to lapse. It stood next to the Sadler Gate elevation of the *George*, and may have been later incorporated into that inn.
DM 26/9/1755

SUSUMI**
9-11 (21-22) Wardwick   *2001*
A Japanese theme bar opened in the former premises of Golden Gains, once Melia's grocery store by the same partnership that operate *Foobaa* in Blacksmith's Yard. The stone-fronted building was built in the 1880s as the County Club, with Linnell & Co, furnishers, occupying the shop units below. The façade, which bore Melia's glass façade signage until conversion, now opens out in summer and customers can freeze on the pavement.

(OLD) SWAN*
St Peter's Parish   *by 1762-1791*
Situated 'near to St Peter's Church' (and probably in St Peter's Street) and equipped with a cockpit, much resorted to on race days and market days. Run by Robert Campion in the 1760s – cousin of George, landlord of the nearby *Crown & Anchor* and of John, of the *Bell* – who was the promoter of these contests of 'shakebags' and who was probably there until it was advertised to let in 1772. Probably renamed after 1791.
DM 16/7/1762, 1/7/1763, 11/5/1764, 27/3/1772 & 6/2/1778; *UBD* 1791

SWAN & SALMON*
140 (71) Ashbourne Road (corner Chandos-Pole Street)
                    by 1835
One of several corner pubs on the West End side of Ashbourne Road, and probably one of a pair of anonymous

beerhouses listed in 1835 and 1846. First named when for sale as a going concern in 1856, and sold again in 1871. In 1874 it was listed merely as the *White Swan,* the badge of the great mediaeval house of Stafford, landowners in cadet branches, at Egginton, Eyam and Mellor in Derbyshire (as their crests) and collaterals of the Longfords and the Gresleys. The badge itself came from their common ancestors, the de Toenis, and is associated with the ancient German legend of the *Schwannritter* – the Swan Knight, a theme enlarged dramatically upon by Wagner, no less. By 1878 it was the *Swan & Salmon* once again – its other title being either the whim of a landlord or a directory compiler's error. In the hands of Offiler's by 1937. A large brewhouse survives behind. In 2002 it extended into the small cottage next door on Ashbourne Road, but still retains the small front bar and dividing wall.

Swan and Salmon, Ashbourne Road, 2002.

SWAN WITH TWO NECKS*

24 St James's Lane   *by 1761-1867*

One of the coaching inns of the town, it first appears on record as one of the watering holes favoured by Sir Harry Harpur for enticing his constituents. The name is said to derive from the mediaeval and later tradition of marking swans on the Thames. This was done by 'nicking' their bills, the Crown's swans being distinguished by two 'nicks', hence by corruption and mutation to the sign as here. The most famous inn of this name was that in Lad Lane, City of London, to which John Campion's coaches ran from the *Bell;* the service must have originated at this inn before transferring to the former, for this was in John Campion's proprietorship from before 1772 and still in 1774 when he transferred to the Sadler Gate inn. He eventually sold it in 1777 when he bought the freehold of the *Bell.* Note that there are, however, one or two prominent English families who actually bear a swan with two necks as a crest, and even the Habsburgs used the device at one time. Thus the traditional explanation may not always have held good. The inn was for sale in 1820 and to let in 1856 before being closed and swept away to make way for the widening of St James' Street in 1867.

DM 4/12/1772, 31/1/1777, 13/12/1820 & 30/7/1856

TAILORS' ARMS

96-8 (28) Green Lane   *by 1833-1960*

Stood next door from the corner of Haarlem Street, Little City, but listed as in Burton Road in 1843. The name is

derived from the arms of the Worshipful Company of Merchant Taylors *(sic),* a livery company chartered in 1327 and incorporated 6 January 1603. The arms were granted 23 December 1586 and the shield is blazoned: *Argent a pavilion Imperial purple garnished or lined ermine between two mantles of the second also lined ermine on a chief azure a lion passant guardant or.* In the 1930s this inn was owned by Marston's (although the rate book of 1937 names Zachary Smith's of Shardlow as owners, despite including a photograph with 'Marston's' clearly showing on the façia boards!) The two-storey pub, which latterly consisted of two single-bay cottages flanking one double-fronted one, all stuccoed over and with replaced ground floor windows, was compulsorily purchased by the Borough Council for £7,025 in March 1960, when the inn closed, being torn down soon afterwards.

TALBOT

Full Street   *by 1750-1755*

Known only from two references, five years apart. The talbot was an old English hunting dog, a type of mastiff, in a Derbyshire context, notable for being the crest and supporters of the Talbots, Earls of Shrewsbury and Waterford, great local landowners until 1617. Bess of Hardwick was (by her fourth marriage) the most notable local member of the dynasty, albeit by marriage.

DM -/1750 & -/1755

(OLD) TALBOT*

23 Iron Gate   *by 1676-1876*

A notable coaching inn, in a 16th-century timber-framed and jettied building which survived, albeit covered in

Talbot, Iron Gate, by R.Keene, c.1858.

stucco, until 1876, when the inn was demolished to make way for Messrs Crompton & Evans' new bank, now the *Standing Order.* In the later 17th century, it was a meeting place of the Derby Mercers' Company, but by the 1730s it was owned by Alderman Samuel Cooper, Mayor of Derby 1725, 1735 and 1744, who died there in February 1746 aged 47. His brother Francis (1711-1751) a London merchant, left a son, who was then 'partner in a brewery with Sir Benj. Trueman', thus reinforcing the family connection with the licensed trade.

Another of Francis's sons, Robert, was a wine-shipper at Oporto, Portugal, too, and the fourth brother, David was a carrier running wagons to Derby – doubtless carrying Robert's port for their uncle's inn! The *Talbot* probably remained in the family, passing to Samuel's second son of the same name who died in 1782. His elder brother Thomas (1728-1783) however was a poacher-turned-gamekeeper, having been appointed Collector of Excise for Derby in the 1750s.

The calling of coaches is recorded as early as 1722 when a London-Manchester service had called here daily. In 1764 the coach to London, called the 'Flying Machine' – with steel springs (a great innovation) – departed for the capital

three times a week. In 1804, the former landlord of the *George,* George Woodward, took it, calling it the *George & Talbot,* which it so continued until sold in 1828, despite his acquisition of the *King's Head* (with all its consequences, *qv*) in 1814. It was sold again in 1839, its new landlord again retitling it, this time the *Talbot Inn & Nottingham House.* When in 1871 the Corporation began demolishing the Piazzas in the Market Place, draper and hatter James Haskew was displaced, and by 1873 he had taken the inn, and reopened his hatter's shop in a redundant portion, the decline of the coaching trade having had a deleterious impact upon it. Even then he was able to advertise stabling for 24 horses.

DM 7/10/1736, 12/2/1747, 25/3/1774, 25/10/1804, 23/4/1828, 9/10/1839 & 16/4/1873.

TANKARD*

41 Nuns' Street 1873-1910

A beerhouse which made its licence application in 1873, taking its name from an important piece of its own equipment; beer was brewed on the premises. Closed between 1910 and World War One.

DM 1/10/1873

TANNERS' ARMS*

2 William Street   *by 1833-1871*

Probably named after the arms of the Worshipful Company of Curriers, the existence of which was recognised by charters of 1272, 1415, 1516, 1517 and which was incorporated 30 April 1606. The arms were granted 8 August 1583 and the shield was blazoned: *Azure a cross engrailed or between four pairs of shaves in saltire argent handled of the second.* There were several noisesome tanneries nearby at the time. The inn, which was situated next to the *(Old) Dove*, was adapted to form an early Co-op shop in 1871, the Derby Society buying both in the process, selling the latter on once their transactions were complete. Effectively this new grocery was an expansion from a first floor lock-up behind the *Old Dove*, into which they had originally moved in June, 1862.
Holyoake & Scotton (1900) 55-59.

(JOLLEY'S) TAP HOUSE*

4 Rotten Row   *by 1818-1877*

Occupied the rear of an early 18th-century building on the west side of the Market Place, known until the demolition of The Piazzas in 1871 as Rotten Row. Thereafter the address was 1½ Market Place! It was undoubtedly a much older house than the record would suggest and was probably renamed some time before 1818. Known as *Jolley's Taphouse* in 1850 (when the landlord was William Jolley) until the 1870s and occasionally misprinted as *Top House*. From the 1840s, the entrance was through an arch under the pretty Italianate building next door to the north which still survives, albeit shorn of its French style dormers. Pulled down in 1877 to make way for the rebuilt Smith's Bank (now Market Place branch of the NatWest Bank).

TAVERN, (THE)

See NEW STATION, TRIDENT

TELEGRAPH*

Morledge   *1822-1907*

Town centre pub 'old established and for sale' in 1838. It was probably considerably older than the 1822 entry in Pigot might suggest, and may have been renamed. The name's origin will be found under *Royal Telegraph*. It was situated on the Shot Tower Corner in what were once a pair of three-storey stuccoed cottages with replacement ground floor fenestration, perhaps hiding an earlier core. It was closed, possibly after Temperance Society pressure, in 1907 and demolished on 13 July 1908.
DM 20/6/1838

TELEGRAPH

See (ROYAL) TELEGRAPH

THOMAS-A-BECKET*

Green Lane (corner Gower Street)   *1979*

The building is a former chapel, gothic in rock-faced ashlar, designed by J. Tait of Leicester in 1868 and built that year for the Presbyterians. The extraordinary Eleanor Cross-like spire and pinnacles were later removed, prior to its closure as a place of worship in the early 1970s. After a period standing idle, it was purchased and refurbished imaginatively as a pub, opened in 1979 as the *Thomas-a-Becket*. In 1981 it was refurbished and renamed *Sloanes*, initiating a new role as a 'fun pub', which it retains, despite becoming (February 1986) *Becket's* and then in 1989 *Derby Steam Bar/Old Ale House* (a separate bar to the left of the Gower Street entrance, catering for the real ale market). By 1995 it had become *Bar 101* (all drinks £1.01) and, through inflation, quickly *Bar 121*! Then *Jerry Lee's* (presumably after the American rock star of the 1950s and 60s, Jerry Lee Lewis), then Bar *121* again and (main entrance) *Sin* (an establishment that promoted female 'podium dancers'). By August 2002 it had been closed for some time, but reopened, 4 October as *Divas* disco bar.

THORN TREE (I)

Gaol Bridge (St Peter's Street)   *by 1710-1787*

In around 1710 the historian William Woolley wrote of the *Thorn Tree*: 'It has the best ale in town without a doubt.' It was built on the old bridge over the Markeaton Brook opposite the Tudor gaol, which itself was demolished in 1755. In 1787 the ancient bridge was replaced by a new, balustraded stone one designed by William Strutt, and in clearing its predecessor, the venerable inn (taking its name from the street which connected the bridge to the Morledge: Thorn Tree Lane, an ancient name deriving from a 'a huge hawthorn tree' which once grew near the spot) was destroyed, although the business was transferred to a new site very close by.
DM 1/6/1744, 27/10/1749 & 14/4/1775

THORN TREE (II)

Thorntree Lane (St Peter's Street)   *1787-1845*

So famous was the Thorn Tree in the area that Strutt's rebuilding of the old bridge failed to kill it. The landlord removed a few yards to Thorntree Lane, opposite the *Castle*, although the address is given as St Peter's Street in 1835; in fact it was just behind Strutt's brother Joseph's house, Thorn Tree House. It was for sale in 1842. However, a further improvement scheme (Albert Street) forced a second closure in 1848 and it migrated to:

THORN TREE (III)*

11-12 Tenant Street   *1845-1932*

The landlord of the *Thorn Tree II*, Joseph Wright (no relation) in 1845 purchased the *Dog and Partridge*, on the east

Thorn Tree, Tenant Street.

side of Tenant Street. This was built as a coaching inn (but does not seem to have functioned as one for very long) and was housed in a splendid two-and-a-half-storey five-bay building with a stuccoed façade grooved to resemble rusticated ashlar, replacing an earlier edifice around 1780. This

Thorn Tree, Tenant Street.

then became the third *Thorn Tree*. 'Joseph Wright begs most respectfully to return his most sincere thanks to all friends that have given him their support since conducting the [old *Thorn Tree*] and begs to inform them that he has disposed of the same for the improvement of the Town of Derby, and has taken the Dog & Partridge Inn, Tenant Street, Derby, which will in future be called the THORN TREE INN.'

It was sold in 1858 and, as business contracted in the 20th century, its end portions were let as shops. A token survives from the mid-19th century, however, to remind us of more prosperous days: a brass 4d by Edwin Cottrill was issued in the name of T.W. Starkey, the landlord. It finally closed in early 1932, the licence being transferred to the *Grange*, Normanton-by-Derby in February of that year, ending a very long tradition. A new hotel was planned for the site in the 1985-92 period (for the inn was demolished in the mid-1930s to make way for a redevelopment which has yet to happen) which might have deserved to revive this venerable name, but the three schemes proposed were all out-of-scale for the site, and in the end a recession killed the idea, the site becoming a deep water-logged pit until the creation of the Sir Peter Hilton memorial garden there in 1999.

DM 14/10/1845 & 15/9/1858; Ward, J. *Notes of Reminiscences of Old Derby,* i. V

THREE CRANES**
Unknown location - 1778 -
Jewitt. This sign is almost certainly heraldic, and represents the (unauthorised) arms of the Storers of Kirk Ireton, the heiress of which family married into the Blackwalls of Blackwall. The herald Isaac Heard confirmed the Blackwall's arms with the Storer coat as a quartering in 1764, thus legitimising them. They were: *Per fesse argent and gules on a pale counterchanged three cranes of the first.* Anthony Storer, Gent, of All Saints' parish, Derby (died 1726) was a member of this family and may have been the inn's owner or initiator.

(OLD) THREE CROWNS*
68 (24) Bridge Gate *by 1690-1898*
Situated on the lower part of the south side of Bridge Gate with Court 6 and Court 7 on either side. The sign is said to represent the biblical three kings but more likely reflects the three kingdoms of England, Scotland and Ireland, but in a local context may even reflect the arms of the Leighs of Egginton, the Leches of Chatsworth or the Lyttons of Litton all of which bore three crowns in some manner. William Hutton tells us that the future Lord Chancellor, the 1st Earl of Macclesfield, lived in a house next to the *Three Crowns* for many years from the time he first set up in Derby as a young lawyer, around 1690. This implies that the Three Crowns then existed, although it is not proof. The next evidence of its existence is in 1771, and the inn remained in existence until around the turn of the 20th century when it appears to have been cleared to extend Walley's boiler factory. Referred to as 'Old' in 1835/43, suggesting the existence then or previously of another house of this name, but of less long foundation. It was to let in 1855 and 1877.

DM 9/8/1771, 1/5/1855 & 24/1/1877; Hutton (1791) 284

THREE HORSESHOES**
Brook Street - 1835 -
This beer house appears only in Pigot's directory for 1835, and was probably renamed.

THREE HORSESHOES
location unknown -1740-
Mentioned only in 1740; the name relates to the arms of

the ancient Norman family of de Ferrers, Earls of Derby to 1268, and local landowners for some four centuries afterwards whose earliest coat-of-arms seems to have featured a varying number of horseshoes. Several of the families who were the Ferrers' feudal sub-tenants bore three horseshoes somewhere on their arms, too.

DM 11/9/1740

THREE JOLLY BUTCHERS*
91 (36) Traffic Street *by 1827-1862*
Presumably the inn at no. 36, Traffic Street advertised in 1862 to let as 'the oldest [public house] in the street'- but not specifically named. This address was an anonymous beer house in 1846, and the name only appears in 1827 and 1835. All are likely to refer to the same house rather than the *Druids', Mazeppa* or *Stag,* which enjoyed different addresses. By 1874 it was merely a house, and by the time renumbered, a shop.

DM 15/1/1862

THREE JOLLY COLLIERS
See JOLLY COLLIERS

THREE LOGGERHEADS
location unknown -1873-
Jewitt. The sign apparently showed a pair of bucolic simpletons, the viewer making up three 'loggerheads'.
Reliquary XIV (1873-4) 50

THREE NUNS*
84 (31, 25) Nuns' Street (corner Mundy Street) *by 1827-1963*
Named, in a whimsical way, from the street, itself deriving its name from Nuns' Green (the former estate of the convent of St Mary de Pratis, alias King's Mead) across which it ran. Called the *Nuns' Inn* in 1852. For sale in 1869 with a contents sale two years later. In 1871, the new landlord, Benjamin Newbold (formerly of the *Black Horse)* transferred the name of his previous inn, the *Dove,* to this establishment, but the new name lapsed with the departure of John Newbold, its initiator's son, around 1880. Owned by Pountain's in 1937, but cleared in 1963 under a CPO. Latterly run by the Gagaro family.

DM 25/8/1869 & 5/4/1871; Palmer (1996) (ii)

THREE PIGEONS
St Peter's Parish -1772-
Known only from a notice of 1772. The sign derived either from the arms of the family of Alsop of Alsop-en-le-Dale, the Tunsteads of Tunstead, or the Columbells of Darley (cf. *Dove).* Another alternative is the arms of Sir John Porte of Etwall, founder of Etwall Hospital and Repton School, who

had a town house in St Peter's Parish. All these families bore arms with three pigeons or doves, only the Portes having any other additional device thereon. Probably renamed. *DM 27/3/1772*

THREE STAGS' HEADS

St James's Lane   *by 1756-1759*
In 1756 this inn was taken over by Richard Salt formerly of the *Black Boy*, and he was still landlord in 1759. It may have later suffered renaming, although such a development might have been construed as a serious slight on the Borough's hereditary High Steward, the Duke of Devonshire whose arms are: *sable three stags' heads argent attired or.* *DM 29/10/1759*

THREE SWANS

Sadler Gate Bridge   *by 1732-1754*
Possibly changed its name later to the *White Horse* and then to the *Flying Horse*: the dates fit, at least. The inn is first mentioned in 1732. The name derived from the arms of the Charltons of Breaston, Sandiacre and Risley: *azure on a chevron or between three swans argent as many cinquefoils gules,* a family with fairly strong Derby connections, which is more than could be said for the only other candidate, the Swanns of Hurdlow: *azure a chevron ermine between three swans in the beak of each a mascle.* *DM 23/3/1732*

THREE TUNS*

40-41 Sadler Gate   *by 1791-1883*
Probably quite an old established inn, to let in 1855 and 1865, which was eventually swept away by demolition to make way for the building of the Strand Arcade by John Somes Story, 1883. The name derives from the arms of the Worshipful Company of Vintners: *sable a chevron between three wine tuns argent*. These were granted 17 September 1447 and the Company was incorporated 23 August 1437, although they had received Royal Letters Patent as early as 15 July 1364. It may well be that the man who founded the establishment was, in fact, a speculative vintner, like Charles Brentnall (cf. *Wine Vaults*). *DM 30/5/1855 & 19/4/1865; UBD 1791*

(OLD) TIGER*

52 City Road (corner Union Place)   *by 1835-1925*
It first appears as the *Old Tiger* in 1843, although listed as an anonymous beer house here in 1835 and was no doubt founded to serve the adjacent works of James Fox & Co, later incorporated in the adjacent Haslam's Foundry, renamed in consequence the Union Foundry. In 1878 it was listed as the *Leopard*. Closed between 1921 and 1924 and demolished in 1925.

Tiger, Cornmarket, as designed and built by Joseph Pickford.

TIGER (INN) (VAULTS)

41 Cornmarket   *by 1737*
Once a coaching inn with a Cornmarket frontage, and even in the 1830s the coach office was attached to the inn. By 1764 the meeting place of the Derby Society of Musicians. In that year, too, a new building to house the inn was put up. This is a five-bay, two-and-a-half-storey brick Palladian edifice with the central bay breaking slightly forward where it straddles Lock-up Yard (originally Tiger Yard), the rusticated depressed arch being ensigned by a Venetian window with a Diocletian superimposed under a plain pediment. The building, restored in 1990, is by Joseph Pickford, and an elaborately plastered room still exists behind the central Venetian window. Originally the parapet was decorated with ball finials and the pediment rested upon a bracket modillion cornice. Later additions were made behind the inn on the north side of the yard, possibly by Pickford's pupil, Thomas Gardner, *c.*1795, including an assembly room with an orchestra gallery, and this was still being advertised for hire in the 1930s, according to a contemporary pamphlet. Also then on offer was the wireless, a library including newspapers and magazines, gramophone (with a library of records) and amateur dramatics. Prices then included Graham's Port (1890) 16s per bottle,

Tiger, Cornmarket, now in Lock-up Yard (formerly Tiger Yard), occupying it's own outbuildings, 2002.

Cockburn's (1912) 14s 6d and best bitter 9d and mild 7d a pint. It was also a free house. The coach which called in the 18th century was the London-Manchester *Defiance*. In 1781 Henry Tomlinson took the lease, and there was a partial contents dale in 1826, at which period, Glover tells us, the 'Masonic Lodge' met here – presumably the Tyrian lodge, then Derby's only one – although their official history only mentions the George, by then closed. In 1837 the 3rd AGM of the South Derbyshire Conservative Association was held here, a Coronation Dinner in 1838, and a further Conservative function in 1846. The owners by the 1870s were Orme and Renals, vintners, but in 1936 the freeholders were William Deacon's Bank Ltd (now Royal Bank of Scotland) by which time the Cornmarket building had long been vacated, although a property around the angle in Market Place had been acquired to provide a street access. With wartime and post-war decline, it removed further back down the yard, now occupying quite modest quarters near the Market Hall/Guildhall corner of Lock-up Yard; now Bass. Since 1981 the landlord has been David Foulk, the longest-serving landlord at a single pub in the city centre.
DM 3/11/1737, 18/4/1771, 11/1/1837, 4/7/1838 & 2/9/1846; Glover (1831/33) II. 539.

(OLD) TIGER*

41 (35) Queen Street   *by 1761-1912*
Stood opposite St Michael's House, one door from the corner of Walker Lane, and features in the list of inns supplying free refreshment for the potential supporters of

Sir Harry Harpur in the 1761 election. It was probably renamed from the *Plaisterers' Arms*. The address was given as in King Street when it was for sale in 1791, but qualified by the remark 'nearly opposite St Michael's Church'. It was to let in 1832 and for sale in 1863. A Tiger Friendly Society met here during the 1820s, when it was known as the *Old Tiger*, a qualification which still applied in 1835 and probably suggests that it was considered of earlier foundation than the Cornmarket inn. It was for sale in 1863 and Samuel Cotton, the new landlord, made a spirit licence application in 1871; seven years later he was also described as a brewer. Although not listed in the 1925 *Directory*, the inn probably closed at around this time to facilitate widening the west side of Queen Street. The Queen Street Baths occupy what is left of the site.
DM 20/10/1791, 27/9/1832, 23/9/1863 & 26/8/1871; Glover (1831/33) II. 539; *UBD* 1791.

TIGER*

Walker Lane   *-1743-*
This might refer to the same inn as that above; it may well be that in the 18th century it had an access (and an address) onto Walker Lane, having been situated only a door or two down from the junction with that street. If, however, the Queen Street pub was indeed previously the *Plaisterers' Arms* in 1755, then this name may have migrated from Walker lane with a new landlord subsequent to that date. The name in all these cases probably refers to the crest of the Pagets, Marquesses of Anglesey: *a demi heraldic tiger sable maned ducally gorged and tufted argent.* They were considerable landowners in Burton upon Trent, South Derbyshire and, to a limited extent, Derby – this last because the 1st Lord Paget was granted all the property in the area of the recently dissolved Abbey of Burton.

TIGER
See also LEOPARD

TIGER'S HEAD

Willow Row   *by 1849-1850*
The sign derives from the arms of the Catholic family of Hunloke of Wingerworth Hall: *Azure on a fesse between three tigers' heads erased or as many mullets of the field.* Its existence is only attested over about a year. Possibly to be identified with the *Bull's Head*.

TONIC**

9 Friar Gate   *1995*
Opened as a 'brasserie bar and restaurant' in the courtyard which was once cabinet makers' workshops, and restored as a retail area in the early 1980s. The courtyard is available to sit out in during clement weather.

TOP HOUSE
See LITCHURCH INN, TAP HOUSE

TOWN ARMS*

The Spot   *by 1744-1775*

For sale as a going concern in 1744, where the location was given as 'at the Spot' – almost the earliest reference to this enigmatic Derby toponym. Later recorded as being in Upper St Peter's Parish in 1749 and in one source (of 1748) as the *Buck in the Park*; therefore the 'town arms' were those of Derby itself.

DM 7/9/1744, 24/2/1749 & 6/1/1775

TOWN HALL CELLARS
See GLOBE

TRAVELLERS' REST*

185 (108, 28) Ashbourne Road   *by 1852*

Traditionally-named inn, listed anonymously at this address in 1850 and which appears on the 1852 Board of Health map. It subsequently acquired a new building, probably in the later 1880s. Owned by nearby Stretton's in 1937, later Ansells/Allied. Relatively unspoilt child-free zone today, with excellent Pedigree served from a jug.

TRAVELLER'S REST*

Walker Lane   *1846-1857*

Recorded only for 1857, although an anonymous beer house listed 11 years before is almost certainly the same. Perhaps a renaming, or later renamed.

TRENT BOAT**

Navigation Row (Nottingham Road)   *by 1818-1820*

Possibly the forerunner of the *Jolly Colliers* and probably established not long after the opening of the canal in 1796, probably then called the *Navigation*. The Trent Boat was a passenger craft which took people, usually on market days, to Derby from points along the canal from Swarkestone, where the canal met the Trent & Mersey, by the River Trent itself.

TRIDENT*

Albion Street   *1967-1991; 1992-1994*

A new pub in modernist style opened by Ind Coope (Allied/Ansell's) in December 1967 to replace the *Newmarket* and which closed again in 1991. In May 1992 it was refurbished and reopened as *The Tavern* but in 1994 closed again and was demolished (visually no loss) to make way for the felicitous rebuilding of the whole street. Interestingly, two tridents appear on the arms of the brewing family of Worthington, a member of which lived at Derwent Bank in the 1880s.

TRINIAN'S
See (ROYAL) TELEGRAPH

TUDOR**

Midland Road   *1994*

A free house. [no information at all!]

TURF
See SARACEN'S HEAD

TYLER'S
See STATION INN

UNICORN

All Saints' Parish   *-1724-*

Location unknown. Most pubs with this name date from the union of the crowns of England and Scotland in 1603, the unicorn being the Stuart supporter added to the revised royal arms at that time and which has featured on them ever since.

Deed, 14/6/1724

UNION BAR
See DIAL BAR

UNION FLAG*

1 Stepping Lane (corner Uttoxeter Old Road)by 1827-1850

Only recorded in 1827, but probably the beer house anonymously listed in Old Uttoxeter Road (but not the *Bay Horse*) in 1850. The inn is possibly somewhat older, for both Stepping Lane (then a field lane) and Uttoxeter Old Road are ancient thoroughfares; by 1852 the stretch of the lane between Fowler Street (of 1845) and Uttoxeter Old Road was also incorporated into the former. The name might well date from the introduction of the present Union flag on the Act of Union in 1801.

UNION OF HEARTS*

39 (20) John Street   *by 1846-1971*

Delightfully-named inn. It started as an anonymous beer house in one very mean artisan's cottage with glazing bar sashes and ended up occupying two adjoining, whitewashed over to give a semblance of 'union!' Perhaps its name change was inspired by the wedding of Edward, Prince of Wales, and Alexandra of Denmark in 1863, in which case it is to be identified with the *Engine Tavern*, previously at this address. Owned in 1937 by Offilers', and a beerhouse which gained a full licence in 1950. Not recorded in the 1952 *Directory*, but the licence was certainly renewed in June 1961 and until at least 1971 it still ran a darts team.

UPPER GREEN MAN
See GREEN MAN

UPPER SHIP
See SHIP

VARSITY**

21-23 Friar Gate *(2002)*

An application was lodged with the City Council for change of use and listed building consent to turn this elegant pair of three-storey Regency shops (and the adjacent late 19th century gabled one) into a 'chain-pub' named the *Varsity* by Messrs Barracuda Inns of Marlow, Bucks. It is probably the fourth such application relating to the site, the others having either failed or stalled. The scheme involved gutting all three properties internally, it being considered inadvisable to have small rooms in pubs any more; a couple of CCTV cameras can scan an open plan one with ease. A poor reflection on the proprietors' view of their likely clientele. Due to open in November 2002.

VAULTS
See NEW MARKET (Albert Street), WINE VAULTS

VICTORIA

2 Cowley Street (corner Watson Street) *1895*

For the old West End, quite a lavish two-storey brick building embellished with two large eared coped gables and a high hipped roof named after the reigning Queen, built by Offilers' and in the 1930s still in their hands, later Bass.

VICTORIA

8-9 Graham Street *by 1874-1965*

An Alton's establishment in 1937 and closed in the later 1960s when the area began to be cleared.

VICTORIA**

Market Place *1880*

Only listed in 1880 and thus perhaps a temporary renaming of either the *Wine Vaults* or the *Greyhound* – most likely the latter which not so long afterwards became the *Criterion*.

(QUEEN) VICTORIA (INN)*

12 Midland Place (corner Wellington Street) *by 1855*

Opened after 1855, although situated in a row of buildings contemporary with the Railway Cottages (thus, earlier 1840s) further along the street. For sale and 'in the occupation of the proprietor Mrs Mansfield for 19 years' in 1874, having been to let in 1856. Called the *Queen Victoria* in 1878. Owned by James Eadie Ltd, but sold to Bass by 1937. Note in the rate book, dated 27 August 1933, says:

Victoria, Midland Place, 2002.

Victoria, Midland Place. The conservatory in the mid-1930s. This part of the pub survived for almost 50 years with little change.

'Under the old management this inn was a resort for prostitutes'. Nowadays it is mainly a pub offering live music seven nights a week.
DM 16/4/1856 & 22/4/1874

VICTORIA**

Victoria Street *by 1846-1871*

Probably the anonymous beer house recorded for an unspecified address in Victoria Street in 1846, but only referred to by name in January 1870 when it was to let

'doing capital business' and not heard of after 1871. Probably closed and turned to retail use and swept away in the early 20th century by the building of the new range opposite the *Royal Hotel*.
DM 12/1/1870 & 15/2/1871

VINE*

119-121 Abbey Street (corner Wilson Street)by 1862-1991
Set in a brick stuccoed four-square building of late Regency type with (until 1994) glazing-bar sashes. Owned by Alton's in 1937, it probably benefited from the closure of the *Lifeboat* further up the street. Closed in April 1991, after police had investigated an obscenity complaint, and empty and boarded up until offered sold by Allied in 1994 when it was renovated (and given ugly UPVC windows) and turned into the offices of a printing firm called the Anvil Press. One third of the original building (never part of the pub) demolished to make way for the planned Inner Ring Road extension. Former Vine regulars will remember the next-door barber's shop of Phil Vidofsky; he moved to London in 1958 after being told that he would lose his shop to the ring road. In 1962 he returned, to a former tobacconist's at the corner of Gerard Street and Wilson Street, and stayed there until he retired in the 1980s. The road has yet to be built!

VINE*

22 (28, 78) Ford Street (corner Cavendish Street)
by 1835-1992; 1994
Founded by 1835, it was offered for sale by its landlord, Alfred Pymm, in 1877 when it was acquired by Stretton's. Stuccoed over and grooved to resemble ashlar but the fenestration much altered in the 1920s. Closed, July 1992, refurbished and reopened in 1994.

VINE

Leather Lane (Market Place) –1829–
Only a single reference exists to this inn. Possibly renamed from the *Nottingham Post* and therefore originally the *Crane*; in 1828 (bearing in mind that directories were compiled and accurate, as far as they ever were, to a year or two before the date they bear) Leather Lane, formerly Breadleaps, was destroyed by the demolition of the 1731 Guildhall and the building of its successor.

VINE

See COOPERS' ARMS, MIDLAND ARMS

VINE

Lower Dale Road – 1895–
No further information; the house number fails to appear in the relevant directory.

VINE*

37-8 (29) Whitaker Street (corner Corden Street)
by 1874-2001
The significance of this otherwise ordinary corner pub, formed from a pair of artisans' cottages, is that in 1877, George Offiler (1838-1899) – formerly landlord of the *Shoulder of Mutton*, Radford Road, Nottingham, who came to Derby in 1876 – began to sell surplus beer which he had already been brewing on the premises. Nevertheless, it was offered for sale as a 'freehold old licensed public house now in the occupation of George Offiler'; why, one wonders? Did he wish to move to larger premises, and did it fail to sell, or did his business suddenly take off, causing him to take it off the market? This date has, nevertheless, always subsequently been taken to mark the beginning of Offilers' Brewery (see introduction), which went on to be Derby's last old independent one. Naturally it remained an Offilers' pub until Bass took over in the mid-1960s. When brewing expanded beyond the limitations of the curtilage, Offiler moved to the former Ordnance depot on Normanton Road (by James Wyatt, 1806) for long then a silk mill. Original and historic brewhouse subsequently destroyed. Acquired by Punch Inns in 1998 and closed by them in 2001. It suffered a serious fire when boarded up 1 April 2002, and its fate is, at the time of writing, very uncertain.
DM 6/6/1877; Ward (1890) 1-4

VINE

See also DOVE, MIDLAND ARMS

VINES

51a Sadler Gate 1980
Founded in a former brush manufacturers' yard near to the *Bell* by the Thompson family of Ingleby in 1980.

VIRGIN'S INN

Market Place *by 1708-1767*
Probably the most venerable of the inns of Derby, with a name suggesting an existence going back to pre-Reformation times, although specific mentions of it are non-existent or equivocal until a deed of 1708. At this stage the inn appears to have been old, timber-framed and built around a courtyard. On 20 March 1741, however, it burned down, and was replaced by a plain, well-proportioned brick three-storey edifice of six bays, the ground floor windows being equipped with folding jalousies to protect them from the excesses of the Derby Football, which 'kicked off' from in front of it. It included a 'great room' for the holding of assemblies, auctions, and theatrical performances, copious stabling for the coaches which plied the turnpikes, as well as those of the fashionable. On race weeks, entries for the races were entered at

the *Virgin's*. In 1752, it was purchased by William Brentnall (cf. *Spread Eagle*, London Street) and he ran it until 1767, when it was sold to William Cox of Brailsford Hall, lead entrepreneur, who used it partly as a townhouse and partly as a business headquarters. He also seems to have acquired at least a share in Brentnall's vintner's business, which he built up over the next 50 years (see *Admiral Rodney)*. He also founded the lead works in the Morledge in about 1800, building the Shot Tower in 1809. Thus the inn became but a memory from 1767, although Cox's businesses, in the hands of his numerous sons, proliferated as Cox & Bowring, Cox & Malin and Cox & Garrard, thriving into the 20th century. The inn, however, was sold to Pountain's in the late 1870s, was the subject of an unsuccessful attempt to revive the licence, but was then demolished in around 1884, being replaced with a new, aggressively Victorian edifice by James Wright and T.H. Thorpe, itself demolished in 1971.

DLSL Local deed 8824; *DM* 1/6/1732, 26/3 & 15/10/1741, 6/9/1751, 18/9/1767 & 6/10/1880

VULCAN ARMS

1 St Thomas's Road (corner Prince's Street)   *by 1874*
Situated not so far from Ley's Vulcan foundry, which without doubt inspired the name, an appropriate classical figure, whom the landlord then whimsically endowed with arms! A meeting foregathered here in 1881 to ask the tramway company to extend their line to this point. Owned by Home Ales in 1937, refurbished 1963.
Harrison (c.1952)

VULCAN (ARMS) INN*

25 (13) John Street   *by 1846-1931*
A modest beer house, listed anonymously in 1846-62 and first mentioned by name (as the *Vulcan Arms*) in 1878, later the *Vulcan Inn*, which closed at the start of the Great Depression. Offered for sale as as 'an old established beer house called the *Vulcan Arms'* in 1881. Like the entry above, it was in an area not so far removed from foundries, in this case those of the former Midland Railway.
DM 17/8/1881

WAG(G)ON & HORSES*

149 (121, 33) Ashbourne Road   *by 1833*
Probably a place from which 'fly waggons' left, plying for cargo to various places in the locality, hence the name. 'Waggon' when referring to these vehicles was always spelt thus, although the pub now spells it in the modern fashion. Rebuilt in the later 19th century by Pountain's and brewing on the premises in 1956. On 15 July 1879 PC Moss was shot dead in the yard by the police station in Lock-up Yard (*qv Tiger*) by an upper class young tearaway called Gerald

Mainwaring of the Whitmore Hall (Staffs.) family. He was challenged by the constable whilst drunkenly driving off on a jolly from this inn in a gig accompanied by a local doxy, and waved a hand-gun he had acquired not long before on a visit to the USA, fatally shooting the unfortunate policeman in the process. He escaped the gallows at his trial because the jury was deadlocked and settled the matter of his guilt with a ballot – highly improper. A juror told the home secretary, Derby MP Sir William Vernon Harcourt, who had no alternative but to commute the sentence to life, a move that proved extremely unpopular locally. Mainwaring – whose great nephew Sir Jock Delves Broughton, Bt, was, by coincidence, the celebrated victim of the *Black Mischief* slaying of Joss, 22nd Earl of Errol, in Kenya in 1941 – served only a few years before being released and returning (permanently) to America. As a result, the landlord, John Smith, sold up in 1881; perhaps the crime had affected trade. Now Burtonwood.
DET Bygones 31/10/2001 & *DET* 12/11/2001; *DM* 16/7/1879 & 14/12/1881

WAGGON & HORSES

Siddals Road   *–1849–*
Nothing further known of this inn; its name, at least, was short-lived and was probably replaced, cf *Plasterers' Arms,* which is probably to be differentiated from it.

WALBROOK INN

115 Walbrook Road   *by 1991*
A recent conversion of a detached house on the south side of the street, not far from the Cavendish.

WALKABOUT

See JACKIE STAMPS

WARDWICK TAVERN*

15 (19) Wardwick   *1969*
The building occupied by this pleasant inn, was built for Samuel Alsop (a scion of the family of Alsop of Alsop-en-le-Dale) in c.1708-12; a stylish and well-proportioned red brick building with a sophisticatedly panelled parapet, three storeys and seven bays. The sashed fenestration has gauged brick lintels centred with grooved keyblocks. Parts of an earlier (stone) building remain in the fabric visible from Victoria Street, and inside in the shape of an enormous stone bressumered fire-place and an extension ending in a canted bay of c.1770 exists at the rear. The plan looks very much as if Alsop amalgamated two adjacent burgage plots, removed both houses thereon and started afresh, for the south wing (facing E-W) looks to be on the footprint of a typical end-to-the-road burgage plot messuage. In the early 19th century it was stuccoed over

and had pediments added to the windows, but these features have since been removed, although the replacement fenestration leaves something to be desired. The entrance is down some steps from the street (whereas it would once have been up, but the road surface has been raised considerably) under a pretty stone hood. To the left of the entrance is a surviving iron plaque marking the height of the Great Flood of 1 April 1842 (another is fixed in the yard, but was originally elsewhere entirely); the rise in street level has lessened the impact of this too, however. There was once a 'pretty entrance hall and a fine oak staircase. The dining room was 23ft by 15ft, there was a breakfast room, library, drawing room (15ft 6in by 20ft), large kitchen, wash house etc. and housekeeper's room on the ground floor. Upstairs there were nine bedrooms or dressing rooms, two attic rooms and two large closets; there was also a secondary staircase. After the Alsops sold up and retired to Worcestershire, it was bought by Thomas Heaford, who started a brewery on the premises. Heaford tried to let it in 1767, sold it the following year and departed to Tattershall, Lincs, taking with him a particularly fine long-case clock with a barometer built into the trunk door by John Whitehurst FRS; the clock is now in Derby Museum. Heaford's advertisements feature 'a large commodious dwelling house and good gardens in one of the most pleasant situations in Derby and fit for a gentleman's family; a complete new Brewhouse with utensils good cellars and all other offices contiguous, stable for 6 horses, a chaise house, a cold bath and other conv. Out buildings and yards.' He then goes on to itemise his professional accoutrements:

'12 excellent new standing ale casks, iron hooped, hold 150 galls. each, 100 new hogsheads, half hogsheads, 20 gallons, 18 gals, 16 galls. and some smaller casks of English oak. A very large parcel of good dry English oak hogsheads, half hogsheads and barrel headings, hambro' pipe and hogshead staves; 100 dozen white hoops, cooper's shop tools, 10 pockets of fine Kentish hops, two new coppers, one holds 320 galls the other 210 gals, 30ft copper pipes of 2½in and 50ft of ditto 1¼ ins, two large coolers, four brewing squares 600 galls each, a pair of very good cast metal malt rollers [which] turn easily by hand, new cart and gears, a parcel of dressed flagstones, bricks, deals, iron and other articles.'

Wardwick Tavern, Wardwick.

The purchaser on this occasion was Thomas Lowe (1753-1831), four times mayor of Derby, and son of Richard, a King Street maltster. His brother John continued the King Street business. Thomas had six sons, of whom the third son, Revd Henry Lowe (1779-1877) was Mayor of Derby in 1821 and vicar of Hawnby, Yorks, whilst the sixth was George Lowe, FRS (1788-1868) a pioneer of gas lighting. The fifth son, Alderman Charles Matthew Lowe (1784-1871) inherited the brewery, and served as Mayor in 1831. He ran it until 1837 when it was sold to Moreton Charles Wedge (1798-1881), trading as M.C. Wedge & Co. At that time the rear gardens accommodated upper and lower counting houses, 40ft by 45ft brew house, 86ft by 16ft cooling room, fermenting room, tun room, two 60ft long store rooms cellars, coopers' shops, four hop & malt rooms and a yeast room. There was, in addition a separate double malthouse of three storeys, but this was in Babington Lane. There were still an acre and a quarter of gardens left. Wedge were taken over by William Alton and Edward Barnett in 1863, although he remained in the business as the firm's accountant until his death.

William Alton was the eldest son of George, of Heage, maltster, of an old yeoman family from that village. He was successively landlord of the *Lion & Tiger* and the *Golden Lion* before establishing the brewery in Derby and in Castle Donington. His brother, James, also a brewer had been landlord successively of the *Brown Bear, Seven Stars* and *Boar's Head* (both King Street) and the *Castlefields*.

In 1869, the firm became just Alton's, and greatly enlarged the brewery under the Union system, which they named the Wardwick Brewery. It was in operation after William's death around 1887 under Hepworth Tropolet Alton (died 1903), nephew of William, and under Reginald Tijou (who was adopted by H.T. Alton and took his surname) until 1922. The brewery buildings were all demolished in the following decade to build the telephone exchange, (itself replaced in the 1970s). In 1927, Stretton's (see introduction), who had taken it over, were, in their turn, taken over by Samuel Allsopp's of Burton upon Trent, then headed by Lord Hindlip, a direct lineal descendant of Samuel Alsop, who had built the house. In 1968 they (by this time Allied Breweries) closed their Derby offices and refurbished them extensively, the architect being G.A. Salkeld of Loughborough, opening them as a pub on 2 December 1969. That the building (listed Grade II*) was always (until 1969) a house, counting house or offices, saved it from being shop-fronted, making it a precious survival. By the late 1990s it was part of Festival Inns and Taverns (*New Zealand, White Swan*, Littleover). By 2002 it had been disposed of by Carlsberg-Tetley, refurbished twice, and remains one of the more civilised and agreeable city centre public houses.

Craven (1987) 34-35; *DAT&I* (1891) 47; *DET* 3 & 5/12/1969, 4/8/1990; *DM* 18/9/1767, 12/2/1768, 15 & 22/3/1837 & 14/10/1863; Glover (1831/3) II. 599; Hutton (1791) 28

WARREN ARMS
Nottingham Road   c.*1880*
Depicted on a photograph c.1880 in Derby Museum (L.481) where it is stated to be Derby, but evidence to support the identification is lacking. Sir John Borlase Warren, GCB, Bt, (d.1822) of Stapleford Park, Nottinghamshire, was an admiral educated at Derby School.

Waterfall, Railway Terrace, formerly the Railway Institute, 2002.

WATERFALL**
Railway Terrace (corner Midland Place)   *1996*
Opened by Frazer and Karl Sanders (of an old farming family from Stenson) in the former Midland Railway Institute. This was designed by MR architect Charles Trubshaw and built in 1892 in a mixture of brick and terra-cotta banding, with an octagonal tower at the angle topped a copper-sheathed bell-shaped roof and cupola. The 15-bay long side, facing the railway has two straight coped gables and a tall flamboyant pedimented entrance at the north end.

It opened 16th February 1894. It had a lecture hall to seat 500, three classrooms, a magazine and newspaper room, games room, coffee room and a café, but its chief glory was its fine and extremely well-stocked library. Membership at a minimal weekly sum was open to all the Company's employees. The library was closed and the books sold (or given away to members) in 1963, and the Derby Railway Institute (as it had by then been named) became a branch of the British Railways Staff Association, but by the 1980s it had been sold off to a property company and leased to the Post Office Social Club. That closed and plans in 1994 to turn it into an arts complex failed too.
Billson (1996) 127-8, 142

WATERLOO
See APOLLO

WAVERLEY HOTEL
20 Midland Road (corner Park Street)   *1870-1980*
Established (according to terracotta work on the exterior) in 1870, and survived just over 110 years before being absorbed by the *Clarendon*. Demolition of the entire block between Park Street and Carrington Street for a vast replacement to the *Clarendon* was commenced in May 1992 (see *European Inn*).

WEAVERS' ARMS*
7-8 Leaper Street   *1849-1878*
Sandwiched in between the *Seven Stars* and the *Mundy Arms*. The Worshipful Company of Weavers occurs as early as c.1155 and arms were granted 4 August 1490: *Azure on a chevron argent between three leopards' heads each holding in the mouth a shuttle or, three roses gules*. The proliferation of tape and silk mills, with their attendant outworkers doubtless inspired the name. Listed anonymously in 1850 and closed after 1878.

WELCOME
66 Nottingham Road   *by 1874-1965*
A small pub opposite the racecourse and backing on to the canal. Owned by Offilers' in 1937, but cleared for the inner ring road system in the later 1960s.

WELLINGTON*
6 Regent Terrace (116 (58) London Road)   *by 1812-1868*
In 1812 this inn was the *Silver Lion*, and had been in existence for an indeterminate period. The name may have referred, if of late 18th-century origin, to the Colviles; if late 17th or early 18th, to the powerful Derby family of Dalton. At about the time of the Peninsular War, however, it was renamed the *Wellington*, after the hero of the hour: Arthur Wellesley, then Lord Wellington, later 1st Duke, when reopened after refurbishment 30 November 1853 'late the Silver Lion.' In fact it was again advertised as the *Silver Lion* a month later, when to let in March 1855 and for sale the following year. Did the new name fail to 'take'? Yet in advertising a contents sale in 1854 and when to let in 1859 and 1862, it is referred to by its new name. The consistency of the address and the November 1853 advertisement confirm that the same pub is being referred to, though. It was again for sale, this time at closure and without the licence, as 'Wellington House' in 1868 and, as such, from 1878 and until his death in June 1908, it was the home and consulting rooms of Surg. Lt-Col. & Cllr Thomas Lawrie Gentles VD, FRCP, LSA, a distinguished local surgeon.

DM 30/11 & 28/12/1853, 26/4/1854, 7/3/1855, 19/3 & 24/9/1856, 25/5/1859, 15/8/1862 & 12/8/1868

WHEATSHEAF*
Bold Lane   *by 1792-1797*
For sale twice in five years, but otherwise not heard of. No obvious candidates are discernable as possible re-namings, unless it survived unrecorded for upwards of five decades to become the *Elephant & Castle*.
DM 1/1/1793 & 12/1/1797

WHEATSHEAF*
6-8 (90) Liversage Street   *by 1843-1969*
A beerhouse situated close to the corner of Siddals Road beside the 25 houses which formed the terrace known as Liversage Cottages. The name is a very ancient one, reflecting the armorial bearings of the mediaeval Earls of Chester. To let in 1843, and still brewing on the premises 99 years later. In 1931 the inn was let to Offilers', although the property of the Liversage Trust; it gained a full licence in 1950, but closed 9 April 1969 in advance of clearance of the area.
DM 29/11/1843

WHEATSHEAF*
Market Place   *by 1733-1791*
This inn occurs in Sir Harry Harpur's famous list of 1761 and it was quite an important market inn in its day, possibly renamed in the Regency period. In 1742 the weekly 'Flying Waggon' to London began, making the journey a day faster than that from the *Red Lion*.
DM 22/11/1733, 2/8/1777; *UBD* 1791

(OLD) WHEATSHEAF*
32-33 (32) Walker Lane (corner Goodwin Street) *by 1818-1937*
Probably of old foundation, and certainly in an ancient building, being jettied and timber-framed, with a carved dragon post, if somewhat rebuilt and stuccoed over. By 1874 it had been united with the late 18th century No.33, a three-storey brick building. To let in 1855 and for sale March 1877 for £1,600. One shop up from the corner of Goodwin Street up to 1878, but later on the corner, as the intervening building was demolished to improve the angle. Closed by Alton's 31 January 1937 and licence transferred in the February to the *Broadway*, Duffield Road; it was then demolished and the road widened.
DM 12/12/1855

(OLD) WHEEL INN*
68 Friar Gate   *by 1722*
The premier inn of the Friar Gate market area, often thought to have gained its name from the discovery of a

wheel or wheels from a piece of ordnance left behind by Bonnie Prince Charlie's troops, 6 December 1745; however, the earlier occurrence of the name clearly belies this. The landlord in 1726, Francis Ward, laid out a bowling green of 1,078 square yards area, which survived until the Bridgart/Parker building works was built upon it in 1876 (cf. *Pymm's*). In 1800 it was taken over by Benjamin Hewitt, the inn having been kept for many years previously and successively by his father, Thomas, uncle, Benjamin, and cousin (another Benjamin). Acquired 1811 by the powerful Ward family, who sold it on in in January 1826 as the *Wheel* and it was for sale again in 1867. The rebuilding of 1880 (see below) was accompanied by a contents sale. It was on the market yet again in 1886 as the *Old Wheel*, being acquired by to Alton's, from which concern the latter passed to Stretton's.

The building, although comprehensively rebuilt by Robert Bridgart (whose builder's yard was practically next door) in 1880, is older, being largely of *c*.1790-1800 with even older parts embedded in the rear fabric. The Regency portion is of two bays to the east of two and a half storeys, the windows having rusticated lintels and triple keyblocks. The part refronted to Bridgart's designs, which angles back somewhat towards the Uttoxeter Old Road junction, is of three slightly lower storeys with a paired arched window to the left of the Lombardic doorcase and with a window rather like a shop's to the right, with single sashes above in architrave surrounds, whilst there is a triple window over the left hand part and a paired window above it. The brickwork has been painted in recent years.

In about 1972, this venerable old inn was unexpectedly renamed the *Garrick*; the eminent 18th-century actor, David Garrick was a Lichfield man, with marriage connections to a West Derbyshire family, hardly a particularly inspired choice, quite apart from the unnecessary change from a name of at least 250 years' standing and originating in the contraption on which St Catherine was martyred at Alexandria *c*.AD 310. Being a religious sign, the inn may even be of early foundation. In 1997, the owners Burtonwood Brewery, jumping on the bandwagon started rolling by the elevation of the HE College to University status in 1992, renamed it the *Thirsty Scholar*: pathetic.
BBA 1880; DM 3/12/1741, 23/3/1753, 13/3/1800,24/10/1811, 24/7/1867 & 24/3/1880

WHITE BEAR*

18 Derwent Row (corner Exeter Street)   by 1824-1969
A complete set of deeds survives for this inn, given by the late Mr N.R. Beckett to Derby Museum in 1990. From them we learn that the land was part of the Exeter House estate, passing from Lord Exeter to Alderman John Bingham in 1758, and divided from the demesne of that house in 1796,

White Bear (right), Derwent Row, with the Derby Canal, Derwent Row Bridge leading into Exeter Street and the lock beyond, c.1952.

when it was sold to Revd Thomas Manlove of Derby School. It was reunited with Exeter House by sale to William Eaton Mousley in 1819, and he built the inn between that date and 1824, when it was purchased 'newly built' by Alexander Street, the landlord. He was a boat builder by profession with a yard on the canal right behind the inn. Street bought the inn on a mortgage from Joseph Bloor, then co-proprietor of the china factory. When Street died in 1827, leaving several sons, who continued with the boat-building business, his widow Ann ran it until 1830 when her son-in-law John Smedley took it on; he later became a prosperous jeweller with a new house in Leonard Street. In 1854, his son, Alexander Smedley took over, but in 1877 he and the other heirs of Street sold for £1,060 to Reuben Grocock (d.1889). Grocock was a canal carrier's agent, and had probably worked with the Streets fixing up cargoes to be conveyed in the boats they built and, one suspects, operated by this time. By this time, too, the Bloors' mortgage on the inn had been transferred first to the painter John Raynor of Mugginton (son of Samuel and brother of Louise) and then to Fanny Boorman of Shepherd's Bush, Middlesex, the great-granddaughter of the illustrious china painter, Zachariah Boorman, thus continuing this odd link with the old China factory, which had stood nearby. From her the mortgage was transferred to Richard Rice, Alexander Smedley's brother-in-law. Later, this long-standing charge was held by Harpur-Crewe cousin the Revd J.A Whitaker, rector of Breadsall, of all people, who held it on behalf of J.H. Cotton, a tenant who bought the freehold in 1902 for £850, in his turn also installing a tenant. In 1913 this was F.P. Wildsmith, previously of the *Seven Stars*, Nottingham Road, another inn

White Bear, with later signage, towards the end of its days in the late 1960s.

with strong China Factory links. The freehold was sold in 1918 to William Beckett, whose family owned it until this venerable free house (which brewed on the premises almost until the end) was compulsorily purchased in 1969 to make way for the new ring road and closed in November that year, although the last landlord was Herbert Ferneyhough. It was demolished in May 1970.

In most contexts, the name drives from the badge of the mediaeval Earls of Warwick, although they never amounted to much in Derbyshire. The only local family to sport a white bear was the powerful Chesterfield family of Clarke, of Ashgate and Brampton, who did have Derby connections in the 18th century and before.
Deeds, at Derby Museum; *DET* 24/4/2000; *DM* 28/2/1877

(OLD) WHITE HART*

40 (12) Bridge Gate (corner Court No.2)   *by 1717-1935*
The White Hart was the badge adopted by Richard II and it continued in occasional use amongst his Yorkist successors. In Derby Museum there is a drawing of a 1717-dated rain-water head from this inn, which stood two doors down from the *Orange Tree*. The London weekly wagon later went from here, the service having previously departed from the *Red Lion*, Cornmarket. For sale in 1777 and 1787 and to let as a beerhouse in 1842, something of a comedown after the esteem it enjoyed in earlier times. It had 'Old' added to its title by 1818, perhaps to differentiate itself from the pub in Queen Street, if that had been founded by then and for which little evidence exists. In 1856, a year after a further sale, the anniversary was held here of the Poor Man's Friend Lodge of the Derby Midland United Order of Oddfellows – the Oddfellows were anything but united, splitting into several different independent groupings at an early date. It was again sold in 1864. It was run from the early 1870s until World War One by Emmanuel Cheeseborough who was succeeded by his son, Joseph until

it closed in 1935 and was purchased by Frederick King who absorbed it and no. 42 into his furnishing business. Demolished in 1965.
Derby Museum, Goodey Cat. 315; *DM* 25/1/1771, 26//7/1787, 20/7/1842, 29/9/1855, 2/7/1856 7 27/7/1864

(OLD) WHITE HART

Irongate (corner St Mary's Gate)   *by 1660-1799*
For many years this hostelry was owned by the Franceys family, apothecaries of Cornmarket and it is mentioned in the Fenny Bentley parish register for 1660. On the death of Alderman Henry Franceys in 1747, it passed to his heir, a priest, and his trustees sold it in 1751 to Thomas Mountney, who in 1754 pulled it down and rebuilt it. Thereafter it became well-known for staging wild beast shows. In 1799 it and surrounding houses were purchased by Mrs Richardson, a banker's widow, who pulled it down to undertake a property development, built 1800-1: this is the pleasing range which today stretches from the Probate Court, St Mary's Gate, round into Irongate, where stands the former Clulow's bookshop. It may, in consequence, have migrated to a nearby site, and be represented by the inn of this name only recorded in 1835. The occasional prefix 'Old' suggests that this inn predated that in Bridge Gate, so both are likely to have been 17th century at least.
Deeds, Private Collection; *DM* 14/7/1737, 8/4/1742, 6/1/1745, 8/2/1751, 25/1/1754, 20/3/1778 & 14/7/1785

WHITE HART

Sadler Gate   *–1761–*
Only known from a mention in Sir Harry Harpur's list of inns providing refreshment at his expense during the 1761 election; probably underwent previous and subsequent name changes.

WHITE HART**

Queen Street   *–1835 –*
Possibly a migration of the White Hart in Iron Gate after its original site was 're-developed' in 1799-1800. Either way probably subsequently renamed.

WHITE HART**

Wardwick   *–'1672'–*
A single reference, received at second hand, allegedly from the *DM*. However, as that paper was not founded until 1732, the date might have been intended for 1772. No other references found.

(OLD) WHITE HORSE*

96 Friar Gate   *by 1732-1876*
Probably a very old inn indeed, the picturesque building being mediaeval and reputedly cruck-framed; it was

White Horse, Friar Gate, c.1875 and as demolition started for the construction of Friar Gate Bridge in the autumn of 1876.

thatched until its demise. It was one of the many inns built to serve the cattle and beast markets at the upper end of Friar Gate.

It was also the home of the murderous virago Ellen Beare, at one stage of her evil career as abortionist, adultress and fraudster. She kept what Glover described as a 'paltry' public house – the *White Horse* – and was married to a 'cipher' of a husband, Ebenezer Beare. She was 'a handsome woman [of about 30 years of age] with an education superior to her rank, and was mistress to that persuasive eloquence which insensibly wins over the hearer to her own side...she was remarkably expert at procuring qualifications for the men; an exit for those women who were troublesome wives; an abortion for those who were

not.' A Stepping Lane butcher, John Hewitt, and his wife were regular customers, and Hewitt took a shine to Rosamond Ollerenshaw, the serving girl at the inn, and Mrs Beare provided poison by which in the spring of 1732, Mrs Hewitt was silenced for ever. At the subsequent trial of Hewitt, Beare and Ollerenshaw, Hewitt and the girl, rather by accident than design, shielded Mrs Beare from the evidence of her part in the squalid plot, and she was acquitted; the other two hanged. Yet at the next assizes, she was indicted on two counts of abortion and one of yet again providing poison for a man to do away with his wife, this time foiled by indiscretion. Even then she only received two days in the pillory for it. But shortly afterwards she received three years in gaol for yet another offence.

In 1735, Mrs Beare, now using the alias Merriman, and lately released from gaol, was again locked up for receiving stolen goods. On 10 July 1740, she was the ringleader of a mob which stopped two wagons en route for Ashbourne loaded with 24 sacks of fine flower and ransacked the cargo, an event which led to a full-scale riot. She and her co-conspirator, Elizabeth Bell got seven years' transportation; she left Liverpool 'for His Majesty's plantations abroad' on 31 August that year; no doubt the town breathed a sigh of relief!

A sheep roast was held here in 1856 to celebrate the ending of the war with Russia. In 1876 it was acquired by the Great Northern Railway, being on the line of the Handyside Bridge which was to carry the tracks over Friar Gate at this point, and it closed for demolition on 13 October the same year. At that time it was believed to be the oldest inn in Derby. A great loss. The last landlady, Ann Taylor, applied for the licence to be transferred elsewhere but was refused. Her late husband had run the pub before her and at the time of its closure she had been remarried, to William Rowley, whose father had kept the *Rising Sun* at the town end of Friar Gate.

DM 21/5/1856; Glover (1831/3) II.616-620

WHITE HORSE**

High Street   *by 1827-1857*

The address does not provide us with a house number, so it is difficult to know if it continued later in another guise;

the *High Street Tavern* is likely, being only recorded under that name from 1862. The malt house in the pub's yard was the subject of a sale in 1843.
DM 19/7/1843

White Horse, Morledge (as the Court House 2002). The Noah's Ark is to the right.

Thorntree Lane; side elevation of the White Horse of 1920. Pictured in 2002.

WHITE HORSE*

27-29 (18) Morledge (latterly corner Thorntree Lane)   *by 1779*

Originally one of a line of three small inns: the *Noah's Ark*, the *Cossack* and the *Bishop Blaze*. The latter was originally so named because the wool merchants plied their trade at the Morledge markets and fairs (on the name, cf. *Bishop Blaze,* Cornmarket). It was to let in 1779 and for sale in 1814 with a malthouse 'capable of malting 40 q[uarts] per week and two counting houses, stables, etc... late in the possession of Messrs Hollingshead.' The sale included all the land along Thorntree Lane, consisting of 4,700 [square] yards 'presenting a most desirable situation for a brewery or any extensive mercantile concern and comprising 22 dwelling houses...' It was to let in 1824, on the latter occasion being advertised as still having 'an extensive frontage in Thorn Tree Lane', despite then still not actually including the corner plot. Between 1874 and 1878 it was renamed the *White Horse.* Most inns of this name in Derby and, generally, elsewhere, took the name after the main charge in the arms of the Electorate of Hanover, added to the royal arms of Britain when George I succeeded in 1714: *gules a horse rampant argent,* deriving from the same Germanic source as the white horse of the Kingdom (later County) of Kent. It was acquired by Pountain's, which company also bought the *Cossack* from the Melland Thompson family, pulling both down in 1920, and reopening the *White Horse* in a grandiose new building, faced in terracotta-faced blocks, here and there with joggled voissoirs, and decorated with a giant Doric order of pilasters on a plinth to sill height supporting a substantial entablature and modillion cornice, all enclosing a single bay at the ends of the Morledge façade and two pairs in the centre. The curved frontispiece on the junction with Thorntree Lane has a bracketed segmental pediment over the entrance with a round headed window above enclosed by further pilasters and a pedimented attic above. It also incorporated the site of a small shop on the corner of Thorntree Lane. It took some time to build, the reopening not being achieved until early in 1923.

About the time of World War Two, it was taken over by George R. Baker – universally known as 'the old Scholar' on account of his unrivalled omniscience and his wife Alice, daughter of William Parnell of the *Royal Standard,* which they had previously run in succession to her father. She was the secretary of the Derby Ladies LVA, in which she was succeeded by her daughter Doreen, who had taken over the *Royal Standard.*

It was painted externally in 1990, which resulted in a loss of the sober tones of the terracotta, and introduced a garish note. In May 1994 it was sold by Carlsberg-Tetley, acquired by the concern who owned the *Flamingo & Firkin* pub in Becket Street and renamed the *Foal & Firkin.* It reverted to *White Horse* again before a second sale and refurbishment resulted in its once more being renamed, in December 2001, the *Court House,* the name being inspired by the Crown Court building opposite, and the idea no doubt being to attract lawyers, bolstered by fat expense accounts. In the event, the customers seem more accurately to reflect their less well-favoured clientele; appropriately, the interior has all the stark, Spartan simplicity of the institutions to which some of them are doubtless consigned following their appearances in the building opposite. *DET* 21/12/1996, 3/11/1998 (*Bygones* Suppl.) 19/12/01 & 12/2/2002 (*Bygones* Supplement); *DM* 12/11/1779, 17/3/1814 & 24/11/1824

WHITE HORSE*

85 Regent Street   *by 1857-1958*

As the second inn on this street, the *White Horse* failed to survive as long as the *Prince Regent Tavern*. It was originally of three bays and two storeys, with rusticated lintels over glazing-bar sashes, but at some stage the easternmost bay was reduced to a single storey. Listed anonymously at this address in 1857 and 1862. It was owned by Pountain's from at least 1937.

WHITE HORSE**

Rotten Row, Market Place   *1630-1737*

Known from a passing reference in the records of All Saints' Church (now Derby Cathedral), 1630. *DM* 20/10/1737

WHITE HORSE*

Sadler Gate (Bridge)   *-1765-*

To let in 1765, 'near to Sadler Gate Bridge'. The name is printed as the White House, but this is almost certainly a misprint (cf. *Crown & Cushion*). The description of its situation matches that of the *Half Moon* very closely, and possibly this was its previous name. *DM* 1/2/1765

WHITE HORSE

See CROWN & CUSHION

WHITE LION*

Cornmarket   *by 1732-1836*

Stood adjacent to the *Red Lion*, and was first mentioned in 1732; it faced Brookside and was jointly owned with the Red Lion by Francis Dawson until 1767, when the *White Lion* was advertised to let separately. It was for sale in 1785 and the new owner must have been keen to diversify, for we find him hiring shows, a menagerie appearing here in 1789. In 1804 another new landlord appeared and he sold up 11 years later having added 'newly built stables' and the inn itself 'lately rebuilt'. In 1820 the *Peveril* coach stopped here to change horses and for the passengers to be refreshed, only 15 minutes being allowed. In 1823-4 it was also the meeting place of the Independent Lodge of Oddfellows – George the Fourth. It was demolished in 1836 to make way for the culverting of

Markeaton Brook and the erection of the *Royal Hotel*. *DM* 26/10/1732, 28/8/1767, 16/12/1774, 14/4/1785, 31/12/1789, 31/1/1804, 15/6 & 24/8/1815

WHITE LION*

18 Derwent Street East (corner Exeter Street)
                    by 1874-1933

On almost as acute an angle as the *Royal Standard*, and at the other end of the row, almost next to the Congregational Chapel. The two-and-a-half-storey building was contemporary with Exeter Street, thus c. 1815/20, and if not built as a pub, must have been intended as a corner shop. It had massive stone lintels, first floor sill band and a high hipped roof, and a quadruple arcade was added to the Exeter Street ground floor frontage when it was converted into an inn around 1870. A spirit licence application was made in 1874, implying that it had existed previously as a beer house, rather than having been newly opened. White Lion Yard was a row of four minuscule cottages behind, within the angle. The White Lion was a badge of Edward V, but also of the Mowbrays, Lords Mowbray and Duke of Norfolk, a great mediaeval family which owned Bretby for a time in the 15th century. It also appeared on the arms of Alderman Henry Browne, apothecary and Mayor of Derby 1799 and 1808, descended from an old Loughborough family. Altons in 1927. Closed 1933 and demolished, the site being given over to industrial purposes, by 1936. *DM* 26/8/1874

(OLD) WHITE LION*

(14) Friar Gate   *by 1750-1861*

The 1827-9 *Directory* of Stephen Glover lists this inn, as well as the better known one (below); it is the only place where both are listed together, otherwise the entirely reasonably speculation would be that they were one and the same; the landlord was John Albrighton. It was for sale in 1851, and again 'with a brewery attached' in 1861, after which it vanishes from record. *DM* 14/5/1851, 31/3/1858 & 23/10/1861

WHITE LION*

2 Ashbourne Road (corner Brick Street)   *by 1732-1898*

One of the market taverns which once flourished at the west end of Friar Gate, and in a building of considerable age, on a site with deeds going back to mediaeval times, and still today retaining traces of its timber fabric. First recorded in 1732 (deed) and marketed in 1772 as being 'at the top of Nuns' Green' and in 1823 'at the top of Friar Gate'. For sale in 1779 and 1785, and to let in 1833. The advertisement in the latter year adds: 'The above inn stands in the centre of the Cattle fairs and is well adapted for an extensive business.' With the decline of the market after

White Lion, Ashbourne Road, c.1920 as a shop.

1861, it dwindled into a beerhouse, many such being soon converted into separate freeholds, which became shops. The same fate befell this free house shortly after the turn of the century. It is now divided between a betting shop and Luigi's Italian restaurant.
DM 18/9/1772, 24/6/1779, 1/12/1785, 10/11/1823 &
2/10/1833

WHITE SWAN
See SWAN & SALMON

WHITE SWAN*

57-59 (52) St Peter's Street   *by 1818-1913*
Situated a little up on the east side from East Street, opposite St Peter's Church Yard. It had a spacious yard on the south side, with several other businesses established in it. A large bowling green was an added attraction by 1830 when to let, and appears on the 1852 Board of Health Map. From the bowling green Emmanuel Jackson (1818-1883) a silk throwster and celebrated Derby aeronaut, made his first balloon ascent in 1850. He made ascents thereafter all over the world, from Derby Arboretum to Australia, but murdered his wife and died by his own hand at his home at 112, Burton Road 26 June 1883, leaving two sons. Closed in 1913 and later taken down to build the White Hall cinema opened in 1914.

WHITE STOUP*

Duffield Road (King Street)   *by 1757-1800*
Not certainly an inn at all. It is referred to ambiguously in the *Derby Mercury* (11 March 1757) '...at the commencement of the Duffield Turnpike' which might indicate a toll bar; nevertheless, a pub beside the toll bar is just as likely. The turnpike was inaugurated in 1739 and improved in 1756, so either date might apply to the founding of an inn by the toll bar. In 1804 another clue appears: 'To be let, a new erected dwelling house situated at the White Stoup, near Derby'. This might well refer to The Elms, the listed Georgian House surviving at Five Lamps between the

Duffield and Kedleston Roads and built in 1800. If there was a pub, it was probably demolished to build The Elms. Perhaps it migrated and survived later under a different name, in which case the *New Inn* later the *St Helen's* would be the only candidate, although if it started as the *New Inn* the implication is that it was just that.
DM 11/3/1757 & 27/9/1804

WHO CAN TELL?
See CARRINGTON ARMS

WILLIAM IV
See DUKE OF CLARENCE

WILMOT ARMS

39 (47) Normanton Road (corner Wilmot Street)
                                      by 1846-2000
Corner pub named after the street, which took its name from either the Wilmots of Chaddesden Hall or those of Osmaston Hall; the latter being more likely, especially in view of the fact that Sir Robert Wilmot-Horton, 3rd Bt, was Colonial Secretary. The inn was acquired by Offilers' who rebuilt it completely in brick with stone dressings in 1913, the date being carried on the parapet of the odd projecting full-height bay added on the angle. It is named in the 1850 directory and in a notice of 1865 and is probably to be identified with an anonymous beer house in Normanton Road recorded in 1846. Owned by Bass in 1994 but subsequently closed and boarded up. Re-opening as a private member club, not a pub.
DM 1/3/1865

WINDMILL HOTEL

Railway Terrace   *-1965-*
Only recorded for 1965, and not necessarily in possession of a full licence.

(OLD) WINDMILL*

29 (26) Willow Row   *by 1818-1935*
So called perhaps because of the possibility that a windmill existed nearby (see *Northern Star*), and the reason why the Lodge Lane establishment was called the *Old Windmill*. But then in 1818, this pub was also prefixed 'Old'! It was to let in 1844 and for sale in 1861. A spirit licence was subsequently granted in 1873. Latterly in the hands of Stretton's, it appears to have closed in the very late 1920s, although the building survived to become an eating house which opened at 6am to provide breakfast for night shift workers as Cooper's Café until demolition, although this establishment does not show in the directories – probably it was an 'unofficial' business operating from what was, in essence, a private residence. It was painted for a picture in the

Windmill, Willow Row, 1933. The doorway of the inn is to the right of Arnold Woodhouse's fruit shop.

Museum's Goodey Collection in 1935, when it appears to have been the only building then left standing on that part of the street.
DM 1/10/1873; Goodey (1936) no.166; Palmer (1996)(i) 12

WINDMILL
See also CAMBRIDGE, NORTHERN STAR

(Old) Wine Vaults, Market Place.

(OLD) WINE VAULTS*

17 (11) Market Place   *by 1734-1970*
Situated on the north side of the Market Place, by 1754 it was in the hands of George Brentnall, who had it until 1769, and called it *Brentnall's Wine Vaults*. His successor was Miss Bowyer and it thus became *Bowyer's Wine Vaults*, although she was in fact Brentnall's tenant. In 1872 it was acquired by, and became the HQ of, J.T. Pountain & Co, vintners, but when they moved to the site of the former *Virgin's Inn,* it was sold to Offiler's and by 1898 had retreated into premises behind no. 11 (later 17). Universally known as 'The Sough' from at least that date until it was demolished to make way for the Assembly Rooms in 1970.

(Old) Wine Vaults. 1924.

A sough is, of course, local dialect for a tunnel, (especially for the draining of lead mines, and indeed a drain is an analogy), the name being prompted by the noisesome alley by which one latterly gained access.
DM 6/11/1872

WINE VAULTS

35 Iron Gate   *–1857–*
Seemingly a fairly ephemeral establishment, situated almost next to Robin Hood Yard. Later a shop.

WINE VAULTS
See WRIGHT'S VAULTS

WOOD LARK*

76-80 (84, 71) Bridge Street   *by 1850*
Once a small inn, close to two others (cf. *Maypole* and *Ram*) at the intersection of Bridge Street and Brook Street, listed anonymously in 1850 and all three today miraculous survivors from the wholesale destruction of the old West End. It now occupies the whole of a pair of double-fronted two-and-a-half-storey houses with four-over-four glazing bar sashed windows and a sill band at first floor level, subsequently harled and with the ground floor windows

Wood Lark, Bridge Street, 2002.

altered. The portion furthest from the intersection had once been the *Mechanics' Arms,* absorbed by subsequent expansion. Acquired by Offilers' in 1926, thence to Bass and a free house latterly. From 1934 the landlord was the legendary Joe Rostron (1910-1993). He was born at Heywood, Lancs, and was a professional boxer who fought 133 bouts until his retirement in 1934, the year he came to Derby, losing only 13; he was never knocked out in 113 bouts. He went on to run the *Old Angel,* Cornmarket and then the *Post Office Hotel,* retiring from it in 1963. His successor, Edward Carter, Mr Motley tells us, was still brewing on the premises in 1939 in a malthouse shared with the *Ram.* Named after the bird. The lark (Jewitt reminds us) is 'the early bird picks up all the worms, so the early-opened public house catches all the stray customers in the morning'.
Reliquary XI (1871) 177.

WOODMAN'S STROKE
See BEECH TREE

WOOLPACK
See DURHAM OX

WOOLSACK

164-6 Parliament Street   *by 1874-1977*
A very modest beerhouse on the east side of the street, in the hands of Stretton's in 1937 (thus later Ind Coope) and granted a full licence in 1951. In 1955 it was sold to the Stone family who recommenced brewing their own ale on the premises. Cleared in the St Luke's rebuilding scheme at the end of the 1970s. Name from the Lord Chancellor's ceremonial seat in the Lords.

WRIGHT'S VAULTS*

24 Railway Terrace (Railway Parade) (corner Midland Place)   *by 1874*
Originally called the *Wine Vaults* in 1874 when the landlord was W.J. Wright, hence its later name, but only a beer-

Wright's Vaults, now the Merry Widows, Railway Terrace.

house converted from an off-licence. Run by Frederick William Ragg from the later 1880s until World War One, whose widow – who succeeded him – led to its colloquial name of 'the merry widow's'. Later taken over by Samuel Allsopp & Co. Taken on, briefly, by the Barker dynasty (having acquired a full licence in 1950) in 1990, and accordingly renamed the *Merry Widows* in 1992, the new sign showing two women, a slight misunderstanding of the original soubriquet! Carlsberg-Tetley by 1994.

Yates's Wine Lodge, Iron Gate, formerly Brigden's outfitters, 2002.

YATES WINE LODGE**

22, Iron Gate   *1998*
Installed in the former premises of Geo. Brigden & Co, for over a century outfitters to the gentry of the County. The Grade II listed building, of Queen Anne type but a decade or so later in date, in brick with wavy stone lintels, is of five bays and four storeys, topped with a parapet. Brigden shop-fronted it in about 1882 in a very respectful way with stone rusticated pilasters, the entrance being at the east end of the façade, the remainder consisting of a large saloon. When this firm moved in 1996, the building was sold to Yates's who not only gutted what was left of the interior, and moved the entrance to the central bay, but added a

huge extension to the rear, where the elevation had survived completely intact from the early 18th century, a shocking solecism, and one of which the City Council should be thoroughly ashamed. It opened in 1998.

York Hotel, Midland Road.

YORK HOTEL*

22 Midland Road (corner Railway Terrace)   *by 1857*

Set in quite what was once quite a distinguished early Victorian building. Of three storeys, it has sill bands and entablatures over the once-glazing-bar sashed windows supported on consoles. In 1859 it was taken by the appropriately named James Boosey, former head waiter of the *Midland Hotel*, who is reported to have made 'extensive alterations.' It expanded into two neighbouring, later and less distinguished Victorian buildings round the corner in Railway Terrace after World War One, and the whole was stuccoed.

It was extensively altered in 1929 by Allsopp's and again modernised in 1937, this time with black marble sheathed ground floor, Crittall windows and the title in stainless steel applied lettering. Taken over in the early 1980s, refurbished yet again and renamed, unnecessarily one might think, the *Aston Court Hotel.* Interior now entirely gutted and soulless.

DM 30/1/1859

YORK TAVERN

23 (10) York Street   *by 1846*

Small inn converted from a well-proportioned double-fronted brick house built a decade or two before by Thomas and Joseph Cooper, masons. In 1854 for sale as a 'well accustomed old public house' so conceivably purpose-built, although it doesn't show on record before 1846. For sale again in 1865 and 1881. Later owned by Stretton's, but a free house by 1994. Named after the street, itself perhaps named after the ecclesiastical province in which Derby lies.

DM 11/10/1854, 4/10/1865 & 1/6/1881

York Tavern, York Street, 1936.

Suburban Pubs

ALLENTON

CROWN*
Chellaston Road   *1879*

Built by Isaac Allen, founder of the settlement which was later named after him, and built at a cost of £1,200. At first it only had a 6-day licence. Next door, in Upper Moor Road, Allen built Boulton Fields Farm, but, by 1895, when Offiler's took over, the two buildings were linked together and form part of the same edifice. Today pebble-dashed. A prehistoric hippopotamus's remains were discovered when a well was being dug in March 1895. Henry Bemrose excavated an entire hippopotamus skeleton between 8-11 April that year and gave them to Derby Museum, where they are still on display.
DM 8/8/1882; Longdon (2000) 22

MITRE
Osmaston Road   *1930*

Designed and built by T.H. Thorpe for Zachary Smith's brewery in a watered-down 'by-pass' Tudor, on land acquired from 1924, by Marston's. Remarkably little altered since. Deliberately named the *Mitre* to reflect the nearby *Crown*, to reflect church and state. Licence transferred from the *Dog & Duck* Haarlem Street.
Longdon (2000) 81-2.

ALLESTREE

ALLESTREE HOTEL
See MARKEATON HOTEL

ALLESTREE INN**
Duffield Road   *by 1826-1846*

A notice of this in appears in 1826, and in 1846 it was announced that it was 'discontinued and sold up'. Probably of old establishment, however, being on the main road.

MARKEATON HOTEL
Kedleston Road   *1938*

Built to a design by Naylor & Sale as the *Allestree Hotel* and opened in 1938. Renamed since the war and more recently rebuilt drastically, a process being repeated at the time of writing. In 2002 an Ember Inn.
DA 13/5/1938

NEW INN
Duffield Road   *by 1771-1846*

Stood opposite Allestree Park gates on the turnpike road, but divided into two cottages *c.*1860 by the anti-drink Evans family of Allestree Hall. Legend has it that the inn was founded in the early 16th century and that the eloping Dorothy Vernon and John Manners stopped here in 1567. Unfortunately, there are few facts to support the story of the lovers' flight, and none whatsoever to associate the inn with the event.

PARK FARM
Birchover Way (Park Farm Centre)   *1968*

Opened in September 1968 as an integral part of the new shopping centre there. Designed by Montague & Associates. Named after the farm which once stood nearby.

Red Cow, St Edmund's Close, Allestree, 2002.

RED COW*
St Edmund's Close   *by 1753*

Pleasant vernacular inn with a white stuccoed façade of three bays and two storeys probably rebuilt into its present form around 1800, but retaining an earlier core. A lower 1930s extension is attached to the right hand side. Stocks once stood outside, and a mortuary behind, we are told. Inside a stuffed dog once graced the bar, with a bone ring round its neck. Born in 1903, it was put down by the landlord because it began to get too portly for the non-adjustable collar!

WOODLANDS

Blenheim Drive   *1965*

Apparently the last Offiler's house to be opened before that brewery was absorbed by Bass on 12 March 1965. Named after a farm which once stood on the site. It is worth noting that there were four licences granted for Allestree 1761-71, but only two inns can be identified.

ALVASTON & CREWTON

Alvaston Hotel, London Road, Alvaston.

ALVASTON HOTEL

1196 London Road (corner Brighton Road)   *1891*

A fairly pretentious curved structure of two storeys and seven bays curving around the angled site, the steep tiled roof retaining its iron decoration. Four sets of paired sashes on ground floor. Named after the settlement by Alton's, who built the pub which was designed by Naylor & Sale. Later sold to Home Ales. Renamed the *Round House* (after its apparent shape and local nickname) 1995.

BLUE PETER*

London Road (corner Harvey Road)   *1934*

The first of Offiler's three Art Deco style hotels using the word 'Blue' as a prefix in their titles and designed by George Morley Eaton PRIBA (died 1940). White stuccoed symmetrical wireless-set style building situated today by a busy roundabout, but built on the site of a wheelwright's shop of which the last proprietor was Henry Sherwin, and in his family since at least the early 19th century. Named after the well-known maritime signal flag. A Toby Inn from 1980 and refurbished without its curved steel glazing, which has somewhat marred its appearance. Now an Arena Inn.

DET 18/8/1982

CORNISHMAN

Holbrook Road   *1968*

Opened February 1968; modern open-plan estate pub. Named in deference to the profusion of local roads bearing Cornish place names, doubtless so called by the developer for reasons of his own. Confusingly, the road in which it stands bears the name of former local landowners, the Holbrook family of Nunsfield House.

CORONATION

Baker Street (Crewton)   *1939*

Nominally a Strettons' house, planned in 1937 (hence the name; George VI was crowned that year) and opened in 1939. Spacious brick building on a prominent corner site. The sign was repainted in 1992 to show George V.

DOG & HARE

Unknown locale   *by 1846-1855*

Little known about this apparently short-lived hostelry. Familiar bucolic name from coursing and also an Aesop fable.

HARRINGTON ARMS*

1240 London Road   *by 1854-1966;1967*

Possibly the *Dog & Hare* renamed, as their dates run consecutively. The (re-)naming was clearly in honour of Leicester FitzGerald Charles Stanhope, 5th Earl of Harrington (1784-1862), who succeeded to the nearby Elvaston Castle estate in 1851. This inn was demolished in August 1966, rebuilt and reopened 14 September 1967; it is now a lowish, undistinguished modern brick box bearing the modified soubriquet of *The Harrington*.

JAMES WYATT

Keldholme Lane   *1985*

Opened to serve a new estate on former Elvaston estate land, 23 March 1985, and named as the result of a competition, after the architect of Elvaston Castle, James Wyatt (1746-1813), who was born near Burton upon Trent.

JOINERS' ARMS

London Road   *by 1846-1857*

Once on the site of *Stanhope Lodge*, but enjoying no continuity, since this inn reverted to being a private house in the 1860s.

LODGE

See STANHOPE LODGE

NEEDLES

Bembridge Drive   *1984*

Opened by Banks's to serve the west portion of the same

estate as the *James Wyatt*, 19 November 1984, and named after the famous Isle of Wight headland due to a misunderstanding of the origin of Bembridge Drive. This road took its name from a prominent yeoman family, originally cadets of the eminent Bainbrigge family of Lockington Hall and Derby; the name mutated to Bembridge and whoever named this unconventionally designed pub, plainly assumed that the street took its name from the Isle of Wight town.

NEW INN
London Road   *by 1791-1827*

A low, vernacular, mediaeval-looking three-bay building set at right angles to the turnpike road, known from a vignette on a map and probably founded when the road was turnpiked 40 years earlier.

ROUNDHOUSE
See ALVASTON INN

SILVER GHOST
Field Drive   *1965*

Opened 17 December 1965 to serve expanding housing and named after the most famous Derby-built automotive product of Messrs Rolls-Royce. At one time, though, the inn sign amusingly showed the car on one side and a spook on the other!

(STANHOPE) LODGE
Shardlow Road (corner of Grange Road)   *1962*

Opened, newly-built in brick, 12 December 1962, on the site of the former *Joiners' Arms* and again named after the Stanhopes, Earls of Harrington, for many centuries owners of the land in this part of the parish. Renamed *The Lodge*, December 1988.

SWAN
Unknown locale   *–1753–*

Known only from an advertisement of 1753.
DM 16/11/1753

WELCOME
Brighton Road   *1891-1952*

A temperance hotel, but one by force of circumstance rather than design. It was built as an inn, but consistently failed to secure a licence. The compromise was to open as a temperance establishment. The distinguished looking two-storey brick house with stone dressings and half-timbered gables was designed by Naylor & Sale, and it went on to enjoy an unlicenced existence of some 60 years. It was later demolished.

WHEEL*
London Road   *by 1817-1877*

Situated on the turnpike road opposite the New Inn. The 1827 map shows it with a cart wheel as a sign, bracketed out from the wall. For sale in 1817 and granted a full licence in 1877, after which it inexplicably fades from view.
DM 9/1/1817, 26/9/1877

BOULTON

BRACKENS HOTEL
Brackens Lane   *by 1955*

Built in a post-war version of the style of the *Mitre*, Allenton to serve the burgeoning Boulton Lane estate, and named after the street, which itself was named after the farm across the pastures of which it was pitched.

BREADSALL

PADDOCK
391 Mansfield Road   *1987*

Opened October 1987 to serve the west side of the Oakwood development. Named after a field name. Note that the remainder of the inns in Breadsall Parish are outside the city.
For Breadsall Hilltop see under Chaddesden and Oakwood.

CHADDESDEN

BLUE BOY*
Wiltshire Road   *1936*

The best preserved of the three Art Deco style white stuccoed hotels built for Offiler's to the designs of George M. Eaton in the inter-war years with themed names. Much use inside and out of curvilinear walling and Crittall wrap-around fenestration, although the lounge bar is decoratively firmly rooted in the non-Art Deco 1920s' tradition. Built 1935 and opened January 1936 with licence transferred from the *Pheasant*, Traffic Street. Presumably named after Gainsborough's famous painting.

(CHADDESDEN) PARK HOTEL*
Nottingham Road   *1931-1995; 1996*

Opened December 1931 and built to a design by T.H. Thorpe, at the corner of Chaddesden Lane and named after the parkland of Chaddesden Hall (then but recently demolished) on the fringes of which it lay. Renamed *Beau*

Park Hotel, Nottingham Road, Chaddesden, 1935.

Brummell (after the Regency Buck, George Bryan Brummell, 1778-1890) January 1972, and later merely *The Park*. Much transformed from its original appearance, and given a £300,000 refurbishment in April 1992, in 1950s American speakeasy style, and renamed (yet again) *Rosie O'Brien's Pumphouse*, the origin of which is elusive, to say the least. In June 1995 it was refurbished, the name reverted to being *The Park* and was reopened as such in January 1996. In 2001 it became a Toby Carvery.
DET 7/5/1992

CHERRY TREE HOTEL
Cherry Tree Hill   -(1938)-
Proposed but was not approved by the council and was never built.
DA 11/2/1938

DUCK
Chaddesden Lane   by 1791-1849
Stood on the west side of the lane, near the Nottingham Road, and owned (or tenanted) by the Bailey family through most of its life. Sarah Bailey, widow, died in 1849 and by the 1851 census it fails to appear, so was presumably sold as a residence or demolished.

JOHN F. KENNEDY*
Ellendale Road   1967-1995
Opened 3 May 1967 and named after the US President assassinated in November 1963 and four years later still a much-admired figure. It was for sale in September 1993 and was closed in 1995 prior to demolition for new housing after only 28 years of existence.

KINGFISHER
Lexington Road   by 1977
The address would be more suitable for the previous entry, being named (along with others in this part of Chaddesden), after an American city! The pub, though, was named after the waterbird.

PARK
See CHADDESDEN PARK HOTEL

PENGUIN
Wollaton Road   1963
As the previous entry, named after the (flightless) bird. An estate pub opened in 1963.

RHINO
Max Road   by 1965
Another inn named after an animal seemingly plucked at random from the reference books. Brick estate pub.

RISING SUN
Unknown locale   by 1719-1762
Nothing known about this inn.

ROCKET
St Andrew's View, Breadsall Hill Top   by 1977
Typical estate pub, named after George Stephenson's well-known locomotive when opened.

ROSIE O'BRIEN'S PUMPHOUSE
See CHADDESDEN PARK HOTEL

ROYAL CROWN (DERBY)
7 Cavan Drive   by 1977
Another mundane looking late 1950s style building with a later front extension. Refurbished to the tune of £45,000 and reopened in May 1992 with the word 'Derby' omitted from the title, thus losing the china manufacturing connection.
Derby Herald & Post 13/5/1992

SHOULDER OF MUTTON
Unknown locale   1773
Referred to only in an advertisement of 1773.
DM 29/10/1773

SPINNING WHEEL
96 Wood Road   1777, 1939
A *Spinning Wheel* was mentioned as early as 1777 but it is unclear whether this had any connection with the current establishment, which was proposed in February 1938 (along with the *Cherry Tree Hotel*, and similarly turned down). Permission was granted upon reapplication on a new site in 1939 and built that year in brick with a hipped roof, the elevations now unfortunately painted over. Hardy Hansons at present.

TAP HOUSE**
Unknown location   1835
Landlord, Thomas Bailey. Directory entry is only reference.

TRAVEL INN**

Stanier Way, Wyvern Park   *2000*

A modern soulless hotel for a certain level of business clientele; exact licensing situation unclear. The street is named after the late Sir William Stanier, FRS, chief mechanical engineer of the LMS from 1933 to 1946.

WHEEL

See WILMOT ARMS

Wilmot Arms, Morley Road, Chaddesden, c.1930.

WILMOT ARMS*

Morley Road (corner Chapel Lane)   *by 1770*

A double pile 18th-century structure, end-on to the road with three bays, two storeys and segmental headed Regency sashes, originally called the *Wheel* (as in 1770) and the main village pub since that time, being near Church and Hall and renamed the *Wilmot Arms* when the Chaddesden Hall estate acquired it at the beginning of the 19th century. The Wilmots lived at the Hall 1626-1926. Stretton's in the earlier part of the 20th century, during which time for the most part the landlords were members of the Frith family, Mrs Sarah M. Frith dying there in harness in 1917. Now a Burtonwood Inn.

Cholerton (1999) 92; *DM* 1/6/1770

CHELLASTON

BONNIE PRINCE**

166 Swarkestone Road   *1999*

A large new 'family pub' built by Hardy Hansons to cater for the passing trade brought to its doorstep by the new Southern Derby Link Road (A50), and named after Bonnie Prince Charlie, whose advance guard reached Swarkestone on the evening of 4 December 1745, and which placed a picquet on the southern approach of Swarkestone Bridge. The core of the building is a later Victorian villa of some pretension, now almost wholly swamped by neo-vernacular additions. The interior is – inevitably – open plan and a little soulless.

DET 1/4/1999

New Inn (later the Corner Pin), Swarkestone Road, Chellaston, 1938.

CORNER PIN*

Swarkestone Road   *1863*

A very ancient cruck timber-framed structure lies beneath the banal stuccoed exterior of this inn's lower wing. Rest built early in the 19th century: brick, two storeys, three bays, with four-pane sashes and stone lintels. The inn was established as the *New Inn*, the local histories tell us, in 1863, but it seems likely from its appearance that it was purpose built, and may previously have been the *Gate* (see below) named because the turnpike gate once stood here. It was for sale in 1870. The name changed to the *Corner Pin* post-war, probably harking back to its probably original name; perhaps there was an hiatus between the closure of the *Gate* and its reopening in 1863, for neither appears in the 1857 directory. Restoration to the cruck timbers took place, autumn 2002.

DM 23/2/1870

GATE*

Unknown locale   *by 1827-1846*

Nothing further known of this inn; possibly an earlier name for the *Corner Pin* (*New Inn*), for both names recall the forgotten *lingua franca* of the turnpikes. Listed as an anonymous beer house in 1846 run by William Pegg.

LAWNS HOTEL

High Street   *1977*

A conversion from a medium-sized Victorian villa, after which it was named; externally an architectural nightmare.

Subsequently sold and renamed *The Lawns*. Opened in June 1977 by Derek Cash, who converted the coach house and stables into a bar. Prior to this the buildings had been used as a bakery and laundry. The work was carried out by J. M. Hobson of Derby, who had recently built the new brew-house at the *John Thompson Inn* at Ingleby. Initially a stone-and-wood 'old-style' bar, it was extended in the late 1980s.

DET 8/6/77

NEW INN
See CORNER PIN

Red Lion, Derby Road, Chellaston.

RED LION*
Derby Road   *1829*

A fine old inn built on the main road in 1829, into which was built the former staircase from the former Manor House in the 1840s. Demolished and replaced by Bass in 1964, the replacement being banal in the extreme, considering that the former structure was easily the handsomest of Chellaston's inns. Stuccoed, of two storeys and attics with a wide end-gable to the road, quoins, four over four pane sashes and entrance with attractive if eccentric stone hood; lower extension to right. The traditional name is said to derive from the arms of Richard Plantagenet, Earl of Cornwall and King of the Romans (1209-1272), second son of King John.

Craven & Stanley (1984) 29

A Frank Gresley painting from c.1880 of a very rural Chellaston, showing an inn, the Rose and Crown.

ROSE & CROWN*
Swarkestone Road   *by 1753*

Probably the original main village pub and a one-time local coaching inn, 18th century, two storeys, of brick, and apparently incorporating a smaller dwelling to the east to make three bays, with a much earlier, lower extension to the south, last thatched in 1930 but now tiled. As with the *Red Lion*, almost totally rebuilt in recent times. Perhaps to be equated with the *Gate*. Alton's early in the last century, but later (and still) Marston's. Modern rebuilding has robbed it of all vestiges of antiquity.

DARLEY ABBEY

Abbey Inn, Darley Abbey, 2002.

ABBEY
Darley Street   *1979*

Adapted from a monastic stone-built edifice of unclear original purpose (and long abandonment after use as tenements) and opened 5 October 1979; architect for sympathetic alterations was Richard Wood. There was a great deal of opposition from local residents to the opening of this inn; from 1782 to 1979 no pub had existed in the village due to the attitude of the Evans family of Darley Hall, who owned the mill and created the village. Most people actually born and bred in Darley therefore welcomed the coming of a pub!

HASLAM'S

Haslam's Lane   *2002*

In the summer of 2002, Derby Rugby Club were relocated to the old Qualcast Sports Ground on Haslam's Lane after the controversial redevelopment of their former ground on Kedleston Road. The club opened their bar on 8 August – run by an organisation called Concept 15 – as *Haslam's* – named after the throughfare, itself named after the local family of Haslam, later celebrated foundrymen. Although membership is presumably required for the rugby club itself, entrance to the bar appears to be free to all, thus qualifying it for inclusion in this book.

LITTLEOVER

ARGOSY*

Manor Road (corner Constable Drive)   *1956*

Built on the Derby Ring Road 1955-6 to the designs of Edward Saunders for Morrison & Associates of brick and roughcast with a battered attached chimney breast and slightly chalet-style clay tile roofs. It has since been extended three times, most recently in 1984 and in July 1996, at first spoiling the original design – which had a stratifying compactness about it – and subsequently almost obliterating it.

Named after mediaeval merchant ships originating from Ragusa. Bearing in mind the impenetrable qualities of the old Derby Ring Road the *Flying Dutchman* might have been a more appropriate choice! It became a Harvester in the mid-1990s.

BLUE BALL

Littleover Common (Huffin Heath)   *–1773–*

In an advertisement of 1773 it was described as 'newly built' in brick and for sale with an acre of garden. The area, now mainly built over or destroyed by the A38, was heathland, but handy to attract travellers on the turnpike road to Uttoxeter. Possibly to be identified with the *Plough*. Name unclear.

COPPICE
See CREST MOTEL

CREST MOTEL*

Pastures Hill   *1951-2001*

Originally a large private house called The Coppice, built for ironfounder Luther Russell in 1898 in brick with stone dressings, to a design by Arthur Coke-Hill (1847-1907). Of two storeys and attics, it was built in brick with lavish stone dressings, mullioned and transomed windows some in curved and square projecting bays, the whole producing a sort of Arts-and-Crafts Jacobethan edifice of some dignity and distinction, with a recessed entrance under a curved stone hood. The interior was replete with light oak panelling with decorative chimney-pieces and a certain amount of good plaster decoration. The fine gardens were embellished with a pretty stable block, or motor house, for the family had a car from very early on. Russell was the youngest son of Alderman Robert Russell (Mayor of Derby in 1882-3), initiator of the Peel Foundry in 1857. On Luther Russell's death in 1941, it was sold to H.C. Offiler who at first planned to live there, stabling the Offiler's Brewery show horses there. After the war, and seeing the potential of the adjacent A38, he decided to convert it to an hotel, failing at first to obtain a licence. He finally obtained one in 1950 and it opened in 1951, briefly the *Crescent*, presided over by the elegant and efficient Mrs Tipping. After a few years it became once again the *Coppice* until renamed the *Crest* in November 1970. It was later sold to Forte Hotels and in 1991 became the *Forte Posthouse* and vastly expanded in such a way as visually to swamp the original architecture although the link between the house and the extensions was a modest one. It was the only hostelry in Derby with a Roman road (Rykneild Street) running through it, a Scheduled Ancient Monument (SAM). After the sale of Forte it was renamed merely the *Posthouse* and closed after just 50 years with less than a month's warning on 24 December 2001 (wrecking numerous Christmas period festivities), when the owners were told by their marketing men that it would fetch more as a building site than as an hotel. Sold to a local firm for a housing redevelopment (which the SAM would somewhat circumscribe), but no application to demolish and build has yet materialised at the time of writing. An enlightened developer would, without doubt, be prepared to convert the house as dwelling units and build where the extensions were, taking slightly less profit, but attracting much goodwill. A serious fire in September 2002 destroyed the roof and much of the interior, leaving the old house's future in more doubt.
DET 3/1/2002

HALF MOON

Burton Road   *by 1577*

Allegedly founded in (or by) 1577 (landlord William Carter)

and said to have been a coaching inn in the 18th century, it was for sale in 1835 and to let nine years later. It was almost entirely rebuilt in the early 20th century and gutted internally in 1984; the stables partly survive. Last landlord before the brewery (Bass) imposed a manager in 1991 was the efficient and memorable Ted Goodall. Refurbished 1985 and in 1997 won the City Council's Best Pub Garden competition.

DM 7/10/1835 & 13/3/1844; Scott (1916) 8

HOLLYBROOK TAVERN**

Rykneld Road, Heatherton   *1994*

Built to serve a new suburb built to the south-west on farm land once part of the Heathcote's estate, hence, perhaps the odd hybrid name of the area. It is a two-storey neo-vernacular brick edifice, with 'family' facilities, and pantiled roofs with terracotta finials sweeping low to eaves at ground floor level, with lower side and rear extensions. It occupies the site of the former Pastures Farm, home farm of The Pastures, now the Independent Grammar School for Boys. The Holly Brook, which crossed the site, was only noticed by the architects once construction was under way, but it was diverted in front and turned into a 'feature'. It is prone to periodic and disastrous flooding, so one hopes that Bass have taken adequate precautions! The first landlords were Mr and Mrs Les Lowe, previously at the *Navigation*, Wilmorton and the *Stenson Fields*. Opened July, 1994. It is an Ember Inn, now owned by Six Continents Retail, who applied for planning permission to extend it in February 2002.

DT 14/7/1994

PANTHER

Oaklands Avenue   *1961*

Modern pub built to serve a new housing development by Ind Coope and opened on 12 August 1961. A traditional heraldic name treated in a literal way.

PLOUGH*

Huffin Heath   *by 1827-1872*

Almost certainly the same as the *Blue Ball* under another name and for sale with 2 acres of land in 1839, and again in 1866, having been let five years previously, being acquired by William Ratcliffe of an old Normanton farming family most memorably connected with Cotton's Farm. He advertised it for sale in 1871 getting £610 for it a year later when it probably closed, when it became a small holding. It was abandoned by the 1940s and cleared less than a decade later. Named either after the heavenly body or, more likely in this context, the agricultural implement.

Deeds, Private collection; *DM* 25/9/1839, 17/7/1861, 4/4/1866 & 20/9/1871

RISING SUN*

Burton Road   *by 1577-c.1820*

Mentioned in the same 16th-century source as the *Half Moon* and stood nearby, on the parish boundary with Derby, on the east side of Littleover Hill, until the early 19th century. The conjunction of the two inns bearing moon and sun in their names is more common than might be expected, and not necessarily the result of a happenstance. The 1577 landlord was William Dakeyne.

Scott (1916) 8

[UNKNOWN]**

The Hollow   *before 1850*

The Old Cottage is said to have once been a pub owned by the Page family.

Watson (1993)

(WHITE) SWAN

Shepherd Street   *by 1768*

The main village inn, outside which fairs were traditionally held; occasionally listed (*eg* in 1827) merely as the *Swan*. The sign here represents a heraldic badge of the de Tonei/de Stafford family, powerful nearby, south of the Trent, in the early mediaeval period. For sale in 1839 by the Heathcote family of the Old Hall who sold the *Plough* at the same time, along with a large amount of other property, workshops and building land. The tenant was Joseph Ratcliffe of the same family as the later owner of the *Plough*. It was sold again in 1879. Building replaced early in the 20th century.

DM 28/2/1839 & 10/12/1879

MACKWORTH

(NEW) BULL & BUSH

Henley Green   *1965*

Built to serve the Corporation's large post-war estate at Mackworth, near the site of the former Humbleton Farm, once all part of the Markeaton estate, in 1965. Two-storey banal brick building with steel windows.

KINGSWAY HOTEL

Brackensdale Avenue   *1954 (1958)*

The first pub to be built on the estate, a commodious building completed and opened, according to one account, on 11 November 1954, although, like the estate itself, planned before the war and designed by Sam Morrison & Partners. J. Farmer, RIBA of Morrisons, however, avers that it was commissioned by Offilers around 1956 and opened in spring 1958.

WOODPECKER

Woodford Road   *by 1965*

Another modern and architecturally undistinguished estate pub.

MARKEATON

COCK

Unknown locale   *–1764–*

Recorded only in 1764. Possibly on the site of the Kedleston Road Toll Bar, near where Maxwell Avenue was until the A38 was widened at this point, or perhaps another name for the inn following. Crest of the Cokaynes of Ashbourne, or merely a bucolic name.

DM 15/6/1764

NIMROD & HOTSPUR

Markeaton Lane   *to c.1904*

A brick two-storey edifice of three wide bays attached to one of the farms in the hamlet of Markeaton, just outside the park gates. It is not listed anywhere. Engagingly named after an odd combination of a dashing early 15th century member of the Percy family and the legendary 'mighty hunter' from near-eastern myth; perhaps a pair of (race) horses once owned by the Mundys. According to Don Farnsworth it closed *c.*1904.

Farnsworth (1987) 95

BELL

Unknown locale   *–1770–*

Nothing known other than the fact that the landlord at this date was John Campion, of a notable Derby family of landlords. Perhaps to be identified with the *Three Pigeons/Vine* Mickleover, (*qv*).

DM 18/5/1770

MICKLEOVER

FREEMASONS' ARMS

See MASON'S ARMS

(GREAT) NORTHERN HOTEL

Station Road   *by 1891*

Built shortly after the opening of the Mickleover station of the Great Northern Railway's Derby extension to Egginton Junction in 1878. Brick with stone dressings, two storeys with two wide square full-height bays flanking the entrance. Recorded in 1908 as the *Northern Hotel*. Stands virtually on top of the GNR line, now closed, by the road bridge.

HONEYCOMB

Ladybank Road   *1974*

Built by Everard's on two levels with partly hexagonal plan form to serve the (then) new Silverhill Estate and opened on All Saints' Day (1 November) 1974. Run for many years

Great Northern, Station Road, Mickleover.

by the late Dennis ('Danny') Craven (no relation to the author), who died in April 1989.

MASONS' ARMS*

1 Etwall Road (The Square)   *by 1724*

Main village pub in all probability; like the *White Swan* at Littleover and the *Wilmot Arms* at Chaddesden, it lies in close proximity to the Church and Manor House. The main range is tall and comparatively narrow with a round headed shaped gable to the road, a ground floor canted bay beneath and a much rebuilt wing to the east. Named after the armorial bearings of the Worshipful Company of Masons, but since displaying those of the English Grand Lodge of Freemasons and, indeed, actually called the *Freemasons' Arms* in 1874 and 1878. Rebuilt in the 19th century, when the Mickleover Sick Benefit Club met there on the first Saturday of the month and refronted c.1920. Refurbished 1974.

Watson (1993)

MICKLEOVER COURT HOTEL*

Etwall Road   *1993*

Large, Post-Modernist hotel overlooking the bypass in yellow brick and blue-painted steel decorations under slate roofs. Two wings angle forward either side of a central rotunda. Planned opening was for 1991 but delayed several times thereafter. Empty (although complete) in June 1992, due in part to problems over planning permission for an additional car park on the opposite side of the road. The delay was unfortunate for the promoters who were forced to sell to Virgin Hotels after it finally opened in 1993. It is now part of the independent Belper-based Menzies Hotel chain.

Nag's Head, Uttoxeter Road, Mickleover, 1931.

NAG'S HEAD

Cawdy Hill (Uttoxeter Road)   *by 1774*

It was for sale in 1774, 1775 and 1805. It then stood just east of the Market Square in an 18th-century brick range.

Old Nag's Head (left) and Mason's Arms (in distance), Mickleover.

It was a two-storey, three-bay vernacular brick edifice, terraced in with its neighbours. In 1827 it was run by Sam Roome of a Mickleover family traceable back to the late 16th century, but in 1874 by Thomas Hodgkinson who doubled as a plumber. Demolished in 1928 to make way for a garage and rebuilt further east at the top of Cawdy Hill by T.H. Thorpe & Partners in a half-timbered style, with a certain amount of good interior decorative features, mainly removed removed during a 1970s refurbishment. From the late 19th century run by Frederick Storer, whose granddaughter's husband, Edward Hinckley, took over in 1923, and moved with the pub. In 1946 its landlord was former Derby County player Stuart McMillan, who took over the Rams when the previous manager, Ted Magner, went to coach abroad. Four months later Derby beat Charlton at Wembley and the landlord of the *Nag's Head* went into the history books as the only manager ever to win the FA Cup for the club, although most of the credit had gone to a team which was essentially Magner's. McMillan remained as manager of the club until it was relegated from the old First Division in 1953. About 1970 the pub acquired a car from the much-lamented ex-Southern Railway *Brighton Belle* electric Pullman train as a restaurant. Named from the crest of the locally prominent Meynell family. Underwent a drastic refurbishment from July 1993 which resulted in some months' closure. In the summer of 2002 it was again refurbished and reopened on 10 July that year, selling a good range of real ales in addition to its other fare.

DM 11/2/1774, 10/4/1775 & 14/11/1804

ROBIN

Devonshire Drive   *1959*

Opened by Offiler's to serve a new housing development in September 1959; brick with artificial dressings. Ornithological name.

THREE PIGEONS

Unknown locale   *–1776–*

Known from a *notice of* 1776, possibly to be identified with the *Vine*.
DM 6/12/1776

VINE

Uttoxeter Road   *by 1846*

The building is a brick vernacular one with traces of internal timber-framing, suggesting a date of at least 17th century; name not recorded in any but the most modern directories, however, and thus possibly the victim of a change of name, cf. *Three Pigeons* and *Bell.* Note also William Redfern, who ran a beerhouse (name not given) in 1846 and 1857; this may be the *Vine.* Indeed, a large vine was rambling across the façade a century ago and later was a living inn-sign. The interior has every appearance in layout of having been an inn for some considerable time. Note a second, un-named beerhouse run in Mickleover by Thomas Wallis, a wheelwright, in 1846.

WHITE HART

Unknown locale   *–1770–*

Recorded only in 1770.
DM 17/8/1770

NORMANTON-BY-DERBY

BLUE POOL

Stenson Road   *1936*

The last and finest of the three Offiler's Blue-themed pubs to open, the licence having been transferred from the *Mazeppa*, Traffic Street. Designed, like the others, by George Morley Eaton, PRIBA, it cost £10,259 to build, cf. *Blue Boy* (Chaddesden), *Blue Peter* (Alvaston). Named after topographical feature, cf. that of the Isle of Purbeck. Of two storeys it is long and low with curved ends and an off-set entrance under a flat concrete canopy topped by a tower. The fenestration is set between bands and the steel windows were originally separated by black marble panels, lending a dramatic horizontal emphasis, all now lost through insensitive refurbishment. Stair tower at the southern end of the façade and a lower extension to the north. Interior largely altered, too.

GRANGE (HOTEL)

Ingleby Avenue   *1932*

The building started life as a pleasant Regency stuccoed residence standing in its own grounds on the site of a farm owned, up until the Reformation, by the Abbot of Darley.

The house was extended in the Victorian era, but in 1931 was purchased from its last owner, Mr Newton, by Offiler's and opened 26 March 1932 as a pub with the licence transferred from the *Thorntree*, Tenant Street, obtained from the corporation. On 23 February 1933 it was greatly extended and reopened as an hotel.

GREYHOUND

Derby Lane (corner Village Street)   *by 1928*

Built on the site of Rose Farm, in standard 'bypass Tudor'. Taken over by the Barker dynasty 1989 but under brewery control from 1993.

Norman Arms, Normanton-by-Derby, c.1930.

NORMAN(TON) ARMS

Village Street   *by 1846*

The only village pub here throughout the 19th century, run as an un-named beerhouse by Rayner Beckett in 1846, although an inn with the name *Norman Arms* under the same management in 1857. Possibly named after the Normans, erroneously, as the village name is actually a corruption of 'Norse men's town', referring to the Viking occupation. There was a local family called Norman, but they were neither particularly prominent nor armigerous. It is listed in 1874 and 1878, however (whether by false assumption or from accurate knowledge), as the *Normanton Arms.* Purchased from the estate of minor landowner Benjamin Edge by Strettons 12 November 1884 with one acre. Rebuilt on a slightly different site with the stimulus from the coming of the ring road as the *Greyhound* c.1930 in lavish style, all close-studded timber framing, jettied gables and oriel windows but with absurdly skinny Tudor-style brick chimney stacks. In the 1960s the landlord was former Derby-based professional boxer, Harry Brown.

UNKNOWN**

'Church Street' (Village Street)   *1878*

The 1878 directory has under Normanton-by-Derby for Edward Newbold (son of Benjamin of the *Black Horse* and *Dove*) 'Innkeeper, Church Street'. The *Norman(ton) Arms* is listed separately with another landlord. Probably he ran a fairly minor domestic beerhouse nearby.

WILLIAM CAXTON

Caxton Street   *1977*

Modern and quite restrained-looking brick pub opened to serve the lower part of the former Austin Estate. Why the street should have been named after England's first printer is quite unclear, although it was logical enough to name the pub after the street! Many other streets hereabouts are, however, named after authors or poets and Caxton, as the author of the first *History of England*, certainly counts!

OAKWOOD

KING'S CORNER**

Lime Lane   *1993*

Planned by Wolverhampton & Dudley Brewery and announced as the *Oak Tree* as 'about to be built', but eventually named as a result of a competition after a family of turners called King who once lived opposite the site. Opened by the then Derbyshire cricket captain, Kim Barnett 19 March 1993.

Derby Drinker XLV (4/1993); *DET* 8/4/1992; *Derby Herald & Post* 11/3/1993

OAK & ACORN

District Centre, Danebridge Crescent   *c.1989*

Unlovely Bass pub in yellow brick with blue brick bands and a central gabled block. The name is associative with that of the estate which took its name from a once prominent bosky feature.

OAK TREE

See KING'S CORNER

WINDMILL**

Mansfield Road, Breadsall Hill Top   by 1827

A pleasant late 18th-century brick built two-storey vernacular inn, run by John Walker, who doubled as the local blacksmith when it was for sale in 1827. Now officially in Oakwood, but then in Breadsall.

DM 8/8/1827

OSMASTON-BY-DERBY (WILMORTON)

Navigation, Wilmorton, 2002.

NAVIGATION*

805 London Road   *by 1846*

Probably built shortly after the Derby Canal (opened 1796) although not recorded in the directories of 1827/29/35. Replaced on a new site, with a new brick building by James Wright in 1895 for James Eadie Ltd; now Bass. It started out with a good quality wrought-iron sign by Edwin Haslam now, of course, vanished. It also had 'one of the best bowling greens in Derby' but, like that at the *Coach & Horses*, Little Chester, it was later sacrificed to the automobile and is now an asphalted car park. The previous inn ended up as part of Holmes's building yard next door.

DET Bygones Supplement 16/3/1999

NIGHTINGALE HOTEL

506 Osmaston Road   *1966*

Built to catch the trade from Rolls-Royce workers. It stands at the corner of Nightingale Road, taking its name from the locally-born angel of mercy, although it is the bird which has graced the sign! In 1936 it was the site of William Lebeter's grocery store and a doctors' surgery.

OSMASTON PARK HOTEL*

187 Osmaston Park Road   *1930*

Opened by Alton's in 1930 to serve the municipal housing then spreading along the new arterial road (ring road) in the vicinity, using land purchased from the Wilmot-Horton family, once the parkland of nearby Osmaston Hall (demolished 1938). Typical 'by-pass' pub: brick with symmetrically gabled front and recessed entrance under a 'timber-framed' two-storey porch with barrell-vaulted upper room, canted bays, mullioned steel-framed windows and a timbered gable to the east. From c.1998 to 2001 called *Bramwell's* – perhaps (for what reason, goodness only knows) named after the brother of the Brontë sisters, good West Riding folk all. Renamed *Osmaston Park* (but losing *Hotel*) in 2001.

PORTLAND HOTEL*

603 (1) London Road (corner of Dickenson Street) by 1884
Originally a three-storey three-bay stuccoed late Regency villa with top cornice, architrave surrounds to its windows and tripartite ground floor windows. The entrance, ensigned by a curly pediment, sported an extremely fancy lamp and swan-necked bracket following conversion into a 'family & Commercial hotel' after 1878. Rebuilt in an equally grand style, possibly to designs by Alexander MacPherson, in the Edwardian period. Home Ales in 1936, by which time it had for long been the watering-hole of local MP Rt. Hon. Jimmy Thomas, PC. The Duke of Portland was a substantial Derbyshire landowner.
Hodgkin (1996) 84

The same inn, before demolition, used by Clayborn's the builders.

SHELTON LOCK

Bridge Inn, Chellaston Road, Shelton Lock, c.1900.

(NEW) BRIDGE INN*

Chellaston Road   *by 1827*
Quite an elegant brick public house of two storeys and seven bays, the central three breaking forward and containing the then obligatory two entrances to lounge and public bars respectively set in classical aedicules. It has plate glass sashes (now replaced to no good effect) with gauged brick lintels under a hipped roof, all built c.1920. Since 1990 it has borne the prefix 'New' because it replaced a much smaller establishment, at the turn of the century called for a while the *Shelton Lock Inn* (recorded 1891). The latter was a beerhouse separated from the lock on the Derby Canal bearing this name by an attractive lock-keeper's cottage and George Wootton's alabaster kiln. It without doubt dated back to the opening of Derby Canal in 1796, a two-storey building of brick with wide Regency sashes

under heavy stone lintels. A pair of earlier agricultural labourers' cottages of early 18th-century date and once very handsome, formed a rear extension and may, indeed, have been the original pub before the later elevation facing the road was built in the 1820s. There was a contents sale in 1881. After the completion of the new pub adjacent, the old inn became R. Clayborn's building firm's yard and offices, since demolished. Now Marston's.

CROWN & ARROWS

Sinfin Avenue   *by 1976*
Modern low, brick-built pub named after the crest of the Derby historian, William Hutton (1723-1815), who claimed descent from a distinguished Northumbrian family. Hardy Hanson's.

GOLDEN PHEASANT**

Derby Road   *1986*
Originally a popular restaurant adapted with spurious timber framing and awkward extensions from an existing house. The builder and developer in the early 1950s was Kenneth Gresley, son of artist Cuthbert Gresley of Chellaston (1876-1963) and opened as the *Travellers' Joy*. Sold after his death and later renamed the *Golden Pheasant* by the late 1960s. Sold to the Laurel Pub Co and turned into an inn in the 1980s and which applied for planning consent for further extensions in March 2002.

SHELTON LOCK INN
See BRIDGE

SINFIN

COCK 'N' BULL
See SINFIN HOTEL

COUNTY HOTEL

Sinfin Lane   *1934*
Modern pub for its time, but of unexciting appearance, by G.M. Eaton, opened by Offiler's Brewery in 1934.

Sinfin Hotel, Sinfin Lane.

CROWN

Sinfin Moor by 1770-1804

Opened only when the races were held on Sinfin Moor from early in the 18th century until 1804, when the event moved to the Siddals. Possibly based in an agricultural building, suitably adapted, or in a temporary structure, as with the numerous booths erected on the Moor on race days for bookies, visitors and sideshows.

FERRERS ARMS

Sinfin District Centre 1979

Opened as part of the shopping precinct for this part of the Sinfin area in 1979. The arms shown are those of the Shirley, Earls Ferrers; the suggestion, by the author (after a request by the Co-operative Society, the developers, to the Museum for three likely names), was for the arms of the Ferrers, Earls of Derby, the mediaeval lords of Sinfin. However, a year or two later, after a lecture on heraldry, attended by an executive of Everard's, the sponsors of the inn, in 1978, the arms as shown were drawn up for the executive in ignorance of the reason for the brewery's interest. Hence the question to the author from the present Lord Ferrers, at the opening: 'Why us?' Thus do bizarre inn signs evolve!

FIGHTING COCKS

Arleston Lane 1977-1998

Opened 1977, using another of the author's suggestions, this time without accident! Elaborate cockfights were staged on Sinfin Moor on race days in the 18th century, as well as at selected inns in the town. Demolished 1998, due partly to the expansion of the Walmart-Asda supermarket.

GRAMPIAN, THE**

2A Cromarty Close by 1978

Built in the 1970s to help cater for the sprawling Sinfin estate.

SAXON INN

See SINFIN HOTEL

SINFIN HOTEL

Sinfin Lane 1934

Opened by Stretton's in a new building to serve (like its rival the nearby *County Hotel*) the expanding municipal housing nearby on 6 March 1934. An impressive design, brick and render, of two storeys, the upper one much lower, like a half-storey, interrupted by a raised and projecting centre with a wide bay and wrap-around angle bays. The wings are of three bays each, the entrance being set in a raised surround in the centre all under hipped roofs with green pantiles. In the 1970s it was known as the *Saxon*. Rebuilt, renamed the *Cock 'n' Bull* and reopened in August 1982 by Ansell's.

SPONDON

(OLD) ANGLERS' ARMS*

Nottingham Road by 1891

The present inn was built in a relentlessly suburban style by Hardy Hansons in 1938 to replace an earlier building, further west on the opposite side of the road which thereafter became a café and then an upholsterer's works. Ridiculous and unconvincing heraldic sign. The earlier inn, of brick and two storeys with three bays, which was a horse-changing station for coaches on the Nottingham turnpike, was sold in 1916 to (Hardy) Hansons, who

installed Samuel Lewsley, whose family ran it for at least two generations. It is now an Italian restaurant.
Watson (1989) 48

BEEHIVE

38-40 Moor Street –1850–

Little known about the history of this house, which seems to have escaped all the directories. Note that Wilde's, a Derby (soft) drinks manufacturer, sported a beehive trademark, the sign associated with industriousness. The building survives as a decorator's shop.
Watson (1989) 47

BRICKMAKERS' ARMS

Locko Road –c.1860–

One of a row of old cottages, and replaced on an adjacent site by the *Vernon Arms*. It took its name from nearby brickyards (at the end of Windmill Lane, Royal Hill Road), from the products of which it was undoubtedly built. After closure in the mid-19th century it was occupied by G. Thompson, joiner and undertaker, there in 1896. Elusive in the local directories. See p.36 for name.
Watson (1989) 47

CANAL TAVERN*

Near Station Road *by 1806-1929*

A pleasant looking two-storey four-bay inn built shortly after the opening of the Erewash arm of Derby Canal in all probability, erected on its banks beside a bridge and renamed the *Station Inn* with the coming of the railway in 1839. It had something of a mini boom during World War One when a colony mainly of Irishmen was brought in and housed in Nissen huts nearby to help build British Celanese's works. Demolished in 1929 when it was replaced on a new site as the *Moon*, the last landlord being Thomas William Porter, who moved to the *Greyhound*, Friar Gate when it closed. However, it must have been closed beforehand because the licence was not transferred to the *Moon* from the *Station* as one might expect, but from the *Union*. Mr Porter's daughter, Mabel (whose husband Tony was the son of Fred Ward of the *White Swan* in Spondon) recalled a fishing party from the *Ram* arriving from Derby in a canal boat and calling at the *Station*. 'They were so eager to disembark', she was quoted as saying, 'that the boat capsized and they all had to wade out of the canal.' The Porters also ran something of a grocery store from the inn as well.
Brighouse (1990) 39; *DET* 7/10/1997

CROWN

Stoney Cross *1979*

Built c.1890 as a house for Henry Ranby, founder of the Derby department store. It has a four-bay, two-storey

façade with extensions and was converted to a club as the *Crown Inn* post-war and reopened as a public house under the same name in 1979 by Marston's.
Watson (1989) 50

FOX & HOUNDS**

Moor Street *c. 1860*

Part of a farmhouse, like the *Nimrod & Hotspur*, Markeaton, and later a private residence; perhaps a renaming of the *Harrow*.
Watson (1989) 47

GREGORY'S**

Aspen Drive *c.1992*

Established for a decade and handy for exhausted shoppers at Asda. Presumably named after the founding proprietor.

HARROW*

Unknown locale *by 1770-1771*

Known only from two notices in 1770 and 1771. Name from the agricultural implement: logical in a farming community. Possibly became the *Fox & Hounds*.
DM 12/10/1770

MALT SHOVEL*

Potter Street *by 1777*

There is no documentary evidence for the existence of the Malt Shovel before the 18th century, but the fire which destroyed most of Spondon in 1340 started at a malting house on the site. The building is basically an 18th-century vernacular farmhouse in brick with a somewhat earlier core, said to date from 1680, and containing a single ashlared doorcase of much greater antiquity, the whole having been rebuilt and extended c.1800 and altered again in the late 19th century. The 1800 extensions and alterations – on much earlier foundations and attached to a short wing to the left of earlier date – were, without doubt, the work of William Harrison, who was also a maltster here, being succeeded by his son, Joseph, who retained the malthouse, but who, by 1857, had let the inn, although this does not explain a sale of lease notice of 1845; perhaps it failed to generate any offers. Owned by the Drury-Lowe (Locko) estate, and rent dinners were held here until 1955, early in the reign of landlords Tony and Betty Woodyet which lasted from 1950 until 1985. The future of this inn was under some question early in 1992, due to the brewers (Bass) having been faced with a colossal repairs bill to the listed building; their response was to consider selling it. It occurred to many to wonder why they had failed to adequately maintain it in the first place. Fortunately, they relented and did the repairs. Locko Estate rents were received here for very many years.
DM 1/10/1845; Watson (1989) 47-8

MOON (HOTEL)*

Station Road 1929

Largish mock-Tudor pub built in 1929 to replace the *Station Inn* (cf. *Canal Tavern*) by Offiler's. Two bottles of brown ale were built high up into the fabric at the behest of the whimsical Henry C. Offiler and the inn was provided with its own bowling green since, needless to say, sacrificed to make a car park. The licence had a permanent extension to 10.30pm to cater for the workers at British Celanese, over the railway, whose shift ended at 10pm.

Brighouse (1990) 2, 39; Watson (1989) 50

Prince of Wales, Chapel Street, Spondon with the White Swan, Moor Street, in the background.

PRINCE OF WALES*

Chapel Street by 1867

Probably named in honour of the marriage in 1863 of Edward, Prince of Wales with Queen Alexandra. On a site recorded back to 1720. Run by the Goff family from 1867 and for sale in 1880 'now used as a beer house' (no takers, apparently) by Sarah Ann Goff, daughter of William, on his death and sold in 1895 as the 'beerhouse known by the name or sign of the Prince of Wales' to Alton's, by whom totally rebuilt in Arts & Crafts style but still only a beerhouse, although it acquired a full licence later.

DM 14/7/1880; Watson (1989) 50

SPONDON CROSS

Old Nottingham Road –(1950)–

Planned by Mitchell's & Butler's for the approximate site of the *Old Anglers' Arms*, but never proceeded with.

STATION INN

See CANAL TAVERN, MOON HOTEL

UNION INN*

Potter Street by 1826-1928

May date to 1801 when the Act of Union in which Ireland was incorporated into the United Kingdom, or even 1707 when that between England and Scotland took place, although the lack of mention of it in the *Derby Mercury* during the 18th century would seem to favour the first suggestion. However, it is said locally to reflect the 'union' with New Zealand, but the date 1826 (when the pub is named) is far too early for this, especially as South Africa was the only official union in the Empire. For sale in 1826, 1839 and 1878 and to let in 1860 and 1861. For sale by Robert Ford, the landlord, as 'well accustomed' with eight nearby cottages and a half share in a pew in the parish church. Statutes fairs once held in front of the inn, which was not far from the *Malt Shovel*. Closed about 1928 and licence transferred to *Moon Hotel*, which suggests that Offiler's were then the owners.

DM 26/7/1826, 18/12/1839, 26/9/1860, 18/12/1861 & 30/10/ 1878; Watson (1989) 47

VERNON ARMS

21 Locko Road 1899

Adapted from a pair of cottages and before 1899 known as Oak House. Unclear why it was named after Lord Vernon's Arms, as these local peers had no connection with Spondon. On the death of landlord Thomas Holloway it was acquired by Stretton's. Called 'Top House' by the locals, and in the early 1990s acquired by Burtonwood's.

Watson (1989) 49

(WHITE) SWAN*

Moor Street by 1774

Fine old inn in much altered 18th-century building of two storeys and two bays but fitted by 1900 with mullion and transom cross windows and a pretty gabled porch; the *Swan* only in 1787 (sale at) and for sale in 1842, by John Bennet who had been there since at least 1827. From this period cotton from Darley Mills was brought here for distribution to outworkers in the village, who would wind it onto bobbins and left for collection the week following. Every fifth Sunday in the 19th century services would be held here in lieu of the church, although it is not clear why. Taken on by Thomas Coxon, of a family of blacksmiths, in 1857, of whom Peter Coxon, junior was a later landlord. Tony, the son of Frederick Lewis Ward, landlord in 1926, married the daughter of T. W. Porter of the *Station* (ex-*Canal* later the *Moon)*

DET 7/10/1997; Hughes (1997) 23; Watson (1989) 49-50

YARNSPINNER

Borrowash Road 1961

Built in 1961 and named to mark the proximity of the British Celanese (Courtauld's) works, nearby, which opened in 1916. The sign depicts a yokel, spinning a yarn.

Appendix

The directories from 1835 to 1862 list beer houses separately from 'Inns, Taverns and Public Houses' in alphabetical order of licensee plus addresses. In the 1835 (Pigot's) directory a handful are equipped with street numbers, the process of numbering the streets being then incomplete. Later, the addresses are more or less complete, and it is possibly to match the majority of them with existing named pubs. Those that could not be matched up and named are listed below, with their *earlier* street numbers, in street order. Some clearly are represented in the main text, but without sufficient precision. A dash between dates means that the beer house is listed continuously; a slash, that it occurs only on the dates either side and not in the directories for those intervening.

8 Bag Lane	1850-62
23 Bag Lane	1857-62
30 Bag Lane	1857-62
63 Bag Lane	1857-62
Bath Street	1835
23 Bold Lane	1850-62
25 Bold Lane	1857-62
30 Bold Lane	1846-50
17 Bridge Gate	1835
58 Bridge Street	1835
36 Brook Street	1846-57
51 Brook Street	1835
Brook Street (Upper)	1846-57
Chester Place	1835/50
Chester Place	1835/50
84 Devonshire Street	1835
46 Eagle Street	1846/62
48 Friar Gate	1835
17 Henry Street	1850-62
10 King Street	1835*

13 King Street	1835*
16 King Street	1862
Leonard Street	1835
43 London Street	1835-50
17 Lodge Lane	1846-62
Mill Street	1835
14 Mansfield Road	1857-62
31 Mansfield Street	1857-62
37 Mansfield Street	1857-62
Monk Street	1862
35 Nelson Street	1857/62
Nottingham Rd, Cowsley Cottage	1850
10 Nuns' Street	1846
35 Nuns' Street	1846-57
62 Osmaston Street	1850-57
86 Park Street	1846/62
Pool Street (unlocated)	1835
5 Siddals Lane	1835
4 Wright Street	1862
5 Wright Street	1835/50

*One or other of these could be the *Coach & Horses* and/or the *Mechanics' Arms*

Street Index

Inn names of non-suburban pubs are listed here in alphabetical order of streets. Dates in brackets are the approximate dates of the pitching of the relevant streets, plus or minus five years. In most cases the date is the first known record of the street: 'early' tends to mean before the 17th century; 'ancient' tends to mean from Roman times until the late Middle Ages.

As in the main text, former street numbers are expressed within brackets.

Abbey Street (1825)
54 Abbey
18 Curzon Arms
201 Free Trade House
245 (255) Lord Belper
174 Pelican
201 (191) Richard Cobden
210 (204) (Old) Spa
119 Vine

Agard Street (1800)
Derby Temperance
55 (27) Golden Eagle
59 (29) Leopard
29 (16) Old Oak
(16) Royal Oak

Albert Street (1848)
6 (3) Albert Vaults
21 Castle
2 Central
12 City Inn
12 Exchange
2 George & Dragon
2 King's Head
21 Mayfair
2 Metro Bar
27 New Market
27 Spencer's Vaults
26 Star Vaults

Albion Street (1816)
9-10 Albion
(10) Black Boy
(9) (Free) Mason's Arms
Trident

All Saint's Parish
Unicorn

Amen Alley (ancient)
7 (6) Bath
(7) (Crown &) Mitre

Amy Street (1890)
1 Roebuck

Ashbourne Road (early)
110 Gallant Hussar
32-34 Georgian House
110 Hope & Anchor
140 (71)Swan & Salmon
185 (108, 28) Travellers' Rest
109 (121, 32-3) Wagon & Horses
(1) White Lion
7 White Swan

Babington Lane (1789)
11-13 Babington Arms
34 (5) Babington Arms

Back Parker Street (1851)
14 Palmerston Arms

Baker Street (1900)
Coronation

Becket Street (1852)
Berlin's
127 Flamingo & Firkin

Bedford Street (1869)
2 Bedford Arms
55 Dog & Partridge

Bold Lane (1570)
3-4 Alexandra Vaults
23 Dun Cow
30 (Old) Elephant & Castle
3-4 Jolly Dogs
17 (19) (Old) Shakespeare
Wheatsheaf

Borough's Walk (1840)
25 (14) Elm Tree

Boyer Street (1871)
12 Buxton

Brackensdale Avenue (1948)
Kingsway

Bradshaw Street (1820)
Hawk & Buckle
42 (30) (Lion &) Tiger(ess)
27 (36) Ring o' Bells

Brick Street (early)
1 Brick & Tile

Bridge Gate (by 1226)
Admiral Vernon
Bell
48-9 British Arms
Crown
Five Alls
61 (43) Fox & Owl
5/6 Golden Lion
Navigation
Nevill's Wine Vaults
58 (21) Nottingham Arms
10 (Old) Orange Tree
Pack Horse
Pheasant
Reindeer
Rising Sun
35 Roebuck
Seven Stars
Shearman's Arms
Sir John Falstaff
68 (24) Three Crowns
12 (Old) White Hart

Bridge Street (1792)
142 (84, 95) Hollybush
30 (70) Mechanics' Arms
153 Northern Star
112 (81) Pheasant
82 (59, 72) Ram
74 (84-5) Red Lion
Ring o'Bells
76-80 (71) Woodlark

Broadway
Clovelly/Jokers

Brook Street (Upr/Lwr) (1796)
26 (58 Lwr) British Queen
72 (Lwr) Cross Keys
60 (Lwr) Duke of Wellington
16 (60 Lwr)(Great Northern) Bridge Inn

69 (Upr) Holy Friar
Leopard
42-4 (47) Maypole
Scarsdale Arms
33 (Upr) Seven Stars
88 (92) Sir Charles Napier
25 (2 Lwr) Stag & Pheasant

Brook Walk (1795)
1 Quiet/Silent Woman

Burton Road (early)
2 Angel
86-92 (43) Bell & Castle
112 Burton
17 (3, 56, 69) Duke of York
124 (110) Durham Ox
288 International
(New) Orange Tree
70 Ordnance Arms

Canal Street (1833)
105 (47) Barleycorn
52-3 Black Bull
52-3 Canal
48 Dyers' Arms
53 Locomotive
Mulberry Tree
93 (41) New
9-11 (2-3) Queen Adelaide
2 (117) Railway
33 (14) Red Lion
107 (48) Royal Albert

Carrington Street (1843)
Borough Arms
25 British Oak
5 Carrington Arms
112 (32) Rutland Arms
5 Who Can Tell?

Castle Street (1826)
40 Castle
21 (Fox &) Grapes
Sawyers' Arms
17-18 Sir Henry Wilmot Arms

Chapel Street (1804)
13 Blessington Carriage

(5) Crown & Cushion
25 (7) Rose & Thistle

Cheapside (c.1806)
10 Butchers' Arms
10 Marquess of Anglesey

Chequers Road (1967)
Meadows

Chester Place – See Mansfield St.

City Road
37 Leopard
52 (37) Old Tiger

Clifton Street (1872)
10 Carpenters' Arms
7 New Station Inn

Clover Street (1872)
38 Lord Raglan

Cobden Street (c.1870)
45 Cobden Arms

Cockpit Hill (1760) (previously Copecastel, 1085)
32 (Old) Boat
10 Canal
1 Castle & Falcon
Chequers
38 (18) Cock
Derby Pride
33 Dusty Miller

Colyear Street (c.1855)
8 Bay Cob
9 Scarsdale Arms

Copeland Street (1845)
1 Buck in the Park
37 (18) Copeland Arms
61 (27) Dog & Partridge
9 Garibaldi

Cornmarket (1510)
30 Admiral Rodney
29 (Old) Angel
Bishop Blaze
45 Cross Keys
Crown & Cushion
Elephant & Castle
George & Dragon
37 George Wine Vaults

Green Dragon
Grasshopper
35 Hotel & King's Head
10 King's Head
36 Knotted Snake
Maypoll
Plough
Ramsden's
Red Lion
Rising Sun
15 Rose & Crown
(Upper/Nether) Ship
Spread Eagle
37 (40) Tiger
White Lion

Cowley Street (1885)
2 Victoria

Crompton Street (1862)
46 Crompton
46 Public House
46 (70) Queen's

Curzon Street (1820) (previously Dayson Lane, ancient)
68 (1) Buck in the Park
58 Crown
101 Freddie's
101 (Great Northern) Refreshment House

Dairy House Road (1890)
86 Cambridge
86 Windmill

Darley Lane (ancient)
5 Grove

Derwent Row (1792)
(18) White Bear

Derwent Street (1827)
4-6 Market Tavern
1 Royal Standard
18 White Lion

Devonshire Street (1816)
90 Bee Hive
30 Black Horse
30 Black's Head
27 (12) Devonshire Arms
30 Oatsheaf

Dog Kennel Lane (c.1800)

(now Great Northern Road)
Fox & Hounds

Duckworth Square (1962)
1-2 Merlin

Duffield Road (1756)
Broadway
25 Five Lamps
25 New Inn
25 St Helen's
White Stoup

Duke Street (1828)
9 Furnace Arms

Eagle Street (1802)
Castle
43 Chequers
24-5 Reindeer

East Street (1882) (formerly Bag Lane c. 1220)
35 Barley Mow
60 Beech Tree
Brick Cart
55 Don Cossack
13-14 Football
Green Man
Jolly Boatman
54 New Market
8 Oddfellows' Arms
28 (30) Plumbers' Arms
(Old) Ship
61 Woodman's Stroke

Edward Street (c.1835)
2 (6) Masons' Arms

Elm Street (1844)
48 (24) Horse & Groom

Erasmus Street (1826)
26 Hare & Hounds

Exeter Place (1827)
13 Exeter Arms

Exeter Street (1820)
Cherry Tree
4 Nag's Head

Fleet Street (1885)
3 (1) Fleet

Ford Street (ancient)
13 (6, 9) Apollo

2 Steam Mill
22 (28) Vine
13 (9) Waterloo

Fowler Street (1845)
1 (70-1) Brickmakers' Arms

Franchise Street (1852)
64 Freehold
17-19 (7-9) Gisborne Arms

Friar Gate (1332/1768) (part formerly Nuns' Green)
14 Bank Tavern
Blue Boar
16 Boater's
Chequers
Courtyard
Crown
18 Fat Cat
11 Fox & Goose
114 Friar Gate
Friary
68 Garrick
75-6 Greyhound
49 Howard
Lamb
Maypole
Pymm's
Red Lion
114 (Rising) Sun
68 Thirsty Scholar
68 Wheel
110A Where House
96 (86) White Horse
(Old) White Lion
White Lion

Full Street (c.1250)
David & the Harp
43-4 Horse & Trumpet
Leopard
Pelican
Ship
19 (21) (Old) Silk Mill
Talbot

Gerard Street (1853)
84 (124) Marquis of Granby
111 (45) (Old) Ship

Gilman Street (1890)
17 Star

Goodwin Street (1818)
55 Duke of Devonshire
59 Shamrock

Gower Street (*c*.1861)
Gower's Arms

Graham Street (1853)
8-9 Victoria

Green Lane (1510)
20 (8) Brown Bear
15 (45) (Bunch of) Grapes
12 Crù
12 Green Lane House
12 Jelly Roll's
12 Ranby's
28 (96-8) Tailors' Arms
86 Thomas-à-Becket

Green Street (1792)
20 (6) Eagle
51 Hallam's Vaults
Rainbow

Grove Street (1821)
16 Arboretum
19 (16) Leopard
59 Old English Gentleman
19 (16) Tiger

Haarlem Street (1815)
34 (13) Dog & Duck

Harrington Street (1880)
193 Pear Tree

Henry Street (*c*.1835)
29-30 (10-11) Great Northern
1 Park Fountain

High Street (1816)
85 Allies
33 High Street
85 Prince Albert
33 White Horse

Hill Street – see Ossian
    Street

Hope Street (1818)
10 (14) Derby Volunteer
32 London
32 St George & Dragon

Iron Gate (1318)
12-14 Bowring's Vaults
11 Casa
George

30 George & Talbot
41 (34) Globe
11-12 Henly's
11-12 Henry's
11-12 Irongates
41 Lafferty's
41 Mr Jorrocks
38 (31) Robin Hood (& Little
    John)
30 Standing Order
29 (25) Talbot
White Hart
35 Wine Vaults
27 Yates's Wine Lodge

John Street (1843)
20 Engine Tavern
8 Prince of Wales
39 (20) Union of Hearts
25 (13) Vulcan

Junction Street (1868)
19 (6) Great Northern
17 Jolly Soldier
12 Junction

Jury Street (c. 1100)
1 Bird

Kedleston Road (1770s)
Jonty Farmer

Kedleston Street (1852)
44 Malt Shovel

Kensington Street (1820)
36 Globe
32 (28) Green Man

King Street (ancient)
21 Boar's Head
15 Coach & Horses
Hare & Setter
Mechanics' Arms
40 New Flower Pot
12 (16) New Inn
13 (18) Odd Fellows' Arms
25 (9) Old Flower Pot
97 (23) Seven Stars
34 Shamrock

King Alfred Street (1894)
98 Dunkirk

Kingsway (1928)
Derbyshire Yeoman

King's High Way

Langley Street (1854)
2, New Zealand Arms
Large's Street (1817)
73 (12) Old House at Home

Leaper Street (1844)
13 Seven Stars
8 Weavers' Arms

Leather Lane (*c*.1483) (later
    part of Market Place)
Dog & Partridge
Nottingham Post
Vine

Leonard Street (1822)
36 George IV

Litchurch Lane (ancient)
Derby Volunteer

Litchurch Street (1826)
83 Coopers' Arms
1A Vine

Liversage Street (1815)
90 (6-8) Wheatsheaf

Lodge Lane (ancient)
3 Boat/Boot
55 (3) (Brown) Bear
24 (Old) Windmill

London Road (*c*.1739) (North
    part formerly London
    Street)
Big Ship
72 (Old) Black Swan
116 Carlton
115 Cloisters
45 Coliseum
51 Commercial
10 Crown & Cushion
51 (62) Crown Vaults
13/15 Derwent
Eagle
111-2 Florence Nightingale
119 Gables
Golden Lion
110 (61) Leviathan
154 Locomotive
23 Louis Napoleon
111-2 Nottingham Arms
119 Periquito

33 (71, 27) Plough
603 Portland
73 (5) Prince of Wales
Railway
Regent
119 Royal Stuart
69 (1, 54) (Royal) Telegraph
Salisbury
116 (58) Silver Lion
Spread Eagle
116 (58) Wellington

Loudon Street (1868)
4 Loudon Arms
4 Rose Hill

Lower Dale Road (1882)
80 Byron
1 Normanton
Vine

Lower Parliament St (1854)
102 Joiners'
102 Prince Arthur

Macklin Street (1845)
    (previously Cross Lane,
    ancient)
Pennine
54 (24) Stork

Malcolm Street (1843)
1 Grange

Mansfield Road (ancient)
2-3 Bridge
Coach & Horses
Crown
87 (22) Duke of Clarence
22 William IV

Mansfield Street (Chester
    Place) (1842)
Junction Tavern
31 Moulders' Arms
37 Red Lion

Market Place (*c*.1100)
Arkwright's
Blackamoor's Head
Blue Stoops
Central Commercial
Corporation
Crane
13 Criterion
35 Cross Keys
Cryer

Dog & Partridge
13 (5, 1 Rotten Row)
    Greyhound
11-12 Jackie Stamps
Mermaid
Nottingham Carrier
26 Ramsden's
30 (24) Royal Oak
1 (9 Rotten Row) (Jolley's)
    Tap House
13 Victoria
Virgin's
11-12 Walkabout
Wheatsheaf
17 (11) (Old) Wine Vaults

Market Street (1865)
(Star) Vaults

Meadow Road (1883)
(Cattle) Market
Smithfield

Meteor Centre (1994)
Master Locksmith

Middleton Street (1894)
34 Sun

Midland Place (1841)
Nelson
12 Victoria

Midland Road (1839)
    (formerly Station Street)
22 Aston Court
18 Caledonia
15-18 Clarendon
15-18 European Inn (Hotel)
13 George
44 Midland Arms
44 Sir Charles Colvile
11 Station
Tudor
Vine
20 Waverley
22 York

Milton Street (1869)
2 Lord Napier

Morledge (1525)
Bird in Hand
18 Bishop Blaze
Black Swan
Cattle Market

3 Coach & Horses
17 Cossack
22 (Old) Crown
Curriers' Arms
23 Durham Heifer
Freemasons' Arms
John Wilkes
King of Prussia
23 (17) Noah's Ark
16 (Old) Noah's Ark
Plume of Feathers
5 Telegraph
27 (18) White Horse

Mundy Street (1847)
31 Druids' Retreat
31 Mundy Arms

Navigation Row (1792)
China Punch Bowl
Peacock
Trent Boat

Nelson Street (1852)
Rutland Arms

Newlands Street (1869)
1 (Royal) Drill Hall
1 New Vaults

Normanton Road (ancient)
113 City Inn
206 Douglas Bar
264 Lyndhurst
205 Malin
113 Melbourne Arms
201 Phoenix
39 (47) Wilmot Arms

North Street (1846)
Park Fountain

Nottingham Road (early)
Boat
Bowling Green
74 Chesterfield Arms
Cricketers' Arms
Grandstand
27 Hearty Good Fellow
Jolly Colliers
27 Jolly Toper
63 (18) Liversage Arms
123 (50) New Station
87 (71, 34) Peacock
44 Plough
53 (13) Punch Bowl

29 (1) Seven Stars
Warren Arms
66 Welcome

Nuns' Green See Friar Gate

Nuns' Street (1793)
1 Black Horse
33 Brickmakers' Arms
41 Tankard
84 (25) (Three) Nuns

Old Chester Road (AD 80)
1 Coach & Horses
Duke's Head

Osborne Street (1880)
1 Bridge

Osmaston Road (ancient)
192 Arboretum
Barley Mow
1 Bricklayers' Arms
26 Carlton Bar
25 (17, 20) City of London
    Arms
273-5 Football
83 (57) Fountain
Garrick
Green Man
256-8 Hilton Arms
Jubilee City
1 (Old) Leather Bottle
Marquess of Granby
10 (5) (Old) Neptune
Plough
83 Prince Leopold
13 Queen's Vaults
67 (63) Rising Sun
Robin Hood
180 Sir Walter Scott

Ossian Street (1807) (later
    Hill Street)
22 (18) Milton's Head
17 Saddle

Oxford Street (1850)
21 Crown

Park Street (1832)
88 Feathers
Foresters' Arms
84 (60) Lamb
46 (81) Melancthon's Head
85 (39) Park

Parker Street (1829)
103 (99) Napoleon

Parliament Street (1855)
21 (1) Marquis of Hastings
164-6 Woolsack

Pear Tree Road (1875)
131-3 Sir Frederick Roberts

Porter Road (1901)
129 (Mafeking &) Bowling
    Green

Portland Street (1885)
Chestnut Tree

Pride Park
Baseball Bar and Grill
Harvester

Prince's Street
89 Portland Arms

Quarn Street (1844)
34 Quarn

Queen Street (early)
29 (25/26) Acorn
Bishop Blaze
9 (7/8) Bull's Head
Cavern
10 Devonshire Arms
6 (Old) Dolphin
51 Hallam's Vaults
12 (9) Nottingham Castle
Plaisterers' Arms
41 (35) (Old) Tiger
White Hart

Railway Terrace (1839)
1 Brunswick
24 Merry Widows
Midland
25 Nelson
Waterfall
Windmill
24 Wine Vaults
24 Wright's Vaults

Regent Street (1843)
57 Prince Regent
85 (68) White Horse

River Street (1818)
4 Britannia

19-20 (Old) Britannia

Rivett Street (1827)
50 Sir Henry Wilmot's Arms
47 Spread Eagle

Rosehill Street (1867)
42 Crystal Palace
Depot
42 New Inn

Rotten Row (early)
Angel
Barleycorn
1 Greyhound
Hare & Hounds
Salutation
4 (9) (Jolley's) Tap House
White Horse

Russell Street (1856)
1 Barley Mow
1 Jubilee City
44 Litchurch
28 New

Sacheverel Street (1827)
49 (46) Globe
Prince of Wales
(41) Sitwell (Arms)
46 Town Hall Vaults

Sadler Gate (1248)
Barley Mow
53 Bell
Bell & Castle
8/7 Black Boy
9 Coach & Horses
Forty Second Street
Golden Hart
30 Half Moon
21 Horse & Jockey
16 Ostrich
Punch Bowl
8 Saddler's
16 Shakespeare
Sun
40 Three Tuns
51A Vines
White Hart

Sadler Gate Bridge (early)
Crispin
Five Alls
Flying Horse
7 Lord Byron

Three Swans
White Horse

St Alkmund's Church Yard (ancient)
1-2 Eagle & Child
17 Golden Lion
11 Lamb

St Helen's Street (1817)
18 (4) Foresters' Arms
4 Joiners' Arms
4 Minnitt's Vaults
New
18 (4) Old Vaults/Minutes Vaults
47 (26) (Old) Spot(ted Horse)

St James's Lane (ancient; Street, 1868)
21 (Old) Coach & Horses
Hole in the Wall
13 Jimmy's
13 Knights
22-23 Saracen's Head
13 St James's Hotel
(24) Swan With Two Necks
Three Stags' Heads
Wine & Spirit Vaults

St Mary's Gate (ancient)
Bishop Blaze
Buck in the Park
Bunker's Hill
30 Crown
20 King's Arms County
26 (Duke of) Marlborough's Head
Miners' Arms
Roebuck
21 Star & Garter
White Hart

St Michael's Lane (ancient)
Ship

St Michael's Parish (ancient)
Crown

St Peter's Church Yard (ancient)
Eagle
1-2 (Upper) Green Man

St Peter's Parish (ancient)
(Blue) Bell

(Lower) Green Man
Ostrich
Peacock
Red Ball
Shoulder of Mutton
Spotted Boar
Three Pigeons
Town Arms

St Peter's Street (c.1250)
63 Anchor
56 Barley Mow
41 Cheshire Cheese
Commercial
Crown & Anchor
571/2 Durham Ox
35 Green Dragon
Marquess of Anglesey
64 Nag's Head
Plough
Spread Eagle
Sun
Swan
Thorn Tree (1)
57-9 (52) White Swan
Woolpack

St Thomas's Road (1881)
155 Pear Tree
85 Sherwood Forester
1 Vulcan Arms

Shaftesbury Crescent (1886)
173 Baseball
2 Crescent

Shaftesbury Street (1886)
16 Shaftesbury

Short Street (1792)
2 Lord Hill

Siddals Road (1806; previously Siddals Lane, early)
203 Alexandra
48 Arms of the IoM & Moira
49 (15) Black Swan
24 British Lion
19 (14) Castle Fields
25/6 Cooke's Temperance
159 (51) Magnet
35 (11) Melbourne Arms
19 Plasterers' Arms
105 (23) Star
Wagon & Horses

Silver Hill Road (1890)
74 Falstaff

Sitwell Street (1827)
21 (11) Sitwell

South Street (1818)
10 Golden Fleece

Stepping Lane (1893)
1 Union Flag

Stockbrook Street (1850)
114 (37) Parliament House
110 Stockbrook

Talbot Street (1825)
22 Kensington

Tenant Street (1483)
11-12 Dog & Partridge
11-12 Thorn Tree

Traffic Street (1821)
99 (33) Druids' Arms
65 (58) Mazeppa
57 (21) Pheasant
109 (52, 46) Stag (& Thorn)
36 Three Jolly Butchers

Union Street
Dog & Duck

Unknown Locale
Antelope
Black Cow
British Grenadier
Brown Jug
Brown Cow
Farmers' Arms
Golden Cross
Grinding Young
Irish Harp
Jews' Harp
Last Inn
Live & Let Live
Lord Macclesfield
Magpie
(Old) Mitre
Monkey
Monks' Tavern
Naked Boy
Oak & Acorn
Pig of Lead
Sugar Loaf
Three Cranes

Three Horseshoes
Three Loggerheads

Upper Dale Road (1885)
Cavendish

Upper South Street (1847)
78 (Blue) Bell
77 Earl Grey

Uttoxeter Old Road (ancient)
1 Bay Horse

Uttoxeter Road (1819)
Mallard
246 Rowditch

Victoria Street (1839)
   (previously Brookside,
   early)
5 Pig & Truffle
5 Lloyd's
5 Post Office
25 Queen's Head
1 Royal
12 Saracen's Head
5 Spotted Horse
12 Turf
Victoria Vaults

Vivian Street (ancient)
(Garden) City

Walbrook Road (1897)
115 Walbrook

Walker Lane (1263)
14 Barrell
Black Bull
43 George & Dragon
26 (Old) Hen & Chickens
King's Arms
Marquis of Granby
Star & Garter
Tiger
Travellers' Rest
32-33 (Old) Wheatsheaf

Wardwick (1085)
Crown
The Haus
11 (10) (Old) Lord Nelson
Nag's Head
4 Old Institute
1 Revolution
Sir Walter Scott
20 Wardwick
White Hart

Watson Street (1851)
11 Elm Tree

Wellington Street (1856)
Nottingham Castle
45 Sir Robert Peel

Whitaker Street (1871)
1 Minstrel Boy
37-38 (29) Vine

Whitecross Street (1852)
2-4 Albert
34 Duke of Cambridge
97 Prince of Wales

Wild Street (1884)
83 Crescent

William Street (1844)
1 Dove
2 Tanners' Arms
Vine
Willow Row (early)
(Old) Bell
Bird
30 (New) Bull's Head
50 (41) Chequers
(34) Cobblers' Rest

Goat's Head
24 (21) Golden Ball
11 Horse & Groom
29 (26) Windmill

Wilson Street (1812)
30 Lifeboat

York Street (1827)
29 (2) Alma
23 (10) York Tavern
Quoted in the text by author +
   (date) + reference except
   where indicated below in
   square brackets.
ALLEN, J.W., *Bygone Derby*
   Vol.1. Coaching, Days,
   Derby, n.d.

Bibliography

ANON., *Universal British Directory*, London, 1791 [*UBD* 1791]

ANON., *Derby, its Arts, Trades and Industries*, Derby n.d.(1891) [DATI]

BAGSHAW, S., *Directory of Derbyshire*, London, 1846.

BEMROSE, W., *Life & Works of Joseph Wright*, Derby, 1885.

BILLSON, P., *Derby and the Midland Railway*, Derby, 1996.

BRADBURY, E., & KEENE, *R.*, *All About Derby*, 2nd Edn., Derby, 1884.

BREWER'S *Derby Circular Guide & Common Directory 1823/4*, Derby 1824

BRIGHOUSE, G. *Memories of Spondon*, 2nd Edn., Derby, 1990.

BROADWOOD, G, & CHERRY, M., *Men of Property*, Leicester, 1990

BULMER'S *Directory of Derbyshire*, London, 1895.

BURTON, C.H. *Little Chester*, Derby, n.d., (1989).

BYNG, HON. J., *The Torrington Diaries*, (Ed., Andrews, C.B.) 4 Vols, London, 1934-8.

CAMERON, K., *The Place Names of Derbyshire*, 3 Vols., *English Place Name Society* Vol. XXIX, Cambridge, 1959.

CHELLASTON LOCAL HISTORY GROUP, *Chellaston Recollections*, Derby, 1990

CHELLASTON LOCAL HISTORY GROUP, *Chellaston, Then and Now*, Derby, 1992

CHRISTIAN, R. in *Derbyshire Advertiser* 7/10/1960

CHOLERTON, P., *Chaddesden*, Stroud, 1999

COOK'S *Directory of Derby*, London, 1898

COX, J.C. & HOPE, W.H. St J., *The Chronicles of the Collegiate Church of All Saints'*, Derby, 1881.

COX, T., *Magna Britannica*, London, 1730.

CRAVEN, M. A. J. B., *John Whitehurst of Derby*, Mayfield, 1996

CRAVEN, M. A. J. B., *The Derby Town House*, Derby, 1987

CRAVEN, M. A. J. B., *The Illustrated History of Derby*, Derby, 1988

CRAVEN, M. A. J. B. & STANLEY, M. F. *The Derbyshire Country House Vol II*, Matlock, 1984

CUNNINGHAM, J., *The Brewer, Innkeeper and Publican's Guide*, London, 1765.

DARLINGTON, R.R., (Ed.), *The Cartulary of Darley Abbey*, Kendal, 1945.

DAVISON, A. W., *Derby, Its Rise and Progress*, Derby, 1906

DEFOE, D., *A Tour Through the Whole Island of Great Britain*, 2 Vols., London, 1967.

DERBY BOROUGH *Directory of Derby*, 1935, 1952, 1965.

DERBY & CHESTERFIELD REPORTER [*DCR*]

DERBY EVENING TELEGRAPH [*DET*]

DERBY LOCAL STUDIES LIBRARY:

  Building Byelaw Approvals 1859-1947 [*BBA*]

  Deeds [DLSL, Deeds]

DERBY MERCURY, *Newspaper*, from 1732-1832 [*DM*]

DERBY TRADER [*DT*]

DERBYSHIRE ADVERTISER [*DA*]

DERBYSHIRE LIFE & COUNTRYSIDE, from 1932 [*DLC*]

EARDLEY SIMPSON, Ll., *Derby and the Forty-Five*, London, 1933

FARINGTON, J., *The Farington Diary*, (Ed. Grieg, J.) Vol.V., London, 1925.

FARNSWORTH, D., *From Mearca to Clark-Maxwell*, Derby, 1987.

FEARNEYHOUGH, H. W., *Chaddesden, A History*, Ashbourne, n.d.

FIENNES, C., *The Journeys of Celia Fiennes*, (Ed. Morris, C.) London, 1967.

FREEBODY'S *Directory of the Towns of Derby[shire]* Derby 1852

GLOVER, S., *Directory of Derbyshire*, Derby, 1827-9.

GLOVER, S., *Directories of Derby*, Derby, 1843, 1849.

GLOVER, S., *History and Gazetteer of Derbyshire*, 2 Vols., Derby, 1829/31.

GOODEY, A.E., *The Alfred E. Goodey Collection of Old Derby Pictures*, Derby, 1936.

GOODHEAD, E. E., *The West End Story*, Matlock, 1983

GOODHEAD, E. E., *West End Tales*, Derby, 1986

GRIFFITHS, I., *Littleover, Portrait of a Village*, Derby, 1990.

HARRISON, J., *Some Account of the History of Normanton-by-Derby and Its Church*, Derby, nd. (1958).

HASLEM, J., *The Old Derby China Factory*, Derby, 1876

HIGGINSON, M., *The Friar Gate Line*, Derby, 1989.

HODGKIN, A, *Wilmorton*, Derby, 1996

HOLYOAKE, G.J. & SCOTTON, A., *A Jubilee History of the Derby Co-operative Provident Society*, Derby, 1900.

HUGHES, J.R. *Around Spondon*, Stroud, 1997

HUTTON, W., *History of Derby*, Derby, 1791.

HUTTON, W., *The Life of William Hutton*, Birmingham, 1816.

JEWITT, Ll. (Ed.), *The Reliquary*, VII (1866) – XIV (1873). [Jewitt]

JEAYES, I. H., *The Records of the County Borough of Derby*, London, 1904

KELLY & CO., *Directories of Derbyshire*: London, 1888, 1891, 1903, 1908, 1912, 1925, 1926, 1932, 1936 & 1941.

KEYS, J., *Sketches of Old Derby & Neighbourhood*, London, 1895.

LEE, G. T., Craft *Freemasonry in Derbyshire*, Derby, 1926

LONGDON, A. *Early Allenton and its Environs*, Derby, 2000

MORITZ, C.P., *Journeys of a German in England in 1782* (Ed. & Trans, Nettel, R.) London, 1965.

MOZLEY, T., *Reminiscences*, 2 Vols., London, 1885.

NEWCOMBE, R., *Derbyshire Ale: the CAMRA Guide to Derbyshire*, Derby, 1990.

PALMER, D., *Derby's Old West End in Pictures*, Derby, 1996 [Palmer 1996 (i)]

PALMER, D., *Derby's West End...Derby's Best End*, Derby, 1996 [Palmer 1996 (ii)]

PALMER, D., *Westenders*, Derby, 1998

PHILLIPS, SIR R., *A Personal Tour Through the United Kingdom*, London, 1828, Vol. XI, Derbyshire and Nottinghamshire.

PIGOT & CO.: *Directories of Derbyshire*, London, 1818/20, 1822, 1829, 1835.

RAVEN, J., *Normanton-by-Derby: A Glimpse of the Past*, Derby, 1988.

RIPPON, A. C., *Taverns in the Town*, Derby, 1982.

SAMPLE, E., in *Derbyshire Countryside*, 4/1956.

SAUNDERS, E.J.., *Joseph Pickford of Derby*, Stroud, 1993.

SLATER'S *Directory of Derbyshire*, London, 1850, 1862.

SCOTT, A.B., *Littleover and its Church* (Ed. Robotham, E.,) Derby, 1978.

SIMPSON, R., *A Collection of Fragments Illustrative of the History and Antiquities of Derby*, 3 Vols., Derby, 1826.

WARD, J., *Billingsley & Pardoe*, Derby, 1896.

WARD, J., *Almanack for 1890*, Derby, 1890.

WARD, J., *Notes of Reminiscences of Old Derby*, Derby Museum MS, c.1890.

WARD, J., *Derby from Age to Age*, Derby 1892.

WATSON, S., *Spondon, A History*, Spondon, 1989.

WELLING, M., *Portrait of a Village, Mickleover*, Derby, 1997

WHITE'S *Directory of Derbyshire*, London, 1857.

WILKINS, G., *A Walk Through Derby*, Derby, 1827.

WILKINS & ELLIS, *New Borough of Derby Directory*, Derby, 1878

WILLIAMSON, F., *Old Derby Street Names*, Derby, 1942.

WILLIAMSON, F.S., *The Midland Railway, Its Rise & Progress*, London, 1876.

WOOLLEY, W., *History of Derbyshire* (Ed. Glover., C & Riden, P.) DRS VI, Chesterfield, 1981.

WRIGHT'S *Directory of Derbyshire*, London, 1874.

YOUNG, J.A., *An Introduction to the History of Chellaston and Its Parish Church*, rev. edn., Derby, 1983